SAN
FRANCISCO
HANDBOOK

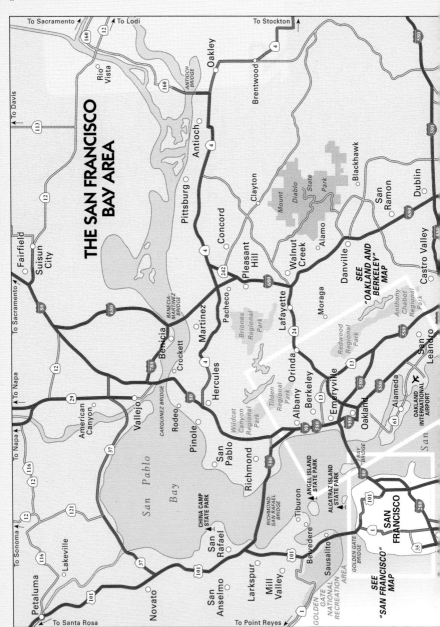

THE SAN FRANCISCO BAY AREA

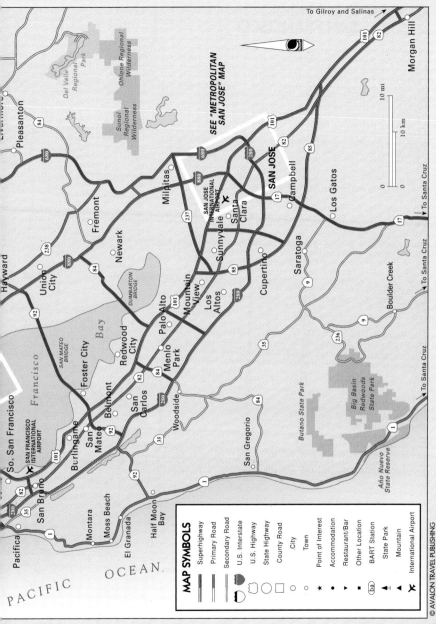

MAP SYMBOLS

▬▬	Superhighway
──	Primary Road
──	Secondary Road
◗	U.S. Interstate
◯	U.S. Highway
◯	State Highway
○	County Road
★	Point of Interest
●	City
▶	Town
■	Accommodation
▸	Restaurant/Bar
●	Other Location
(ba)	BART Station
▲	State Park
▲	Mountain
✈	International Airport

SEE "METROPOLITAN SAN JOSE" MAP

To Gilroy and Salinas

Morgan Hill

SAN JOSE

PACIFIC OCEAN

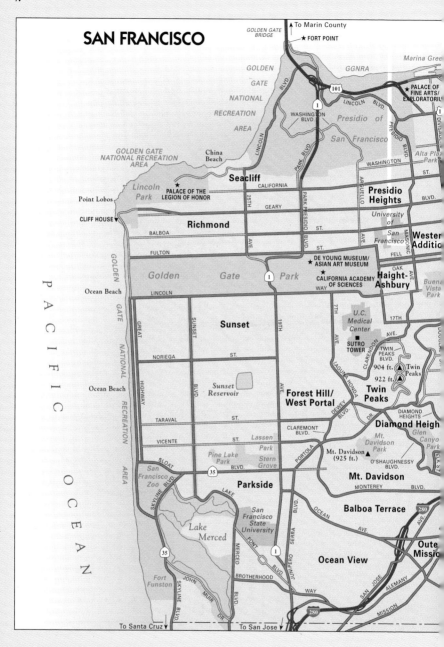

SAN FRANCISCO

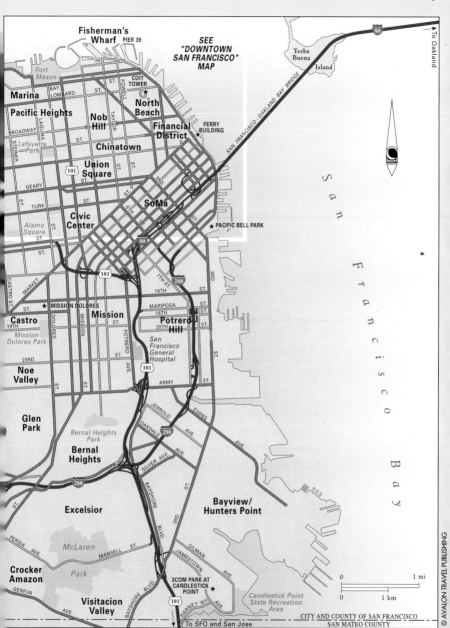

DOWNTOWN SAN FRANCISCO AND VICINITY

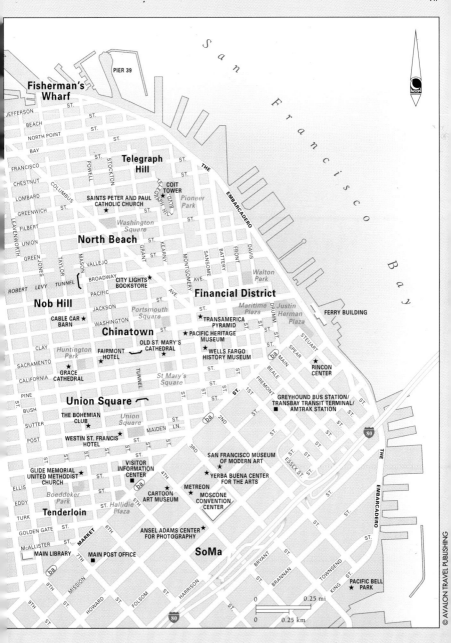

PIER 39

Fisherman's Wharf

JEFFERSON ST.
BEACH ST.
NORTH POINT ST.
BAY ST.
FRANCISCO ST.
CHESTNUT ST.
LOMBARD ST.
GREENWICH ST.
FILBERT ST.
UNION ST.
GREEN ST.

Telegraph Hill

COIT TOWER
Pioneer Park

SAINTS PETER AND PAUL CATHOLIC CHURCH

Washington Square

North Beach

THE EMBARCADERO

San Francisco Bay

Walton Park

Financial District

CITY LIGHTS BOOKSTORE

Nob Hill

CABLE CAR BARN

Portsmouth Square

Chinatown

OLD ST. MARY'S CATHEDRAL

Huntington Park

FAIRMONT HOTEL

GRACE CATHEDRAL

TRANSAMERICA PYRAMID

PACIFIC HERITAGE MUSEUM

WELLS FARGO HISTORY MUSEUM

Maritime Plaza
Justin Herman Plaza

FERRY BUILDING

RINCON CENTER

St Mary's Square

Union Square

THE BOHEMIAN CLUB

Union Square

WESTIN ST. FRANCIS HOTEL

GREYHOUND BUS STATION/
TRANSBAY TRANSIT TERMINAL/
AMTRAK STATION

GLIDE MEMORIAL UNITED METHODIST CHURCH

VISITOR INFORMATION CENTER

Boeddeker Park

St. Hallidie Plaza

CARTOON ART MUSEUM

METREON

SAN FRANCISCO MUSEUM OF MODERN ART

YERBA BUENA CENTER FOR THE ARTS

MOSCONE CONVENTION CENTER

Tenderloin

MAIN LIBRARY

MAIN POST OFFICE

ANSEL ADAMS CENTER FOR PHOTOGRAPHY

SoMa

MARKET ST.

PACIFIC BELL PARK

THE EMBARCADERO

0   0.25 mi

0   0.25 km

© AVALON TRAVEL PUBLISHING

SAN FRANCISCO HANDBOOK

FIRST EDITION

KIM WEIR
WITH PAT REILLY

MOON
HANDBOOKS

SAN FRANCISCO HANDBOOK
FIRST EDITION

Published by
Avalon Travel Publishing, Inc.
5855 Beaudry St.
Emeryville, CA 94608, USA

Printed by
RR Donnelley

Please send all comments, corrections,
additions, amendments, and critiques to:

**SAN FRANCISCO HANDBOOK
MOON TRAVEL HANDBOOKS
AVALON TRAVEL PUBLISHING, INC.
5855 BEAUDRY ST.
EMERYVILLE, CA 94608, USA
e-mail: info@travelmatters.com
www.travelmatters.com**

ISBN: 1-56691-195-8
ISSN: Library of Congress Cataloging-in-Publication Data has been applied for.

Printing History
First edition—2000

5 4 3 2 1 0

Editors: Steve Fahringer, Marion Harmon, Emily Kendrick
Map Editor: Mike Ferguson
Production & Design: Amber T. Pirker, Bob Race
Cartography: Chris Folks, Mike Morgenfeld
Index: Vera Gross

Front cover photo: © Christian Heeb/Gnass Photo Images, Inc. ©2000

Distributed in the United States and Canada by Publishers Group West

Printed in U.S.A.

CONTENTS

MAPS

EXPRESS YOURSELF

Not on just any topic, though. This being California, most things change faster than traffic lights. Because of this unfortunate fact of life in the fast lane of travel writing, comments, corrections, inadvertent omissions, and update information are always greatly appreciated. Though every effort was made to keep all current facts corralled and accounted for, it's no doubt true that *something* will already be inaccurate by the time the printer's ink squirts onto the paper at press time.

Just remember this: whatever you divulge may indeed end up in print—so think twice before sending too much information about your favorite hole-in-the-wall restaurant, cheap hotel, or "secret" world's-best swimming hole or hot springs. Once such information falls into the hands of a travel writer, it probably won't be a secret for long. Address all correspondence to:

San Francisco Handbook
c/o Moon Travel Handbooks
Avalon Travel Publishing
5855 Beaudry Street
Emeryville, CA 94608
E-mail: info@travelmatters.com

ABBREVIATIONS

AAA	—	American Automobile Association
Ave.	—	Avenue
AYH	—	American Youth Hostel
B&B	—	bed and breakfast inn
Dr.	—	Drive
F	—	Fahrenheit
Hwy.	—	Highway
Ln.	—	Lane
Mt.	—	Mount
Pt.	—	Point
Rd.	—	Road
Rt.	—	Route
RV	—	recreational vehicle
St.	—	Street

ACCOMMODATIONS RATINGS

Accommodations in this book are rated by price category, based on double-occupancy, high-season rates. Categories used are:

Budget: 35$ and under
Inexpensive: $35-60
Moderate: $60-85

Expensive: $85-110
Deluxe: $110-150
Luxury: $150 and up

ACKNOWLEDGMENTS

MY DEEPEST APPRECIATION TO SAN FRANCISCO DENIZEN PAT REILLY, TRAVEL WRITER AND researcher extraordinaire, who did such fine work in helping me complete *San Francisco Handbook*. From what I hear, it's quite possible that the hotelkeepers, restaurateurs, and shopkeepers she met along the way enjoyed the trip as much as she did. Pat's keen eye, genuine appreciation of cultural zaniness, dogged attention to detail, and subtle Brit wit have all contributed immense creative and practical value to this particular book. I'm particularly grateful for her enthusiasm and gracious good humor in the midst of all the hard work it takes to make an easy read.

I am also eternally grateful to the brave team of editors who helped this book on its way, beginning with Emily Kendrick, whose generous assistance and stalwart support were, and are, greatly appreciated. A deep bow also to Karen Bleske, who helped gather the parts into a recognizable whole, and to series editor Steve Fahringer, who bravely coordinated all of our efforts.

At the top of my thank you list, too, is Avalon Travel Publishing's business whiz Bill Newlin, who has long been committed to "making it work" so I might complete my longer-term task—telling the entire California story in travel book form. As Walt Whitman would say: "Oh Captain! my Captain! Our fearful trip is done." Yet another book has weathered the rack. Thanks to Bill, perhaps we'll all still be cheering after the next book is made, and the next one after that.

I reserve a special category of gratitude for the many Moon Travel Handbook authors who helped me learn the ropes, particularly now-departed Joe Bisignani ("Mr. Hawaii"), Jane King, Steve Metzger, and Bob Nilsen. I also want to thank Tim Moriarty—wherever he is now—both for his diligent research and for his own written contributions to *San Francisco Handbook*. For their contributions to this book's editorial content, I offer my appreciation, too, to Ed Aust and Taran March.

My thanks also to those whose dedication and skill helped turn the words in this book into the physical object you now hold in your hands. It's a bit confusing to correctly call the roll—and to give appropriate credit where it is due—now that Moon's administrative (and part of its editorial) staff are subsumed within the greater whole of Avalon Travel Publishing, in Emeryville. But at last report an impressive team of hard-working bookmakers, of both the editorial and production persuasions, was still at home in the Chico office, bravely flailing away at the immense tasks before them.

Again, my personal thanks to Karen Bleske, for her conscientious stewardship of this book's text—a task not nearly as simple as it looks—and to series editor Steve Fahringer, who assisted with rounding up all those last-minute details. My thanks, too, to Marion Harmon for copyediting.

Snapping off a few dozen rolls of fascinating photographs would be the best way to express my gratitude to the production crew. Words, however, will have to suffice at the moment. I particularly appreciate layout artists Amber Pirker and Jon Knolle, for their keen sense of balance, design, and overall visual aesthetics as well as their patient attention to all those picayune graphic details. Special thanks to Chris Folks, Mike Ferguson, and Kim Marks for such fine work on the maps, and to Bob Race for his outstanding artistic contributions and dedication in organizing all the book's graphic elements.

Thanks, too, to associate publisher Donna Galassi, marketing director Amanda Bleakley, as well as promotion and sales wizards Mary Beth Pugh and Patty Chiavola, for doing everything possible to help us all make a living in this business.

My special thanks to photographer Aislinn Race, who has contributed her work to this work, not to mention the city of San Francisco Arts Commission and the California Department of Parks and Recreation. Thank you also to Christian Heeb for the fine cover photo.

In addition, I extend my heartfelt thanks to Fred Sater, media relations manager for the California Division of Tourism. I appreciate his personal encouragement and support, not to mention that refreshing sense of humor. I am also grateful for the generous assistance of the San Francisco Convention and Visitor Bureau, with thanks in particular to Laurie Armstrong, vice president of public relations. Their contributions and thoughtful suggestions have greatly improved this book's practical focus and (I hope) its overall usefulness.

—*Kim Weir*

East is East, and West is San Francisco.
–O. Henry

SAN FRANCISCO CONVENTION AND VISITORS BUREAU/MICHAEL MOESON

SAN FRANCISCO: AN INTRODUCTION

LIFE ON THE EDGE

"When I was a child growing up in Salinas we called San Francisco 'The City,'" California native John Steinbeck once observed. "Of course it was the only city we knew but I still think of it as The City as does everyone else who has ever associated with it."

San Francisco is The City, a distinction it wears with detached certitude. San Francisco has been The City since the days of the gold rush, when the world rushed in through the Golden Gate in a frenzied pursuit of both actual and alchemical riches. It remained The City forever after: when San Francisco started, however reluctantly, to conceive of itself as a civilized place; when San Francisco fell down and incinerated itself in the great earthquake of 1906; when San Francisco flew up from its ashes, fully fledged, after reinventing itself; and when San Francisco set about reinventing almost everything else with its rolling social revolutions. Among those

the world noticed this century, the Beatniks or "Beats" of the 1940s and '50s publicly shook the suburbs of American complacency, but the 1960s and San Francisco's Summer of Love caused the strongest social quake, part of the chaos of new consciousness that quickly changed the shape of everything.

Among its many attributes, perhaps most striking is The City's ability, still, to be all things to all people—and to simultaneously contradict itself and its own truths. San Francisco is a point of beginning. Depending upon where one starts, it is also the ultimate place to arrive. San Francisco is a comedy. And San Francisco is tragedy.

See color maps of San Francisco and Downtown San Francisco at front of book.

As writer Richard Rodriquez observes: "San Francisco has taken some heightened pleasure from the circus of final things. . . . San Francisco can support both comic and tragic conclusions because the city is geographically *in extremis,* a metaphor for the farthest flung possibility, a metaphor for the end of the line." But even that depends upon point of view. As Rodriquez also points out, "To speak of San Francisco as land's end is to read the map from one direction only— as Europeans would read or as the East Coast has always read it." To the people living on these hills before California's colonialization, before the gold rush, even before there was a San Francisco, the land they lived on represented the center, surrounded on three sides by water. To Mexicans extending their territorial reach, it was north. To Russian fur hunters escaping the frigid shores of Alaska, it was south. And to its many generations of Asian immigrants, surely San Francisco represented the Far East.

The precise place The City occupies in the world's imagination is irrelevant to compass points. If San Francisco is anywhere specific, it is certainly at the edge: the cutting edge of cultural combinations, the gilt edge of international commerce, the razor's edge of raw reality. And life on the edge is rarely boring.

THE LAND: NATURAL SAN FRANCISCO

Imagine San Francisco before its bridges were built: a captive city, stranded on an unstable, stubbed toe of a peninsula, one by turns twitching under the storm-driven assault of wind and water, then chilled by bone-cold fog.

The city and county of San Francisco—the two are one, duality in unity—sit on their own appendage of California earth, a political conglomeration totaling 46.4 square miles. Creating San Francisco's western edge is the Pacific Ocean, its waters cooled by strong Alaskan currents, its rough offshore rocks offering treachery to unwary sea travelers. On its eastern edge is San Francisco Bay, one of the world's most impressive natural harbors, with deep protected waters and 496 square miles of surface area. (As vast as it is, these days the bay is only 75% of its pre-gold rush size, since its shoreline has

been filled in and extended to create more land.) Connecting the two sides, and creating San Francisco's rough-and-tumble northern edge, is the three-mile-long strait known as the Golden Gate. Straddled by the world-renowned Golden Gate Bridge, this mile-wide river of sea water cuts the widest gap in the rounded Coast Ranges for a thousand miles, yet is so small that its landforms almost hide the bay that balloons inland.

Spaniards named what is now considered San Francisco Las Lomitas, or "little hills," for the landscape's most notable feature. Perhaps to create a romantic comparison with Rome, popular local mythology holds that The City was built on seven hills—Lone Mountain, Mt. Davidson, Nob Hill, Russian Hill, Telegraph Hill, and the two Twin Peaks, none higher than 1,000 feet in elevation. There are actually more than 40 hills in San Francisco, all part and parcel of California's Coast Ranges, which run north and south along the state's coastline, sheltering inland valleys from the fog and winds that regularly visit San Francisco.

City on a Fault Line

The City has been shaped as much by natural forces as by historical happenstance. Its most spectacular event involved both. More than any other occurrence, San Francisco's 1906 earthquake—estimated now to have registered 8.25 on the Richter scale—woke up residents, and the world, to the fact that The City was built on very shaky ground. California's famous, 650-mile-long San Andreas Fault, as it is now known, slips just seaward of San Francisco. In the jargon of tectonic plate theory, The City sits on the North American Plate, a huge slab of earth floating on the planet's molten core, along the San Andreas earthquake fault line. Just west is the Pacific Plate. When earth-shaking pressure builds, sooner or later something has to give. In San Francisco, as elsewhere in California, a rumble and a roar and split-second motion announces an earthquake and the fact that an interlocking section of the earth's crust has separated, a movement that may or may not be visible on the earth's surface. San Francisco's most recent major quake, on October 17, 1989, reminded us that The City's earthquake history is far from a finished chapter.

City in a Fog

San Francisco's second most famous physical feature is its weather—mild and Mediterranean but with quite perverse fog patterns, especially surprising to first-time summer visitors. When people expect sunny skies and warm temperatures, San Francisco offers instead gray and white mists, moist clouds seemingly filled with knife-sharp points of ice when driven by the wind.

Poets traditionally call forth all nine muses to honor the mysteries of fog. Scientists are much more succinct. Summer heat in California's central valley regions creates a low-pressure weather system, while cooler ocean temperatures create higher atmospheric pressure. Moving toward equilibrium, the cool and moist coastal air is drawn inland through the "mouth" of the Golden Gate and over adjacent hills, like a behemoth's belly breath. Then, as the land cools, the mists evaporate. So even during the peak fog months of July and August, wool-coat weather dissipates by midafternoon—only to roll back in shortly after sundown. Due to microclimates created by hills, certain San Francisco neighborhoods—like the Mission District, Noe Valley, and Potrero Hill—may be quite sunny and warm when the rest of the city still shivers in the fog.

San Francisco Weather

The coast's strong high-pressure system tends to moderate San Francisco weather year-round: expect average daytime temperatures of 54-65° F in summer, 48-59° F in winter. (Usually reliable is the adage that for every 10 miles you travel inland from the city, temperatures will increase by 10 degrees.) September and October are the warmest months, with balmy days near 70 degrees. The local weather pattern also prevents major rainstorms from May through October. Despite the water-rich imagery associated with the San Francisco Bay Area, the region is actually semiarid, with annual (nondrought) rainfall averaging 19-20 inches. Snow is a very rare phenomenon in the region.

HISTORY AND CULTURE: HUMAN SAN FRANCISCO

At its most basic, the recorded history of San Francisco is a story of conquest and curiosity.

The region's original inhabitants, however, were generally content with the abundant riches the land provided quite naturally. Descendants of mysterious nomads who first crossed the Bering Strait from Asia to the North American continent some 20,000 or more years ago, California's native peoples were culturally distinct. The language groups—"tribes" doesn't serve to describe California Indians—living north of the Golden Gate were classified by anthropologists as the Coast Wiwok people. Though the barren and desolate site of San Francisco attracted few residents, the dominant native population throughout the greater Bay Area was called Costanoan ("coast people") or Ohlone by the Spanish, though the people called themselves Ramaytush.

In precolonial days, the region was the most densely populated on the continent north of Mexico, with a population of 10,000 people living in 30 or more permanent villages. Though each village considered itself unique, separated from others by customs and local dialect, the Ohlone intermarried and traded with other tribes and shared many cultural characteristics. Though dependent on shellfish as a dietary staple, the Ohlone also migrated inland in summer and fall to hunt game, fish, and collect acorns, which were valued throughout California for making bread and mush. Thousands of years of undisturbed cultural success created a gentle, gracious, unwarlike society—a culture that quickly passed away with the arrival of California's explorers and colonizers.

Early Explorations

Discoveries of dusty manuscripts, ancient stone anchors, and old coins now suggest that Chinese ships were the first foreign vessels to explore California's coastline, arriving centuries before Columbus bumbled into the new world. The Portuguese explorer Juan Cabrillo (João Cabrilho) was the coast's first official surveyor, though on his 1542 voyage he failed to discover the Golden Gate and the spectacular bay behind it. In 1579 the English pirate Sir Francis Drake took the first foreign step onto California soil, quite possibly near San Francisco, and claimed the land for Queen Elizabeth I. (Where exactly Drake landed is a subject of ongoing controversy and confusion. For a further discussion, see Point Reyes National Seashore.)

And even Drake failed to see the Golden Gate and its precious natural harbor, perhaps due to the subtle subterfuge of landforms and fog.

The Arrival of Spain, Mexico, Russia, and America

In 1769, some 200 years after Drake, a Spanish scouting party led by Gaspar de Portolá discovered San Francisco Bay by accident while searching for Monterey Bay farther south. After Monterey was secured, Capt. Juan Bautista de Anza was assigned the task of colonizing this new territorial prize. With 35 families plus a lieutenant and a Franciscan priest, de Anza set out on a grueling trip from Sonora, Mexico, arriving on the peninsula's tip on June 27, 1776, just one week before the American Revolution. The first order of business was establishing a military fortress, the Presidio, at the present site of Fort Mason. And the second was establishing a church and mission outpost, about one mile south, on the shores of a small lake or lagoon named in honor of Nuestra Señora de los Dolores (Our Lady of Sorrows). Though the mission church was dedicated to Saint Francis of Assisi, it became known as Mission Dolores—and the name "San Francisco" was instead attached to the spectacular bay and the eventual city that grew up on its shores.

Though Spain, then Mexico, officially secured the California territory, underscoring ownership by means of vast government land grants to retired military and civilian families, the colonial claim was somewhat tenuous. By the 1830s, Americans were already the predominant residents of the settlement at Yerba Buena Cove (at the foot of what is now Telegraph Hill), the earliest version of San Francisco. Yerba Buena was first a trading post established by William Anthony Richardson, an Englishman who married the Presidio commandant's daughter. In the early 1800s, Russian fur hunters established themselves just north along the coast, at the settlement of Fort

A well-supplied prospector heads for mining camp.

Ross. They sailed south to trade. English, French, and American trading ships were also regular visitors. By the 1840s, Yankees were arriving by both land and sea in ever greater numbers, spurred on by the nation's expansionist mood and the political dogma of "Manifest Destiny!" The official annexation of the California territory to the United States, when it came in mid-1846, was almost anticlimactic. After the 13-man force at the Presidio surrendered peacefully to the Americans, the citizens quickly changed the name of Yerba Buena to that of the bay, San Francisco—a shrewd business move, intended to attract still more trade.

The World Rushes In: The Gold Rush

Events of early 1848 made the name change all but irrelevant. San Francisco could hardly help attracting more business, and more businesses of every stripe, once word arrived that gold had been discovered on the American River in the foothills east of Sacramento. Before the gold rush, San Francisco was a sleepy port town with a population of 800, but within months it swelled to a city of nearly 25,000, as gold seekers arrived by the shipload from all over the globe. Those who arrived early and lit out for the goldfields in 1848 had the best opportunity to harvest California gold. Most of the fortune hunters, however, arrived in '49, thus the term "forty-niners" to describe this phenomenal human migration.

As cosmopolitan as the overnight city of San Francisco was, with its surprisingly well-educated, liberal, and (not so surprisingly) young population, it was hardly civilized. By 1849 the ratio of men to women was about 10 to one, and saloons, gambling halls, and the notorious red-light district—known as the Barbary Coast—were the social mainstays of this rootless, risk-taking population. Though early San Francisco was primarily a tent city, fire was a constant scourge. The city started to build itself then burned to the ground six

DOVER PUBLICATIONS, INC.

times by 1852, when San Francisco was recognized as the fourth largest port of entry in the United States. And though eccentricity and bad behavior were widely tolerated, unrestrained gang crime and murder became so commonplace that businessmen formed Committees of Vigilance to create some semblance of social order—by taking the law into their own hands and jailing, hanging, and running undesirables out of town.

More Barbarians and Big Spenders
By the late 1850s, the sources for most of California's surface gold had been picked clean. Ongoing harvesting of the state's most precious metal had become a corporate affair, an economic change made possible by the development of new technologies. The days of individualistic gold fever had subsided, and fortune hunters who remained in California turned their efforts to more long-lasting development of wealth, often in agriculture and business.

The city, though temporarily slowed by the economic depression that arrived with the end of the gold rush, was the most businesslike of them all. A recognizable city and a major financial center, no sooner had San Francisco calmed down and turned its attentions to nurturing civic pride than another boom arrived—this time silver, discovered in the Nevada territory's Comstock Lode. Silver mining required capital, heavy equipment, and organized mining technology; this was a strictly corporate raid on the earth's riches, with San Francisco and its bankers, businesses, and citizenry the main beneficiaries. Led by the silver rush "Bonanza Kings," the city's nouveau riche built themselves a residential empire atop Nob Hill and set about creating more cultured institutions.

Confident California, led by San Francisco, believed the future held nothing but greater growth, greater wealth. That was certainly the case for the "Big Four," Sacramento businessmen who financed Theodore Judah's dream of a transcontinental railroad, a development almost everyone believed would lead to an extended boom in the state's economy. Soon at home atop Nob Hill with the city's other nabobs, Charles Crocker, Mark Hopkins, Collis Huntington, and Leland Stanford also set out to establish some political machinery—the Southern Pacific Railway—to generate power and influence to match their wealth.

Bad Times and Bigotry
But the transcontinental railroad did little to help California, or San Francisco, at least initially. As naysayers had predicted, the ease of shipping goods by rail all but destroyed California's neophyte industrial base, since the state was soon glutted with lower-cost manufactured goods from the East Coast. A drought in 1869—a major setback for agricultural production—and an 1871 stock market crash made matters that much worse.

Legions of the unemployed, which included terminated railroad workers all over the West, rose up in rage throughout the 1870s and 1880s. They attacked not those who had enriched themselves at the expense of the general populace but "outsiders," specifically the Chinese who had labored long and hard at many a thankless task since the days of the gold rush. Mob violence and the torching of businesses and entire Chinese communities, in San Francisco and elsewhere, wasn't enough to satisfy such open racist hatred. Politicians too bowed to anti-Chinese sentiment, passing a series of discriminatory laws that forbade the Chinese from owning land, voting, and testifying in court, and levying a special tax against Chinese shrimp fishermen.

A near-final bigoted blow was the federal government's 1882 Oriental Exclusion Act, which essentially ended legal Asian immigration until it was repealed during World War II. (For more information, see Angel Island State Park.) San Francisco's Chinese community, for the most part working men denied the opportunity to reunite with their families, was further damaged by the Geary Act of 1892, which declared that all Chinese had to carry proper identification or face deportation. The failure of American society to support traditional Chinese culture led to rampant crime, gambling, and prostitution—acceptable diversions of the day for bachelors—and a lawless reign of terror by competing tongs who fought to control the profits. Only the gradual Americanization of the Chinese, which minimized tong influence, and the disastrous events during the spring of 1906 could change the reality of Chinatown. But the year 1906 changed everything in San Francisco.

The scene at 18th and Howard Streets after the 1906 earthquake: not everything was lost to fire.

WELLS FARGO BANK HISTORY ROOM

The World Ends: Earthquake and Fire

By the early 1900s, San Francisco had entered its "gilded age," a complacent period when the city was busy enjoying its new cosmopolitan status. San Francisco had become the largest and finest city west of Chicago. The rich happily compounded their wealth in downtown highrises and at home on Nob Hill and in other resplendent neighborhoods. The expanding middle class built rows of new Victorian homes, "painted ladies" that writer Tom Wolfe would later call "those endless staggers of bay windows," on hills far removed from the low life of the Barbary Coast, Chinatown, and the newest red-light district, The Tenderloin. But the working classes still smoldered in squalid tenements south of Market Street. Corruption ruled, politically, during the heyday of the "paint eaters"—politicians so greedy they'd even eat the paint off buildings. The cynical reporter and writer Ambrose Bierce, sniffing at the status quo, called San Francisco the "moral penal colony of the world." But the city's famous graft trials, a public political circus that resulted in 3,000 indictments but shockingly little jail time, came later.

Whatever was going on in the city, legal and otherwise, came to an abrupt halt on the morning of April 18, 1906, when a massive earthquake hit. Now estimated to have registered 8.25 on the Richter scale, the quake created huge fissures in the ground, broke water and gas mains all over the city, and caused chimneys and other unsta-

ble construction to come tumbling down. The better neighborhoods, including the city's Victorian row houses, suffered little damage. Downtown, however, was devastated. City Hall, a shoddy construction job allowed by scamming politicians and their contractor cohorts, crumbled into nothing. Though a central hospital also fell, burying doctors, nurses, and patients alike, the overall death toll from the earthquake itself was fairly small. Sadly for San Francisco, one of the fatalities was the city fire chief, whose foresight might have prevented the conflagration soon to follow.

More than 50 fires started that morning alone, racing through the low-rent neighborhoods south of Market, then into downtown, raging out of control. The flames were unchecked for four days, burning through downtown, parts of the Mission District, and also demolishing Chinatown, North Beach, Nob Hill, Telegraph Hill, and Russian Hill. The mansions along the eastern edge of Van Ness were dynamited to create an impromptu firebreak, finally stopping the firestorm.

When it was all over, the official tally of dead or missing stood at 674, though more recent research suggests the death toll was more than 3,000, since the Chinese weren't counted. The entire city center was destroyed, along with three-fourths of the city's businesses and residences. With half of its 450,000 population now homeless, San Francisco was a tent city once again. But it was an optimistic tent city, bolstered by relief and rebuilding funds sent from around the world. As reconstruction began, San Francisco also set out to clean house politically.

Modern Times

By 1912, with San Francisco more or less back on its feet, Mayor James "Sunny Jim" Rolph, who always sported a fresh flower in his lapel, seemed to symbolize the city's new era. Rolph presided over the construction of some of San Francisco's finest public statements about itself. These included the new city hall and Civic Center, as well as the 1915 world's fair and the Panama-Pacific International Exposition, a spectacular 600-acre temporary city designed by Bernard Maybeck to reflect the "mortality of grandeur and the vanity of human wishes." Though the exposition was intended to celebrate the opening of the Panama Canal, it was San Francisco's grand announcement to the world that it had not only survived but thrived in the aftermath of its earlier earthquake and fire.

During the Great Depression, San Francisco continued to defy the commonplace, dancing at the edge of unreal expectations. Two seemingly impossible spans, the Golden Gate Bridge and the Bay Bridge, were built in the 1930s. San Francisco also built the world's largest man-made island, Treasure Island, which hosted the Golden Gate International Exposition in 1939 before becoming a U.S. Navy facility. (In 1997, the Navy abandoned ship and ceded the island to the city of San Francisco; now it's a venue for occasional concerts and a regular flea market.)

No matter how spectacular its statements to the world, San Francisco had trouble at home. The 1929 stock market crash and the onset of the Depression reignited long-simmering labor strife, especially in the city's port. Four longshoremen competed for every available job along the waterfront, and members of the company-controlled Longshoremen's Association demanded kickbacks for jobs that were offered. Harry Bridges reorganized the International Longshoremen's Association, and backed by the Teamsters Union, his pro-union strike successfully closed down the waterfront. On "Bloody Thursday," July 5, 1934, 800 strikers battled with National Guard troops called in to quell a riot started by union busters. Two men were shot and killed by police, another 100 were injured, and the subsequent all-city strike—the largest general strike in U.S. history—ultimately involved most city businesses as well as the waterfront unions. More so than elsewhere on the West Coast, labor unions are still strong in San Francisco.

Other social and philosophical revolutions, for iconoclasts and oddballs alike, either got their start in San Francisco or received abundant support once arrived here. First came the 1950s-era Beatniks or "Beats"—poets, freethinkers, and jazz aficionados rebelling against the suburbanization of the American mind. The Beats were followed in short order by the 1960s, the Summer of Love, psychedelics, and rock groups like the legendary Grateful Dead. More substantial, in the '60s, the Free Speech Movement heated up across the bay in Berkeley, not to mention anti-Vietnam War protests and the rise of the Black Panther Party. Since then, San Francisco has managed to make its place at, or near, the forefront of almost every change in social awareness, from women's rights to gay pride. And in the 1980s and '90s, San Franciscans went all out for baby boomer consumerism; young urban professionals have been setting the style for quite some time. But there are other styles, other trends. You name it, San Francisco probably has it.

San Francisco as Destination

Tourism is the city's top industry these days; in 1995, San Francisco hosted more than 16 million visitors. Earthquake anxieties aside, it's not difficult to understand San Francisco's appeal. The city offers almost everything, from striking scenery and sophisticated shopping to fine hotels and restaurants. Even budget travelers can arrive, and stay, with exceptional ease, at least compared to elsewhere in California. And the city's multiethnic cultural, artistic, and entertainment attractions are among its most undervalued treasures.

Downtown San Francisco, which serves as the city's corporate and financial headquarters as well as tourist central, is a world of skyscraping office towers and imposed isolation. Surely it's no accident that the city's homeless live here. But the most authentic spirits of San Francisco live elsewhere, out in the neighborhoods. So do get out—out past the panhandlers and the polished glass buildings, past the

WALKING ON WATER ACROSS THAT GOLDEN GATE

Nothing is as San Francisco as the city's astounding **Golden Gate Bridge,** a bright, red-orange fairy pathway up into the fog, a double-necked lyre plucked by the wind to send its surreal song spiraling skyward. The bridge stands today as testimony to the vision of political madmen and poets, almost always the progenitors of major achievements. San Francisco's own **Emperor Norton**—a gold rush-era British merchant originally known as Joshua A. Norton, who went bankrupt in the land of instant wealth but soon reinvented himself as "Norton I, Emperor of the United States and Protector of Mexico"—was the first lunatic to suggest that the vast, turbulent, and troublesome waters of the Golden Gate could be spanned by a bridge. The poet and engineer **Joseph Baermann Strauss,** a titan of a man barely five feet tall, seconded the insanity, and in 1917 he left Chicago for San Francisco, plans and models in hand, to start the 13-year lobbying campaign.

All practical doubts aside, San Francisco at large was aghast at the idea of defacing the natural majesty of the Golden Gate with a manmade monument; more than 2,000 lawsuits were filed in an effort to stop bridge construction. California's love of progress won out in the end, however, and construction of the graceful bridge, designed by architect Irwin F. Morrow, began in 1933. As Strauss himself remarked later: "It took two decades and 200 million words to convince the people that the bridge was feasible; then only four years and $35 million to put the concrete and steel together."

Building the Golden Gate Bridge was no simple task, rather, an accomplishment akin to a magical feat. Some 80,000 miles of wire were spun into the bridge's suspension cables, a sufficient length to encircle the earth (at the equator) three times, and enough concrete to create a very wide sidewalk between the country's West and East coasts was poured into the anchoring piers. Sinking the southern support pier offshore was a particular challenge, with 60-mile-an-hour tidal surges and 15-foot swells at times threatening to upend the (seasick) workers' floating trestle. Once the art-deco towers were in place, the *real* fun began—those acrobats in overalls, most earning less than $1 an hour, working in empty space to span the gap. Safety was a serious issue with Strauss and his assistant, Clifford Paine. Due to their diligence, 19 men fell but landed in safety nets instead of in the morgue, earning them honorary membership in the "Halfway to Hell Club." But just weeks before construction was completed, a scaffolding collapsed, its jagged edges tearing through the safety net and taking nine men down with it.

When the Golden Gate Bridge was finished in 1937, the world was astonished. Some 200,000 people walked across the virgin roadbed that day, just to introduce themselves to this gracious steel wonder. At that time, the bridge was the world's longest and tallest suspension structure—with a single-span, between-towers distance of 4,200 feet—and boasted the

the Golden Gate
Bridge

SAN JOSE CONVENTION AND VISITORS BUREAU

highest high-rises west of New York's Empire State Building. Its total length was 1.7 miles, and its 746-foot-tall towers were equivalent in total height to 65-story buildings. Even now, the bridge's grace is much more than aesthetic. As a suspension bridge, the Golden Gate moves with the action of the immediate neighborhood. It has rarely been closed for reasons of safety or necessary repairs, though it was closed, in 1960, so French President Charles de Gaulle could make a solo crossing. Even in treacherous winds, the bridge can safely sway as much as 28 feet in either direction, though standing on a slightly swinging bridge of such monstrous dimensions is an indescribably odd sensation.

Perhaps the best thing about the Golden Gate Bridge, even after all these years, is that people can still enjoy it, up close and very personally. Though the bridge toll is $3 per car (heading south), for pedestrians it's a free trip either way. The hike is ambitious, about two miles one-way. For those who don't suffer from vertigo, this is an inspiring and invigorating experience, as close to walking on water as most of us will ever get. (But it's not necessarily

a life-enhancing experience for the seriously depressed or suicidal. The lure of the leap has proved too tempting for more than 900 people.) Parking is available at either end of the bridge.

Though the Golden Gate Bridge is the Bay Area's most royal span, credit for San Francisco's propulsion into the modern world of commerce and crazy traffic actually goes to the **Bay Bridge** spanning San Francisco Bay between downtown San Francisco and Oakland/Berkeley. Completed in 1936, and built atop piers sunk into the deepest deeps ever bridged, the Bay Bridge cost $80 million to complete, at that time the most expensive structure ever built. And in recent history, the Bay Bridge has made front-page and nightly news headlines. The whole world watched in horror when part of the bridge collapsed amid the torqued tensions of the 1989 earthquake, a pre-rush-hour event. There were deaths and injuries, but fewer casualties than if the quake had come during peak commuter traffic. Despite the quake, the bridge still remained structurally sound, and the more critically necessary repairs have been made. A new span for the Bay Bridge is in the planning stages.

pretty shops and the prettier shoppers—to see San Francisco.

Even out in the neighborhoods, though, San Franciscans have started to suspect that things aren't quite as wonderful as they once were. Their beloved city suffers from the same problems as other major cities, from staggering demands on urban services to worsening traffic problems and astronomical housing costs.

But at last report—and despite some notable historical lapses—the city's deepest traditions, liberalism and tolerance, are still going strong. And freedom is still the city's unofficial rallying cry.

JUST THE FACTS

USEFUL INFORMATION

The clearinghouse for current visitor information is the **San Francisco Convention & Visitors Bureau,** 900 Market St. (at Powell, downstairs—below street level—outside the BART station at Hallidie Plaza), P.O. Box 429097, San Francisco, CA 94142-9097, tel. (415) 391-2000, www.sfvisitor.org. Here you can pick up official visitor pamphlets, maps, booklets, and brochures about local businesses, including current accommodations bargains and various coupon offers. Multilingual staffers are available to answer questions. The Visitor Information Center is open

for walk-ins weekdays 9 a.m.-5 p.m., Sat.-Sun. 9 a.m.-3 p.m.; closed Thanksgiving, Christmas, and New Year's Day.

If you can't make it to the Visitor Information Center or are planning your trip in advance and need information, you have a couple of options. To find out what's going on in town, from entertainment and arts attractions to major professional sports events, you can call the city's free, 24-hour visitor hot line, available in five languages. To get the news in English, call (415) 391-2001; in French, tel. (415) 391-2003; in German, tel. (415) 391-2004; in Japanese, tel. (415) 391-2101; and in Spanish, tel. (415) 391-2122. The information is updated weekly. You can also

BOOKSHOP SAN FRANCISCO

...isco is a well-read city, judging ...om the number of booksellers here. ...s most famous is that bohemian bookshop of lore in North Beach, **City Lights,** 261 Columbus Ave. (at Broadway), tel. (415) 362-8193, founded in 1953 by Lawrence Ferlinghetti and Peter Martin. The small press and poetry sections here are especially impressive. The **Sierra Club Bookstore,** 85 Second St. (near Mission), tel. (415) 977-5600, offers a great selection of outdoor, ecology, nature, and travel books. Nearby and also well worth a stop is **A Clean, Well Lighted Place for Books,** 601 Van Ness Ave. (between Golden Gate and Turk), tel. (415) 441-6670.

Theater aficionados, take a side trip to **Fantasy Etc.,** 808 Larkin (at O'Farrel, on the edge of the Tenderloin), tel. (415) 441-7617. In the same general neighborhood, you'll find the **European Book Company,** 925 Larkin (between Geary and Post), tel. (415) 474-0626, offering a selection of books in French, German, and Spanish, as well as a good travel section including English-language titles.

At Union Square, you'll find a four-story outpost of **Borders Books and Music,** 400 Post (at Powell), tel. (415) 399-1633 (books) or (415) 399-0522 (music). The store stocks more than 200,000 titles and has its own coffee shop. Open Mon.-Thurs. 9 a.m.-11 p.m., Fri.-Sat. 9 a.m.-midnight, Sunday 9 a.m.-9 p.m.

Probably the best downtown San Francisco stop for travel and maps is the Financial District's **Rand McNally Map and Travel Store,** 595 Market St. (at Second), tel. (415) 777-3131. Worthwhile elsewhere are the **Complete Traveler,** 3207 Fillmore (at Lombard), tel. (415) 923-1511; and **Get Lost—Travel Books, Maps, and Gear,** 1825 Market St. (at Guerrero), tel. (415) 437-0529, which offers travel guides, travel literature, luggage and travel accessories, maps, atlases, and author events. It's open Mon.-Fri. 10 a.m.-7 p.m., Saturday 10 a.m.-6 p.m., Sunday 11 a.m.-5 p.m.

Two good Union Square-area antiquarian bookshops include **Jeremy Norman & Co., Inc.,** 720 Market (near New Montgomery), tel. (415) 781-6402; and **Brick Row Bookshop,** 49 Geary, tel. (415) 398-0414, specializing in 18th- and 19th-century British and American literature.

Some unusual specialty or neighborhood bookstores include pulp-fiction bookseller **Kayo Books,** downtown at 814 Post (near Leavenworth), tel. (415) 749-0554; the **San Francisco Mystery Book Store,** 4175 24th St. (Noe Valley, near the Mission District), tel. (415) 282-7444; and **Marcus**

---

write to the SFCVB to request current information on accommodations, events, and other travel planning particulars. For $3 postage and handling, you can get a copy of the SFCVB's semiannual **The San Francisco Book,** which contains thorough information about sights, activities, arts, entertainment, recreation, shopping venues, and restaurants, as well as a detailed map. (And then some.) If you'll be in town awhile, it's worth the money to request in advance.

The **Redwood Empire Association** operates an International Visitors Center in the Cannery at Fisherman's Wharf, 2801 Leavenworth (at Columbus), tel. (415) 394-5991, open Tues.-Sat. 10 a.m.-6 p.m. Visitors can visit and view the original Ansel Adams prints taken for the Redwood Empire Association in the 1960s; this extensive archive holds photos dating back to 1920, when the REA was founded. The center offers an impressive amount of information—brochures, maps, and pamphlets on member towns, counties, attractions, accommodations, and eateries—in San Francisco and vicinity, and north to the Oregon border. The association publishes the **Redwood Empire Adventures** guide, which you can pick up for a token amount at the visitor center, and also operates a helpful website at www.redwoodempire.com.

Available free at hotels, restaurants, and some shops around town is the small, magazine-style **Key: This Week San Francisco,** which is chock-full of the usual information and has a thorough and current arts, entertainment, and events section. Though focused primarily for permanent Bay Area residents, **San Francisco Focus** magazine also offers regular food and entertainment columns, plus in-depth feature articles about the real world of San Francisco and environs.

Where-San Francisco is a slick, free magazine full of useful information on accommodations, dining, shopping, and nightlife. It's available at the Hallidie Square visitor center and else-

Book Store, 1712 Fillmore St. (at Post, in the Western Addition), tel. (415) 346-4222, specializing in African-American books. Foreign-language book specialists include: **Kinokuniya,** 1581 Webster St. (at Fillmore in the Japan Center), tel. (415) 567-7625; **Russian Books,** 332 Balboa (Richmond District), tel. (415) 668-4723; and **Znanie Book-** store, 5237 Geary (at 11th Ave.), tel. (415) 752-7555, also in the Richmond and also specializing in Russian titles.

Bookstores are also covered in individual districts in The Lay of the Land below. Keep in mind, too, that museums and other major sites sometimes offer impressive selections of books and gifts.

Don't miss a
visit here.

where around town. You can also order a subscription ($30/year) by contacting: Where Magazine, 74 New Montgomery St., Ste. 320, San Francisco, CA 94105, tel. (415) 546-6101.

Even more real: the *San Francisco Bay Guardian* and *SF Weekly* tabloid newspapers, available free almost everywhere around town. The Guardian's motto (with a hat tip to Wilbur Storey and the 1861 *Chicago Times,* as interpreted by Editor/Publisher Bruce Brugmann), "It is a newspaper's duty to print the news and raise hell," is certainly comforting in these times and also generates some decent news/feature reading, along with comprehensive arts, entertainment, and events listings. The Guardian also publishes *FYI San Francisco,* a tourist-oriented guide to the city with some of the same punchy, irreverent writing. It's free and widely available around town. The Weekly also offers what's-happening coverage and—to its everlasting credit—Rob Brezsny's "Real Astrology" column.

While roaming the city, look for other special-interest and neighborhood-scope publications. The *San Francisco Bay Times* is a fairly substantive gay and lesbian biweekly. For comprehensive events information, pick up a copy of the *Bay Area Reporter.* Widely read throughout the Sunset and Richmond Districts is *The Independent.* Other popular papers include the award-winning, hell-raising, *Street Sheet,* published by the Coalition on Homelessness in San Francisco and distributed by the homeless on San Francisco's streets; the *New Mission News;* and the *Noe Valley Voice.*

The city's major dailies are universally available at newsstands and in coin-op vending racks. The morning paper is the *San Francisco Chronicle,* and the afternoon/evening paper is the *San Francisco Examiner.* In late 1999, the *Chronicle* was sold to the Hearst Corporation, and the new owners said they would try to sell the *Examiner,* which they already own. Because the two papers have been linked in a federally approved joint operating agreement since the 1960s, the sale must be accepted by the Justice Department before it's final. But at present, the *Examiner* and *Chronicle* share printing facilities (and classified ads) and also combine forces every week to produce the humongous Sunday paper. That edition's pink "Datebook" section is packed with readable reviews, letters from sometimes demanding or demented Bay Area readers, and the most comprehensive listing of everything going on in the coming week. San Francisco's major non-English and ethnic newspapers include the *Chinese Times,* the *Irish Herald,* and the African-American community's *Sun Reporter.*

If you are so inclined, the newish, high-tech, and highly controversial **San Francisco Main Library,** downtown at 100 Larkin (at Grove), tel. (415) 557-4400, is a good place to start becoming familiar with the local public-library system. For better or worse, the old card catalogs are gone—replaced by a computerized system— and the computers here offer free Internet access. But many users decry the seemingly low percentage of space in the expensive, expansive building actually devoted to stacks of books.

A complete listing of neighborhood branch libraries is offered in the white pages of the local phone book, under "Government Pages—SF City & County—Libraries."

Consulates, Passports, Visas

San Francisco is home to some 70 foreign consulates, from Argentina, Botswana, and Brazil to Indonesia, Malta, the Philippines, and what was once Yugoslavia. For a complete listing, contact the San Francisco Convention & Visitors Bureau (above). The **Australian Consulate** is downtown at 1 Bush St., Seventh Floor, tel. (415) 362-6160 (in emergencies: tel. 415-330-7347); the **British Consulate** is at 1 Sansome St. (at Sutter), Ste. 850, tel. (415) 981-3030 (emergencies: tel. 415-550-6244); and the **Canadian Consulate** is at 50 Fremont St., Ste. 2100, tel. (415) 834-3180. The **French Consulate** is at 540 Bush St., tel. (415) 397-4330 (emergencies: tel. 415-425-6172); the **German Consulate** is at 1960 Jackson St., tel. (415) 775-1061 (emergency callers must leave a message during nonbusiness hours); and the **Hong Kong Economic and Trade Office,** essentially the

Chinese consulate here, is at 130 Montgomery, tel. (415) 835-9300. The **Irish Consulate** is at 44 Montgomery St., Ste. 3830, tel. (415) 392-4214; the **Italian Consulate** is at 2590 Webster St., tel. (415) 931-4924; and the **Japanese Consulate** is at 50 Fremont St., Ste. 2200, tel. (415) 777-3533, and open weekdays 9 a.m.-5 p.m. (closed noon-1 p.m. for lunch). The **Mexican Consulate** is at 870 Market St., Ste. 528, tel. (415) 392-5554; the **New Zealand Consulate** is at 1 Maritime Plaza, tel. (415) 399-1255 (call before coming); and the **Spanish Consulate** is at 1405 Sutter St., tel. (415) 922-2995.

For passports and visas, go to the **U.S. Department of State Passport Agency,** 95 Hawthorne St. (at Folsom), tel. (415) 538-2700; open weekdays 9 a.m.-4 p.m. For customs information and inquiries, contact the **U.S. Customs Service,** 555 Battery St., tel. (415) 782-9210.

For help in locating a foreign-language translator, or for information about San Francisco's foreign-language schools, contact the Convention & Visitors Bureau, which maintains a current listing of member public and private schools.

Other Helpful Information Contacts

For current **weather information,** call (415) 936-1212. For current San Francisco **time,** call that old-time favorite POPCORN (767-8900). For current **road conditions** anywhere in California, call toll-free (800) 427-7623. The free **DOC** (Directory On Call) service, tel. (415) 808-5000, offers a prerecorded summary of local news, sports, stocks, entertainment, and weather information.

The **International Diplomacy Council** is at 312 Sutter St., Ste. 402 (between Grant and Kearny downtown in the financial district), tel. (415) 986-1388. This nonprofit organization promotes international understanding and friendship; foreign visitors are welcome to visit headquarters and to participate in the "Meet Americans at Home" program.

On the third floor of the Chinatown Holiday Inn, the **Chinese Culture Center,** 750 Kearny (at Washington), tel. (415) 986-1822, is the community clearinghouse for Chinese educational and cultural programs, including classes, lectures, workshops, and current events—from the arts and upcoming performances to festivals. Check out the gallery here for shows of Chinese art and artifacts; open Tues.-Sun. 10 a.m.-4 p.m.

BEING PREPARED FOR SAN FRANCISCO

San Francisco's weather can upset even the best-laid plans for a frolic in the summertime California sun. For one thing, there may not be any sun. In summer, when most visitors arrive, San Francisco is enjoying its citywide natural air-conditioning system, called "fog." When California's inland areas are basting in blast-furnace heat, people here might be wearing a down jacket to go walking on the beach. (Sometimes it does get hot—and "hot" by San Francisco standards refers to anything above 80° F.) Especially during the summer, weather extremes even in the course of a single day are normal, so pack accordingly. Bring warm clothing (at least one sweater or jacket for cool mornings and evenings), in addition to the optimist's choice of shorts and sandals, and plan to dress in layers so you'll be prepared for anything. The weather in late spring and early autumn is usually sublime—balmy, often fog-free—so at those times you should bring two pairs of shorts (but don't forget that sweater, just in case). It rarely rains May-Oct.; raingear is prudent at other times.

Most buildings in San Francisco and most public-transit facilities should be accessible to people in wheelchairs and those with other physical limitations; many hotels, restaurants, and entertainment venues will make special accommodations, given some advance notice.

All of San Francisco's (and California's) public buildings and restaurants are nonsmoking. Most motels and hotels have nonsmoking rooms, and many have entire floors of nonsmoking rooms and suites.

Unless otherwise stated on a restaurant menu, restaurants do not include a gratuity in the bill. The standard tip for the wait staff is 15% of the total tab, though truly exceptional service may merit 20%. The average tip for taxi drivers is 15%. It's also customary to tip airport baggage handlers and hotel porters ($1 per bag, one way, is an acceptable standard), parking valets, and other service staff. When in doubt about how much to tip, just ask someone.

While Japan Center or Japantown in its entirety is the center of Japanese-American cultural life, the **Japanese Cultural and Community Center** is here, too, at 1840 Sutter St. (between Buchanan and Laguna), tel. (415) 567-5505.

The **Alliance Française de San Francisco,** 1345 Bush St. (between Hyde and Larkin), tel. (415) 775-7755, is an international cultural center committed to promoting French culture and language. The center's facilities include a café, library, school, theater, and satellite television services. In the Richmond District, the **Booker T. Washington Community Service Center,** 800 Presidio Ave. (at Sutter St.), tel. (415) 928-6596, sponsors a variety of educational, recreational, scouting, and sports activities of specific interest to the black community. **La Raza Information and Translation Center,** 474 Valencia (near 16th in the Mission District), tel. (415) 863-0764, is useful for Latino community information, as is the **Mexican Museum,** clear across town at Fort Mason, tel. (415) 441-0404 or (415) 202-9700. The **Jewish Community Information and Referral Service,** 121 Steuart St. (between Mission and Howard), tel. (415) 777-4545, offers information on just about everything Jewish, from synagogue locations to special-interest community events. For **Senior Citizen's Information and Referrals,** call (415) 626-1033 or stop by the office at 25 Van Ness Ave. (at Market).

The **Women's Building of the Bay Area,** 3543 18th St. (in the Mission District, just off Valencia), tel. (415) 431-1180, serves as the region's central clearinghouse for feminist and lesbian arts, entertainment, and other information. This is the place to contact for a variety of nonprofit women's services (and for advice about where to go for others). **The Names Project Foundation,** headquartered at 310 Townsend St. (near Fourth), tel. (415) 882-5500, is a nonprofit group dedicated to preserving the memory of those lost to AIDS. Its efforts have included the creation of the world-renowned AIDS Quilt. The group's Bay Area Chapter office and visitor center is at 2362 Market St. (near Castro), tel. (415) 863-1966. Berkeley's **Pacific Center for Human Growth,** tel. (510) 548-8283, provides information about everything from local gay and lesbian clubs to current community events, in addition to its counseling service.

For special assistance and information on the city's disabled services, contact the **Mayor's Office of Community Development** (Attn.: Disability Coordinator), 25 Van Ness Ave., Ste. 700, San Francisco, CA 94102, tel. (415) 252-3100, or the helpful local **Easter Seal Society,** 6221 Geary Blvd., tel. (415) 752-4888. To understand the ins and outs of disabled access to local public transit, request a copy of the *Muni Access Guide* from Muni Accessible Services Program, 949 Presidio Ave., San Francisco, CA 94115, tel. (415) 923-6142 weekdays or (415) 673-6864 anytime.

SAFETY, ESSENTIAL SERVICES

Safeguarding Your Self

San Francisco is a reasonably safe city. Definitely unsafe areas, especially at night, include The Tenderloin, some areas south of Market St., parts of the Western Addition, and parts of the Mission District (including, at night, BART stops). For the most part, drug-related gang violence is confined to severely impoverished areas. The increased number of homeless people and panhandlers, particularly notable downtown, is distressing, certainly, but most of these people are harmless lost souls.

Definitely not harmless is the new national crime craze known as "carjacking." As the scenario usually goes, you're sitting in your car at an intersection or at a parking garage when an armed stranger suddenly appears and demands that you get out. Though there have been highly publicized cases involving successful driver heroism, the best advice is, don't try it. If a criminal demands that you get out of your car or give up your car keys, do it. Losing a car is better than losing your life. Though there is no sure-fire prevention for carjacking, locking all car doors and rolling up windows is often suggested. Another good idea: avoid dubious or unfamiliar neighborhoods.

If your own vehicle isn't safe, keep in mind that no place is absolutely safe. And sadly, in general it still holds true that female travelers are safest if they confine themselves to main thoroughfares. As elsewhere in America, women are particularly vulnerable to assaults of every kind. At night, women traveling solo, or even with a friend or two, should stick to bustling, yuppie-happy areas like Fisherman's Wharf and Union Street. The definitely street-savvy, though, can get around fairly well in SoMa and other nightlife areas, especially in groups or by keeping to streets with plenty of benign human traffic. (You can usually tell by looking.)

Emergency Assistance: Safety and Health

In any emergency, get to a telephone and dial 911—the universal emergency number in California. Depending upon the emergency, police, fire, and/or ambulance personnel will be dispatched. Runaways can call home free, anytime, no questions asked, by dialing the **California Youth Crisis Line,** toll-free tel. (800) 843-5200. Other 24-hour crisis and emergency hot lines include: **Helpline,** 772-HELP; **Rape Crisis** (operated by Women Against Rape, or WAR), tel. (415) 647-7273, the number to call in the event of any violent assault; **Suicide Prevention,** tel. (415) 781-0500; **Drug Line,** tel. (415) 834-1144 or (415) 362-3400; **Alcoholics Anonymous,** tel. (415) 621-1326; **Narcotics Anonymous,** tel. (415) 621-8600; and **Poison Control,** toll-free tel. (800) 876-4766.

The San Francisco Police Department (general information line: 415-553-0123) sponsors several Japanese-style kobans—police ministation neighborhood kiosks—where you can get law-enforcement assistance if you're lucky enough to be nearby when they're open. The Hallidie Plaza Koban is in the tourist-thick cable-car zone at Market and Powell; open Tues.-Sat. 10 a.m.-6 p.m. The Chinatown Koban is on Grant between Washington and Jackson; open daily 1-9 p.m. The Japantown Koban is at Post and Buchanan; open Mon.-Fri. 11 a.m.-7 p.m.

San Francisco General Hospital, 1001 Potrero Ave. (at 22nd St., on Potrero Hill), tel. (415) 206-8000 (911 or 415-206-8111 for emergencies), provides 24-hour medical emergency and trauma care services. Another possibility is **UCSF Medical Center,** 505 Parnassus Ave. (at Third Ave.), tel. (415) 476-1000. (The UCSF dental clinic is at 707 Parnassus, tel. (415) 476-1891 or (415) 476-5814 for emergencies.) Convenient for most visitors is **Saint Francis Memorial Hospital** on Nob Hill, 900 Hyde St., tel. (415) 353-6000, which offers no-appointment-needed clinic and urgent-care medical services as well as a **Center for Sports Medicine,** tel. (415)

353-6400, and a physician referral service, toll-free tel. (800) 333-1355.

For nonemergency referrals, call the **San Francisco Medical Society,** tel. (415) 561-0853, or the **San Francisco Dental Society,** tel. (415) 421-1435.

Post Offices, Banks, Currency Exchanges
San Francisco's main post office is the Rincon Annex, 180 Steuart St. (just off the Embarcadero, south of Market), San Francisco, CA 94105. It's open weekdays 7 a.m.-6 p.m., Saturday 9 a.m.-2 p.m. For help in figuring out local zip code assignments, and for general information and current postal rates, call toll-free (800) 275-8777 or log on to www.usps.gov. Regional post offices are also scattered throughout San Francisco neighborhoods. Some branches are open extended hours, such as 7 a.m.-6 p.m. weekdays, or with limited services some Saturday hours, and some have after-hours open lobbies, so customers can purchase stamps via vending machines. Public mailboxes, for posting stamped mail, are available in every area. Stamps are also for sale in major hotels (usually in the gift shop) and, increasingly, even in major grocery stores.

Branches of major national and international banks are available in San Francisco; most offer automated cash-advance facilities, often accessible through various member systems. Getting mugged while banking is a potential disadvantage of getting cash from an automated teller. Always be aware of who is nearby and what they're doing; if possible, have a companion or two with you. If the situation doesn't feel "right," move to another location—or do your banking inside.

Most currency exchange outlets are either downtown or at the San Francisco International Airport (SFO). **Bank of America Foreign Currency Services,** 345 Montgomery St., tel. (415) 622-2451, is open Mon.-Fri. 9 a.m.-6 p.m. Another possibility is the Bank of America at the Powell St. cable car turnaround, 1 Powell (at Market), tel. (415) 622-4498 (same hours). **Thomas Cook Currency Services, Inc.,** 75 Geary, tel. (415) 362-6271 or toll-free (800) 287-7362, is open weekdays 9 a.m.-5 p.m., Saturday 10 a.m.-4 p.m. (Another location is at 1 Powell Street.) To exchange currency at the airport,

head for the International Terminal, where **Bank of America,** tel. (650) 615-4700, offers currency exchange for both in- and out-bound travelers daily 7 a.m.-11 p.m.

For cardmembers, the **American Express Travel Agency** is another possibility for check cashing, traveler's-check transactions, and currency exchange. There are three San Francisco offices: 455 Market (at First), 560 California St. (between Kearny and Montgomery), and 333 Jefferson (at Jones); tel. (415) 536-2600 for all. In Northern California, the American Automobile Association (AAA) is known as the California State Automobile Association (CSAA), and the San Francisco office is near the Civic Center at 150 Van Ness Ave., tel. (415) 565-2012. The CSAA office is open weekdays for all member inquiries and almost endless services, including no-fee traveler's checks, free maps and travel information, and travel agency services.

San Francisco's major hotels, and most of the midrange boutique hotels, have a fax number and fax facilities; some offer other communications services. For telex and telegrams, you can pop into one of the many **Western Union** branches throughout the city.

TRANSPORTATION: GETTING TO AND FROM TOWN

At least on pleasure trips, Californians and other Westerners typically drive into San Francisco. The city is reached from the north via Hwy. 101 across the fabled Golden Gate Bridge ($3 toll to get into the city, no cost to get out); from the east via I-80 from Oakland/Berkeley across the increasingly choked-with-traffic Bay Bridge ($2 toll to get into the city, no cost to get out); and from the south (from the coast or from San Jose and other South Bay/peninsula communities) via Hwy. 1, Hwy. 101, or I-280/19th Avenue. Whichever way you come and go, avoid peak morning (7-9 a.m.) and afternoon/evening (4-6 p.m.) rush hours at all costs. The Bay Area's traffic congestion is truly horrendous.

Airports
About 15 miles south of the city via Hwy. 101,

San Francisco International Airport (SFO), tel. (650) 876-2377 (general information) or (650) 877-0227 (parking information), perches on a point of land at the edge of the bay. (That's one of the thrills here: taking off and landing just above the water.) Each of the three terminals—North, Central (or International), and South—has two levels, the lower for arrivals, the upper for departures. San Francisco's is the fifth busiest airport in the U.S. and seventh busiest in the world; its 80 gates handle some 32 million passengers per year. More than 40 major scheduled carriers (and smaller ones, including air charters) serve SFO. There's protected parking for 7,000 cars, best for short-term car storage.

San Francisco International has its quirks. For one thing, its odd horseshoe shape often makes for a long walk for transferring passengers; the "people movers" help somewhat, but people seem to avoid the second-floor intraterminal bus. (In all fairness, though, since SFO is primarily an origin/destination airport, so for most travelers this isn't a problem.) And with such a high volume of air traffic—an average of 1,260 flights per day—delays are all too common, especially when fog rolls in and stays.

People complain, too, that the airport always seems to be under major construction. A multibillion-dollar expansion project is underway, which at some point will result in a new international terminal. If you've got some time to kill, check out the permanent "Images of Mexico" cultural display, with masks and such, in the South Terminal connector (beyond the security check) and the outstanding changing exhibits along United's North Terminal connector. Or you can make use of the AT&T Communications Center, upstairs in the International Terminal; it's open 8 a.m.-10 p.m. and offers special phone facilities to allow callers to pay the attendants (multilingual) in cash, as well as a six-person conference room set up for teleconferencing (fax, too). Other airport facilities include restaurants (the Bay View Restaurant in the South Terminal, the North Beach Deli in the North), the South Terminal's California Marketplace (where you can get some wine and smoked fish or crab to go with that sourdough bread you're packing), and the North Terminal's Author's Bookstore, which prominently features titles by Bay Area and California writers.

Due to its excellent service record and relatively lower volume, many travelers prefer flying into and out of efficient, well-run **Oakland International Airport** just across the bay, tel. (510) 577-4000. It's fairly easy to reach from downtown San Francisco on either public transit or one of the convenient shuttle services.

Airport Shuttles

If flying into and out of SFO, avoid driving if at all possible. Airport shuttles are abundant, fairly inexpensive, and generally reliable. Most companies offer at-your-door pick-up service if you're heading to the airport (advance reservations usually required) and—coming from the airport—take you right where you're going. The usual one-way fare, depending upon the company, is around $15 per person for SFO/San Francisco service. (Inquire about prices for other shuttle options.)

The blue-and-gold **SuperShuttle** fleet has some 100 vans coming and going all the time, tel. (415) 659-2547. When you arrive at SFO, the company's shuttle vans (no reservation needed) to the city are available at the outer island on the upper level of all terminals. To arrange a trip to the airport, call and make your pick-up reservation at least a day in advance. (And be ready when the shuttle arrives—they're usually on time.) Group, convention, and charter shuttles are also available, and you can pay on board with a major credit card. (Exact fare depends on where you start and end.)

SFO Airporter, tel. (415) 641-3100, offers nonstop runs every 20 minutes between the airport and the Financial District or Union Square. No reservations are required in either direction. **City Express Shuttle** in Oakland, tel. (510) 638-8830, offers daily shuttle service between the city of San Francisco and Oakland International Airport. **Bayporter Express, Inc.,** tel. (415) 656-2929, (415) 467-1800, or toll-free (800) 287-6783 (from inside the airport), specializes in shuttle service between most Bay Area suburban communities and SFO, and offers hourly door-to-door service between any location in San Francisco and the Oakland Airport. **Marin Airporter** in Larkspur, tel. (415) 461-4222, provides service every half hour from various Marin communities to SFO daily, 4:30 a.m.-11 p.m., and from SFO to Marin County daily, 5:30 a.m.-midnight.

San Mateo County Transit (SamTrans), toll-free tel. (800) 660-4287, offers extensive peninsula public transit, including express and regular buses from SFO to San Francisco. It's cheap, too (about $1). Buses leave the airport every 30 minutes from very early morning to just after midnight; call for exact schedule. The express buses limit passengers to carry-on luggage only, so heavily laden travelers will have to take one of the regular buses—a 10-minute-longer ride.

Buses and Trains

The **Transbay Terminal,** 425 Mission St. (just south of Market St. between First and Fremont), tel. (415) 495-1551 or (415) 495-1569, is the city's regional transportation hub. An information center on the second floor has displays, maps, and fee-free phone lines for relevant transit systems. Bus companies based here include **Greyhound,** tel. (415) 495-1569, with buses coming and going at all hours; **Golden Gate Transit,** tel. (415) 455-2000, offering buses to and from Marin County and vicinity; **AC Transit,** tel. (415) 817-1717, which serves the East Bay; and **San Mateo County Transit** (SamTrans), toll-free tel. (800) 660-4287, which runs as far south as Palo Alto. Shuttle buses here also take passengers across the bay to the Amtrak station at 245 Second St. in Oakland's Jack London Square, tel. (510) 238-4306 or toll-free (800) USA-RAIL, www.amtrak.com, where you can make train connections both north and south.

Primarily a regional commute service, **Cal-Train,** toll-free tel. (800) 660-4287 within Northern California, runs south to Palo Alto and the Amtrak station in San Jose, where you can get a bus connection to Santa Cruz. The San Francisco CalTrain depot is at Fourth and Townsend Streets.

Ferries

Since the city is surrounded on three sides by water, ferry travel is an unusual (and unusually practical) San Francisco travel option. Before the construction of the Golden Gate Bridge in 1937, it was the only way to travel to the city from the North and East Bay areas. Nowadays, the ferries function both as viable commuter and tourist transit services. (See Delights and Diversions for more about ferry tours and other oceangoing entertainment.)

The **Blue & Gold Fleet,** tel. (415) 773-1188 (recorded schedule) or (415) 705-5555 (reservations and information), based at Fisherman's Wharf, Piers 39 and 41, offers roundtrip service daily between San Francisco (either the Ferry Building or Pier 41) and Oakland (Jack London Square), Alameda (Gateway Center), Sausalito, Tiburon, Angel Island, and Vallejo (via high-speed catamaran). The company also offers bay cruises, tours of Alcatraz, an "Island Hop" tour to both Alcatraz and Angel Island, and various land tours (Muir Woods, Yosemite, Monterey/Carmel, Wine Country).

Golden Gate Ferries, headquartered in the Ferry Building at the foot of Market St., tel. (415) 923-2000, specializes in runs to and from Sausalito (adults $4.70) and more frequent large-ferry (725-passenger capacity) trips to and from Larkspur. Family rates available, and disabled pasengers and seniors (over age 65) travel at half fare.

Red & White Fleet at Fisherman's Wharf, Pier 43$\frac{1}{2}$, tel. (415) 447-0597 or toll-free (800) 229-2784, offers bay cruises and various land tours, as well as a commuter run to Richmond.

TAKING A TAXI

Taxis from SFO to San Francisco cost around $30. Standard San Francisco taxi fare, which also applies to around-town trips, is $2.50 for the first mile, $1.80 per additional mile (plus tip, usually 15%). Among the 24-hour taxi companies available:

DeSoto Cab Co.	tel. (415) 673-1414
Luxor Cab	tel. (415) 282-4141
Veteran's Taxicab Company	tel. (415) 552-1300
Yellow Cab	tel. (415) 626-2345

TRANSPORTATION: GETTING AROUND TOWN

San Francisco drivers are among the craziest in California. Whether they're actually demented, just distracted, insanely rude, or perhaps intentionally driving to a different drummer, walkers beware. The white lines of a pedestrian crosswalk seem to serve as sights, making people easier targets. Even drivers must adopt a heads-up attitude. In many areas, streets are narrow and/or incredibly steep. Finding a parking place requires psychic skills. So, while many people drive into and out of the Bay Area's big little city, if at all possible many use public transit to get around town.

But some people really want to drive in San Francisco. Others don't want to, but need to, due to the demands of their schedules. A possible compromise: if you have a car but can't stand the thought of driving it through the urban jungle yourself, hire a driver. You can hire a chauffeur, and even arrange private sightseeing tours and other outings, through companies like **WeDriveU, Inc.,** 60 E. Third Ave. in San Mateo, tel. (650) 579-5800 or toll-free (800) 773-7483. Other local limousine companies may be willing to hire-out just a city-savvy driver; call and ask.

Though those maniacal bicycle delivery folks somehow manage to daredevil their way through downtown traffic—note their bandages, despite protective armor—for normal people, cycling is a no-go proposition downtown and along heavy-traffic thoroughfares. Bring a bike to enjoy the Golden Gate National Recreation Area and other local parks, though it may be easier to rent one. Rental outlets around Golden Gate Park include **Lincoln Cyclery,** 772 Stanyan (near Waller), tel. (415) 221-2415; **Start to Finish Bicycles,** 672 Stanyan (near Page), tel. (415) 750-4760; and **Avenue Cyclery,** 756 Stanyan, tel. (415) 387-3155. In Golden Gate Park, you can rent a bike, rollerblades, or a pedal-powered surrey at **Golden Gate Park Bike & Skate,** 3038 Fulton, tel. (415) 668-1117.

Car Rental Agencies

Some of the least expensive car rental agencies have the most imaginative names. Near the airport in South San Francisco, **Bob Leech's Auto Rental** 435 S. Airport Blvd., tel. (650) 583-3844, specializes in new Toyotas, from $25 per day with 150 fee-free miles. (You must carry a valid major credit card and be at least 23 years old; call for a ride from the airport.) Downtown, family-owned **Reliable Rent-A-Car,** 349 Mason, tel. (415) 928-4414, rents new cars with free pick-up and return for a starting rate of $19 per day ("any car, any time"). That all-American innovation, **Rent-A-Wreck,** 2955 Third St., tel.

(415) 282-6293, rents out midsize used cars for around $29 per day with 150 free miles, or $159 per week with 700 free miles.

The more well-known national car rental agencies have desks at the airport, as well as at other locations. Their rates are usually higher than those of the independents and vary by vehicle make and model, length of rental, day of the week (sometimes season), and total mileage. Special coupon savings or substantial discounts through credit card company or other group affiliations can lower the cost considerably. If price really matters, check around. Consult the telephone book for all local locations of the companies listed below.

Agencies with offices downtown include: **Avis Rent-A-Car,** 675 Post St., tel. (415) 885-5011 or toll-free (800) 831-2847; **Budget Rent-A-Car,** 321 Mason, tel. (415) 775-5800 or toll-free (800) 527-0700; **Dollar Rent-A-Car,** 364 O'Farrell (opposite the Hilton Hotel), tel. (415) 771-5301 or toll-free (800) 800-4000; **Enterprise,** 1133 Van Ness Ave., tel. (415) 441-3369 or toll-free (800) 736-8222; **Hertz,** 433 Mason, tel. (415) 771-2200 or toll-free (800) 654-3131; and **Thrifty Rent-A-Car,** 520 Mason (at Post), tel. (415) 788-8111 or toll-free (800) 367-2277.

For a transportation thrill, all you wannabe easy riders can rent a BMW or Harley-Davidson motorcycle from **Dubbelju Tours & Service,** 271 Clara St., tel. (415) 495-2774. Rates start at $92 a day and include insurance, 100 free miles, and road service. Weekly and winter rates available. Open Mon.-Fri. 9 a.m.-noon and 4-6 p.m., Saturday 9-noon, or by appointment. German spoken.

Parking Regulations and Curb Colors

If you're driving, it pays to know the local parking regulations as well as rules of the road—it'll cost you if you don't.

Curbing your wheels is the law when parking on San Francisco's hilly streets. What this means: turn your wheels toward the street when parked facing uphill (so your car will roll into the curb if your brakes and/or transmission don't hold), and turn them toward the curb when facing downhill.

Also, pay close attention to painted curb colors; the city parking cops take violations seriously. Red curbs mean absolutely no stopping or parking. Yellow means loading zone (for vehicles with commercial plates only), half-hour time limit; yellow-and-black means loading zone for trucks with commercial plates only, half-hour limit; and green-yellow-and-black means taxi zone. Green indicates a 10-minute parking limit for any vehicle, and white means five minutes only, effective during the operating hours of the adjacent business. As elsewhere in the state, blue indicates parking reserved for vehicles with a California disabled placard or plate displayed. Pay attention, too, to posted street-cleaning parking limits, to time-limited parking lanes (open at rush hour to commuter traffic), and avoid even a quick-park at bus stops or in front of fire hydrants. Any violation will cost $25 or more, and the police can tow your car—which will cost you $100 or so (plus daily impound fees) to retrieve.

Parking and Parking Garages
If you're driving, you'll need to park. You also need to find parking, all but impossible in North Beach, the Haight, and other popular neighborhoods. San Franciscans have their pet parking theories and other wily tricks—some even consider the challenge of finding parking a sport, or at least a game of chance. But it's not so fun for visitors, who usually find it challenging enough just to find their way around. It's wise to park your car (and leave it parked, to the extent possible), then get around by public transit. Valet parking is available (for a price, usually at least $15 per day) at major and midsize hotels, and at or near major attractions, including shopping districts.

Call ahead to inquire about availability, rates, and hours at major public parking garages, which include: **Fisherman's Wharf,** 665 Beach (at Hyde), tel. (415) 673-5197; **Fifth and Mission Garage,** 833 Mission St., tel. (415) 982-8522; **Downtown,** Mason and Ellis, tel. (415) 771-1400 (ask for the garage); **Moscone Center,** 255 Third St., tel. (415) 777-2782; **Chinatown,** 733 Kearny (underground, near Portsmith Square), tel. (415) 982-6353; and **Union Street,** 1550 Union, tel. (415) 673-5728. For general information on city-owned garages, call (415) 554-9805.

And good luck.

Public Transportation: Muni
The city's multifaceted San Francisco Municipal Railway, or Muni, headquartered at 949 Presidio Ave., tel. (415) 673-MUNI weekdays 7 a.m.-5

p.m., Sat.-Sun. 9 a.m.-5 p.m., is still the locals' public transit mainstay. One of the nation's oldest publicly owned transportation systems, Muni is far from feeble, managing to move almost 250 million people each year. Yet even small glitches can wreak havoc when so many people depend on the system; heated criticism regularly crops up on local talk-radio shows and in the Letters to the Editor sections of local newspapers.

The city's buses, light-rail electric subway-and-surface streetcars, electric trolleys, and world-renowned cable cars are all provided by Muni. It costs $2 to ride the cable car. (It's odd that people stand in long lines at the Powell and Market turnaround, since it actually makes much more sense—no waiting, unless there's absolutely no space available—to grab on at Union Square or other spots en route.) Otherwise, regular Muni fare is $1 ($0.35 for seniors and youths, children under 5 free), exact coins required, and includes free transfers valid for two changes of vehicle in any direction within a two-hour period. If you'll be making lots of trips around town, pick up a multitrip discount Muni Passport (which includes cable car transit), available for sale at the Muni office, the Convention & Visitors Bureau information center downtown, Union Square's TIX box office, the City Hall information booth, and the Cable Car Museum. A one-day pass costs $6, a three-day pass $10, a seven-day pass $15, and a monthly pass $35.

Muni route information is published in the local telephone book yellow pages, or call for route verification (phone number listed above). Better yet, for a thorough orientation, check out one of the various Muni publications, most of which are available wherever Muni Passports are sold (and usually at the Transbay Terminal). A good overview and introduction is provided (free) by the *Muni Access Guide* pamphlet and the useful, seasonally updated *TimeTables,* which list current route and time information for all Muni transit. Especially useful for travelers is Muni's *Tours of Discovery* brochure, which lists popular destinations and possible tours with suggested transit routes (including travel time) and optional transfers and side trips. But the best all-around guide, easy to carry in pocket or purse, is the official annual *Muni Street & Transit Map* ($2), available at bookstores and grocery stores in addition to the usual outlets. The Muni map ex-

RIDING THE CABLE CARS

With or without those Rice-a-Roni ads, Muni's cable cars are a genuine San Francisco treat. (Don't allow yourself to be herded onto one of those rubber-tired motorized facsimiles that tend to cluster at Union Square, Fisherman's Wharf, and elsewhere. They are not cable cars, just lures for confused tourists.) San Francisco's cable cars are a national historic landmark, a system called "Hallidie's Folly" in honor of inventor Andrew S. Hallidie when these antiques made their debut on August 2, 1873. The only vehicles of their kind in the world, cable cars were created with the city's challenging vertical grades in mind. They are "powered" by an underground cable in perpetual motion, and by each car's grip-and-release mechanism. Even though maximum speed is about nine mph, that can seem plenty fast when the car snaps around an S-curve. (They aren't kidding when they advise riders to hold onto their seats.) After a complete $67.5 million system overhaul in the early 1980s, 26 "single-enders" now moan and groan along the two Powell St. routes, and 11 "double-enders" make the "swoop loop" along California Street. (New cars are occasionally added to the city's collection.) To get a vivid education in how cable cars work, visit the reconstructed **Cable Car Barn and Museum.**

cable cars: a time-honored way to climb the city's steep streets

SAN JOSE CONVENTION AND VISITORS BUREAU

plains and illustrates major routes, access points, frequency of service, and also shows BART and Muni Metro subway stops, along with the CalTrain route into San Francisco. As a city map, it's a good investment, too.

San Francisco's Muni buses are powered by internal-combustion engines, and each is identified by a number and an area or street name (such as #7 Haight or #29 Sunset). Similarly numbered local trolleys or streetcars are actually electrically operated buses, drawing power from overhead lines, and are most notable downtown and along the steepest routes. The summers-only Historic Trolley Festival is actually a do-it-yourself party, achieved by climbing aboard Muni's international fleet of vintage electric streetcars (F-Market) that start at the Transbay Terminal and run along Market St. to and from Castro.

The Muni Metro refers to the five-line system of streetcars or light-rail vehicles, often strung together into trains of up to four cars, that run underground along Market St. and radiate out into the neighborhoods. Metro routes are identified by letters in conjunction with point of destination (J-Church, K-Ingleside, L-Taraval, M-Oceanview, and N-Judah).

Public Transportation: BART
The Bay Area's 95-mile Bay Area Rapid Transit, or BART, system headquartered in Oakland, tel. (510) 464-6000 or (650) 992-2278 (transit information), calls itself "the tourist attraction that gets people to the other tourist attractions." Fair enough. Heck, it is pretty thrilling to zip across to Oakland and Berkeley underwater in the Transbay Tube. And at least as far as it goes, BART is a good get-around alternative for people who would rather not drive. Currently, there isn't much BART service on the San Francisco side of the Bay, with 10 BART stations in San Francisco, the

line ending at Colma. Some day in the not-too-distant future, a line will extend south to the airport; work is underway and is expected to be completed in 2001. But the system can take you to Oakland/Berkeley, then north to Richmond, south to Fremont, or east to Pittsburg or Pleasanton. (BART Express buses extend transit service to other East Bay communities.)

Helpful publications include the annual *All About BART* (with fares, travel times, and other details), *Fun Goes Farther on BART,* and the *BART & Buses* BART guide to connections with the bus system. BART trains operate Mon.-Fri. 4 a.m.-midnight, Saturday 6 a.m.-midnight, and Sunday 8 a.m.-midnight. Exact fare depends upon your destination, but it'll be $4.75 or less. For a special $3.90 "excursion fare," you can tour the whole system; just don't walk through the computerized exits, or you'll have to pay again before you get back on. Tickets are dispensed at machines based at each station. (Change machines, for coins or dollar bills, are nearby.) If you don't have a current Muni map, you can get your bearings at each station's color-keyed wall maps, which show destinations and routes.

SAN FRANCISCO CONVENTION AND VISITORS BUREAU

THE LAY OF THE LAND
DOWNTOWN

In other times, San Francisco neighborhoods and districts had such distinct ethnic and cultural or functional identities that they served as separate cities within a city. It wasn't uncommon for people to be born and grow up, to work, to raise families, and to die in their own insular neighborhoods, absolutely unfamiliar with the rest of San Francisco.

For the most part, those days are long past. Since its inception, the city has transformed itself, beginning as a sleepy mission town, then a lawless gold-rush capital that gradually gained respectability and recognition as the West Coast's most sophisticated cultural and trade center. The process continues. The city's neighborhoods continue to reinvent themselves, and California's accelerated economic and social mobility also erase old boundaries. Just where one part of town ends and another begins is a favorite San Francisco topic of disagreement.

AROUND UNION SQUARE

Named after Civil War-era rallies held here in support of Union forces (California eventually spurned the Confederacy), San Francisco's Union Square is parking central for downtown shoppers, since the square also serves as the roof of the multilevel parking garage directly below. (Other garages within walking distance include the Sutter-Stockton Garage to the north, the Ellis-O'Farrell Garage two blocks south, and, across Market, the huge and inexpensive Fifth & Mission Garage.)

The landmark **Westin St. Francis Hotel** flanks Union Square on the west, its bar a time-honored retreat from nearby major stores like **Saks Fifth Avenue, Tiffany, Bullock & Jones, Macy's,** and **Neiman-Marcus** (which also has its own popular **Rotunda** restaurant for après-shop dropping; open for lunch and afternoon tea).

DEFINING DOWNTOWN

In San Francisco, "downtown" is a general reference to the city's hustle-bustle heart. Knowing just where it starts and ends is largely irrelevant, so long as you understand that it includes Union Square, much of Market St., and the Civic Center government and arts buildings. The Financial District and the Waterfront are also included. Six or seven blocks directly west of the Civic Center is the Alamo Square Historic District, one among other enclaves of gentrified Victorian neighborhoods in the otherwise down-and-out Western Addition, which also includes Japantown. Though purists will no doubt quibble, for reasons of proximity these are included with downtown. And while more "uptown" parts of the South of Market Area (SoMa) are essentially downtown too, as are Nob Hill and Chinatown, those areas are covered in more depth elsewhere below.

Immediately east of Union Square along Post, Maiden Ln., and Geary, you'll find an unabashed selection of expensive and fashionable stores, from **Cartier, Dunhill,** and **Wilkes Bashford** to **NikeTown USA, Eddie Bauer,** and **Brooks Brothers.** Or dress yourself up at **Ralph Lauren, Versace, Chanel, Laura Ashley,** and several other designer emporiums. **Gumps** at 135 Post is the elegant specialist in one-of-a-kind and rare wares, where even the furniture is art. Don't miss a stroll down traffic-free, two-block **Maiden Lane,** a one-time red-light district stretching between Stockton and Kearny, chock-full of sidewalk cafés and shops. Here stands the Circle Gallery building, most ogled for its architecture. Designed in 1949 by Frank Lloyd Wright, with its spiral interior this building is an obvious prototype for his more famous Guggenheim Museum in New York. **Crocker Galleria,** at Post and Montgomery, offers still more shopping.

Heading south from Union Square on Stockton, between O'Farrell and Market, you'll pass the famous **F.A.O. Schwarz** (full of adult-priced toys and still fun for kids); **Planet Hollywood;** and the **Virgin Megastore,** where music lovers can find just about anything to add to their CD collection. At Market St. is the new **Old Navy,** as well as a cheap thrill for shoppers—the eight-story circular escalator ride up to **Nordstrom** and other stores at **San Francisco Shopping Centre,** Fifth and Market, which was built in the late 1980s with the hope of attracting suburbanites and squeezing out the homeless.

Just down a ways from the theater district and skirting The Tenderloin at 561 Geary (between Taylor and Jones) is the odd **Blue Lamp** bar—note the blue lamp, a classic of neo-neon art. Once just a hard-drinkers' dive, now the Blue Lamp is a campy, hipsters', hard-drinkers' dive, most interesting late at night when the neighborhood gets a bit scary. But the real reason to come here is live music, just-starting band badness. Just a few blocks away, near Union Square at 333 Geary (between Powell and Mason), is another world entirely—**Lefty O'Doul's,** a hofbrau-style deli and old-time bar stuffed to the ceiling with baseball memorabilia. Lefty was a local hero, a big leaguer who came back to manage the minor-league San Francisco Seals before the Giants came to town.

The Tenderloin

Stretching between Union Square and the Civic Center is The Tenderloin, definitely a poor choice for a casual stroll by tourists and other innocents. A down-and-out pocket of poverty pocked these days by the city signposts of human misery—drug dealing, prostitution, pornography, and violent crime—the densely populated Tenderloin earned its name around the turn of the century, when police assigned to patrol its mean streets received additional hazard pay—and, some say, substantial protection money and kickbacks. (The extra cash allowed them to dine on the choicest cuts of meat.) The Tenderloin's historic boundaries are Post, Market, Van Ness, and Powell. In reality, however, the city's designated theater district (with accompanying cafés and nightspots, many newly gentrified hotels, even the St. Francis Hotel and most Civic Center attractions fall within this no-man's land, which is especially a no-woman's land. More realistic, better-safe-than-sorry boundaries are Larkin, Mason, O'Farrell, and Market, with an extra caution also for some streets south of Market (especially Sixth) as far as Howard. As a general rule, perimeters are

SAN FRANCISCO ON STAGE

Geary Street near both Mason and Taylor is the official center of the theater district, and the 400 block of Geary serves as the epicenter of the mainstream theater scene. These days the concentration of upscale Union Square hotels downtown roughly duplicates the theater district boundaries. With so many fine theaters scattered throughout the city, it's something of a New York affectation to insist on that designation downtown. But San Francisco, a city that has loved its dramatic song and dance since Gold Rush days, definitely insists. Poetry readings, lectures, opera, and Shakespeare were integral to the 1800s arts scene. Superstar entertainers of the era made their mark here, from spider-dancer Lola Montez and her child protégé Lotta Crabtree to Lillie Langtry, opera star Luisa Tetrazzini, actress Helena Modjeska, and actor Edwin Booth. Today, out-of-towners flock to big musicals like *Phantom of the Opera* and evergreens like the murder mystery *Shear Madness.* Luckily, the best shows are often less crowded. Most shows begin at 8 p.m., and the majority of theaters are closed on Monday.

Theater Information

Finding information on what's going on in the theater is not a difficult task. Listings are printed in the *San Francisco Bay Guardian,* the *SF Weekly,* and the Sunday edition of the *San Francisco Chronicle.* Or check out the arts online at www.citysearch7.com.

And wherever you find it, pick up a free copy of *Stagebill* magazine, www.stagebill.com, for its current and comprehensive show schedules.

Getting Tickets

Theater tickets can be purchased in advance or for half price on the day of the performance at **TIX Bay Area,** on Stockton St. at Union Square, tel. (415) 433-7827, www.tix.com. Payment is cash only, no credit card reservations. A full-service BASS ticket outlet as well, TIX also handles advance full-price tickets to many Bay Area events (open Tues.-Sat. noon-7:30 p.m.). You can get a catalog for ordering advance tickets at half price by calling **TIX by Mail,** at (415) 430-1140. To charge BASS arts and entertainment tickets by phone or to listen to recorded calendar listings, call (415) 478-2277 (BASS). Order full-price tickets in advance with a $2.50 service charge from Ticketmaster, tel. (415) 421-8497 or toll-free (800) 755-4000, www.ticketmaster.com.

Other ticket box offices include: **City Box Office,** tel. (415) 392-4400; **Entertainment Ticketfinder,** tel. (650) 756-1414 or toll-free (800) 523-1515; and **St. Francis Theatre and Sports Tickets,** a service of the Westin St. Francis Hotel, tel. (415) 362-3500, or www.premiertickets.com.

Theater District Venues

For Broadway shows, the **Curran Theatre,** 445

safer than core areas, but since this is San Francisco's highest crime area, with rape, mugging, and other assaults at an all-time high, for tenderfeet no part of The Tenderloin is considered safe—even during daylight hours. Ask local shopkeepers and restaurant or hotel personnel about the safety of specific destinations, if in doubt, and travel in groups when you do venture any distance into The Tenderloin.

But the area has its beauty, too, often most apparent through the celebrations and ministries of the Reverend Cecil Williams and congregation at the renowned **Glide Memorial United Methodist Church,** which rises up at 330 Ellis (at Taylor), tel. (415) 771-6300, www.glide.org. Glide sponsors children's assistance and other community programs, from basic survival and

AIDS care to the Computers and You program, which helps the economically disadvantaged learn computer skills. The Glide Ensemble choir sings an uplifting mix of gospel, freedom songs, and rock at its celebrations, held each Sunday at 9 and 11 a.m.

And some neighborhoods are cleaning up considerably, the indirect influence of commercial redevelopment and the influx of large numbers of Asian immigrants, many from Cambodia, Laos, and Vietnam. The annual **Tet Festival** celebrates the Vietnamese New Year. The Tenderloin also supports a small but growing arts community, as the 'Loin is one of the few remaining pockets of affordable housing in San Francisco. Among the neighborhood's many bars, the **Edinburgh Castle** at 950 Geary (between Polk

Geary (between Mason and Taylor), tel. (415) 551-2000 (information), tel. (415) 478-2277 (BASS) for tickets, is the long-running standard. The repertory **American Conservatory Theater** (ACT), tel. (415) 834-3200 or (415) 749-2228 (box office), performs its big-name-headliner contemporary comedies and dramas in the venerable **Geary Theatre,** 415 Geary (at Mason).

Other neighborhood venues include the **Mason Street Theatre,** tel. (415) 982-5463, at 340 Mason (near Geary); the **Cable Car Theatre,** tel. (415) 255-9772, at 430 Mason (between Post and Geary); the **Golden Gate Theatre,** tel. (415) 551-2000, at 1 Taylor (at Golden Gate), longtime home of the Pulitzer Prize- and Tony-award-winning *Rent;* and the **Marines Memorial Theater,** tel. (415) 551-2000, at 609 Sutter (at Mason). All are good bets for off-Broadway shows. Unusual small theaters include the **Theatre on the Square,** tel. (415) 433-9300, sharing space with the Kensington Park Hotel at 450 Post (between Powell and Mason), and the **Plush Room Cabaret,** tel. (415) 885-2115, inside the York Hotel at 940 Sutter (at Leavenworth).

Performance Spaces Elsewhere

San Francisco is also home to a number of small, innovative theaters and theater troupes, including the **Magic Theatre, Cowell Theater,** and **Young Performers Theatre** at Fort Mason, and the **Asian American Theatre** in the Richmond District, mentioned in more detail in The Avenues

section of this chapter. The **Actors Theatre of San Francisco,** 533 Sutter (between Powell and Mason), tel. (415) 296-9179, usually offers unusual plays. Also popular for progressive dramatic theater is SoMa's **Climate Theatre,** 252 Ninth St. (at Folsom), tel. (415) 978-2345. Another innovator in the realm of performance art is **Theater Artaud,** 450 Florida St. (at 17th), tel. (415) 621-7797. **Theatre Rhinoceros,** 2926 16th St. (between Mission and S. Van Ness), tel. (415) 861-5079, is America's oldest gay and lesbian theater company, est. 1978.

The long-running **Eureka Theatre Company,** 215 Jackson (between Front and Battery), tel. (415) 788-7469 (box office and information), is noted for its provocative, politically astute presentations. **Intersection for the Arts,** 446 Valencia St. (between 15th and 16th), tel. (415) 626-2787 (administration) or (415) 626-3311 (box office), the city's oldest alternative arts center, presents everything from experimental dramas to performance and visual art and dance. One-time "new talent" like Robin Williams, Whoopi Goldberg, and Sam Shepard are all Intersection alumni. **George Coates Performance Works,** 110 McAllister (at Leavenworth), tel. (415) 863-8520 (administration) or (415) 863-4130 (box office), offers innovative multimedia theater presentations in a re-purposed neo-Gothic cathedral.

—Pat Reilly and Kim Weir

and Larkin), tel. (415) 885-4074, stands out, drawing an interesting crowd of Scottish expatriates and young urbanites. The pub specializes in single malt Scotch, lager, and some of the best fish 'n' chips in the city.

MARKET STREET AND THE FINANCIAL DISTRICT

The Financial District features San Francisco's tallest, most phallic buildings, perhaps suggesting something profound about the psychology of the global capitalist thrust. When rolling into town on the river of traffic, via the Golden Gate Bridge or, especially, Oakland's Bay Bridge, this compact concentration of law of-

fices, insurance buildings, investment companies, banks, brokerages, and high-brow businesses rises up from the sparkling waters like some fantastic illusion, the greenback-packed Emerald City of the West Coast. Even if wandering on foot and temporarily lost, to get back downtown one merely looks up and heads off toward the big buildings.

The actual boundaries of the Financial District, built upon what was once water (Yerba Buena Cove), are rather vague, dependent upon both personal opinion and that constant urban flux of form and function. In general, the district includes the entire area from the north side of Market St. to the Montgomery St. corridor, north to the Jackson Square Historic District. Market Street is anchored near the bay by the concrete square of **Justin Herman Plaza** and its either-loved-or-hated **Vaillancourt Fountain,** said to be a parody of the now-demolished freeway it once faced.

Embarcadero Center

Above and behind the plaza is the astounding and Orwellian Embarcadero Center complex, the high-class heart of the Golden Gateway redevelopment project. Here is the somewhat surreal **Hyatt Regency Hotel,** noted for its 17-story indoor atrium and bizarre keyboard-like exterior, as well as the **Park Hyatt Hotel.** But the main focus is the center's four-part shopping complex, **Embarcadero One** through **Embarcadero Four,** stretching along four city blocks between Clay and Sacramento. Inside, maps and information kiosks can help the disoriented. Atop One Embarcadero is San Francisco's equivalent to the Empire State Building observation desk, here called **SkyDeck,** tel. (415) 772-0590 or toll-free (888) 737-5933. This attraction couples basic bird's-eye viewing with art and artifact exhibits, interactive touch screens providing historical and cultural information about the city, and free docent "tours." SkyDeck is open year-round (except major holidays), daily 9:30 a.m.-9 p.m.; admission is $7 adults, $4 seniors/students, $3.50 children 5-12. Wheelchair accessible.

For a hands-on lesson in the **World of Economics,** including the chance to pretend you're president of the U.S. or head of the Fed, stop by the lobby of the **Federal Reserve Bank,** 101 Market (at Spear), tel. (415) 974-2000, open weekdays 9 a.m.-4:30 p.m., to play with the computer games and displays. The **World of Oil** in the Chevron USA Building, 555 Market (at Second), tel. (415) 894-4895, open weekdays 9 a.m.-3:30 p.m., is a small museum with industry-oriented facts, including a computerized "Energy Learning Center." **Robert Frost Plaza,** at the intersection of Market and California, is a reminder that New England's poet was a San Francisco homeboy.

Heading up California St., stop at the **Bank of California** building at 400 California (between Sansome and Battery), tel. (415) 445-0200, for a tour through its basement **Museum of the Money of the American West,** everything from gold nuggets and U.S. Mint mementos to dueling pistols. The **Wells Fargo History Museum,** in Wells Fargo Bank at 420 Montgomery (near California), tel. (415) 396-2619, features an old Concord Stagecoach; a re-created early Wells Fargo office; samples of gold, gold scales, and gold-mining tools; and a hands-on telegraph exhibit, complete with telegraph key and Morse code books. It's open Mon.-Fri. 9 a.m.-5p.m.; admission free. **Bank of America** at California and Kearny also has historical exhibits. In the 1905 **Merchants Exchange** building at California and Montgomery, the bygone boat-business days

the Transamerica Building: once outrageous, now a landmark

AISUNN RACE

are remembered with ship models and William Coulter marine paintings. For a look at more modern mercantile action, climb to the visitors gallery for an insider's view of the action at the **Pacific Stock Exchange** at Pine and Sansome, the largest in America outside New York City.

People were outraged over the architecture of the **Transamerica Pyramid** at Montgomery and Washington, the city's tallest building, when it was completed in 1972. But now everyone has adjusted to its strange winged-spire architecture. Until recently it was possible to ride up to the 27th floor, to the "viewing area," for breathtaking sunny-day views of Coit Tower, the Golden Gate Bridge, and Alcatraz. These days, you'll get only as far as the lobby and the popular new **Virtual Observation Deck,** with its four monitors connected to cameras mounted at the very tip of the Pyramid's spire. What's fun here is the chance to zoom, tilt, and pan the cameras for some fairly unusual views. Back down on the ground, head for Transamerica Center's **Redwood Park** on Friday lunch hours in summer for "Music in the Park" concerts.

Designated these days as the **Jackson Square Historical District,** the section of town stretching into North Beach across Washington St. was once called the Barbary Coast, famous since the gold rush as the world's most depraved human hellhole. Pacific Street was the main thoroughfare, a stretch of bad-boy bawdy houses, saloons, dance halls, and worse—like the "cowyards," where hundreds of prostitutes performed onstage with animals or in narrow cribs stacked as high as four stories. Words like "Mickey Finn," "Shanghaied," and "hoodlum" were coined here. Local moral wrath couldn't stop the barbarity of the Barbary Coast—and even the earthquake of 1906 spared the area, much to everyone's astonishment. Somewhat settled down by the Roaring '20s, when it was known as the International Settlement, the Barbary Coast didn't shed its barbarians entirely until the 1950s. Today it's quite tame, an oddly gentrified collection of quaint brick buildings.

ON THE WATERFRONT

San Francisco's waterfront stretches some six miles along the wide, seawall-straddling **Em-barcadero,** which runs from Fisherman's Wharf in the north to China Basin south of the Bay Bridge. Remnants of bygone booming port days, the docks and wharfs here are today devoted as much to tourism as to maritime commerce. The area is much improved, aesthetically, now that the elevated, view-blocking Embarcadero Freeway is gone (it was razed after being damaged in the 1989 earthquake). Today the Embarcadero is lined with nonnative Canary Island palm trees—a landscaping strategy that initially ired some botanical purists who dismissed the trees as being "too L.A."

Just south of Broadway is the city's only new pier since the 1930s; 845-foot-long **Pier 7** is an elegant public-access promenade for dawdlers and fisherfolk, complete with iron-and-wood benches, iron railings, and flanking colonnades of lampposts, the better for taking in the nighttime skyline. At the foot of Market St. is the **Ferry Building,** completed in 1898. Formerly the city's transportation center, the Ferry Building today is largely office space, including the **World Trade Center.** But the building still features its 661-foot arcaded facade, triumphal entrance arch, and temple-style clocktower echoing the Giralda tower of Spain's Seville cathedral. During commute hours, the area bustles with suits disembarking ferries from Marin. Hop one of the high-speed boats to Sausalito for lunch and you'll get there in about half an hour. Boats leave frequently daily, with extended hours in summer. Tickets $1.35-4.70 one-way.

Across from the updated 1889 Audiffred Building at 1 Mission is city-within-the-city **Rincon Center,** incorporating the former Rincon Annex Post Office, which was saved for its classic New Deal mural art. Note, too, the **36,075-pound brass screw** from a World War II tanker at 100 Spear St., introducing the waterfront exhibits inside. More than elsewhere in the city, except perhaps Nob Hill, the ironies of Financial District art are indeed striking.

The **Waterfront Promenade** stretches from the San Francisco Maritime National Historic Park at the foot of Hyde St. all the way along the bay to the new Giants ballpark. The promenade, built in stages over the last few years, replaces the waterfront's old piers 14 through 22. Named **Herb Caen Way** (complete with three dots) in 1996, for the late *San Francisco Chronicle* columnist, the seawall walkway features grand views of the bay. It's a favorite spot for midday runners and office brownbaggers; literary types enjoy the poems embedded in the sidewalk.

A very long block south of Rincon Center is **Hills Plaza,** a fairly new commercial-and-apartment development with a garden plaza, incorporating the shell of the old Hills Brothers Coffee building. Farther south along the Embarcadero are more new developments also housing restaurants, including **Bayside Village** and the world-renowned drug rehabilitation program **Delancey Street.** Beyond, in China Basin, is **South Beach Marina Pier,** a public fishing pier with a good skyline view of the South Beach Marina.

Rising up at the foot of Second St. is the new **Pacific Bell Park,** www.sfgiants.com, which will replace 3Com Park (better known by its original name—Candlestick Park) as the home of the San Francisco Giants in 2000. Pac Bell Park sits right on the waterfront and will seat 42,000 fans, offering sweeping views of the bay and the city skyline. Designed by Hellmuth, Obata & Kassabaum architect Joe Spear, the fellow responsible for Coors Field in Denver and Camden Yards in Baltimore, the park aims to combine the feel of an old-time ballpark with modern amenities. Quite modern is the potential traffic nightmare of 40,000 fans trying to drive and find parking downtown, so smart fans may find that public transportation is a better option. The ballpark is a fairly short walk from downtown.

CIVIC CENTER AND VICINITY

Smack dab in the center of the sleaze zone is San Francisco's major hub of government, the Civic Center, built on the one-time site of the Yerba Buena Cemetery. (See cautions mentioned under The Tenderloin above, which also apply to almost any section of downtown Market St. after dark.) A sublime example of America's beaux arts architecture, the center's **City Hall,** 401 Van Ness (at Polk), tel. (415) 554-4858, www.ci.sf.ca.us/cityhall, was modeled after St. Peter's Basilica at the Vatican, in the belle epoque style, complete with dome and majestic staircase. Renaissance-style sculptures state the city's dreams—the not necessarily incongruous collection of Wisdom, the Arts, Learning, Truth, Industry, and Labor over the Van Ness Ave. entrance, and Commerce, Navigation, California Wealth, and San Francisco above the doors on Polk Street. After sustaining severe damage in the 1989 earthquake, the building was repaired and meticulously refurbished, and its interior stylishly redone, on the watch of equally stylish Mayor Willie Brown, a project with a price tag of several hundred million dollars. Former state senator Quentin Kopp, never a Brown fan, has called this the "Taj Mahal" of public works projects. See it yourself—free 45-minute tours are available daily.

The **War Memorial Opera House,** 301 Van Ness (at Grove), tel. (415) 865-2000, www.sf-opera.com, is the classical venue for the San Francisco Ballet Company as well as the San Francisco Opera, the place for society folk to see and be seen during the September to December opera season. Twin to the opera house, connected by extravagant iron gates, is the **Veterans Memorial Building.** The **Louise M. Davies Hall** at Van Ness and Grove, which features North America's largest concert hall organ, is the permanent venue for the **San Francisco Symphony.** If in the neighborhood, performing arts aficionados should definitely head west one block to the weekdays-only **San Francisco Performing Arts Library and Museum** at Grove and Gough.

San Francisco's **Main Library,** 100 Larkin (at Grove), tel. (415) 557-4400, is worth a browse, especially for the free Internet access offered at computer stations throughout the library. Free volunteer-led City Guides tours are headquartered here, tel. (415) 557-4266, and some depart from here. Civic Center Plaza, across Polk from the library, is home to many of the area's homeless, and also forms the garden roof for the underground **Brooks Hall** exhibit center and parking garage. **United Nations Plaza** stretches between Market St. and the Federal Building at McAllister (between Seventh and Eighth), commemorating the U.N.'s charter meeting in 1945 at the War Memorial Opera House. On Wednesday and Sunday, the plaza bustles with buyers and sellers of fish and unusual fruits and vegetables when the **Heart of the City Farmer's Market** is in bloom.

Across Market St., technically in SoMa but allied in spirit with the Civic Center, is the stunningly refurbished former San Francisco Post Office and **U.S. Courthouse,** at Seventh and

Mission. This gorgeous 1905 granite masterpiece, full of marble and mosaic floors and ceilings, was damaged in the 1989 earthquake, but it's now back and better than ever after a $91-million earthquake retrofit and rehabilitation. The post office is gone, replaced by an atrium, but the courts are back in session here. The third-floor courtroom is particularly impressive.

In addition to the area's many cafés, restaurants, and nightspots, the **California Culinary Academy,** 625 Polk St. (at Turk), tel. (415) 771-3500 or toll-free (800) 229-2433, is noted for its 16-month chef's training course in Italian, French, and nouvelle cuisine. For the curious, the academy is also an exceptionally good place to eat wonderful food at reasonable prices. The academy operates a bakery and café, the basement **Tavern on the Tenderloin** buffet, tel. (415) 771-3536, and the somewhat more formal **Careme Room,** tel. (415) 771-3535, a glass-walled dining hall where you can watch what goes on in the kitchen. Call for hours and reservation policies, which vary.

WESTERN ADDITION

These central city blocks west of Van Ness Ave. and south of Pacific Heights are certainly diverse. Settled in turn by Jewish, Japanese, and African Americans, the neighborhood's historical associations are with the Fillmore's jazz and blues bars, which hosted greats like John Coltrane and Billie Holiday in the 1950s and '60s.

The area is remarkable architecturally because so many of its 19th-century Victorians survived the 1906 earthquake, though some subsequently declined into subdivided apartments or were knocked down by the wrecking ball of redevelopment. The Western Addition's remaining Victorian enclaves are rapidly becoming gentrified. The most notable—and most photographed—example is Steiner St. facing **Alamo Square** (other pretty "painted ladies" with facelifts stretch for several blocks in all directions), though countrylike **Cottage Row** just east of Fillmore St. between Sutter and Bush is equally enchanting.

Today most of the Western Addition is home to working-class families, though the area south of Geary, considered "The Fillmore," was long composed almost exclusively of heavy-crime, low-income housing projects. Many of those boxy projects have been demolished, and redevelopment here is generally improving the aesthetics of the neighborhood.

The Western Addition's intriguing shops, restaurants, and cultural attractions reflect the neighborhood's roots. For an exceptional selection of African-American literature, check out **Marcus Books,** 1712 Fillmore (at Post), tel. (415) 346-4222, which also hosts occasional readings. On Sunday mornings, the solemn sound of jazz emanates from **St. John's African Orthodox Church,** 351 Divisadero (at Oak), tel. (415) 621-4054, a tiny storefront ministry devoted to celebrating the life of St. John Coltrane. In an interview with *People* magazine, church leader Bishop Franzo Wayne King described first hearing Coltrane play as "a baptism in sound." Services are part celebration and part jam session. For information and updates, check out www.saintjohn-coltrane.org. Fancy dressing like a member of Run DMC? You'll find one of the country's biggest selections of Adidas clothing at **Harput's,** 1527 Fillmore (between Ellis and Geary), tel. (415) 923-9300. And **Jack's Record Cellar** 254 Scott St. (at Page), tel. (415) 431-3047, is the perfect place to browse through obscure jazz and blues records.

Fillmore Street also creates the western border of **Japantown,** or Nihonmachi, an area encompassing the neighborhoods north of Geary, south of Pine, and stretching east to Octavia. This very American variation on Japanese community includes the old-style, open-air **Buchanan Mall** between Post and Sutter, and the more modern and ambitious **Japan Center,** a three-block-long concrete mall on Geary between Fillmore and Laguna. It's inaccessibly ugly from the outside, in the American tradition, but offers intriguing attractions inside, like karaoke bars and the **Kabuki Hot Springs,** tel. (415) 922-6000, a communal bathhouse on the ground floor.

Lined with boutiques selling clothing from small labels, sidewalk restaurants, and oddball furniture stores, **Hayes Street** between Franklin and Laguna is an oasis of funky charm. Stroll over to **560 Hayes,** 560 Hayes St. (at Laguna), tel. (415) 861-7993, for an excellent selection of 1960s and '70s evening wear, including vintage items from top designers like Chanel and Gucci. Find vintage timepieces and watches at **Zeitgeist Timepieces and Jewelry,** 437 Hayes St. (between Gough and Octavia), tel. (415) 864-0185.

BEYOND DOWNTOWN

NOB HILL

Snide San Franciscans say "Snob Hill" when referring to cable car-crisscrossed Nob Hill. The official neighborhood name is purported to be short for "Nabob Hill," a reference to this high-rent district's nouveau riche roots. Robert Louis Stevenson called it the "hill of palaces," referring to the grand late-1800s mansions of San Francisco's economic elite, California's railroad barons most prominent among them. Known colloquially as the "Big Four," Charles Crocker, Mark Hopkins, Collis Huntington, and Leland Stanford were accompanied by two of the "Irish Big Four" or "Bonanza Kings" (James Fair and James Flood, Nevada silver lords) as they made their acquisitive economic and cultural march into San Francisco and across the rest of California.

Of the original homes of these magnates, only one stands today—James Flood's bearish, square Connecticut brownstone, now the exclusive **Pacific-Union Club** (the "P-U," in local vernacular) at 1000 California Street. The rest of the collection was demolished by the great earthquake and fire of 1906. But some of the city's finest hotels, not to mention an exquisite Protestant place of worship, have taken their place around rather formal **Huntington Park.** Huntington's central memorial status atop Nob Hill is appropriate enough, since skinflint Collis P. Huntington was the brains of the Big Four gang and his comparatively simple home once stood here.

Facing the square from the corner of California and Taylor is the charming, surprisingly unique red-brick **Huntington Hotel** and its exceptional **Big Four** bar and restaurant. The **Mark Hopkins Hotel** ("the Mark," as it's known around town) was built on the spot of Hopkins' original ornate Victorian, at 1 Nob Hill (corner of California and Mason). Take the elevator up to the **Top of the Mark,** the bar with a view that inspired the city's song, "I Left My Heart in San Francisco," and perhaps its singer, Tony Bennett, as well. Straight across the street, facing Mason between California and Sacramento, is the famed **Fairmont Hotel,** an architectural extravaganza built "atop Nob Hill" by James Fair's

daughter Tessie (the lobby recognizable to American TV addicts as the one in the short-lived series *Hotel*). Inside, the Tiki-inspired Tonga Room is straight out of *Hawaii Five-O.* Kick back, enjoy a frozen cocktail, and soak in the strange ambience. Simulated rainstorms interrupt the tropical calm every half hour.

The **Stanford Court Hotel** at California and Powell, one of the world's finest, occupies the land where Leland Stanford's mansion once stood. For an artistic rendering of local nabobery, stop for a peek at the Stanford's lobby murals.

The **Bohemian Club** on the corner of Taylor and Post is a social club started by some of California's true bohemians, from Jack London, Joaquin Miller, and John Muir to Ambrose Bierce, Ina Coolbrith, and George Sterling. Though for old-time's sake some artists are invited to join, these days this very exclusive all-male club has a rank and file composed primarily of businessmen, financiers, and politicians. In July each year, these modern American bohemians retreat to the Russian River and their equally private Bohemian Grove all-male enclave for a week of fun and frolic.

Hobnobbing with Spirit: Grace Cathedral

At the former site of Charles Crocker's mansion is Grace Cathedral, facing Huntington Park from Taylor St., an explosion of medieval Gothic enthusiasm inspired by the Notre Dame in Paris. Since the lot *was* cleared for construction by a very California earthquake, Grace Cathedral is built not of carefully crafted stone but steel-reinforced concrete.

Most famous here, architecturally, are the cathedral doors, cast from Lorenzo Ghiberti's Gates of Paradise from the Cathedral Baptistry in Florence, Italy. The glowing rose window is circa 1970 and comes from Chartres. Also from Chartres: Grace Cathedral's spiritual **Labyrinth,** a roll-up replica of an archetypal meditative journey in the Christian tradition. Since Grace is a "house of prayer for all people," anyone can walk the Labyrinth's three-fold path, just part of the cathedral's multifaceted **Veridtas** program. The Labyrinth is open to the public during church hours weekdays and Sunday 7 a.m.-6 p.m., Saturday 8 a.m.-6 p.m. Music is an-

NOB HILL'S INVENTION AND THE CABLE CAR BARN

Not just material wealth and spiritual high spirits are flaunted atop Nob Hill. Technical innovation is, too, and quite rightly, since this is where Andrew Hallidie launched the inaugural run of his famous cable cars, down Clay Street. A free stop at the Cable Car Barn, 1201 Mason (at Washington), tel. (415) 474-1887, open daily 10 a.m.-5 p.m. (until 6 p.m. during the summer), tells the story. No temple to tourist somnambulism, this is powerhouse central for the entire cable car system, energized solely by the kinetic energy of the cables. Electric motors turn the giant sheaves (pulleys) to whip the (underground) looped steel cables around town and power the cars. The idea is at once complex and simple. Feeding cable around corners is a bit tricky; to see how it works, hike down to a basement window and observe. But the "drive" mechanism is straightforward. Each cable car has two operators, someone working the grip, the other the brake. To "power up," heading uphill, the car's "grip" slides through the slot in the street to grab onto the cable, and the cable does the rest. Heading downhill, resisting gravity, the brake gets quite a workout. Also here: a display of historic cable cars and a gift shop.

other major attraction at Grace Cathedral, from the choral evensongs to pipe organ, carillon, and chamber music concerts. Mother church for California's Episcopal Diocese, Grace Cathedral hosts endless unusual events, including St. Francis Day in October, which honors St. Francis of Assisi—the city's patron saint—and the interconnectedness of all creation. At this celebration, all God's creatures, large and small—from elephants and police horses to dressed-up housepets, not to mention the women walking on stilts—show up to be blessed. For more information about Grace Cathedral's current calendar of odd and exhilarating events, call (415) 749-6300. And while you're in the neighborhood, take a peek into the modern **California Masonic Memorial Temple** at 1111 California, with its tiny scale model of King Solomon's Temple and colorful mosaic monument to Freemasonry.

CHINATOWN

The best time to explore Chinatown is at the crack of dawn, when crowded neighborhoods and narrow alleys explode into hustle and bustle, and when the scents, sounds, and sometimes surreal colors compete with the energy of sunrise. Due to the realities of gold rush-era life and, later, the Chinese Exclusion Act of 1882, this very American variation on a Cantonese market town was for too long an isolated, almost all-male frontier enclave with the predictable vices—a trend reversed only in the 1960s, when more relaxed immigration laws allowed the possibility of families and children. The ambitious and the educated have already moved on to the suburbs, so Chinatown today—outside of Harlem in New York, the country's most densely populated neighborhood—is home to the elderly poor and immigrants who can't speak English. It's still the largest community of Chinese anywhere outside China. And it's still a cultural and spiritual home for the Bay Area's expanding Chinese community. Even those who have left come back, if only for a great meal and a Chinese-language movie.

To get oriented, keep in mind that Stockton St. is the main thoroughfare. Grant Avenue, however, is where most tourists start, perhaps enticed away from Grant's endless upscale shops and galleries by the somewhat garish green-tiled Chinatown Gate at Bush, a 1969 gift from the Republic of China. As you wander north, notice the street-sign calligraphy, the red-painted, dragon-wrapped lampposts, and the increasingly unusual roofscapes. Grant goes the distance between Market St. and modern-day Pier 39. This happens to be San Francisco's oldest street and was little more than a rutted path in 1834, when it was dubbed Calle de la Fundación (Foundation St. or "street of the founding") by the ragtag residents of the Yerba Buena pueblo. By the mid-19th century, the street's name had been changed to Dupont, in honor of an American admiral—a change that also recognized the abrupt changing of California's political guard. But by the end of the 1800s, "Du Pon Gai" had become so synonymous with unsavory activities that downtown merchants decided on another name change, this time borrowing a bit of prestige from

Ulysses S. Grant, the nation's 18th president and the Civil War's conquering general. Despite the color on Grant, the in-between streets (Sacramento, Clay, Washington, Jackson, and Pacific) and the fascinating interconnecting alleys between them represent the heart of Chinatown.

Since traffic is horrendous, parking all but impossible, and many streets almost too narrow to navigate even sans vehicle, walking is the best way to see the sights. If you haven't time to wander aimlessly, taking a guided tour is the best way to get to know the neighborhood.

Seeing and Doing Chinatown

At the corner of Grant and California is **Old Saint Mary's Cathedral,** the city's Catholic cathedral from the early 1850s to 1891, still standing even after a gutting by fire in 1906. On Saint Mary's clock tower is sound maternal advice for any age: "Son, Observe the time and fly from evil." (Saint Mary has a square, too, a restful stop just east and south of California St., where there's a Bufano sculpture of Dr. Sun Yat-sen, the Republic of China's founder.) Also at the Grant/California intersection is the **Ma-Tsu Temple of the United States of America,** with shrines to Buddha and other popular deities.

Packed with restaurants and tourist shops, Grant Ave. between California and Broadway is always bustling. Of particular interest is the unusual and aptly named **Li Po Bar** at 916 Grant, a former opium den and watering hole

honoring the memory of China's notoriously romantic poet, a wine-loving warrior who drowned while embracing the moon—a moon mirage, as it turned out, reflected up from a river.

The **Chinese Historical Society of America,** 644 Broadway (between Stockton and Grant), Ste. 402, tel. (415) 391-1188, is the nation's only museum specifically dedicated to preserving Chinese-American history. Chinese contributions to California culture are particularly emphasized. Some unusual artifacts in the museum's huge collection: gold-rush paraphernalia, including a "tiger fork" from Weaverville's tong war, and an old handwritten copy of Chinatown's phone book. Open Monday 1-4 p.m., Tues.-Fri. 10:30 a.m.-4 p.m.; closed weekends and major holidays. Admission is free, but donations are appreciated.

The **Pacific Heritage Museum,** 608 Commercial (between Montgomery and Kearny, Sacramento and Clay), tel. (415) 399-1124, is housed in the city's renovated brick 1875 U.S. Mint building. The museum features free rotating exhibits of Asian art and other treasures; open Tues.-Sat. 10 a.m.-4 p.m. To place it all in the larger context of California's Wild West history, head around the corner to the **Wells Fargo History Museum,** 420 Montgomery, tel. (415) 396-2619.

Portsmouth Square—people still say "square," though technically it's been a plaza since the 1920s—on Kearny between Clay and Washington is Chinatown's backyard.

The Chinatown Gate was a gift from the Republic of China.

AISLINN RACE

SHOPPING CHINATOWN

To a greater extent than, say, Oakland's Chinatown, most shops here are aware of—and cater to—the tourist trade. But once you have some idea what you're looking for, bargains are available. Along Grant Ave., a definite must for gourmet cooks and other kitchen habitués is the **Wok Shop,** 718 Grant (between Sacramento and Clay), tel. (415) 989-3797, the specialized one-stop shopping trip for anything essential to Chinese cooking (and other types of cooking as well). The **Ten Ren Tea Company,** 949 Grant (at Jackson), tel. (415) 362-0656 or toll-free (800) 543-2885, features more than 50 varieties of teas, the prices dependent on quality and (for blends) content. There's a private area in back where you can arrange for instruction in the fine art of a proper tea ceremony. (Notice, on the wall, a photo of former president George Bush, who didn't quite get it right when he tried it.) For unusual gifts, silk shirts, high-quality linens and such, **Far East Fashions,** 953 Grant, tel. (415) 362-0986 or (415) 362-8171, is a good choice.

Finally, musicians and nonmusicians alike shouldn't miss Clara Hsu's **Clarion Music Center,** 816 Sacramento St. (at Waverly Place), tel. (415) 391-1317 or toll-free (888) 343-5374, a treasure trove full of African drums, Chinese gongs, Tibetan singing bowls, Indian sitars, Native American flutes, Bolivian panpipes, Australian didjeridoos, and other exotic instruments from every corner of the world. The store also offers lessons, workshops, and concerts to promote awareness of world musical culture. Open Mon.-Fri. 11 a.m.-6 p.m., Saturday 9 a.m.-5 p.m.

Here you'll get an astounding look at everyday local life, from the city's omnipresent panhandlers to early-morning tai chi to all-male afternoons of checkers, go, and gossip—life's lasting entertainments for Chinatown's aging bachelors. Across Kearny on the third floor of the Financial District Holiday Inn is the **Chinese Culture Center,** 750 Kearny (between Clay and Washington), tel. (415) 986-1822, which has a small gallery and gift shop but otherwise caters mostly to meeting the needs of the local community.

The further actions and attractions of Chinatown's heart are increasingly subtle, from the Washington St. herb and herbalist shops to Ross Alley's garment factories and its fortune cookie company, where you can buy some instant fortune, fresh off the press—keeping in mind, of course, that fortune cookies are an all-American invention. Intriguing, at 743 Washington, is the oldest Asian-style building in the neighborhood, the three-tiered 1909 "temple" once home to the Chinatown Telephone Exchange, now the **Bank of Canton.** But even **Bank of America,** at 701 Grant, is dressed in keeping with its cultural surroundings, with benevolent gold dragons on its columns and doors, and some 60 dragons on its facade. Also putting on the dog is **Citibank** at 845 Grant, guarded by grimacing temple dogs.

Both Jackson and Washington Streets are best bets for finding small and authentic neighborhood restaurants. **Stockton Street,** especially between Broadway and Sacramento and especially on a Saturday afternoon, is where Chinatown shops. Between Sacramento and Washington, **Waverly Place** is referred to as the "street of painted balconies," for fairly obvious reasons. There are three temples here, open to respectful visitors (donations appreciated, picture-taking usually not). **Norras Temple** at 109 Waverly is affiliated with the Buddhist Association of America, lion dancing and all, while the fourth-floor **Tien Hau Temple** at 123 Waverly primarily honors the Queen of Heaven, she who protects sojourners and seafarers as well as writers, actors, and prostitutes. The **Jeng Sen Buddhism and Taoism Association,** 146 Waverly, perhaps offers the best general introduction to Chinese religious tolerance, with a brief printed explanation (in English) of both belief systems.

For a delightfully detailed and intimate self-guided tour through the neighborhood, bring along a copy of Shirley Fong-Torres's *San Francisco Chinatown: A Walking Tour,* which includes some rarely recognized sights, such as the **Cameron House,** 920 Sacramento, a youth center named in honor of Donaldina Cameron (1869-1968), who helped young Chinese slave girls escape poverty and prostitution. Fong-Torres's marvelous and readable guide to San Francisco's Chinese community also covers history, cultural beliefs, festivals, religion and philosophy, herbal medicine (doctors and pharmacists are now licensed for these traditional practices by the state of California), and Chinese tea. It includes a very good introduction to Chinese food—from ingredients, cookware, and techniques to menus and restaurant recommendations.

NORTH BEACH AND VICINITY

For one thing, there isn't any beach in North Beach. In the 1870s, the arm of San Francisco Bay that gave the neighborhood its name was filled in, creating more land for the growing city. And though beatniks and bohemians once brought a measure of fame to this Italian-American quarter of the city, they're all gone now, priced out of the neighborhood.

Quite a number of American poets and writers grubbed out some kind of start here: Gregory Corso, Lawrence Ferlinghetti, Allen Ginsberg, Bob Kaufman, Jack Kerouac, Gary Snyder, Kenneth Rexroth. By the 1940s, North Beach as "New Bohemia" was a local reality. It became a long-running national myth.

Otherwise sound-asleep America of the 1950s secretly loved the idea of the alienated, manic "beat generation," a phrase coined by Jack Kerouac in *On the Road*. The Beats seemed to be everything no one else was allowed to be— mostly, free. Free to drink coffee or cheap wine and talk all day; free to indulge in art, music, poetry, prose, and more sensual thrills just about any time; free to be angry and scruffy and lost in the forbidden fog of marijuana while bopping along to be-bop. But Allen Ginsberg's raging *Howl and Other Poems,* published by Ferlinghetti and City Lights, brought the wolf of censorship— an ungrateful growl that began with the seizure of in-bound books by U.S. Customs and got louder when city police filed obscenity charges. The national notoriety of an extended trial, and Ginsberg's ultimate literary acquittal, brought busloads of Gray Line tourists. And the Beats moved on, though some of the cultural institutions they founded are still going strong.

Nowadays, North Beach is almost choking on its abundance—of eateries, coffeehouses, tourist traps, and shops. Forget trying to find a parking place; public transit is the best way to get around.

Adding to neighborhood stresses and strains— and to the high costs of surviving—is the influx of Asian business and the monumental increase in Hong Kong-money property investment, both marching into North Beach from Chinatown. Old and new neighborhood residents tend to ignore each other as much as possible, in that great American melting-pot tradition. (Before the Italians called North Beach their home turf, the Irish did. And before the Irish lived here, Chileans did. In all fairness, Fisherman's Wharf was Chinese before the Italians moved in. And of course Native Americans inhabited the entire state before the Spanish, the Mexicans, the Russians, and the Americans.) Like the city itself, life here makes for a fascinating sociology experiment.

What with territorial incursions from Chinatown, the historical boundaries of North Beach increasingly clash with the actual. Basically, the entire valley between Russian Hill and Telegraph Hill is properly considered North Beach. The northern boundary stopped just short of Fisherman's Wharf, now pushed back by rampant commercial development, and Broadway was the southern boundary—a thoroughfare and area sometimes referred to as the "Marco Polo Zone" because it once represented the official end of Chinatown and the beginning of San Francisco's Little Italy. The neighborhood's spine is diagonally running Columbus Ave., which begins at the Transamerica Pyramid at the edge of the Financial District and ends at The Cannery near Fisherman's Wharf. Columbus Avenue between Filbert and Broadway is the still-beating Italian heart of modern North Beach.

Seeing and Doing North Beach

Piazzalike **Washington Square,** between Powell and Stockton, Union and Filbert, is the centerpiece of North Beach, though, as the late *San Francisco Chronicle* columnist Herb Caen once pointed out, it "isn't on Washington St., isn't a square (it's five-sided) and doesn't contain a statue of Washington but of Benjamin Franklin." (In terms of cultural consistency, this also explains the statue of Robert Louis Stevenson in Chinatown's Portsmouth Square.) There's a time capsule beneath old Ben; when the original treasures (mostly temperance tracts on the evils of alcohol) were unearthed in 1979, they were replaced with 20th-century cultural values, including a bottle of wine, a pair of Levi's, and a poem by Lawrence Ferlinghetti. In keeping with more modern times, Washington Square also features a statue dedicated to the city's firemen, yet another contribution by eccentric little old Lillie Hitchcock Coit. **Saints Peter and Paul Catholic Church** fronts the square at 666 Filbert, its twin towers lighting up the whole neighborhood come nightfall. Noted for its rococo interior and accompanying graphic statuary of injured saints and souls burning in hell, the Saints also offers daily mass in Italian and (on Sunday) in Chinese.

Two blocks northeast of Washington Square is the **North Beach Playground,** where boccie ball is still the neighborhood game of choice, just as October's **Columbus Day Parade** and accompanying festivities still make the biggest North Beach party. Just two blocks west of the square are the stairs leading to the top of **Telegraph Hill,** identifiable by **Coit Tower,** Lillie Coit's most heartfelt memorial to the firefighters. (More on that below.)

For an overview of the area's history, stop by the free **North Beach Museum,** 1435 Stockton St. (near Green, on the mezzanine of Bayview Bank), tel. (415) 626-7070, open Mon.-Thurs. 9 a.m.-5 p.m. and Friday until 6 p.m., which displays a great collection of old North Beach photos and artifacts in occasionally changing exhibits.

The North Beach "experience" is the neighborhood itself—the coffeehouses, the restaurants, the intriguing and odd little shops. No visit is complete without a stop at Lawrence Ferlinghetti's **City Lights Bookstore,** 261 Columbus (between Broadway and Pacific), tel. (415) 362-8193, on the neighborhood's most literary alley. City Lights is the nation's first all-paperback bookstore and a rambling ode to the best of the small presses; its poetry and other literary programs still feed the souls of those who need more nourishment than what commercial bestsellers can offer. A superb small museum, **Lyle Tuttle's Tattoo Museum and Shop,** is a few blocks up the way at 841 Columbus, tel. (415) 775-4991.

You can shop till you drop in this part of town. And much of what you'll find has something to do with food. For Italian ceramics, **Biordi Italian Imports,** 412 Columbus (near Vallejo), tel. (415) 392-8096, has a fabulous selection of art intended for the table (but almost too beautiful to use). For a price—and just about everything is pricey—the folks here will ship your treasures, too.

NORTH BEACH HANGOUTS

Caffe Greco, 423 Columbus (between Vallejo and Green), tel. (415) 397-6261, is the best of the neighborhood's newish coffeehouses. But for that classic beatnik bonhomie, head to what was once the heart of New Bohemia, the surviving **Caffe Trieste,** 601 Vallejo (at Grant), tel. (415) 392-6739. Drop by anytime for opera and Italian folk songs on the jukebox, or come on Saturday afternoon for jazz, opera, or other concerts. Also-been-there-forever **Vesuvio Cafe,** 255 Columbus Ave. (at Broadway), tel. (415) 362-3370, across Kerouac Alley from the City Lights bookstore (look for the mural with volcanoes and peace symbols), is most appreciated for its upstairs balcony section, historically a magnet for working and wannabe writers (and everyone else, too). It was a favorite haunt of Ginsberg and Kerouac, as well as an in-town favorite for Welsh poet Dylan Thomas. And Francis Ford Coppola reportedly sat down at a back table to work on *The Godfather.* A painting depicts *Homo beatnikus,* and there's even an advertisement for a do-it-yourself beatnik makeover (kit including sunglasses, a black beret, and poem).

Another righteous place to hide in is **Tosca,** 242 Columbus (between Broadway and Pacific), tel. (415) 391-1244, a late-night landmark with gaudy walls and comfortable Naugahyde booths where the hissing of the espresso machine competes with Puccini on the jukebox. Writers of all varieties still migrate here, sometimes to play pool in back. But you must behave yourself: Bob Dylan and Allen Ginsberg got thrown out of here for being unruly. **Cafe Malvina,** 1600 Stockton (at Union), tel. (415) 391-1290, is a good bet, too, especially for early-morning pastries with your coffee.

Serious social history students should also peek into the **Condor Cafe,** Columbus (at Broadway), tel. (415) 781-8222, the one-time Condor Club made famous by stripper Carol Doda and her silicone-enhanced mammaries, and now a run-of-the-mill sports bar. Still, the place offers a memory of the neighborhood's sleazier heyday. Other neighborhood perversion palaces, survivors of the same peep-show mentality, are becoming fewer and farther between, and in any event aren't really all that interesting.

While you're wandering, you can easily put together a picnic for a timeout in Washington Square. Italian delicatessen and meat market **Prudente & Company,** 1460 Grant (at Union), tel. (415) 421-0757, is the place to stop for traditionally cured pancetta and prosciutto. Head to landmark **Molinari's,** 373 Columbus (between Broadway and Green), tel. (415) 421-2337, for cheeses, sausages, and savory salads, or to the Italian and French **Victoria Pastry Co.,** 1362 Stockton St. (at Vallejo), tel. (415) 781-2015, for cookies, cakes, and unbelievable pastries. Other good bakery stops nearby include **Liguria Bakery,** 1700 Stockton (at Filbert), tel. (415) 421-3786, famous for its focaccia, and the **Italian French Baking Co. of San Francisco,** 1501 Grant (at Union), tel. (415) 421-3796, known for its French bread. If you didn't load up on reading material at City Lights—for after you stuff yourself but before falling asleep in the square—stop by **Cavalli Italian Book Store,** 1441 Stockton (between Vallejo and Green), tel. (415) 421-4219, for Italian newspapers, magazines, and books.

North Beach Nightlife

Opened in 1931, **Bimbo's 365 Club,** 1025 Columbus (between Chestnut and Francisco) retains its old-time supper club atmosphere. Bimbo's hosts live music most nights, and if you get there early, you can settle into one of the plush red booths lining the stage. The crowd varies according to the band. The grungy **Purple Onion,** 140 Columbus (at Kearny and Pacific), tel. (415) 398-8415, is a basement dive hosting 1960s punk and retro surf bands. Dressing up is de rigueur at the retro-swing **Hi-Ball Lounge** 473 Broadway (between Kearny and Montgomery), tel. (415) 397-9464, an often packed bar with old-time atmosphere and a juicy selection of cocktails. The Hi-Ball hosts live music nightly, and swing dancers crowd the small dance floor. A fairly inexpensive hot spot, on the site of an old Barbary Coast saloon, is the **San Francisco Brewing Company,** 155 Columbus (between Jackson and Pacific), tel. (415) 434-3344, known for its hearty home brews. **The Saloon,** 1232 Grant (at Columbus), tel. (415) 989-7666, across from Caffe Trieste at Grant and Fresno Alley, is the city's oldest pub, circa 1861. It's a bit scruffy, but still hosts what's

AISUNN RACE

Whatever its symbolism, Coit Tower offers great views and houses a striking collection of Depression-era frescoes.

happening after all these years (blues and rock-abilly, mostly). **Specs 12 Adler Museum Cafe,** across from Vesuvio at 12 Adler Place (off Columbus, between Broadway and Pacific), tel. (415) 421-4112, open daily after 4:30 or 5 p.m., is also a treasure trove-cum-watering hole of eclectic seafaring and literary clutter. For truly odd atmosphere, stroll into a boatlike old timers' hangout, the **Lost and Found Saloon,** at 1353 Grant Ave. (between Vallejo and Green), tel. (415) 392-9126.

Perhaps destined for a long-lasting run is "Beach Blanket Babylon" at **Club Fugazi,** 678 Green St. (at Powell), tel. (415) 421-4222, song-and-dance slapstick of a very contemporary high-camp cabaret style, where even favorite Broadway tunes end up brutally (and hilariously) twisted. Thematic and seasonal changes, like the Christmas revue, make this babbling Babylon worthy of return visits—especially to see what they'll create next in the way of 50-pound decorative headdresses.

Telegraph Hill and Coit Tower

The best way to get to Telegraph Hill—whether just for the view, to appreciate the city's hanging gardens, or to visit Coit Tower—is to climb the hill yourself, starting up the very steep stairs at Kearny and Filbert or ascending more gradually from the east, via either the Greenwich or Filbert steps. Following Telegraph Hill Blvd. as it winds its way from Lombard, from the west, is troublesome for drivers. Parking up top is scarce; especially on weekends you might sit for hours while you wait—just to park, mind you. A reasonable alternative is taking the #39-Coit bus.

Lillie Hitchcock Coit had a fetish for firemen. As a child, she was saved from a fire that claimed two of her playmates. As a teenager, she spent much of her time with members of San Francisco's all-volunteer Knickerbocker Engine Company No. 5, usually tagging along on fire calls and eventually becoming the team's official mascot; she was even allowed to play poker and smoke cigars with the boys. Started in 1929, financed by a Coit bequest, and completed in 1933, Coit Tower was to be a lasting memorial to the firemen. Some people say its shape resembles the nozzle of a firehose, others suggest more sexual symbolism, but the official story is that the design by Arthur Brown was intended to look "equally artistic" from any direction. Coit Tower was closed to the public for many years, due to damage caused by vandalism and water leakage. After a major interior renovation, the tower is now open in all its original glory, so come decide for yourself what the tower symbolizes. Or just come for the view. From atop the 180-foot tower, which gets extra lift from its site on top of Telegraph Hill, you get a magnificent 360-degree view of the entire Bay Area. Coin-op telescopes allow you to get an even closer look. Coit Tower, tel. (415) 362-0808, is open daily 10 a.m.-5 p.m., until 9 p.m. in summer. Admission is free, technically, but there is a charge for the elevator ride to the top: $3.75 adults, $2.50 seniors, $1.50 children ages 6-12.

City Life *(detail) c. 1934 by Victor Arnautoff, from his fresco at Coit Tower*

Another reason to visit Coit Tower is to appreciate the marvelous Depression-era Social Realist interior mural art in the lobby, recently restored and as striking as ever. (At last report, seven of the 27 total frescoes, those on the second floor and along the narrow stairway, weren't available for general public viewing, since quarters are so close that scrapes from handbags and shoes are almost inevitable. You can see these murals on the Saturday guided tour.) Even in liberal San Francisco, many of these murals have been controversial, depicting as they do the drudgery, sometimes despair, behind the idyllic facade of modern California life—particularly as seen in the lives of the state's agricultural and industrial workforce. Financed through Franklin Roosevelt's New Deal-era Public Works Art Project, some 25 local artists set out in 1934 to paint Coit Tower's interior with frescoes, the same year that Diego Rivera's revolutionary renderings of Lenin and other un-American icons created such a scandal at New York's Rockefeller Center that the great Mexican painter's work was destroyed.

In tandem with tensions produced by a serious local dock worker's strike, some in San Francisco almost exploded when it was discovered that the new art in Coit Tower wasn't entirely politically benign, that some of it suggested something less than total support for pro-capitalist ideology. In various scenes, one person is carrying *Das Kapital* by Karl Marx, and another is reading a copy of the Communist-party *Daily Worker;* grim-faced "militant unemployed" march forward into the future; women wash clothes by hand within sight of Shasta Dam; slogans oppose both hunger and fascism; and a chauffeured limousine is clearly contrasted with a Model T Ford in Steinbeck's Joad-family style. Even a hammer and sickle made it onto the walls. Unlike New York, even after an outraged vigilante committee threatened to chisel away Coit Tower's artistic offenses, San Francisco ultimately allowed it all to stay—everything, that is, except the hammer and sickle.

Another Telegraph Hill delight: the intimate gardens along the eastern steps. The **Filbert Steps** stairway gardens are lined with trees, ivy, and garden flowers, with a few terraces and benches nearby. Below Montgomery St., the Filbert stairway becomes a bit doddering—

unpainted tired wood that leads to enchanting Napier Ln., one of San Francisco's last wooden-plank streets and a Victorian survivor of the city's 1906 devastation. (Below Napier, the stairway continues on to Sansome Street.) The brick-paved **Greenwich Steps** wander down to the cliff-hanging Julius' Castle restaurant, then continue down to the right, appearing to be private stairs to the side yard, weaving past flower gardens and old houses to reach Sansome. If you go up one way, be sure to come down the other.

Russian Hill

Also one of San Francisco's rarer pleasures is a stroll around Russian Hill, named for the belief that Russian sea otter hunters picked this place to bury their dead. One of the city's early bohemian neighborhoods and a preferred haunt for writers and other connoisseurs of quiet beauty, Russian Hill today is an enclave of the wealthy. But anyone can wander the neighborhood. If you come from North Beach, head up—it's definitely up—Vallejo St., where the sidewalks and the street eventually give way to stairs. Take a break at **Ina Coolbrith Park** at Taylor, named in honor of California's first poet laureate, a woman remarkable for many accomplishments. A member of one of Jim Beckwourth's westward wagon trains, she was the first American child to enter California by wagon. After an unhappy marriage, Coolbrith came to San Francisco, where she wrote poetry and created California's early literary circle. Many men fell in love with her, the ranks of the hopelessly smitten including Ambrose Bierce, Bret Harte, and Mark Twain. (She refused to marry any of them.) Librarian for both the Bohemian Club and the Oakland Free Library, at the latter Coolbrith took 12-year-old Jack London under her wing; her tutelage and reading suggestions were London's only formal education. Up past the confusion of lanes at Russian Hill's first summit is **Florence Street,** which heads south, and still more stairs, these leading down to Broadway (the original Broadway, which shows why the city eventually burrowed a new Broadway under the hill). Coolbrith's last home on Russian Hill still stands at 1067 Broadway.

To see the second summit—technically the park at Greenwich and Hyde—and some of the reasons why TV and movie chase scenes are

STEVE FAHRINGER

The hundreds of sea lions at Pier 39 have become an attraction in their own right.

frequently filmed here, wander west and climb aboard the Hyde-Powell cable car. Worth exploration on the way up: Green St., Macondray Ln. just north of Jones (which eventually takes you down to Taylor Street), and **Filbert Street,** San Francisco's steepest driveable hill, a 31.5-degree grade. (To test that thesis yourself, go very slowly.) Just over the summit, as you stare straight toward Fisherman's Wharf, is another wonder of road engineering: the one-block stretch of Lombard St. between Hyde and Leavenworth, known as the **Crookedest Street in the World.** People do drive down this snake-shaped cobblestone path, a major tourist draw, but it's much more pleasant as a walk.

FISHERMAN'S WHARF

San Francisco's fishing industry and other port-related businesses were once integral to the city's cultural and economic life. Fisherman's Wharf, which extends from Pier 39 to the municipal pier just past Aquatic Park, was originally the focus of this waterfront commerce. Early on, Chinese fishermen pulled ashore their catch here, to be followed in time by Italian fishermen who took over the territory. After World War II, however, the city's fishing industry declined dramatically, the result of both accelerated pollution of San Francisco Bay and decades of overfishing. Today, Fisherman's Wharf has largely become a carnival-style diversion for tourists. Nevertheless, beyond the shopping centers, arcade amusements, and oddball museums, a small fishing fleet struggles to survive.

Pier 39

At Beach St. and Embarcadero, Pier 39 offers schlock par excellence. If you don't mind jostling with the schools of tourists like some sort of biped sardine, you're sure to find *something* here that interests you. But this place really isn't about San Francisco—it's about shopping and otherwise spending your vacation wad. And you could have done that at home.

Unusual stores include the **Disney Store,** selling licensed Disney merchandise; the **Warner Bros. Studio Store,** selling meep-meeps, cwazy wabbits, and the like; the **NFL Shop,** offering official 49er jerseys and other pigskin paraphernalia; the **City Store,** selling actual bits of San Francisco—old street signs, old bits of cable-car cable, old bricks from Lombard St.—all to benefit San Francisco social-services programs; and **Mel Fisher's Sunken Treasure Museum Store,** displaying artifacts collected by Fisher on his shipwreck dives.

At **Turbo Ride Simulation Theatre,** tel. (415) 392-8872, you'll be thrown around in your spastic, hydraulically controlled seat in perfect time with what's happening on the big screen before you; think armchair Indiana Jones (and three similar adventure scenarios). Open daily. Summer hours are Sun.-Thurs. 10 a.m.-9:30 p.m., Friday 10 a.m.-11 p.m.; Saturday 10 a.m.-midnight. The rest of the year, it's open Sun.-Thurs. 10:30 a.m.-8:30 p.m., Fri.-Sat. 10 a.m.-10 p.m. Admission is $8 general, $5 seniors/children under 12. And at **UnderWater World,** tel. (415) 623-5300, you can travel through a 300-foot-long acrylic tube on a moving walkway, looking out on schools of glittering anchovies, stingrays, leopard sharks, and other sea creatures swimming through the 700,000-gallon Pier 39 Aquarium. UnderWater World is open daily 10 a.m.-6 p.m.; extended summer hours. Admission is $12.95 adults, $9.95 seniors, $6.50 children 3-11.

No, you won't lack for attractions to take your money at Pier 39. But for free you can spend time watching the lolling **sea lions** out on the docks, a fairly recent invasion force. The docks once served as a marina full of pleasure boats—until the sea lions started making themselves at home. It turned out to be a futile effort trying to chase them off, so the powers that be decided to abandon the marina idea and let the pinnipeds (up to 600 of them in the peak Jan.-Feb. herring season) have their way, becoming a full-time tourist attraction. Score: Sea Lions 1, Yachties 0.

Most shops at the pier are open daily 10:30 a.m.-8:30 p.m. Hours are longer in summer. For more information, call (415) 981-7437, or look up www.pier39.com online. Also here are the **Blue & Gold Fleet** ferries to Alcatraz and elsewhere around the bay.

Along Jefferson Street

A culinary treat on the Wharf, especially in December or at other times during the mid-November-to-June season, is fresh **Dungeness crab.** You can pick out your own, live or already cooked, from the vendor stands, or head for any of the more famous Italian-style seafood restaurants here: **Alioto's, Castagliona's, Sabella's,** or the excellent and locally favored **Scoma's,** hidden slightly away from the tourist hordes on Pier 47 (near the intersection of Jones and Jefferson), tel. (415) 771-4383.

If you're in the mood for still more entertainment, Fisherman's Wharf offers a wacky variety. **Ripley's *Believe It Or Not!*** Museum, 175 Jefferson St. (near Taylor), tel. (415) 771-6188, features both bizarre and beautiful items—in-cluding a two-headed cow, a shrunken head, and other grotesqueries—collected during Robert L. Ripley's global travels. Open Sun.-Thurs. 10 a.m.-10 p.m., Fri.-Sat. 10 a.m.-midnight. Admission $8.50 adults, $7 children and seniors.

Around Ghirardelli Square

You can also shop till you drop at elegant **Ghirardelli Square,** 900 North Point (Beach and Larkin), tel. (415) 775-5500, a complex of 50-plus shops and restaurants where you can get one of the best hot fudge sundaes anywhere, or **The Cannery,** 2801 Leavenworth (at Beach), tel. (415) 771-3112, another huge theme shopping center, this one offering outdoor street artist performances as well as the **Museum of the City of San Francisco,** tel. (415) 928-0289; **Cobb's Comedy Club,** tel. (415) 928-4320; and **Quiet Storm,** tel. (415) 771-2929, a jazz club also serving Pacific Rim cuisine. Beer lovers will be in hops heaven at The Cannery, checking out the offerings of **Beach Street Brewhouse,** tel. (415) 775-5110, offering its own housemade beers, and **Jack's Cannery Bar,** tel. (415) 931-6400, a restaurant and bar featuring 83 different beers on tap. Time-honored for imports and the occasional bargain is the nearby **Cost Plus,** 2552 Taylor (at North Point).

Quieter, less commercial pleasures are also available along Fisherman's Wharf—a stroll through **Aquatic Park** perhaps, or fishing out on **Municipal Pier.**

San Francisco Maritime National Historical Park

Historic ships and a first-rate maritime museum make up the core of this national park on the west end of Fisherman's Wharf. To get oriented, first stop by the park's **National Maritime Museum of San Francisco** in Aquatic Park at Beach and Polk, tel. (415) 556-3002, open daily 10 a.m.-5 p.m., free admission. The double-decker building itself looks like an art deco ocean liner. Washed ashore inside are some excellent displays, from model ships and figureheads to historic photos and exhibits on fishing boats, ferries, and demonstrations of the sailor's arts. The affiliated **J. Porter Shaw Library,** tel. (415) 556-9870, housed along with the park's administrative offices west of Fisherman's Wharf in Building E at Fort Mason (a reasonable walk away along a bike/pedestrian path), holds most of the Bay Area's documented boat history, including oral histories, logbooks, photographs, and shipbuilding plans.

Not easy to miss at the foot of Hyde St. are the **Hyde Street Pier Historic Ships,** tel. (415) 556-3002 or (415) 556-6435, an always-in-progress collection that is also part of the national park. Admission $5 adults, $2 youths 12-17, free for children. Here you can clamber across the decks and crawl through the colorfully cluttered holds of some of America's most historic ships.

The Hyde Street fleet's flagship is the three-masted 1886 *Balclutha,* a veteran of twice-annual trips between California and the British Isles via Cape Horn. Others include the side-wheel *Eureka* (the world's largest passenger ferry in her day, built to ferry trains), the ocean-going tugboat *Hercules,* the British-built, gold rush-era paddlewheel tug *Eppleton Hall,* the scow schooner *Alma,* and the three-masted lumber schooner *C.A. Thayer.* Also among the collection, but berthed at Pier 45, is the **U.S.S. Pampanito,** a tight-quarters Balao-class World War II submarine that destroyed or damaged many Japanese vessels and also participated in the tragic sinking of the Japanese *Kachidoki Maru* and *Rayuyo Maru,* which were carrying Australian and British prisoners of war.

Tagging along on a ranger-led tour (complete with "living history" adventures in summer) is the best way to get your feet wet at this national park. Call for tour schedule (guided tours are usually offered daily). But self-guided tours are available anytime the pier is open, which is daily 9:30 a.m.-5 p.m. year-round (until 5:30 p.m. in summer); closed Thanksgiving, Christmas, and New Year's Day. Special activities give you the chance to sing sea chanteys, raise sails, watch the crews "lay aloft," or participate in the Dead Horse Ceremony—wherein the crowds heave a horse doll overboard and shout "May the sharks have his body, and the devil have his soul!"

SS *Jeremiah O'Brien*

Berthed at Pier 45 in summer, Pier 32 the rest of the year, this massive 441-foot-long World War II Liberty Ship made 11 crossings from England to the beaches of Normandy to support the Allied invasion. In 1994, it returned to Normandy for the 50th anniversary of D day. The ship is still powered by its original engines. In fact, the engine-room scenes in the movie *Titanic* were filmed here.

The historic ship is open for self-guided tours year-round, daily 10 a.m.-7 p.m.; admission is $5 adults, $4 seniors/military, $3 children. In addition, the ship makes several day-long cruises each year; you can come along for $100 per person. For more information or for cruise schedule and reservations, call (415) 441-3101.

MARINA DISTRICT, COW HOLLOW, AND PACIFIC HEIGHTS

The neat pastel homes of the respectable **Marina District,** tucked in between Fort Mason and the Presidio, disguise the fact that the entire area is essentially unstable. Built on landfill, in an area once largely bay marsh, the Mediterranean-style Marina was previously the 63-acre site of the Panama-Pacific International Exposition of 1915—San Francisco's statement to the world that it had been reborn from the ashes of the 1906 earthquake and fire. So it was ironic, and fitting, that the fireboat *Phoenix* extinguished many of the fires that blazed here following the 1989 earthquake, which caused disproportionately heavy damage in this district.

The Marina's main attractions are those that surround it—primarily the neighborhood stretch of San Francisco's astounding shoreline Golden Gate National Recreation Area, which includes the **Fort Mason** complex of galleries, museums, theaters, and nonprofit cultural and conservation organizations. (For more information on the park and its many facets, see Golden Gate National Recreation Area in Delights and Diversions.) If you're in the neighborhood and find yourself near the yacht harbor, do wander out to see (and hear) the park's wonderful **Wave Organ** just east of the yacht club on Bay Street. Built of pieces from an old graveyard, the pipes are powered by sea magic. (The siren song is loudest at high tide.) Then wander west toward the Golden Gate Bridge on the **Golden Gate Promenade,** which meanders the three-plus miles from Aquatic Park and along the Marina Green—popular with kite fliers, well-dressed dog walkers, and the area's many exercise freaks—to Civil War-era **Fort Point.** (Be prepared for wind and fog.) The truly ambitious can take a hike across the bridge itself, an awesome experience.

Exhausted by nature, retreat to more sheltered attractions near the Presidio, including the remnants of the spectacular Panama-Pacific International Exhibition of 1915, the Bernard Maybeck-designed **Palace of Fine Arts,** and the indescribable **Exploratorium** inside, fun for children of all ages and a first-rate science museum (see the special topic The Presidio and Fort Point for more area information).

Separating the Marina District from high-flying Pacific Heights is the low-lying neighborhood of **Cow Hollow,** a one-time dairy farm community now noted for its chic **Union Street** shopping district—an almost endless string of bars, cafés, coffeehouses, bookstores, and boutiques stretching between Van Ness and Steiner. Not to be outdone, the Marina boasts its own version: **Chestnut Street.** Other chic areas have included upper **Fillmore Street** near the Heights (and near the still-surviving 1960s icon, the **Fillmore** concert hall, at Geary and Fillmore), and outer **Sacramento Street** near Presidio Avenue. (Who knows where the next trendy block will crop up? The fashion fates are fickle.) **Pacific Heights** proper is the hilltop home pasture for the city's well-shod blue bloods. Its striking streets, Victorian homes, and general architectural wealth are well worth a stroll (for personal guidance, see Walking Tours, in Delights and Diversions, below). Especially noteworthy here is the **Haas-Lilienthal House,** 2007 Franklin (at Jackson), tel. (415) 441-3004, a handsome and huge Queen Anne Victorian, a survivor of the 1906 earthquake and the city's only fully furnished Victorian open for regular public tours. Tours are conducted Wednesday and Sunday; call for times. Admission is $5 adults, $3 seniors and children.

In the Cow Hollow neighborhood, don't miss the unusual 1861 **Octagon House,** 2645 Gough (at Union), tel. (415) 441-7512, owned by the National Society of Colonial Dames of America; it's now restored and fully furnished in colonial and federal period antiques. Open only on the second and fourth Thursday and the second Sunday of each month (closed in January and on holidays). Call to request special tour times. Donations greatly appreciated.

the Palace of Fine Arts

Exploratorium: Sophisticated Child's Play

Scientific American considers this the "best science museum in the world." Good Housekeeping says it's the "number one science museum in the U.S." It's definitely worth spending some time here. Inside the Palace of Fine Arts, 3601 Lyon St. (at Bay), tel. (415) 397-5673, www.exploratorium.edu, the Exploratorium is billed as a museum of science, art, and human perception, and ostensibly designed for children. But this is no mass-marketed media assault on the senses, no mindless theatrical homage to simple fantasy. The truth is, adults also adore the Exploratorium, a wonderfully intelligent playground built around the mysterious natural laws of the universe.

The Exploratorium was founded in 1969 by physicist and educator Dr. Frank Oppenheimer, the original "Explainer" (as opposed to "teacher"), whose research career was abruptly ended during the blacklisting McCarthy era. Brother of J. Robert Oppenheimer (father of the atomic bomb), Frank Oppenheimer's scientific legacy was nonetheless abundant.

"Explaining science and technology without props," said Oppenheimer, "is like attempting to tell what it is like to swim without ever letting a person near the water." The Exploratorium was the original interactive science museum and influenced the establishment of hundreds of other such museums in the U.S. and abroad. Its 650-some three-dimensional exhibits delve into 13 broad subject areas: animal behavior, language, vision, sound and hearing, touch, heat and temperature, electricity, light, color, motion, patterns, waves and resonance, and weather. Everything can be experienced—from a touch-sensitive plant that shrinks from a child's probing hand, to strategically angled mirrors that create infinite reflections of the viewer; from tactile computerized fingerpainting to the wave-activated voice of the San Francisco Bay, as brought to you by the "Wave Organ." The extra special **Tactile Dome,** tel. (415) 561-0362 (reservations recommended), provides a pitch-black environment in which your vision is of no use, but your sense of touch gets a real workout.

Stock up on educational toys, games, experiments, and oddities at the Exploratorium Store. Especially worth purchasing, for teachers and brave parents alike, is the Exploratorium Science Snackbook, which includes instructions on building home or classroom versions of more than 100 Exploratorium exhibits.

The Exploratorium is open in summer daily 10 a.m.-6 p.m. (Wednesday until 9 p.m.). The rest of the year, hours are Tues.-Sun. 10 a.m.-5 p.m. (Wednesday until 9 p.m.). On the first Wednesday of each month, admission is free. Otherwise it's $9 adults, $7 seniors/students with ID, $5 youths 6-17, and $2.50 children 3-5. Admission to the Tactile Dome is $12 per person, which includes museum admission.

THE AVENUES

Richmond District and Vicinity
Originally called San Francisco's Great Sand Waste, then the city's cemetery district (before the bones were dug up and shipped south to Colma in 1914), today the Richmond District is a middle-class ethnic sandwich, built upon Golden Gate Park and topped by Lincoln Park and the Presidio. White Russians were the first residents, fleeing Russia after the 1917 revolution, but just about everyone else followed. A stroll down **Clement Street,** past its multiethnic eateries and shops, should bring you up to speed on the subject of cultural diversity.

The area between Arguello and Park Presidio, colloquially called "New Chinatown," is noted for its good, largely untouristed Asian eateries and shops. Russian-Americans still park themselves on the playground benches at pretty **Mountain Lake Park** near the Presidio. And the gold-painted onion domes of the Russian Orthodox **Russian Holy Virgin Cathedral of the Church in Exile,** 6210 Geary Blvd., along with the Byzantine-Roman Jewish Reform **Temple Emanu-El** at Arguello and Lake (technically in Pacific Heights), offer inspiring architectural reminders of earlier days.

Highlights of the Richmond District include the **University of San Francisco** atop Lone Mountain, an institution founded by the Jesuits in 1855, complete with spectacular **St. Ignatius** church, and the **Neptune Society Columbarium,** 1 Loraine Ct. (just off Anza near Stanyan), tel. (415) 221-1838, the final resting place of old San Francisco families including the newspaper Hearsts and department store Magnins. With its ornate neoclassical and copper-roofed rotunda, the Columbarium offers astounding acoustics, best appreciated from the upper floors. The building is open to the public weekdays 9 a.m.-5 p.m., weekends 10 a.m.-2 p.m.

Seacliff, an exclusive seaside neighborhood nestled between the Presidio and Lincoln Park, is the once-rural community where famed California photographer **Ansel Adams** was raised. West of Seacliff, **Land's End** is the city's most rugged coastline, reached via footpath from Lincoln Park and the Golden Gate National Recreation Area. **China Beach,** just below Seacliff, was probably named for Chinese immigrants trying to evade Angel Island internment by jumping ship, all a result of the Exclusion Act in effect from the 1880s to World War II. During the Civil War, this was the westernmost point of the nation's antislavery "Underground Railroad." You can swim here—facilities include a lifeguard station plus changing rooms, showers, restrooms—but the water's brisk. Northeast is **Baker Beach,** considered the city's best nude beach.

California Palace of the Legion of Honor
The area's main attraction, though, just beyond

Lincoln Park's Municipal Golf Course, is the **California Palace of the Legion of Honor,** on Legion of Honor Drive (enter off 34th and Clement), tel. (415) 750-3600 (office) or (415) 863-3330 (visitor hot line), www.famsf.org. Established by French-born Alma de Bretteville Spreckels, wife of the city's sugar king, this handsome hilltop palace was built in honor of American soldiers killed in France during World War I. It's a 1920 French neoclassic, from the colonnades and triumphal arch to the outdoor equestrian bronzes. Intentionally incongruous, placed out near the parking lot in an otherwise serene setting, is George Segal's testimony to the depths of human terror and terrorism: the barbed wire and barely living bodies of *The Holocaust.* Also here are some original bronze castings from Rodin, including *The Thinker* and *The Shades* outdoors, just part of the Legion's collection of more than 70 Rodin originals. Inside, the permanent collection was originally exclusively French, but now includes the M.H. de Young Museum's European collection—an awesome eight-century sweep from El Greco, Rembrandt, and Rubens to Renoir, Czanne, Degas, Monet, and Manet. Take a docent-led tour for a deeper appreciation of other features, including the Legion's period rooms.

Special events include films, lectures, and painting and music programs, the latter including Rodin Gallery pipe organ concerts as well as chamber music, jazz, and historical instrument concerts in the Florence Gould Theater. The Legion of Honor also features a pleasant café and a gift shop. Museum hours are Tues.-Sun. 9:30 a.m.-5 p.m., and until 8:45 p.m. on the first Saturday of every month. Admission is $7 adults, $5 seniors, $4 youths 12-17, free for everyone on the second Wednesday of each month. Admission may be higher during some visiting exhibitions.

The fit and fresh-air loving can get here on foot along the meandering **Coastal Trail**—follow it north from the Cliff House or south from the Golden Gate Bridge.

Sunset District

Most of San Francisco's neighborhoods are residential, streets of private retreat that aren't all that exciting except to those who live there. The Sunset District, stretching to the sea from south of Golden Gate Park, is one example, the southern section of the city's "Avenues." In summertime, the fog here at the edge of the continent is usually unrelenting, so visitors often shiver and shuffle off, muttering that in a place called "Sunset" one should be able to see it. (To appreciate the neighborhood name, come anytime *but* summer.) The golden gates, both the city and national parks, offer delights and diversions at the fringe. For beach access and often gray-day seaside recreation, from surfing and surf fishing to cycling, walking, and jogging (there's a paved path), follow the **Great Highway** south from Cliff House and stop anywhere along the way.

Stanyan Street, at the edge of the Haight and east of Golden Gate Park, offers odd and attractive shops, as does the stretch of **Ninth Avenue** near Irving and Judah. Just south of the park at its eastern edge is the **University of California at San Francisco Medical Center** atop Mt. Sutro, the small eucalyptus forest here reached via cobblestone Edgewood Ave. or, for the exercise, the Farnsworth Steps. From here, look down on the colorful Haight or north for a bird's-eye view of the **Richmond District,** the rest of the city's Avenues.

Stern Grove, at Sloat Blvd. and 19th Ave., is a wooded valley beloved for its Sunday concerts. Just off Sloat is the main gate to the **San Francisco Zoo,** which offers an Insect Zoo, a Children's Zoo, and the usual caged collection of primates, lions, tigers, and bears. (Mealtime for the big cats, at the Lion House at 2 p.m. every day except Monday, is quite a viewing treat.) Large **Lake Merced** just south, accessible via Skyline Blvd. (Hwy. 35) or Lake Merced Blvd., was once a tidal lagoon. These days it's a freshwater lake popular for canoeing, kayaking, nonmotorized boating (rent boats at the Boat House on Harding), fishing (largemouth bass and trout), or just getting some fresh air.

The Lake Merced area offers one of the newer sections of the **Bay Area Ridge Trail,** a hiking route (signed with blue markers at major turning points and intersections) that one day will total 400 miles and connect over 75 parks in nine Bay Area counties. For more information, contact the **Bay Area Ridge Trail Council,** 26 O'-Farrell St., San Francisco, CA 94108, tel. (415) 391-9300, www.ridgetrail.org. Farther south still is **Fort Funston,** a one-time military installation on barren cliffs, a favorite spot for hang gliders and a good place to take Fido for an outing (dogs can be off-leash along most of the beach here). East of Lake Merced are **San Francisco State University,** one of the state university system's best—noted for its **Sutro Library** and **American Poetry Archives**—and the community of **Ingleside,** home of the 26-foot-tall sundial.

HAIGHT-ASHBURY

Aging hippies, random hipsters, and the hopelessly curious of all ages are still attracted to San Francisco's Haight-Ashbury, once a commercial district for adjacent Golden Gate Park and a solid family neighborhood in the vicinity of Haight Street. The Golden Gate's block-wide Panhandle (which certainly resembles one on a map) was intended as the park's carriage entrance, helped along toward the desired ambience by neighboring Victorian-age Queen Annes. Once abandoned by the middle class, however, Haight-Ashbury declined into the cheap-rent paradise surrounded by parklands that became "Hashbury," "hippies," and headquarters for the 1967 Summer of Love.

Drawn here by the drum song of the coming-of-age Aquarian Age, some 200,000 young people lived in subdivided Victorian crash pads, on the streets, and in the parks that summer, culturally recognizable by long hair, scruffy jeans, tie-dyed T-shirts, granny glasses, peace signs, beads, and the flowers-in-your-hair style of flowing skirts and velvet dresses. Essential, too, at that time: underground newspapers and unrestrained radio, black-lights and psychedelia, incense, anything that came from India (like gurus), acid and mescaline, hashish, waterpipes, marijuana and multicolored rolling papers, harmonicas, tambourines, guitars, and bongo drums. A Volkswagen van was helpful, too, so loads of people could caravan off to anti-Vietnam War rallies, to wherever it was the Grateful Dead or Jefferson Airplane were playing (for free, usually), or to Fillmore West and Winterland, where Bill Graham staged so many concerts. It was all fairly innocent, at first, an innocence that didn't last. By late 1967, cultural predators had arrived: the tourists, the national

media, and serious drug pushers and pimps. Love proved to be fragile. Most true believers headed back to the land, and Haight-Ashbury became increasingly violent and dangerous, especially for the young runaways who arrived (and still arrive) to stake a misguided claim for personal freedom.

"The Haight" today is considerably cleaner, its Victorian neighborhoods spruced up but not exactly gentrified. The classic Haight-Ashbury head shops are long gone, runaway hippies replaced by runaway punks panhandling for quarters (or worse). But Haight St. and vicinity is still hip, still socially and politically aware, still worth a stroll. The parkside Upper Haight stretch has more than its share of funky cafés, coffee shops, oddball bars and clubs, boutiques, and secondhand stores. If this all seems stodgy, amble on down to the Lower Haight in the Western Addition, an area fast becoming the city's new avant-garde district.

Seeing and Doing Haight-Ashbury
Aside from the commercial versions, there are a few significant countercultural sights in the Upper Haight, like the old Victorian **Dead House** at 710 Ashbury (near Waller), where the Grateful Dead lived and played their still-living music (and possibly where the term "deadheads" first emerged for the Dead's fanatic fans), and the **Jefferson Airplane's** old pad at 2400 Fulton (on the eastern edge of Golden Gate Park at Willard). Definitely worth a stop, for organic juice and granola, art to meditate by, and New Age computer networking, is **The Red Victorian** at 1665 Haight (near Belvedere), tel. (415) 864-1978, www.redvic.com, also a fascinating bed-and-breakfast complex that successfully honors The Haight's original innocence. Do climb on up the steep paths into nearby **Buena Vista Park,** a shocking tangle of anarchistically enchanted forest, just for the through-the-trees views.

Otherwise, the scene here is wherever you can find it. **Bound Together,** 1369 Haight St. (at Masonic), tel. (415) 431-8355, is a collective bookstore featuring a somewhat anarchistic collection: books on leftist politics, conspiracy theories, the occult, and sexuality. **Pipe Dreams,** 1376 Haight (at Masonic), tel. (415) 431-3553, is one place to go for Grateful Dead memorabilia and quaint drug paraphernalia, like water pipes and "bongs," but **Distractions,** 1552 Haight (between Clayton and Ashbury), tel. (415) 252-8751, is truest to the form; in addition to the Dead selection, you can also snoop through head shop supplies, an ample variety of Tarot cards, and Guatemalan clothing imports.

Style is another Haight St. specialty. Though secondhand clothing stores here tend to feature higher prices than elsewhere, three of the best are **Wasteland,** 1660 Haight (at Belvedere), tel. (415) 863-3150; the **Buffalo Exchange,** 1555 Haight (between Clayton and Ashbury), tel. (415) 431-7733; and **Aardvarks,** 1501 Haight (at Ashbury), tel. (415) 621-3141. For old-style music bargains—and actual albums, including a thousand hard-to-find ones—head to **Recycled Records,** 1377 Haight (at Masonic), tel. (415) 626-4075. For thousands of used CDs and tapes, try **Reckless Records,** 1401 Haight (at Masonic), tel. (415) 431-3434. Housed in a former bowling alley, **Amoeba Music,** 1855 Haight (between Stanyan and Shrader), tel. (415) 831-1200, is huge and offers an encyclopedic collection of new and used sounds.

Shops of interest in the Lower Haight include: **Zebra Records,** 475 Haight (near Webster), tel. (415) 626-9145, a DJ supply store that's the place to find cutting-edge hip hop, acid jazz, and Latin House; the **Naked Eye,** 533 Haight (between Fillmore and Steiner), tel. (415) 864-2985, which specializes in impossible-to-find videos; and **Used Rubber U.S.A.,** 597 Haight (at Steiner), tel. (415) 626-7855, which makes durable, hip, high-style handbags out of otherwise unrecycled car tires (a bit expensive). Well respected in the neighborhood for more organic personal decoration is **Erno's Tattoo Parlor,** 252 Fillmore (between Haight and Waller), tel. (415) 861-9206. Shop the Lower Haight, too, for stylish used clothing stores with good pickings, low prices, and zero crowds.

Haight-Ashbury Nightlife

In the 1980s, the Haight was known as a rock nightspot, but the Haight's pulse has slowed considerably in the last 10 years. The I-Beam, Kennel Club, and Nightbreak are no more, gone along with the street's ability to attract big talent. In their place, the Haight's comfortable bars

make great hideouts from elbow-to-elbow crowds found elsewhere.

A laid-back bar popular with young and old is **The Gold Cane,** 1569 Haight St. (between Ashbury and Clayton), tel. (415) 626-1112, serving the cheapest drinks in town. More typical of modern Haight is the **Trophy Room,** 1811 Haight (between Shrader and Stanyan), tel. (415) 752-2971, full of self-styled hippies and punks as well as unusual combinations of leather jackets, long hair, and tattoos. **Martin Macks,** 1568 Haight (between Ashbury and Clayton), tel. (415) 864-0124, is cleaner, quieter, and a bit more upscale than the usual Haight bar scene, with at least 10 imported beers on tap. Retro-swing bars are all the rage in San Francisco these days, and **Club Deluxe,** 1511 Haight (at Ashbury), tel. (415) 552-6949, is one of the best.

Wilder by far are the bars and clubs in the Lower Haight. No matter what the weather, **Mad Dog in the Fog,** 530 Haight (between Fillmore and Steiner), tel. (415) 626-7279, is packed every night, the very mixed clientele attracted by the English pub-style dart boards as much as the live music. Across the street, serious drinking is the main agenda at the loud and boisterous **Toronado,** 547 Haight (between Fillmore and Webster), tel. (415) 863-2276. **Nickie's Haight Street BBQ,** 460 Haight (between Fillmore and Webster), tel. (415) 621-6508, serves barbecue by day, red-hot DJed dance music by night—everything from hip-hop and salsa to world beat and the music of Islam. (And the bar jumps, too.) Quieter and perhaps a tad too self-conscious for this very natural neighborhood is the **Noc Noc,** 557 Haight (between Fillmore and Steiner), tel. (415) 861-5811, a cavelike, romantically gloomy environment simultaneously inspired by *The Flintstones* cartoons and *Star Trek* reruns. For genuine cultural inspiration, though, that now-gone mural of former president George Bush shooting up at The Kennel Club was a classic.

MISSION DISTRICT

Vibrant and culturally electric, the Mission District is one of San Francisco's most exciting neighborhoods. The fact that most tourists never discover the area's pleasures is a sad commentary on our times. To the same extent people fear that which seems foreign in America—a nation created by foreigners—they miss out on the experience of life as it is. And the country becomes even more hell-bent on mandating social homogenization despite ideals and rhetoric to the contrary.

On any given day in the Mission District, especially if it's sunny, the neighborhood is busy with the business of life. The largely Hispanic population—Colombian, Guatemalan, Mexican, Nicaraguan, Peruvian, Panamanian, Puerto Rican, Salvadorean—crowds the streets and congregates on corners. Whether Mission residents are out strolling with their children or shopping in the many bakeries, produce stores, and meat markets, the community's cultural energy is unmatched by any other city neighborhood—with the possible exception of Chinatown early in the morning. This remains true now that gentrification has arrived even in the Mission.

Before the arrival of the Spanish, the Bay Area's Ohlone people (they called themselves Ramaytush) established their largest settlement here in the sheltered expanse later known as Mission Valley. Largely uninhabited until the 1860s, the valley attracted a large number of Irish immigrants and became one of the city's first suburbs. Most of the Mission District was spared the total devastation otherwise characteristic in the fiery aftermath of the 1906 earthquake, so some of San Francisco's finest Victorians are still area standouts.

Even with onrushing gentrification, the Mission's ungentrified modern attitude and still relatively low rents have also created a haven for artists, writers, social activists, and politicos. The Latino arts scene is among the city's most powerful and original. This is one of San Francisco's newest New Bohemias, a cultural crazy quilt where artists and assorted oddballs are not only tolerated but encouraged. Businesses catering to this emerging artistic consciousness are becoming prominent along Valencia St., already considered home by the city's lesbian community.

Technically, the Mission District extends south from near the Civic Center to the vicinity of Cesar Chavez (Army). Dolores or Church St. (or thereabouts) marks the western edge, Alabama St. the eastern. Mission Street, the main thoroughfare

(BART stations at 16th and 24th), is lined with discount stores and pawnshops. Main commercial areas include 16th St. between Mission and Dolores, 24th St. between Valencia and York, and Valencia St.—the bohemian center of social life, lined with coffeehouses, bars, bookstores, performance art venues, and establishments serving the lesbian and women's community. For the latest word on feminist and lesbian art shows, readings, performances, and other events, stop by the nonprofit **Women's Building**, 3543 18th St. (just off Valencia), tel. (415) 431-1180.

Mission Dolores

With the Mission District's return to a predominantly Hispanic ethnic attitude, a visit to the city's oldest structure seems especially fitting. Completed in 1791, Mission San Francisco de Asis at Dolores and 16th Streets, tel. (415) 621-8203, is open daily 9 a.m.-4:30 p.m. A donation of $2 or more is appreciated. (The best time to arrive, to avoid busloads of tourists and the crush of schoolchildren studying California history, is before 10 a.m.) This is the sixth mission established in California by the Franciscan fathers. Founded earlier, in 1776, the modest chapel and outbuildings came to be known as Mission Dolores, the name derived from a nearby lagoon and creek, Arroyo de Nuestra Señora de los Dolores, or "stream of our lady of sorrows."

And how apt the new shingle proved to be, in many ways. In the peaceful cemetery within the mission's walled compound is the "Grotto of Lourdes," the unmarked grave of more than 5,000 Ohlone and others among the native workforce. Most died of measles and other introduced diseases in the early 1800s, the rest from other varieties of devastation. After California became a state, the first U.S. Indian agent came to town to take a census of the Native American population. It was an easy count, since there was only one, a man named Pedro Alcantara who was still grieving for a missing son. Near the grotto are the vine-entwined tombstones of pioneers and prominent citizens, like California's first governor under Mexican rule, Don Luis Antonio Arguello, and San Francisco's first mayor, Don Francisco de Haro.

The sturdy mission chapel—the small humble structure, not the soaring basilica adjacent—survived the 1906 earthquake due largely to its four-foot-thick adobe walls. Inside, the painted ceilings are an artistic echo of the Ohlone, whose original designs were painted with vegetable dyes. And the simple altar offers stark contrast to the grandeur next door. For a peek at the collection of mission artifacts and memorabilia, visit the small museum.

Potrero Hill

East of the Mission District proper and southeast of the SoMa scene is gentrifying (at least on the north side) Noe Valley-like Potrero Hill, known for its roller-coaster road rides (a favorite spot for filming TV and movie chase scenes) and the world-famous **Anchor Brewing Company** microbrewery, 1705 Mariposa St. (at 17th), tel. (415) 863-8350, makers of Anchor Steam beer. Join a free weekday tour and see how San Francisco's famous beer is brewed. If you drive to Potrero Hill, detour to the "Poor Man's Lombard" at 20th and Vermont, which has earned the dubious honor of being the city's second twistiest street. This snakelike thoroughfare is not festooned with well-landscaped sidewalks and flowerbeds, but instead an odd assortment of abandoned furniture, beer bottles, and trash. Not yet socially transformed is

the south side of the hill, which is close to **Bayview-Hunters Point;** these once-industrialized neighborhoods were left behind when World War II-era shipbuilding ceased and are now ravaged by poverty, drugs, and violence.

Mission District Shopping

Clothes Contact, 473 Valencia (just north of 16th), tel. (415) 621-3212, sells fashionable vintage clothing for $8 per pound. (Consumer alert: those big suede jackets in the back weigh more than you might imagine.) Worth poking into, too, is the **Community Thrift Store,** 623-625 Valencia (between 17th and 18th), tel. (415) 861-4910, a fundraising venture for the gay and lesbian Tavern Guild. It's an expansive, inexpensive, and well-organized place, with a book selection rivaling most used bookstores. (The motto here is "out of the closet, into the store.") Cooperatively run **Modern Times Bookstore,** 888 Valencia (between 19th and 20th), tel. (415) 282-9246, is the source for progressive, radical, and Third World literature, magazines, and tapes.

If you're down on your luck, head up to **Lady Luck Candle Shop,** 311 Valencia (at 14th), tel. (415) 621-0358, a small store selling some pretty big juju, everything from high-test magic can-

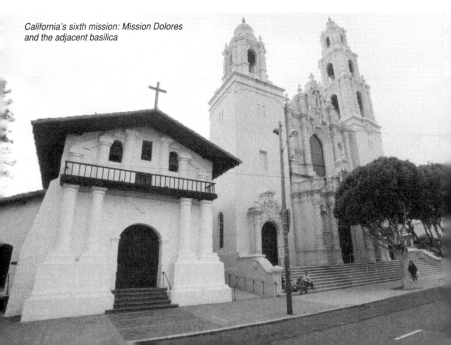
California's sixth mission: Mission Dolores and the adjacent basilica

MISSION DISTRICT MURALS

The entire Mission District is vividly alive, with aromas and sounds competing everywhere with color. And nothing in the Mission District is quite as colorful as its mural art. More than 200 murals dot the neighborhood, ranging from brilliantly colored homages to work, families, and spiritual flight to boldly political attacks on the status quo.

Start with some **"BART art,"** at the 24th St. station, where Michael Rios' columns of humanoids lift up the rails. Another, particu-

Mission District mural

larly impressive set, is eight blocks down, off 24th St. on the fences and garage doors along **Balmy Alley,** and also at **Flynn Elementary School** at Precita and Harrison. At 14th and Natoma is a mural honoring Frida Kahlo, artist and wife of Diego Rivera.

Walking tours of the neighborhood murals (with well-informed guides) are led by the **Precita Eyes Mural Arts Center,** a charming gallery at 2981 24th St. (at Harrison), tel. (415) 285-2287, www.precitaeyes.org. The tours are offered every Saturday at 11 a.m. and 1:30 p.m., Sunday at 1:30 p.m.; $7 general, $4 seniors, $1 youths 18 and under.

Call for information on the center's many other tours. Other good art stops in the area include the nonprofit **Galeria de la Raza,** 2857 24th St. (at Bryant), tel. (415) 826-8009, featuring some exciting, straight-ahead political art attacks; the affiliated **Studio 24** gift shop adjacent, with everything from books and clothing to religious icons and Day of the Dead dolls; and the **Mission Cultural Center for Latino Arts,** 2868 Mission (between 24th and 25th Streets), tel. (415) 821-1155, a community cultural and sociopolitical center that can supply you with more information on area artworks.

---

dles and religious potions (like St. John the Conqueror Spray) to Lucky Mojo Oil and Hold Your Man essential oil. **Good Vibrations,** 1210 Valencia (at 23rd), tel. (415) 974-8980, home of the vibrator museum, is a clean, user-friendly, liberated shop where women (and some men) come for adult toys, and to peruse the selection of in-print erotica, including history and literature.

More common in the Mission District are neighborhood-style antique and secondhand stores of every stripe. Bargains abound, without the inflated prices typical of trendier, more tourist-traveled areas.

Mission District Nightlife
The Roxie, 3117 16th St. (at Valencia), tel. (415) 863-1087, www.roxie.com, is the neigh-

borhood's renowned repertory film venue, with a full schedule of eclectic and foreign films as well as special programs, including live audience interviews with filmmakers. Most of the Mission's coffeehouses, bars, and clubs are equally entertaining. An offshoot of the Spanish restaurant Esperpento on 22nd, **Cafe Picaro,** 3120 16th St. (between Valencia and Guerrero), tel. (415) 431-4089, is an unpretentious new bohemian coffeehouse-cum-used bookstore (read or buy) which also serves authentic hot and cold tapas. For good coffee and Ethiopian food (including some vegetarian selections), head to **Cafe Ethiopia,** 878 Valencia St. (at 20th), tel. (415) 285-2728. **Radio Valencia,** 1199 Valencia (at 23rd), tel. (415) 826-1199, puts a musical spin on the coffeehouse scene, serving up the latest releases from a broad range of genres along with inventive pizzas, perfect foccacia sandwiches, and homemade soups. In addition to coffee drinks, Radio Valencia offers 12 beers on tap and a good selection of wine. On weekend nights, the café hosts live experimental jazz.

The Mission District may seem to have a bar on every block, but some are more appealing than others. Scoring high marks on the cool-o-meter is the **Latin-American Club** (aka "the Latin"), 3286 22nd St. (between Mission and Valencia), tel. (415) 647-2732. The Latin has a truly neighborhood vibe, funky but comfortable clubhouse atmosphere and good people-watching. Just across the way and favored by local musicians is the **Make-Out Room,** 3225 22nd (between Mission and Valencia), tel. (415) 647-2888. Easy to miss

TOURING LEVI STRAUSS

If you're curious about how the West's most historic britches evolved, stop by **Levi Strauss & Co.,** 250 Valencia St. (between Clinton Park and Brosnan), tel. (415) 565-9100, for a free tour (Tuesday and Wednesday only, at 9 a.m., 11 a.m., and 1:30 p.m., reservations required —and make them well in advance). This, Levi's oldest factory, was built in 1906 after the company's original waterfront plant was destroyed by earthquake and fire. The company is the world's largest clothing manufacturer, and most of its factories are fully automated. But at this site you can hear the riveting story of how Levi's 501's were originally made, and see it, too. Skilled workers cut, stitch, and assemble the button-fly jeans, as in the earlier days of the empire that Bavarian immigrant Levi Strauss built. During the boom days of the California gold rush, miners needed very rugged pants, something that wouldn't bust out at the seams. Strauss stitched up his first creations from tent canvas; when he ran out of that, he switched to sturdy brown cotton "denim" from Nimes, France. Levi's characteristic pocket rivets came along in the 1870s, but "blue jeans" weren't a reality until the next decade, when indigo blue dye was developed. After the tour, you can shop in the on-site company store.

from the outside, the small, windowless storefront entrance is painted all black (look for the bar's flickering sign out front). Inside, the dark bar extends back to a pool table and a small stage covered with red velvet curtains.

Shot straight from the glittering heart of NYC (the original site is in Manhattan's East Village), the **Beauty Bar,** 2299 Mission (at 19th), tel. (415) 285-0323, offers an odd and intoxicating mix of cocktails and 1950s beauty parlor ambience. The walls are pink, the chrome blow-dryers sparkle, and the crowd is a mix of Mission trendsetters and fashion victims. Specialty drinks are named after beauty products, like the Aqua Net made with blue curaçao and the Prell made with crème de menthe. Come on a weeknight and you may even score a complimentary manicure with your cocktail. A neon sign outside **Doc's Clock,** 2575 Mission (at 21st), tel. (415) 824-3627, announces it's "Cocktail Time," but the vibe down here is more relaxed, and flannel shirts outnumber silver pants 10 to 1.

Up on 16th St., **Doctor Bombay's,** 3192 16th St. (at Guerrero), tel. (415) 431-5255, is dim and diminutive, the clientele quite happy to talk the night away while downing the good doctor's award-winning specialty drink, the melon-flavored Pixie Piss. Across the street is the **Albion,** 3139 16th (between Valencia and Guerrero), tel. (415) 552-8558, a popular corner bar complete with pool table and degenerative art—home-away-from-home for a hip but friendly, artsy crowd, with occasional live music. **Esta Noche,** 3079 16th (between Mission and Valencia), tel. (415) 861-5757, is the red-hot Latino answer to the almost-all-white gay bars in the Castro.

La Rondalla, 901 Valencia (at 20th), tel. (415) 647-7474, is the most festive bar around, what with the year-round Christmas lights, smoke-stained tinsel, and revolving overhead disco ball. (Good traditional Mexican food is served in the restaurant.) Down at the foot of Mission St., hole-in-the wall **El Rio,** 3158 Mission St. (at Cesar Chavez), tel. (415) 282-3325, sports a big welcome sign outside announcing this is "Your Dive," and indeed the feeling here is warm yet slightly seedy. The outdoor deck, shuffleboard set-up, and pool tables make it an excellent warm-weather hangout. Next door is **Roccapulco,** 3140 Mission (at Cesar Chavez), tel. (415) 648-6611, a supper club where you can dine and dance salsa to live Latino bands.

Live, new theater is the specialty of **The Marsh,** 1062 Valencia St. (near 22nd), tel. (415) 826-5750. A neighborhood classic, the Marsh isn't glitzy, fashionable, or expensive (tickets usually cost around $6-12). But it has heart. The performers (and audiences) here are serious about art. Experimentation is de rigueur, meaning you're never at risk of encountering formula productions. You won't need your tux here, and your applause will be well-deserved gold to the performers, some of whom may go on to fame and fortune. Definitely check it out.

CASTRO STREET AND VICINITY

The very idea is enough to make America's righteous religious right explode in an apoplectic fit, but the simple truth is that San Francisco's Castro St. is one of the safest neighborhoods in the entire city—and that's not just a reference to sex practices.

This tight-knit, well-established community of lesbian women and gay men represents roughly 15% of the city's population and 35% of its registered voters. Nationally and internationally, the Castro District epitomizes out-of-the-closet living. (There's nothing in this world like the Castro's Gay Freedom Day Parade—usually headed by hundreds of women on motorcycles, the famous Dykes on Bikes—and no neighborhood throws a better street party.) People here are committed to protecting their own and creating safe neighborhoods. What this means, for visitors straight or gay, is that there is a response—people get out of their cars, or rush out of restaurants, clubs, and apartment buildings—at the slightest sign that something is amiss.

Who ever would have guessed that a serious revival of community values in the U.S. would start in the Castro?

Actually, there have been many indications. And there are many reasons. The developing cultural and political influence of the Castro District became apparent in 1977, when openly gay Harvey Milk was elected to the San Francisco Board of Supervisors. But genuine

acceptance seemed distant—never more so than in 1978, when both Milk and Mayor George Moscone were assassinated by conservative political rival Dan White, who had resigned his board seat and wanted it back. (White's "diminished capacity" defense argument, which claimed that his habitual consumption of high-sugar junk food had altered his brain chemistry—the "Twinkie" defense—became a national scandal but ultimately proved successful. He was sentenced to a seven-year prison term.)

The community's tragedies kept on coming, hitting even closer to home. Somewhat notorious in its adolescence as a safe haven for freestyle lifestyles, including casual human relationships and quickie sex, the Castro District was devastated by the initial impact of the AIDS epidemic. The community has been stricken to the center of its soul by the tragic human consequences of an undiscriminating virus. But otherwise meaningless human loss has served only to strengthen the community's humanity. Just as, after Milk's assassination, greater numbers of community activists came forward to serve in positions of political influence, Castro District organizations like the Shanti Project, Open Hand, and the Names Project have extended both heart and hand to end the suffering. And fierce, in-your-face activists from groups like Act Up, Queer Nation, and Bad Cop No Donut have taken the message to the nation's streets.

So, while Castro District community values are strong and getting stronger, the ambience is not exactly apple-pie Americana. People with pierced body parts (some easily visible, some not) and dressed in motorcycle jackets still stroll in and out of leather bars. Its shops also can be somewhat unusual, like **Does Your Mother Know,** a seriously homoerotic greeting card shop on 18th St. near Castro.

Seeing and Doing the Castro

The neighborhood's business district, both avant-garde and gentrified Victorian, is small, stretching for three blocks along Castro St. between Market and 19th, and a short distance in each direction from 18th and Castro. This area is all included, geographically, in what was once recognizable as **Eureka Valley.** (Parking can be a problem, once you've arrived, so take the Muni Metro and climb off at the Castro St. Station.) Some people also include the gentrifying **Noe Valley** (with its upscale 24th St. shopping district) in the general Castro stream of consciousness, but the technical dividing line is near the crest of Castro St. at 22nd Street. Keep driving on Upper Market St., and you'll wind up into the city's geographic center. Though the ascent is actually easier from Haight-Ashbury (from Twin Peaks Blvd. just off 17th—see a good road map), either way you'll arrive at or near the top of **Twin Peaks,** with its terraced neighborhoods, astounding views, and some of the city's best stairway walks. More challenging is the short but steep hike to the top of Corona Heights Park (at Roosevelt), also noted for the very good **Josephine D. Randall Junior Museum,** 199 Museum Way (at Roosevelt), tel. (415) 554-9600, a youth-oriented natural sciences, arts, and activities center open Tues.-Sat. 10 a.m.-5 p.m. Admission free; donations welcome.

Down below, **A Different Light,** 489 Castro St. (between Market and 18th Streets), tel. (415) 431-0891, is the city's best gay and lesbian bookstore, with literature by and for. Readings and other events are occasionally offered; call for current information. Truly classic and quite traditional is the handsome and authentic art deco **Castro Theater,** 429 Castro (at Market), tel. (415) 621-6120, built in 1923. San Francisco's only true movie palace, the Castro is still a favorite city venue for classic movies and film festivals. Another highlight is the massive house Wurlitzer organ, which can make seeing a film at the Castro a truly exhilarating experience. **Cliff's Variety,** 479 Castro (at 18th), tel. (415) 431-5365, is another classic, a wonderfully old-fashioned hardware store where you can buy almost anything, from power saws to Play-doh. Retro kitsch **Uncle Mame,** 2241 Market (between Noe and Sanchez), tel. (415) 626-1953, is another Castro gem. Packed to the rafters with 1950s, '60s and '70s pop culture ephemera, this is the place to shop for vintage board games, lunch boxes, and Barbies.

Also stop by **The Names Project,** 2362 Market (between 16th and 17th), tel. (415) 863-1966, a museum-like memorial to those felled by AIDS. It's also the original home of the famous AIDS Memorial Quilt, each section created by friends and family of someone who died of the disease. Adjacent (in the same building) is **Under One Roof,** tel. (415) 252-9430, a cool and classy little gift shop with Act Up votive candles, artwork, T-shirts, and more. All money earned goes to support some 50 AIDS service organizations.

Castro Nightlife

Many of San Francisco's 200-plus gay bars are in the Castro District. Those in the know say the best way to find just the scene you're looking for is to wander. **The Cafe,** 2367 Market St. (between 17th and 18th), tel. (415) 861-3846, is the Castro's best lesbian bar, also attracting many gay boys and some straights. From its balcony overlooking Market and Castro, you can get a good overview of the whole Castro scene below. Also featured: an indoor patio, pool tables, and a spacious dance floor. DJs spin a loud mix of techno and house with a few '70s and '80s remixes for a crowd that often packs the floor by 11 p.m. A onetime speakeasy, **Cafe du Nord,** 2170 Market (between Church and Sanchez), tel. (415) 861-5016, is underground, quite literally, in the basement of the Swedish American building. Descend the stairs into a nightspot with the look of a classic supper club: deep red walls and mahogany fixtures. Alternative and swing music make this the best club in the Castro for straights and mixed groups, with excellent cocktails, a good dinner menu, and only moderate pretense. **Josie's Cabaret & Juice Joint,** 3583 16th St. (at Market), tel. (415) 861-7933, is the place to go for healthy relaxation and pure juice intoxication. There's usually a cover charge for the show—the best local and national gay and lesbian performers, from cabaret acts, lounge singers, and drag shows to stand-up comedy.

SOUTH OF MARKET (SoMa)

Known by old-timers as "south of the slot," a reference to a neighborhood sans cable cars, San Francisco's South of Market area was a working- and middle-class residential area—until all its homes were incinerated in the firestorm following the great earthquake of 1906. Rebuilt early in the century with warehouses, factories, train

METREON

Anchoring the corner of Fourth and Mission Streets like a sleek spacecraft, the block-long, four-story-tall **Metreon**, tel. (415) 537-3400, www.metreon.com, is the latest icon of pop culture to land in San Francisco's SoMa district. The Sony Entertainment-sponsored mall features a 15-screen cinema complex, a 600-seat IMAX theatre with 2-D and 3-D capability, and fashion-forward shopping options including a Sony Style store and MicrosoftSF.

Interactive exhibits include **Where the Wild Things Are,** based on Maurice Sendak's magical children's book; an interactive 3-D show titled **The Way Things Work,** based on David Macaulay's book of the same name; and **Airtight Garage,** a futuristic gaming area based on the images of French graphic artist Jean "Mobius" Giraud. The mall's food court features offshoots of several popular local restaurants: LongLife Noodle Co., Buckhorn, Sanraku, and Firewood Café, gathered under the umbrella "a taste of San Francisco." For admission prices, hours, and other current information, call Metreon at (415) 537-3400.

yards, and port businesses at **China Basin,** these days the area has gone trendy. In the style of New York's SoHo (South of Houston), this semi-industrial stretch of the city now goes by the moniker "SoMa."

As is usually the case, the vanguard of gentrification was the artistic community: the dancers, musicians, sculptors, photographers, painters, and graphic designers who require low rents and room to create. Rehabilitating old warehouses and industrial sheds here into studios and performance spaces solved all but strictly creative problems. Then came the attractively inexpensive factory outlet stores, followed by eclectic cafés and nightclubs. The Yerba Buena Gardens redevelopment project sealed the neighborhood's fate, bringing big-time tourist attractions including the Moscone Convention Center, the San Francisco Museum of Modern Art, the Yerba Buena Center for the Arts, and The Rooftop at Yerba Buena Gardens, a multifacility arts and entertainment complex.

Now the city's newest luxury hotel, the 30-story **W San Francisco,** towers over Third and Howard. Sony's futuristic new Metreon holds down Fourth and Mission. Even near the once-abandoned waterfront just south of the traditional Financial District boundaries, avant-garde construction like **Number One Market Street,** which incorporates the old Southern Pacific Building, and **Rincon Center,** which encompasses the preserved Depression-era mural art of the Rincon Annex Post Office, have added a new look to once down-and-out areas. More massive highrises are on the way, and land values are shooting up in areas where previously only the neighborhood homeless did that. The starving artists have long since moved on to the Lower Haight and the Mission District, and in SoMa, the strictly eccentric is now becoming more self-consciously so.

San Francisco Museum of Modern Art
SoMa's transformation is largely due to the arrival of the San Francisco Museum of Modern Art (SFMOMA), 151 Third St. (between Mission and Howard), tel. (415) 357-4000, which moved from its cramped quarters on the third and fourth floors of the War Memorial. Many consider the modern, Swiss-designed building to be a work of art in itself. Love it or hate it, you're not likely to miss the soaring cylindrical skylight and assertive red brick of the new $60-million structure rising above the gritty streets south of Market.

The museum's permanent collection includes minor works by Georgia O'Keefe, Pablo Picasso, Salvador Dali, Henri Matisse, and some outstanding paintings by Jackson Pollock. Mexican painters Frida Kahlo and her husband, Diego Rivera, are represented, as are the works of many Californian artists, including assembler Bruce Connor and sculptor Bruce Arneson. The museum also hosts excellent temporary exhibitions showcasing world-renowned individual artists. There's a hip little café, the **Cafe Museo,** tel. (415) 357-4500, and the **SFMOMA Museum Store,** well stocked with art books and postcards.

The Museum of Modern Art is open 11 a.m.-6 p.m. daily except Wednesday. Additionally, it's open until 9 p.m. on Thursday, and opens at 10 a.m. instead of 11 a.m. from Memorial Day weekend through Labor Day.

The museum is closed on July 4th, Thanksgiving, Christmas, and New Year's Day. Admission is $8 adults, $5 seniors, and $4 students with ID (children under 12 free). Admission is free for everyone on the first Tuesday of each month, and half price Thursday 6-9 p.m. Admission charge is sometimes higher during special exhibitions.

Yerba Buena Center for the Arts

Opposite the museum on the west side of Third St. is the Yerba Buena Center for the Arts, 701 Mission St. (at Third), tel. (415) 978-2700 or (415) 978-2787 (ticket office), www.yerbabuenaarts.org, a gallery and theater complex devoted to showcasing the works of experimental, marginalized, and emerging artists. A YBC classic was the exhibition of a century of drawings for tattoos, *Pierced Hearts and True Love,* featuring drawings by prominent tattoo artists Sailor Jerry and Ed Hardy. A five-acre downtown park surrounds the complex, where a waterfall dedicated to the memory of Martin Luther King Jr. reads: "We will not be satisfied until 'justice rolls down like a river and righteousness like a mighty stream.' " Amen. The Center for the Arts galleries are open 11 a.m.-6 p.m. daily except Monday (until 8 p.m. on the first Thursday of each month). Admission is $5 adults, $3 seniors/students; children 12 and under free. Everyone gets in free on the first Thursday of every month, 6-8 p.m.

The Rooftop at Yerba Buena Gardens

Cleverly built atop the Moscone Center along Fourth, Howard, and Folsom Streets, this parkcum-entertainment complex is the latest addition to the Yerba Buena Gardens redevelopment project. It holds a 1906 carousel, a fullsize indoor ice rink with city-skyline views, a bowling center, and **Zeum,** tel. (415) 777-3727, an interactive art and technology center for children ages 8-18. Hours are Wed.-Fri. noon-6 p.m., Sat.-Sun. 11 a.m.-5 p.m., and admission is $7 adults, $5 youths ages 5-18. The **Ice Skating Center,** tel. (415) 777-3727, is open for public skating daily, 1-5 p.m. Admission is $6 adults and $4.50 seniors and children ($2.50 skate rental).

Other SoMa Sights

Across from the Moscone Center, the **Ansel**

Adams Center for Photography, 250 Fourth St. (between Howard and Folsom), tel. (415) 495-7000 or (415) 495-7242, is a major presence in San Francisco's art scene, with five galleries dedicated to the photographic art, one set aside exclusively for Adams' own internationally renowned black-and-white works. Open daily 11 a.m.-5 p.m. (until 8 p.m. on the first Thursday of every month). Admission is $5 adults, $3 students, $2 seniors/youths.

Less serious is the **Cartoon Art Museum,** 814 Mission (between Fourth and Fifth Streets), tel. (415) 227-8666, which chronicles the history of the in-print giggle, from cartoon sketches and finished art to toys and videos. Open Wed.-Fri. 11 a.m.-5 p.m., Saturday 10 a.m.-5 p.m., Sunday 1-5 p.m. Admission is $5 adults, $3 seniors/students, $1 children.

The **California Historical Society Museum,** 678 Mission St. (between Second and Third Streets), tel. (415) 357-1848, displays rare historical photographs and includes exhibits on early California movers and shakers (both human and geologic), Western art of California, and frontier manuscripts. The museum bookstore features a great selection of books by California authors. The museum and bookstore are open Tues.-Sat. 11 a.m.-5 p.m. Small admission.

Actually closer to the waterfront and Financial District, the **Jewish Community Museum,** 121 Steuart St. (at Mission), tel. (415) 543-8880, features changing, usually exceptional exhibits on Jewish art, culture, and history. (The museum is scheduled to move to the Yerba Buena Gardens area in 2000, so call before going.) The **Telephone Pioneers Communications Museum,** 140 New Montgomery (at Natoma), tel. (415) 542-0182, offers electronic miscellany and telephone memorabilia dating to the 1870s.

SoMa Shopping

Shop-and-drop types, please note: serious bargains are available throughout SoMa's garment district. The garment industry is the city's largest, doing a wholesale business of $5 billion annually. Most of the manufacturing factories are between Second and 11th Streets, and many have off-price retail outlets for their own wares. But you won't necessarily shop in comfort, since some don't have dressing rooms and others are as

CLEAN UP YOUR ACT AT BRAINWASH

No doubt the cleanest scene among SoMa's hot spots is BrainWash at 1122 Folsom, tel. (415) 861-FOOD, (415) 431-WASH, or www.brain-wash.com, a combination café, smart bar, nightclub, and laundromat in a reformed warehouse. The brainchild of UC Berkeley and Free Speech Movement alumna Susan Schindler, BrainWash ain't heavy, just semi-industrial, from the beamed ceilings and neon to the concrete floor. The decor here includes café tables corralled by steel office chairs with original decoupaged artwork on the seats. (Admit it—haven't you always wanted to sit on Albert Einstein's face?) BrainWash also features a small counter/bar area, and bathrooms for either "Readers" (lined with *Dirty Laundry Comics* wallpaper) or "Writers" (with walls and ceiling of green chalkboard, chalk provided for generating brainwashable graffiti). Since literary urges know no boundaries in terms of gender, of course both are open to both basic sexes. And others.

The small café at BrainWash offers quick, simple fare—salads, spinach and feta turnovers, pizza, and decent sandwiches (vegetarian and otherwise)—plus pastries and decadent pies, cakes, and cookies. Try a BrainWash Brownie, either double chocolate or double espresso. There's liquid espresso too, of course, plus cappuccinos and lattes, fresh unfiltered fruit or carrot juice, teas, beer, and wine.

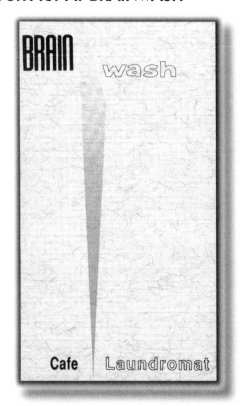

Behind the café (and glass wall) is the Brain-Wash washhouse, a high-tech herd of washers and dryers ($1.50 per load for a regular wash load, $3.50 for a jumbo washer, and a quarter for 10 minutes of dryer time). Ask about the laundromat's wash-and-fold and dry-cleaning services. The whole shebang here is open daily 8 a.m.-12 a.m. (until 1 a.m. on Friday and Saturday nights). "Last call" for washers is 10 p.m. nightly. Call ahead to make sure, but live music is usually scheduled after 9 p.m. on Tues.-Thurs. and Friday or Saturday nights, jukebox available otherwise. BrainWash also sponsors community events, such as the "Take the Dirty Shirt Off Your Back" benefit for the STOP AIDS Project. The place can also be rented for private parties.

So come on down, almost anytime, for some Clorox and croissants.

jam-packed as the post office at tax time. Major merchandise marts, mostly for wholesalers, are clustered along Kansas and Townsend Streets. Some retail discount outlets for clothing, jewelery, and accessories are here, too, also along Brannan St. between Third and Sixth Streets. If at all possible, come any day but Saturday, and always be careful where you park. The parking cops are serious about ticketing violators.

Yerba Buena Square, 899 Howard St. (at Fifth), tel. (415) 543-1275, is an off-price factory mall. **Tower Outlet,** 660 Third St. (at Townsend), tel. (415) 957-9660, offers discounted CDs and tapes. Some of the best places have to be hunted down, however. **Esprit Direct,** 499 Illinois (at 16th), tel. (415) 957-2500, is a warehouse-sized store offering discounts on San Francisco's hippest women's and children's wear. (Try lunch—weekdays only—at **42 Degrees,** tucked behind the outlet at 235 16th St., tel. 415-777-5558.) Neighborhood anchor **Gunne Sax,** 35 Stanford Alley (between Second and Third, Brannan and Townsend), tel. (415) 495-3326, has a huge selection of more than 25,000 garments (including dress-up dresses); the best bargains are way in the back. Nearby, at the border of South Park, **Jeremy's** 2 South Park (at Second), tel. (415) 882-4929, sells hip designer clothes for one-third or more off retail. Consumer alert: because some of the items are returns, be sure to check garments for snags or other signs of wear before buying. **Harper Greer,** 580 Fourth St. (between Bryant and Brannan), tel. (415) 543-4066, offers wholesale-priced fashions for women size 14 and larger.

Since shopping outlets open, close, and change names or locations at a remarkable rate, consult the "Style" section of the Sunday *San Francisco Examiner and Chronicle,* which lists discount centers and factory outlets in SoMa and elsewhere around town.

SoMa Nightlife

Many SoMa restaurants (see Eating in San Francisco) do double-duty as bars and club venues. You won't go far before finding something going on. The classic for people who wear ties even after work is **Julie's Supper Club,** 1123 Folsom (at Seventh), tel. (415) 861-0707, though **Hamburger Mary's,** 1582 Folsom (at 12th), tel. (415) 626-5767, has achieved an almost mythic status among the alternative crowd. The **M&M Tavern,** 198 Fifth St. (at Howard), tel. (415) 362-6386, is a genuine institution, the place to find most of the *Chronicle* or *Examiner* staff, even during the day.

Catch touring and local rock bands at **Slim's,** 333 11th St. (between Folsom and Harrison), tel. (415) 522-0333, the cutting edge for indie rockers; pretty steep cover. Before braving the line, fill up across the street at the **20 Tank Brewery,** 316 11th (at Folsom), tel. (415) 255-9455, a lively brewpub run by the same microbrewery folks who brewed up Triple Rock in Berkeley.

The **Caribbean Zone,** 55 Natoma (between First and Second, Mission and Howard), tel. (415) 541-9465, has a mezzanine cocktail lounge created from an airplane fuselage, so you can sit and down a few while porthole-window television screens and sound effects simulate takeoff (and crash landings). Artistically and genetically expansive, in a punkish sort of way, is the **DNA Lounge,** 375 11th St. (between Harrison and Folsom), tel. (415) 626-1409, serving up dancing nightly after 9 p.m., cover on weekends.

But don't miss the **Paradise Lounge,** 1501 Folsom St. (at 11th), tel. (415) 861-6906, marvelously mazelike and sporting several bars, four separate live stages, and an upstairs pool hall. Upstairs is **Above Paradise,** featuring more music—often acoustic—and occasional poetry readings. Next door is the **Transmission Theatre,** tel. (415) 621-4410, an 800-seat venue for live music and performing arts built in an old auto shop. And all of this adventure for a reasonable cover charge.

Since SoMa in the 1970s was a nighttime playground for the bad-boys-in-black-leather set, the gay bar scene here is still going strong. The original gay bar is **The Stud,** 399 Ninth St. (at Harrison), tel. (415) 252-7883, formerly a leather bar, now a dance bar. For dancing in the gay, country-western style, try the **Rawhide II,** 280 Seventh St. (at Folsom), tel. (415) 621-1197. But the hottest younger-set gay nightclub in the neighborhood, some say in the entire city, is the **Endup** ("you always end up at the Endup"), 401 Sixth St. (at Harrison), tel. (415) 357-0827, famous for serious dancing—"hot bodies," too, according to an informed source—and, for cooling down, its large outdoor deck.

AN OPEN-MINDED GUIDE TO NIGHTCLUBBING IN SAN FRANCISCO

First, ask the basic questions: Who am I? What am I doing here? Where do I belong? To go nightclubbing in San Francisco, at least *ask* the questions. The answers don't really matter; your political, social, sexual, and musical preferences will be matched somewhere. Techno, disco, new wave, house, fusion, industrial, world beat—whatever it is you're into, it's out there, just part of the creative carnival world of San Francisco nightclubbing. Everything goes, especially cultural taboos, leaving only freewheeling imaginations and an unadulterated desire to do one thing and only one thing—dance with total abandon. In the city, heteros, gays, lesbians, blacks, whites, Asians, and Latinos all writhe together, unified in a place where all prejudice drops away: the dance floor.

The hottest dance clubs come and go considerably faster than the Muni buses do, so the key to finding the hippest, most happening spot is to ask around. Ask people who look like they should know, such as young fashion junkies working in trendy clothing shops, used-record stores, or other abodes of pretentious cool. If you're seeking one of those infamous "warehouse" parties, then look for small invitational flyers tacked to telephone poles or posted in the above-mentioned and other likely places (particularly in the Haight, lower Haight, and Castro neighborhoods). The flyers announce a party and list a phone number to call. When you call up—ooh, the intrigue—you'll get directions to that night's secret dance locale. Warning: these roving, nonlicensed dance clubs tend to put on quite crowded parties, very expensive to boot.

Throbbing together with hundreds of other euphorics, experiencing ecstasy en masse, may be the closest we'll ever really get to living in one united world. Still, San Francisco nightclub virgins tend to avoid their initiation, somehow intimidated by the frenzied cosmic collision of electrifying lights, thumping dance tunes, and sweat-drenched bodies. But be not afraid. There are answers to even the three most common worries:

Worry: I can't dance. *Answer:* It wouldn't matter even if you could. The dance floors are so crowded, at best it's possible only to bounce up and down.

Worry: I'm straight (or gay) and the crowd seems to be predominantly gay (or straight). *Answer:* Since the limits of gender and sexuality are hopelessly blurred in San Francisco, and since nobody would care even if they weren't, just dump your angst and dance.

Worry: I'm afraid I'll look like a fool (feel out of place, be outclassed, fall down, throw up, whatever). *Answer:* As we said, nobody cares. You're totally anonymous, being one of more than 728,000 people in town. And no matter what you do, nobody will notice, since narcissism in San Francisco's clubs is at least as deep as the Grand Canyon.

—*Tim Moriarty*

Other SoMa clubs to explore (if you dare) include: **El Bobo,** 1539 Folsom (between 11th and 12th), tel. (415) 861-6822, an elegant supper club open late for nightcaps and midnight munchies; the mostly lesbian **CoCo Club,** 139 Eighth St. (between Mission and Howard), tel. (415) 626-2337; **Covered Wagon Saloon,** 917 Folsom (between Fifth and Sixth), tel. (415) 974-1585, favored by bike messengers; **Holy Cow,** 1535 Folsom (between 11th and 12th), tel. (415) 621-6087; the **Hotel Utah Saloon,** 500 Fourth St. (at Bryant), tel.(415) 421-8308, featuring eclectic live music; and the dance club **1015 Folsom,** 1015 Folsom (at Sixth), tel. (415) 431-1200.

AISLINN RACE

DELIGHTS AND DIVERSIONS

WALKING TOURS

San Francisco is a walking city par excellence. With enough time and inclination, exploring the hills, stairways, and odd little neighborhood nooks and crannies is the most rewarding way to get to know one's way around. Helpful for getting started are the free neighborhood walking-tour pamphlets (Pacific Heights, Union Square, Chinatown, Fisherman's Wharf, the Barbary Coast Trail, and more) available at the Convention & Visitors Bureau Information Center downstairs at Hallidie Plaza (Powell and Market Streets), tel. (415) 391-2000. Also helpful: books such as Adah Bakalinsky's *Stairway Walks in San Francisco,* Randolph Delehanty's *San Francisco: The Ultimate Guide,* and Earl Thollander's *San Francisco: 30 Walking and Driving Tours from the Embarcadero to the Golden Gate.*

Even with substantially less time, there are excellent options. A variety of local nonprofit organizations offer free or low-cost walking tours. Commercial tours—many unusual—are also available, most ranging in price from $15 to $40 per person, more for all-day tours.

Free and Inexpensive Walking Tours
Gold-rush-era San Francisco is the theme behind the city's **Barbary Coast Trail,** a four-mile self-guided walking tour from Mission St. to Aquatic Park, marked by 150 bronze plaques embedded in the sidewalk along the way. Among the 20 historic sites en route are the oldest Asian temple in North America, the western terminus of the Pony Express, and the Hyde Street historic ships. Two different guides to the trail are sold at the Hallidie Plaza visitor information center (Powell and Market).

The **City Guides** walking tours offered by Friends of the San Francisco Public Library, headquartered at the main San Francisco Public Library (Larkin and Grove), include many worthwhile neighborhood prowls. Call (415) 557-4266 for a recorded schedule of upcoming walks (what, where, and when) or try www.walking-tours.com/CityGuides. Most walks include local architecture, culture, and history, though the emphasis—Art Deco Marina, Pacific Heights

Mansions, Cityscapes and Roof Mansions, the Gold Rush City, Victorian San Francisco, Haight-Ashbury, Mission Murals, Japantown—can be surprising. City Guides are free, but donations are definitely appreciated.

Pacific Heights Walks are sponsored by the **Foundation for San Francisco's Architectural Heritage**, headquartered in the historic Haas-Lilienthal House at 2007 Franklin St. (between Washington and Jackson), tel. (415) 441-3000 (office) or (415) 441-3004 (recorded information), and offer a look at the exteriors of splendid pre-World War I mansions in eastern Pacific Heights.

Friends of Recreation and Parks, headquartered at McLaren Lodge in Golden Gate Park, Stanyan and Fell Streets, tel. (415) 263-0991 (for upcoming hike schedule), offers guided flora, fauna, and history walks through the park May-Oct., Saturday at 11 a.m. and Sunday at 11 a.m. and 2 p.m. Group tours are also available.

Precita Eyes Mural Arts Center, at 2981 24th St. (at Harrison), tel. (415) 285-2287, www.precitaeyes.org, offers fascinating two-hour mural walks through the Mission District on Saturday starting at 11 a.m. and 1:30 p.m., and Sunday at 1:30 p.m. Admission is $7 adults, $4 seniors, $1 youths 18 and under. Call for information on the center's many other tours. In addition to its self-guided Mission murals tour, the **Mexican Museum** at Fort Mason, tel. (415) 441-0404 (recorded) or (415) 202-9700, sponsors docent-led tours of San Francisco's Diego Rivera murals. The **Chinese Culture Center,** 750 Kearny (between Clay and Washington), tel. (415) 986-1822, offers both a culinary and a cultural heritage walking tour of Chinatown. (See Useful Information in San Francisco: An Introduction for more about this organization).

The San Francisco Symphony Volunteer Council, San Francisco Opera Guild, and San Francisco Ballet Auxiliary combine their services to offer a walking tour of the three **San Francisco Performing Arts Center** facilities: Davies Symphony Hall, the War Memorial Opera House, and Herbst Theatre. The tour takes about an hour and 15 minutes; costs $5 adults, $3 seniors/students; and is offered every Monday, hourly from 10 a.m. to 2 p.m. Purchase your ticket at the Davies Symphony Hall box office

(main foyer) 10 minutes before tour time. For more information, call (415) 552-8338.

Commercial Walking Tours
Helen's Walk Tours, P.O. Box 9164, Berkeley, CA 94709, tel. (510) 524-4544, offers entertaining walking tours, with a personal touch provided by personable Helen Rendon, tour guide and part-time actress. Tour groups usually meet "under the clock" at the St. Francis Hotel (Helen's the one with the wonderfully dramatic hat) before setting off on an entertaining two-hour tour of Victorian Mansions, North Beach (want to know where Marilyn Monroe married Joe DiMaggio?), or Chinatown. Other options: combine parts of two tours into a half-day Grand Tour, or, if enough time and interested people are available, request other neighborhood tours. Make reservations for any tour at least one day in advance.

Dashiell Hammett Literary Tours, tel. (510) 287-9540, are led by Don Herron, author of *The Literary World of San Francisco and its Environs.* The half-day tours wander through down-town streets and alleys, on the trail of both the writer and his detective story hero, Sam Spade. They're usually offered May-Aug., and other literary themes can be arranged. Shelley Campbell's **Footnotes Literary Walk,** tel. (415) 381-0713 or (415) 721-1763 (recorded), takes guests on a stroll through North Beach, past the former haunts of great writers.

Roger's Custom Tours, tel. (650) 742-9611, offers unusual adventures and custom tours of San Francisco tailored to your specifications. German spoken.

The personable Jay Gifford leads a **Victorian Home Walk Tour** (including a scenic bus trolley ride) through Cow Hollow and Pacific Heights, exploring distinctive Queen Anne, Edwardian, and Italianate architecture in the neighborhoods. You'll see the interior of a Queen Anne and the locations used for *Mrs. Doubtfire* and *Party of Five.* While also enjoying spectacular views of the city, bay, and gardens, you'll learn to differentiate architectural styles. Tours meet at 11 a.m. daily in the lobby of the St. Francis Hotel on Union Square and last about two and a half hours. For reservations and information, call (415) 252-9485 or visit www.victorianwalk.com.

Cruisin' the Castro, historical tours of San Francisco's gay mecca, tel. (415) 550-8110, www.webcastro.com/castrotour, are led by local historian Trevor Hailey and offer unique insight into how San Francisco's gay community has shaped the city's political, social, and cultural development. Everyone is welcome; reservations are required. Tours are offered Tues.-Sat., starting at 10 a.m. at Harvey Milk Plaza, continuing through the community's galleries, shops, and cultural sights, then ending at the Names Project (original home of the AIDS Memorial Quilt) around 2 p.m. Brunch included.

San Francisco's coffeehouse culture is the focus of **Javawalk,** tel. (415) 673-9255, www.javawalk.com, a stroll through North Beach haunts starting at 334 Grant Ave., Saturday at 10 a.m.

Culinary Walking Tours

No matter where else you walk off to, don't overlook San Francisco's fabulous food tours—most of which focus on Chinatown. **Wok Wiz Chinatown Walking Tours,** 654 Commercial St. (between Montgomery and Kearny), tel. (415) 981-8989, www.wokwiz.com, are a local institution. Reservations required. The small-group Wok Wiz culinary and historical adventures are led by founder Shirley Fong-Torres, her husband Bernie Carver, and other tour leaders, starting at 10 a.m. at the Wok Wiz Tours and Cooking Center and ending at 1:15 p.m. after a marvelous dim sum lunch (optional). Stops along the way include: Portsmouth Square; a Chinese temple; herb, pastry, and tea shops (where the traditional tea ceremony is shared); a Chinese open-air market; and a brush-paint artist's studio. Along with taking in the sights along Chinatown's main streets and back alleys, visitors receive a fairly comprehensive history lesson about the Chinese in California, and particularly in San Francisco. Wok Wiz also offers an "I Can't Believe I Ate My Way Through Chinatown!" tour, with an exclusive emphasis on Chinese foods and food preparation, and a shorter (90 minute) "Yin Yang" history tour of Chinatown. (Special group tours can also be arranged.) Serious food aficionados will probably recognize Fong-Torres, well known for her articles, books, and Chinese cooking television appearances. She is also the author of several books, including *San Francisco Chinatown: A Walking Tour, In the Chinese Kitchen,* and the *Wok Wiz Cookbook.*

Combining two cross-cultural tidbits of folk wisdom—"You never age at the dinner table" (Italian) and "To eat is greater than heaven" (Chinese)—**Ruby Tom's Glorious Food Culinary Walk Tours,** tel. (415) 441-5637, stroll through both North Beach and Chinatown, separately or on the same tour. Special walking tours include North Beach Bakeries (an early morning slice of life), North Beach Nightbeat (complete with cabaret, theater, or jazz entertainment), and Lanterns of Chinatown (a stroll under the night-lit red lanterns followed by a hosted banquet). A graduate of the California Culinary Academy, Ruby Tom is an award-winning chef herself. She conducted and organized the first professional chefs exchange between the People's Republic of China and the city of San Francisco. **All About Chinatown Tours,** 100 Waverly Place, tel. (415) 982-8839, conducted by San Francisco native Linda Lee, also walk visitors through Chinatown's past and present; tours include a traditional Chinese lunch or dinner. Call for reservations and current schedule.

Over on the spaghetti-eating side of Columbus, *Chronicle* food writer GraceAnn Walden leads the **Mangia North Beach!** tour through the neighborhood's best trattorias, delis, and bakeries. Along the way, you'll pick up cooking tips, sample Italian cheeses, and learn some local history. The four-hour tour concludes with a multicourse lunch. Tours begin Saturday at 10 a.m.; for reservations, call (415) 397-8530 between 10 a.m. and 8 p.m.

OTHER CITY TOURS

Tours by Land

A Day in Nature, 1490 Sacramento St. (between Hyde and Leavenworth), tel. (415) 673-0548, offers personalized half-day or full-day naturalist-guided tours (groups of just one to four people) of North Bay destinations like the Marin Headlands, Muir Woods, and the Napa Valley wine country, complete with gourmet picnic.

Gray Line, tel. (415) 558-9400 or toll-free (800) 826-0202, www.grayline.com, is the city's largest tour operator, commandeering an impressive fleet of standard-brand buses and red, London-style double-deckers. The company offers a variety of narrated tours touching on the basics, in San Francisco proper and beyond. Unlike most other companies, Gray Line offers its city tour in multiple languages: Japanese, Korean, German, French, Italian, and Spanish. Much more personal is the **Great Pacific Tour Company,** 518 Octavia St. (at Hayes), tel. (415) 626-4499, www.greatpacifictour.com, which runs 13-passenger minivans on four different tours: half-day city or Marin County trips plus full-day Monterey Peninsula and Napa/Sonoma wine country tours (foreign-language tours available). **Tower Tours,** 77 Jefferson (at Pier 43 1/2), tel. (415) 434-8687, is affiliated with Blue & Gold Fleet and offers tours of the city, Marin, Alcatraz, the wine country, Monterey Peninsula, and Yosemite; all tours leave from their office at Fisherman's Wharf. **Quality Tours,** 5003 Palmetto Ave., Pacifica, tel. (650) 994-5054, www.qualitytours.com, does a San Francisco architecture tour and a "whole enchilada" tour in a luxury seven-passenger Chevy suburban. **Three Babes and a Bus Nightclub Tours,** tel. (415) 552-CLUB, www.threebabes.com, caters to visiting night owls, who hop the bus and party at the city's hottest nightspots with the charming hostesses. Many firms create personalized, special-interest tours with reasonable advance notice; contact the Convention & Visitors Bureau for a complete listing.

Though both are better known for their ferry tours, both the Blue & Gold Fleet and the Red & White Fleet (see below) also offer land tours to various Northern California attractions.

Tours by Sea

The **Blue & Gold Fleet** is based at Piers 39 and 41, tel. (415) 705-8200 (business office), (415) 773-1188 (recorded schedule), or (415) 705-5555 (information and advance ticket purchase), www.blueandgoldfleet.com. Blue & Gold offers a narrated year-round (weather permitting) **Golden Gate Bay Cruise** that leaves from Pier 39, passes under the Golden Gate Bridge, cruises by Sausalito and Angel Island, and loops back around Alcatraz. The trip takes about an hour. Fare: $17 adults, $13 seniors over 62 and youths 12-18, $9 children 5-11. The justifiably popular **Alcatraz Tour** takes you out to the infamous former prison (see the special topic Touring the Real Rock for more information). Fare is $12.25 adults with a self-guided audio tour, or $8.75 adults without the audio. Day-use fee on the rock is $1. (Also available is an evening "Alcatraz After Hours" tour, $19.75 adults, which includes a narrated guided tour.) Blue & Gold ferries also can take you to **Sausalito, Tiburon, Oakland, Alameda, Vallejo,** and **Angel Island.**

The **Red & White Fleet,** at Pier 43 1/2, tel. (415) 447-0597 or toll-free (800) 229-2784 (in California), www.redandwhite.com, offers one-hour, multilingual Bay Cruise tours that loop out ito, Angel Is-

cruising the Bay

TOURING THE REAL ROCK

Visiting Alcatraz is like touring the dark side of the American dream, like peering into democracy's private demon hold. At Alcatraz, freedom is a fantasy. If crime is a universal option—and everyone behind bars at Alcatraz exercised it—then all who once inhabited this desolate island prison were certainly equal. Yet all who once lived on The Rock were also equal in other ways—in their utter isolation, in their human desperation, in their hopelessness.

Former prison guard Frank Heaney, born and raised in Berkeley, is now a consultant for the Blue & Gold Fleet's exclusive Alcatraz tour. When he started work as a correctional officer at age 21, Heaney found himself standing guard over some of America's most notorious felons, including George "Machine Gun" Kelly, Alvin "Creepy" Karpis, and Robert "The Birdman of Alcatraz" Stroud. Heaney soon realized that the terrifying reality of prison life was a far cry from Hollywood's James Cagney version.

The job was psychologically demanding, yet often boring. There was terror in the air, too. Inmates vowed—and attempted—to "break him." But he ignored both death threats and too-friendly comments on his youthful appeal. Guards were prohibited from conversing with the inmates—one more aspect of the criminals' endless isolation—but Heaney eventually got to know Machine Gun Kelly, whom he remembers as articulate and intellectual, "more like a bank president than a bank robber." Creepy Karpis,

Ma Barker's right-hand man and the only man ever personally arrested by FBI Director J. Edgar Hoover, was little more than a braggart. And though the Birdman was considered seriously psychotic and spent most of his 54 prison years in solitary confinement, Heaney found him to be "untrustworthy" but rational and extremely intelligent. Many of Heaney's favorite stories are collected in his book *Inside the Walls of Alcatraz,* published by Bull Publishing and available at Pier 39 and the National Park Store gift shop.

Others who remember The Rock, both guards and inmates, are included on the **Alcatraz Cellhouse Tour,** an "inside" audio journey through prison history provided by the Golden Gate National Park Association and offered along with Blue & Gold Fleet tours to Alcatraz.

Among them is Jim Quillen, former inmate, who on the day we visit is here in person. He leans against the rusted iron doors of Cell Block A. His pained eyes scan the pocked walls and empty cells, each barely adequate as an open-air closet. Quillen spent the best years of his life on Alcatraz. "Ten years and one day," he says in a soft voice. "The tourists see the architecture, the history—all I see are ghosts. I can point to the exact spots where my friends have killed themselves, been murdered, gone completely insane."

That's the main reason to visit Alcatraz—to explore this lonely, hard, wind-whipped island of exile.

---

land, and Alcatraz ($17 adults, $13 seniors/youths, $9 kids 5-11, not including the $1 day-use fee). Other offerings include weekend Blues Cruises in summer; an excursion across the bay to Alameda to tour the aircraft carrier USS *Hornet;* and a variety of land tours in Northern California.

Hornblower Cruises and Events, tel. (415) 788-8866, www.hornblowercruises.com, has boats at Pier 33 and elsewhere around the bay. The company offers big-boat on-the-bay dining adventures, from extravagant nightly dinner dances and weekday lunches to Saturday and Sunday champagne brunch. Occasional special events, from whodunit murder mystery dinners to jazz cocktail cruises, can be especially fun. And Hornblower's Monte Carlo Cruises feature casual Las Vegas-style casino gaming tables (proceeds go to charity) on dinner cruises aboard the M/V *Monte Carlo.*

Oceanic Society Expeditions, based at Fort Mason, tel. (415) 474-3385, www.oceanic-society.org, offers a variety of seagoing natural history trips, including winter whalewatching excursions, usually late Dec.-April, and Farallon Islands nature trips, June-November. Reservations are required. Oceanic Society trips are multifaceted. For example, only scientific researchers and trusted volunteers are allowed on the cold granite Farallon Islands, but the Society's excursion to the islands takes you as close as most people ever get. The Farallons, 27 miles from the Golden Gate, are a national wildlife refuge within the Gulf of the Farallons National Marine Sanctuary, which itself is part of UNESCO's Central California Coast Biosphere Reserve. The nutrient-rich coastal waters around the islands are vital to the world's fisheries, to the health of sea mammal populations, and to the success of the breeding

The ghosts here need human companionship.

There is plenty else to do, too, including the ranger-guided walk around the island, courtesy of the Golden Gate National Recreation Area (GGNRA), and poking one's nose into other buildings, other times. National park personnel also offer lectures and occasional special programs. Or take an **Evening on Alcatraz** tour, to see the sun set on the city from the island. For current information, contact the Golden Gate National Recreation Area at (415) 556-0560 or www.nps.gov/goga, stop by the **GGNRA Visitors Center** at the Cliff House in San Francisco (tel. (415) 556-8643), or contact the nonprofit, education-oriented Golden Gate National Park Association, tel. (415) 561-3000. (For more information about the recreation area in general, see that section elsewhere in this chapter and also Point Reyes National Seashore.)

If you're coming to Alcatraz, contact the **Blue & Gold Fleet**, Pier 41, Fisherman's Wharf, tel. (415) 773-1188, www.blueandgoldfleet.com, for general information. To make charge-by-phone ticket reservations—advisable, well in advance, since the tour is quite popular, attracting more than one million people each year—call (415) 705-5555, or make reservations through the Blue & Gold Fleet's website (with seven days' advance notice). At last report, roundtrip fare with audio was $12.25 per adult, $7 per child, plus a $2.25-per-ticket reservation surcharge if you reserve your ticket by phone/Internet; there's also a $1 day-use fee in addition to the ferry price. (Be sure to be there 30 minutes early, since no refunds or exchanges are allowed if you miss the boat.) The entire audio-guided walking tour takes more than two hours, so be sure to allow yourself adequate time. (The audiotape is available in English, Japanese, German, French, Italian, and Spanish.) If at all possible, try to get booked on one of the early tours, so you can see the cellblocks and Alcatraz Island in solitude, before the rest of humanity arrives. Pack a picnic (though snacks and beverages are available), and bring all the camera and video equipment you can carry; no holds barred on photography. Wear good walking shoes, as well as warm clothes (layers best), since it can be brutally cold on Alcatraz in the fog or when the wind whips up.

In the past, the island's ruggedness made it difficult to impossible for those with limited mobility, with moderate to strenuous climbing and limited access for wheelchairs and strollers. Now wheelchair users and others with limited mobility who can't "do" the Alcatraz tour on foot can take SEAT (Sustainable Easy Access Transport) up the 12% grade hill one-quarter mile to the prison. Contact the Blue & Gold Fleet information line for details.

If you're not coming to Alcatraz in the immediate future, you can still take a comprehensive virtual tour, on the web at www.nps.gov/alcatraz/tours.

—Tim Moriarty and Kim Weir

seabird colonies here. Some quarter million birds breed here, among them tufted puffins and rhinoceros auklets (bring a hat). The Oceanic Society trip to the islands takes eight hours, shoving off at 8:30 a.m. (Saturday, Sunday, and select Fridays) from Fort Mason. The 63-foot Oceanic Society boat carries 49 passengers and a naturalist. Contact the nonprofit Oceanic Society for other excursion options.

Tours on Your Own

If you have a car, taking the city's **49 Mile Scenic Drive** is a good way to personally experience the entirety of San Francisco. The route is a bit tricky to follow, though, so be sure to follow the map and directions provided by the Convention & Visitors Bureau—and never try this particular exploration during rush hours or peak weekend commute times.

With enough time, design your own tour or tours, starting with the neighborhood and district information included in this book. Or, using a variety of special-interest books and other resources, design a tour based on a particular theme—such as "literary haunts," "bars throughout history" (best as a walking tour), "stairway tours," "musical high notes," "theatrical highlights," or even "steepest streets."

The **Steepest Streets Tour** is a particular thrill for courageous drivers and/or suicidal cyclists. (However you do this one, take it slow and easy.) As far as vertical grade is concerned, those all-time tourist favorites—Mason St. down Nob Hill, and Hyde St. to Aquatic Park—don't even register in San Francisco's top 10. According to the city's Bureau of Engineering, **Filbert Street** between Leavenworth and Hyde, and **22nd Street** between

.urch and Vicksburg are the city's most hair-.aising roadways, sharing a 31.5% grade. Coming in a close second: **Jones** between Union and Filbert (29%, plus a 26% thrill between Green and Union). So a good way to start this side trip is by shooting down Filbert (a one-way, with the 1100 block a special thrill), then straight up intersecting Jones. It's a scream. For more cheap thrills, try: **Duboce** between Buena Vista and Alpine (a 27.9% grade), and between Divisadero and Alpine, then Castro and Divisadero (each 25%); **Webster** between Vallejo and Broadway (26%); **Jones** between Pine and California (24.8%); and **Fillmore** between Vallejo and Broadway (24%). Whether or not you travel all these streets, you'll soon understand why hard-driving local cabbies burn out—their brakes, that is—every 2,000 miles or so.

A worthy variation is the **Most Twisted Streets Tour,** starting with one-way **Lombard Street** between Hyde and Leavenworth, a route touted as "The World's Crookedest Street," with eight turns within a distance of 412 feet. But San Francisco's truly most twisted is **Vermont Street** between 20th and 22nd Streets, which has six fender-grinding turns within a distance of 270 feet. Better for panoramic views in all directions is **Twin Peaks Boulevard,** with 11 curves and six about-face turns in its one-mile descent.

GOLDEN GATE NATIONAL RECREATION AREA

One of San Francisco's unexpected treasures, the Golden Gate National Recreation Area (GGNRA) starts in the south along Sweeney Ridge near Pacifica, then jumps north to a narrow coastal strip of land adjacent to Hwy. 1, taking in Thornton Beach, Fort Funston, the Cliff House, and other milestones before it pauses at the pilings of the Golden Gate Bridge. The GGNRA also includes Alcatraz Island, one of the nation's most infamous prison sites, and state-administered Angel Island, "Ellis Island of the West" to the Chinese and other immigrant groups. In late 1995, the historic Presidio—1,480 acres of forest, coastal bluffs, military outposts, and residences adjacent to the Golden Gate Bridge—was converted from military to domestic purposes and

formally included in the GGNRA. Vast tracts of the southern and western Marin County headlands, north of the bridge, are also included within GGNRA boundaries, making this park a true urban wonder. Much of the credit for creating the GGNRA, the world's largest urban park, goes to the late congressman Phillip Burton. Established in 1972, the recreation area as currently envisioned includes more than 36,000 acres in a cooperative patchwork of land holdings exceeding 114 square miles. The GGNRA is also the most popular of the national parks, drawing more than 20 million visitors each year.

One major attraction of the GGNRA is the opportunity for hiking—both **urban hiking** on the San Francisco side, and **wilderness hiking** throughout the Marin Headlands. Get oriented to the recreation area's trails at any visitor center (see below), look up the National Park Service website at www.nps.gov/prsf, or sign on for any of the GGNRA's excellent guided hikes and explorations. The schedule changes constantly, depending upon the season and other factors, but the following outings represent a sample of what's available on the San Francisco end of the Golden Gate Bridge: the Sutro Heights Walk, the Presidio's Mountain Lake to Fort Point Hike and Main Post Historical Walk, and the Point of the Sea Wolves Walk. National Park Service rangers also lead other guided tours through the Presidio, including a Natural History of the Presidio hike. A particularly spectacular section of the GGNRA's trail system is the 2.5-mile trek from the St. Francis Yacht Club to Fort Point and the Golden Gate Bridge. This walk is part of the still-in-progress **San Francisco Bay Trail,** a 450-mile shoreline trail system that will one day ring the entire bay and traverse nine Bay Area counties. Ambitious hikers can follow the GGNRA's **Coastal Trail** from San Francisco to Point Reyes National Seashore in Marin County. Once on the north side of the Golden Gate, possibilities for long hikes and backpacking trips are almost endless.

Special GGNRA events include such worthy offerings as a Story of the Golden Gate Bridge tour, a Family Fun at Muir Woods theater workshop, and presentations at the reserve's several former defense installations, including: Women on Military Posts, and Songs and Sounds of the Civil War (at Fort Point); Seacoast Defense (at

Baker Beach); and Rockets to Rangers (at Nike Site 88 on the Marin Headlands).

San Francisco-Side GGNRA Sights

The GGNRA includes the beaches and coastal bluffs along San Francisco's entire western edge (and both south and north), as well as seaside trails and walking and running paths along the new highway and seawall between Sloat Blvd. and the western border of Golden Gate Park.

The original Cliff House near Seal Rocks was one of San Francisco's first tourist lures, its original diversions a bit on the licentious side. That version, converted by Adolph Sutro into a family-style resort, burned to the ground in 1894 and was soon replaced by a splendid Victorian palace and an adjacent bathhouse, also fire victims. Ruins of the old **Sutro Baths** are still visible among the rocks just north. Aptly named **Seal Rocks** offshore attract vocal sea lions.

The current **Cliff House,** across the highway from Sutro Heights Park, dates from 1908 and still attracts locals and tourists alike. The views are spectacular, which explains the success of the building's Cliff House Restaurant, tel. (415) 386-3330, as well as the building's Phineas T. Barnacle pub-style deli and the Ben Butler Room bar. The stairway outdoors leads down the cliff to the GGNRA **Cliff House Visitor Center,** tel. (415) 556-8642, a good stop for information, free or low-cost publications and maps, and books. Open daily 10 a.m.-5 p.m. Also down below just behind the Cliff House is the **Musée**

Méchanique, tel. (415) 386-1170, a delightful and dusty collection of penny arcade amusements (most cost a quarter)—from nickelodeons and coin-eating music boxes to fortune-telling machines—and the odd **Camera Obscura & Hologram Gallery.** The gallery's "camera" is actually a slow revolving lens that reflects images onto a parabolic screen—with a particularly thrilling fractured-light image at sunset.

Wandering northward from Cliff House, Point Lobos Ave. and then El Camino del Mar lead to San Francisco's **Point Lobos,** the city's westernmost point. There's an overlook, to take in the view. Nearby is the **USS *San Francisco* Memorial,** part of the city's namesake ship. Also nearby is **Fort Miley,** which features a 4-H "adventure ropes" course. But the most spectacular thing in sight (on a clear day) is the postcard-pretty peek at the Golden Gate Bridge. You can even get there from here, on foot, via the **Coastal Trail,** a spectacular city hike that skirts Lincoln Park and the California Palace of the Legion of Honor before passing through the Seacliff neighborhood, then flanking the Presidio. From Fort Point at the foot of the Golden Gate, the truly intrepid can keep on trekking—straight north across the bridge to Marin County, or east past the yacht harbors to Fort Mason and the overwhelming attractions of Fisherman's Wharf.

For some slower sightseeing, backtrack to the Presidio's hiking trails and other attractions. The GGNRA's **Presidio Visitor Center,** 102

The views from the Cliff House are spectacular.

THE PRESIDO AND FORT POINT

A national historic landmark and historic military installation, San Francisco's **Presidio** is the nation's newest national park. In 1994, Congress closed the Presidio to the Sixth Army Command, and the Golden Gate National Recreation Area (GGNRA) gained 1,446 acres of the multimillion-dollar real estate. Among other proposals for putting the buildings here to good public use, it's quite possible that 23 acres on the Presidio's eastern border will house studios for filmmaker George Lucas's Industrial Light & Magic, as well as facilities for other Lucas enterprises, on the site of the old Letterman Army Hospital.

The Presidio lies directly south of the Golden Gate Bridge along the northwest tip of the San Francisco Peninsula, bordered by the Marina and Pacific Heights districts to the east and Richmond and Presidio heights to the south. To the west and north, a coastal strip of the Golden Gate National Recreation Area frames the Presidio, which boasts some 70 miles of paths and trails of its own winding along cliffs and through eucalyptus groves and coastal flora. The 1,600 buildings here, most of them eclectic blends of Victorian and Spanish-revival styles, have housed the U.S. Army since 1847.

Founded by the Spanish in 1776 as one of two original settlements in San Francisco, the Presidio had a militaristic history even then, for the area commands a strategic view of San Francisco Bay and the Pacific Ocean. The Spanish garrison ruled the peninsula for the first 50 years of the city's history, chasing off Russian whalers and trappers by means of the two cannons now guarding the entrance to the Officer's Club. After 1847, when Americans took over, the Presidio became a staging center for the Indian wars, a never-used outpost during the Civil War, and more recently, headquarters for the Sixth Army Command, which fought in the Pacific during World War II.

Today the Presidio is open to the public, and visitors may drive around and admire the neat-as-a-pin streets with their white, two-story wood Victorians and faultless lawns or trace the base's history at the **Presidio Army Museum** (one of the oldest buildings, originally the hospital) located near the corner of Lincoln Blvd. and Funston Ave., tel. (415) 561-4131. Pick up a map there showing the Presidio's hiking trails, including a six-mile historic walk and two ecology trails. Museum hours are Wed.-Sun. 12 p.m.-4 p.m., admission free.

Montgomery St. (that's a *different* Montgomery St. than the one downtown), tel. (415) 561-4323, can point you in the right direction. It's open year-round, daily 9 a.m.-5 p.m. One possible detour: the **Presidio Army Museum** at Lincoln and Funston, tel. (415) 561-4331.

Or spend time exploring the coast. At low tide, the fleet of foot can beach walk (and climb) from the Golden Gate Bridge to **Baker Beach** and farther (looking back at the bridge for a seagull's-eye view). Though many flock here precisely because it is a de facto nude beach, the very naked sunbathers at Baker Beach usually hide out in the rock-secluded coves beyond the family-oriented stretch of public sand. Near Baker Beach is the miniature **Battery Lowell A. Chamberlin** "museum," a historic gun hold, home to the six-inch disappearing rifle. Weapons aficionados will want to explore more thoroughly the multitude of gun batteries farther north along the trail, near Fort Point.

For More Information

For information on the GGNRA included elsewhere in this book, see also Touring the Real Rock, The Presidio and Fort Point, and Fort Mason immediately below, and The Avenues in the previous chapter. For more information on the Marin County sections of the GGNRA, see Point Reyes National Seashore and Angel Island State Park in Beyond San Francisco.

For current information about GGNRA features and activities, contact: **Golden Gate National Recreation Area,** Fort Mason, Building 201, tel. (415) 556-0560, www.nps.gov/goga. To check on local conditions, events, and programs, you can also call the GGNRA's other visitor centers: **Cliff House,** tel. (415) 556-8642; **Fort Point,** tel. (415) 556-1693; **Marin Headlands,** tel. (415) 331-1540; **Muir Woods,** tel. (415) 388-2596; and **Presidio,** tel. (415) 561-4323.

To receive a subscription to the quarterly park newsletter and calendar of GGNRA events, join the nonprofit **Golden Gate National Parks As-**

Ranger-led GGNRA guided tours include the **Natural History of the Presidio,** an exploratory lesson in the San Francisco Peninsula's geology, geography, and plant and animal life, featuring an enchanted forest and the city's last free-flowing stream; **Presidio Main Post Historical Walks;** and the **Mountain Lake to Fort Point Hike.**

For more information about the Presidio and scheduled events and activities, look up the National Park Service's website at www.nps.gov/prsf, or call the **Presidio Visitor Center,** at tel. (415) 561-4323.

More businesslike in design but in many respects more interesting than the Presidio, **Fort Point** off Lincoln Blvd. is nestled directly underneath the southern tip of the Golden Gate Bridge and worth donning a few extra layers to visit. Officially the Fort Point National Historic Site since 1968, the quadrangular redbrick behemoth was modeled after South Carolina's Fort Sumter and completed in 1861 to guard the bay during the Civil War. However, the fort was never given the chance to test its mettle, as a grass-roots plot hatched by Confederate sympathizers in San Francisco to undermine the Yankee cause died for lack of funds and manpower, and the more palpable threat that the Confederate cruiser *Shenandoah* would blast its way into the bay was foiled by the war ending before the ship ever arrived.

Nonetheless, military strategists had the right idea situating the fort on the site of the old Spanish adobe-brick outpost of Castillo de San Joaquin, and through the years the fort-that-could was used as a garrison and general catchall for the Presidio, including a stint during WW I as barracks for unmarried officers. During the 1930s, when the Golden Gate Bridge was in its design phase, the fort narrowly missed being scrapped but was saved by the bridge's chief design engineer, Joseph B. Strauss, who considered the fort's demolition a waste of good masonry and designed the somewhat triumphal arch that now soars above it.

Fort Point these days enjoys a useful retirement as a historical museum, open daily 10-5, admission free. While the wind howls in the girders overhead, park rangers clad in Civil War regalia (many wearing long johns underneath) lead hourly tours, 11 a.m.-4 p.m., through the park's honeycomb of corridors, staircases, and gun ports. Cannon muster is solemnly observed at 1:30 and 2:30 p.m., and two slide shows are also offered, at 11:30 a.m. and again at 3:30 p.m. A fairly recent addition is the excellent exhibit and tribute to black American soldiers. At the bookstore, pick up some Confederate money and other military memorabilia. For more information about tours and special events, call Fort Point at (415) 556-1693.

—*Taran March*

sociation, same Fort Mason address, tel. (415) 561-3000, an organization that actively supports educational programs as well as park conservation and improvement. Basic annual membership runs $40, and each year offers five or six members-only events—such as tours of Presidio architecture, moonlight hikes to the Pt. Bonita Lighthouse, or candlelight after-hours tours of Fort Point.

Useful publications and guidebooks published by the Golden Gate National Parks Association, available for less than $10 each at GGNRA visitor center bookstores and elsewhere (such as the National Park Store on Pier 39 at Fisherman's Wharf), include the comprehensive 100-page *Park Guide,* plus *Alcatraz: Island of Change; Fort Point: Sentry at the Golden Gate;* and *Muir Woods: Redwood Refuge.* Also widely available is *The Official Map and Guide to the Presidio* ($2.50), a detailed multicolored map jam-packed with historical and other information.

For a set of maps of the entire San Francisco Bay Trail ($10.95) or detailed maps of specific trail sections ($1.50 each), contact the **San Francisco Bay Trail Project,** c/o the Association of Bay Area Governments, tel. (510) 464-7900, or order the maps online at www.abag.org. About 215 of the Bay Trail's 450 total miles of trails are completed, with planning and/or construction of the rest underway. Call the Association to volunteer trail-building labor or materials, to help with fundraising, or to lead guided walks along sections of the Bay Trail.

Also of interest to area hikers: the **Bay Area Ridge Trail,** a 400-mile ridgetop route that one day will skirt the entire bay, connecting 75 parks. For information, contact the **Bay Area Ridge Trail Council,** 26 O'Farrell St., tel. (415) 391-9300, www.ridgetrail.org. You can order a book about the trail ($14.95) by calling the office.

FORT MASON

Headquarters for the Golden Gate National Recreation Area, Fort Mason is also home to **Fort Mason Center,** a surprisingly contemporary complex of one-time military storage buildings at Marina Blvd. and Buchanan St., now hosting a variety of nonprofit arts, humanities, educational, environmental, and recreational organizations and associations.

Since the 1970s, this shoreline wasteland has been transformed into an innovative multicultural community events center—perhaps the country's premier model of the impossible, successfully accomplished. Several pavilions and the Conference Center host larger group events, though smaller galleries, theaters, and offices predominate. The variety of rotating art exhibits, independent theater performances, poetry readings, lectures and workshops, and special-interest classes offered here is truly staggering.

Expansion plans include the establishment of a marine ecology center, another theater, more exhibit space, and another good-food-great-view restaurant. All in all, it's not surprising that Fort Mason is being studied by the Presidio's national park transition team, and even by other nations, as a supreme example of how urban eyesores can be transformed into national treasures.

Fort Mason Museums

The **San Francisco African American Historical & Cultural Society,** in Building C, Room 165, tel. (415) 441-0640, is a cultural and resource center featuring a library, museum (small admission), speaker's bureau, and monthly lecture series. Open Wed.-Sun. noon-5 p.m.

The **Mexican Museum,** Building D, tel. (415) 202-9700 or (415) 441-0404, www.folkart.com/~latitude/museums, is devoted exclusively to exhibitions of, and educational programs about, Mexican-American and Mexican art. Its permanent collection includes 9,000 items from five periods, including pre-Hispanic and contemporary Mexican art, and rotating exhibits attract much public attention. The changing exhibits typically focus on one particular artist or on a theme, such as "100 Years of Chroma Art Calendars." Open Wed.-Sun. 11 a.m.-5 p.m.; admission $4 adults, $3 students and seniors. The Museum plans to move downtown to the Yerba

Buena Center in the not-too-distant future, so call or check with the website before setting out.

Exhibits at the **Museo ItaloAmericano,** in Building C, tel. (415) 673-2200, foster an appreciation of Italian art and culture. Open Wed.-Sun. noon-5 p.m. Small admission.

Definitely worth a detour is the **San Francisco Craft & Folk Art Museum,** Building A-North, tel. (415) 775-0990, www.sfcraftandfolk.org, which features rotating exhibits of American and international folk art. Open Tues.-Fri. and Sunday 11 a.m.-5 p.m.; Saturday 10 a.m.-5 p.m. Free on Saturday, 10 a.m.-noon, otherwise there's a small admission fee.

In addition to any free hours listed above, all of the museums at the center are free (and open until 7 p.m.) on the first Wednesday of every month.

Fort Mason Performing Arts

Fort Mason Center's 440-seat **Cowell Theater,** tel. (415) 441-3400, is a performance space that hosts events ranging from the acclaimed Solo Mio Festival and the New Pickle Circus to guest speakers such as Spalding Gray and unusual video, musical, and theatrical presentations. Among its showstoppers is the **Magic Theatre,** Building D, tel. (415) 441-8001 (business office) or (415) 441-8822 (box office), which is internationally recognized as an outstanding American playwrights' theater, performing original plays by the likes of Sam Shepard and Michael McClure as well as innovative new writers.

Other Fort Mason performing arts groups include the **Performing Arts Workshop,** Building C, tel. (415) 673-2634, and the **Young Performers' Theatre,** Building C, tel. (415) 346-5550, both for young people. The **Blue Bear School of American Music,** Building D, tel. (415) 673-3600, offers lessons and workshops in rock, pop, jazz, blues, and other genres. **Bay Area Theatresports** (BATS) is an improv comedy group that performs at the **Bayfront Theater,** Building B, tel. (415) 474-8935, and **World Arts West,** Building D, tel. (415) 474-3914, promotes and produces world music and dance festivals.

Fort Mason Visual Arts

The **Fort Mason Art Campus** of the City College of San Francisco, Building B, tel. (415) 561-1840, is the place for instruction in fine arts and crafts. Works of students and faculty are show-cased at the **Coffee Gallery,** in the Building B lobby, tel. (415) 561-1840. The 10-and-under set should head to the **San Francisco Children's Art Center,** Building C, tel. (415) 771-0292. One of the most intriguing galleries here is the **San Francisco Museum of Modern Art Rental Gallery,** Building A-North, tel. (415) 441-4777, representing more than 1,300 artists and offering, in addition to rotating exhibits, the opportunity to rent as well as buy works on display.

Fort Mason Environmental Organizations
The **Endangered Species Project,** Building E, tel. (415) 921-3140, works to protect wildlife and habitat and to prevent illegal poaching and trade of endangered animals. **Friends of the River,** Building C, tel. (415) 771-0400, supports efforts to protect and restore the West's waterways and riparian areas. The **Fund for Animals,** Building C, tel. (415) 474-4020, is an animal-rights organization. The **Oceanic Society,** Building E, tel. (415) 441-1106, offers environmental education programs including whale-watching trips, cruises to the Farallon Islands, and coral-reef and rainforest expeditions. The **Resource Renewal Institute,** Pier 1 North, tel. (415) 928-3774, promotes integrated environmental planning—"Green Plans"—at every level of government, both domestically and internationally. The **Tuolumne River Preservation Trust,** Building C, tel. (415) 292-3531, focuses its efforts on protecting and preserving the Tuolumne River watershed.

Glorious Grazing
No one will ever starve here, since one of the country's best vegetarian restaurants, the San Francisco Zen Center's **Greens,** is in Building A-North, tel. (415) 771-6222. It's open Mon.-Sat. for lunch and dinner and Sunday for brunch. The restaurant also offers **Greens-To-Go** take-out lunches Tues.-Sun.; call (415) 771-6330.
Other Fort Mason Services and Information
Book Bay Bookstore, Building C-South, tel. (415) 771-1076, is run by friends of the San Francisco Public Library. Book sales are regularly held to benefit the city's public-library system.

For more complete information on Fort Mason, including a copy of the monthly *Fort Mason Calendar of Events,* contact the **Fort Mason Foundation,** Building A, Fort Mason Center, tel. (415) 441-3400, www.fortmason.org, open daily 9 a.m.-5 p.m. For **recorded information** 24 hours a day, call (415) 979-3010. To order tickets for any Fort Mason events, call the **Fort Mason box office** at (415) 441-3687.

GOLDEN GATE PARK

Yet another of San Francisco's impossible dreams successfully accomplished, Golden Gate Park was once a vast expanse of sand dunes. A wasteland by urban, and urbane, standards, locals got the idea that it could be a park—and a grand park, to rival the Bois de Boulogne in Paris. Frederick Law Olmsted, who designed New York's Central Park, was asked to build it. He took one look and scoffed, saying essentially that it couldn't be done. Olmsted was wrong, as it turned out, and eventually he had the grace to admit it. William Hammond Hall, designer and chief engineer, and Scottish gardener John McLaren, the park's green-thumbed godfather, achieved the unlikely with more than a bit of West Coast ingenuity. Hall constructed a behemoth breakwater on the 1,000-acre park's west end, to block the stinging sea winds and salt spray, and started anchoring the sand by planting barley, then nitrogen-fixing lupine, then grasses. Careful grading and berming, helped along in time by windrows, further deflected the fierceness of ocean-blown storms.

"Uncle John" McLaren, Hall's successor, set about re-creating the land on a deeper level. He trucked in humus and manure to further transform sand into soil, and got busy planting more than one million trees. And that was just the beginning. In and around walkways, benches, and major park features, there were shrubs to plant, flowerbeds to establish, and pristine lawns to nurture. McLaren kept at it for some 55 years, dedicating his life to creating a park for the everlasting enjoyment of the citizenry. He bravely did battle with politicians, often beating them at their own games, to nurture and preserve "his" park for posterity. He fought with groundskeepers who tried to keep people off the lush lawns, and he attempted to hide despised-on-principle statues and other graven images with bushes and shrubs. In the end he lost this last battle; after McLaren died, the city erected a statue in his honor.

McLaren's Legacy

Much of the park's appeal is its astounding array of natural attractions. The botanic diversity alone, much of it exotic, somehow reflects San Francisco's multicultural consciousness—also transplanted from elsewhere, also now as natural as the sun, the moon, the salt winds, and the tides.

The dramatic **Victorian Conservatory of Flowers** on John F. Kennedy Drive, tel. (415) 641-7978, was imported from Europe and assembled here in 1878. A showcase jungle of tropical plants also noted for its seasonal botanic displays, the Conservatory was heavily damaged in a December 1995 storm and has been closed pending reconstruction. Call for an update.

The 55-acre **Strybing Arboretum and Botanical Gardens,** Ninth Ave. at Lincoln Way, tel. (415) 661-1316, features more than 7,000 different species, incuding many exotic and rare plants. Noted here is the collection of Australian and New Zealand plant life, along with exotics from Africa, the Americas, and Asia. Several gardens are landscaped by theme, such as the Mexican Cloud Forest and the California Redwood Grove. The serene Japanese Moon-Viewing Garden is a worthy respite when the Japanese Tea Garden is choked with tourists. Quite a delight, too, is the Fragrance Garden—a collection of culinary and medicinal herbs easily appreciated by aroma and texture, labeled also in Braille. Any plant lover will enjoy time spent in the small store. The arboretum is open weekdays 8 a.m.-4:30 p.m., weekends 10 a.m.-5 p.m.; admission is free, donations appreciated. Guided tours are offered on weekday afternoons and twice a day on weekends; call for tour times and meeting places. Next door is the **San Francisco County Fair Building,** site of the annual "fair"—in San Francisco, it's a flower show only—and home to the **Helen Crocker Russell Library,** containing some 18,000 volumes on horticulture and plants.

The **Japanese Tea Garden** on Tea Garden Dr. (off Martin Luther King Jr. Dr.), tel. (415) 752-4227 (admission information) or (415) 752-1171 (gift shop), a striking and suitable backdrop to the Asian Art Museum, is an enduring attraction,

The Japanese Tea Garden beckons those in search of serenity.

started (and maintained until the family's World War II internment) by full-time Japanese gardener Maokota Hagiwara and his family. Both a lovingly landscaped garden and tea house concession—the Hagiwaras invented the fortune cookie, first served here, though Chinatown later claimed this innovation as an old-country tradition—the Tea Garden is so popular that to enjoy even a few moments of the intended serenity, visitors should arrive early on a weekday morning or come on a rainy day. The large bronze "Buddha Who Sits Through Sun and Rain Without Shelter," cast in Japan in 1790, will surely welcome an off-day visitor. The Japanese Tea Garden is most enchanting in April, when the cherry trees are in bloom. Open daily March-Dec. 8:30 a.m.-6 p.m., Jan.-Feb. 8:30 a.m.-dusk. The tea house opens at 10 a.m. Admission is $3.50 adults, $1.25 seniors and children 6-12.

Also especially notable for spring floral color in Golden Gate Park: the **Queen Wilhelmina Tulip Garden** on the park's western edge, near the restored (northern) **Dutch Windmill,** and the **John McLaren Rhododendron Dell** near the Conservatory of Flowers. The very English **Shakespeare Garden,** beyond the Academy of Sciences, is unusual any time of year, since all the plants and flowers here are those mentioned in the Bard's works. Poignant and sobering is the expansive **National AIDS Memorial Grove,** at the east end of the park between Middle Drive East and Bowling Green Drive. Regardless of whether or not you personally know anyone with AIDS, this is a good place to wander among the groves of redwoods and dogwoods, quietly contemplating the fragility of life and your place in it. The grove is maintained by volunteers; to volunteer, or for more information, call (415) 750-8340.

Even the **San Francisco Zoo,** 1 Zoo Rd. (Sloat Blvd. at 45th Ave.), tel. (415) 753-7080, has its botanical attractions. The main reason to come, though, is to commune with the 1,000 or so animals in captivity. The zoo is open 365 days a year, 10 a.m.-5 p.m.; admission is $9 adults, $6 youths 12-17 and seniors 65 and over, $3 children 3-11, free on the first Wednesday of every month.

M.H. de Young Memorial Museum

Though plans have been bandied about for years to move both this museum and its incorporated Asian Art Museum downtown, both are currently still housed here in the park. Now merged administratively with the California Palace of the Legion of Honor into the jointly operated Fine Arts Museums of San Francisco, the de Young Museum, 75 Tea Garden Dr. (at Ninth Ave.), tel. (415) 750-3600, www.thinker.org or www.famsf.org, is one of the city's major visual arts venues. The museum, with its Spanish-style architecture, honors San Francisco newspaper publisher M.H. de Young.

The de Young's specialty is American art, from British colonial into contemporary times, and the collection here is one of the finest anywhere. Examine the exhibits of period paintings, sculpture, and decorative and domestic arts; the 20th-century American realist paintings are almost as intriguing as the textile and modern graphic arts collections. Also included in the de Young's permanent collection are traditional arts of the Americas, Africa, and Oceania. Come, too, for changing special exhibits, like "San Francisco's Old Chinatown: Photographs by Arnold Genthe."

Admission (which includes access to the Asian Art Museum) is $7 adults, $5 seniors, $4 youths 12-17 (free for everyone on the first Wednesday of each month). Call about docent-led tours. Open Tues.-Sun. 9:30 a.m.-5 p.m., and until 8:45 p.m. on the first Wednesday of each month. For current information on exhibits, call (415) 863-3330; for information on becoming a museum member, call (415) 750-3636.

Asian Art Museum

Scheduled to move to the site of the old downtown library in 2001, the astounding Asian Art Museum, 75 Tea Garden Dr. (at Ninth Ave.), tel. (415) 379-8801, www.asianart.org, currently shares a wing and the admission charge with the de Young Museum. The museum got its start in 1966 when the late U.S. diplomat Avery Brundage donated his collection to the city. Since then it has expanded greatly. Today, in addition to its vast collections of Chinese and Japanese art, the museum holds masterpieces from some 40 other Asian cultures, including India, Tibet, Nepal, Mongolia, Korea, and Iran. The total collection—more than 12,000 objects in all, spanning 6,000 years of history—is so large that only about 10% can be displayed at any one time. Among the treasures here: the oldest known dated sculpture of Buddha, from China, circa A.D. 338 in Western time; earthenware animals from the Tang Dynasty; and an astounding array of jade artifacts. Special changing exhibits are presented periodically; call for current exhibit schedule.

The Asian Art Museum is open Tues.-Sun. 9:30 a.m.-5 p.m., except on the first Wednesday of each month, when it's open 10 a.m.-8:45 p.m. Admission (which includes access to the adjacent M.H. de Young Museum) is $7 adults, $5 seniors, $4 youths 12-17 (free for everyone on the first Wednesday of each month). Admission is sometimes higher during special exhibitions. Call for information about docent-led tours.

California Academy of Sciences

At home on the park's Music Concourse (between Martin Luther King Jr. and John F. Kennedy Drives), tel. (415) 750-7145, www.calacademy.org, the California Academy of Sciences is a multifaceted scientific institution, the oldest in the West, founded in 1853 to survey and study the vast resources of California and vicinity. In the academy's courtyard, note the intertwining whales in the fountain. These were sculpted by Robert Howard and originally served as the centerpiece of the San Francisco Building during the Golden Gate International Exposition of 1939-40.

Natural History Museum: Dioramas and exhibits include **Wild California,** the **African Hall** (with a surprisingly realistic waterhole), and **Life Through Time,** which offers a 3.5 billion-year journey into the speculative experience of early life on earth. At the **Hohfeld Earth & Space Hall,** the neon solar system tells the story of the universe and the natural forces that have shaped—and still shape—the earth. Especially popular with children is **Earthquake,** a "you are there" experience that simulates two of the city's famous earthquakes. The **Wattis Hall of Human Cultures** specializes in anthropology and features one of the broadest Native American museum collections in Northern California, with an emphasis on cultures in both North America and South America. The **Far Side of Science Gallery** includes 159 original Gary Larson cartoons, offering a hilarious perspective on humanity's scientific research. The **Gem and Mineral Hall** contains some real gems, like a 1,350-pound quartz crystal from Arkansas.

Morrison Planetarium: This 65-foot dome simulates the night sky and its astronomical phenomena; Sky Shows are offered daily, at 2 p.m. on weekdays, and hourly from 11 a.m.-4 p.m. on weekends. The associated Earth & Space Hall features a moon rock, a meteorite, and other exhibits. Admission (over and above Academy admission) is $2.50 adults, $1.25 seniors/youths, children under six free. For more information, call (415) 750-7141. But the planetarium is most noted for its weekend evening **Laserium** shows, tel. (415) 750-7138, where blue beams from a krypton/argon gas laser slice the air to the rhythm of whatever's on the stereo—classical music as well as rock. Tickets are $7 adults, and are available through BASS (tel. 415-478-2277) or at the Academy one-half hour before show time.

Steinhart Aquarium: The oldest aquarium in North America, the 1923 Steinhart Aquarium allows visitors to commune with the world's most diverse live fish collection, including rep-resentatives of around 600 different species (including fish, marine invertebrates, and other sea life). The stunning glass-walled, 100,000-gallon Fish Roundabout here puts visitors right in the swim of things, as if they were standing in the center of the open ocean; it's especially fun at feeding time (daily at 2 p.m.). Altogether there are 189 exhibits here, but some of the most dramatic include: Sharks of the Tropics; the Penguin Environment, featuring an entire breeding colony of black-footed penguins; and The Swamp, featuring tropical critters like alligators, crocodiles, snakes, lizards, and frogs. Fun for some hands-on wet and wild exploring is California Tidepool.

The Academy of Sciences, tel. (415) 221-5100 or (415) 750-7145 (24-hour recorded information), is open daily 10 a.m.-5 p.m. (extended hours from Memorial Day weekend through Labor Day). Admission is free the first Wednesday of the month (when hours are extended until 8:45 p.m.), otherwise $8.50 adults; $5.50 youths 12-17, seniors, and students with ID; and $2 children ages 4-11.

Park Activities, Events, and Information
Kennedy Drive from 19th Ave. to Stanyan is closed to automobile traffic every Sunday; enjoy a walk, bike ride, or rollerblade (bicycle and rollerblade rentals on Stanyan). **Friends of Recreation and Parks,** tel. (415) 750-5105, offers free guided tours throughout the park May-October. But even more active sports fans won't be disappointed. Golden Gate Park action includes archery, baseball and basketball, boating

---

THE CITYPASS

The money-saving **CityPass** provides admission to six of San Francisco's top attractions—the Exploratorium, California Palace of the Legion of Honor, de Young Museum, Museum of Modern Art, California Academy of Sciences/Steinhart Aquarium, and a San Francisco Bay Cruise—for a price, at last report, half of what the individual admissions would cost: $27.75 adults, $19.75 seniors, $17.25 youths 12-17. It's good for seven days and is available at any of the participating attractions or any of the city's visitor information centers.

and rowing, fly-casting, football, horseback riding and horseshoes, lawn bowling, model yacht sailing—there's a special lake for just that purpose—plus polo, roller skating, soccer, and tennis. In addition to the exceptional Children's Playground, there are two other kiddie play areas.

Free **Golden Gate Band Concerts** are offered at 2 p.m. on Sunday and holidays at the park's Music Concourse. The **Midsummer Music Festival** in Stern Grove, Sloat Blvd. at 19th Ave., is another fun, and free, park program. Scheduled on consecutive Sundays from mid-June through August, it's quite popular, so come as early as possible. (For exact dates and program information, call the park office, listed below.) A variety of other special events are regularly scheduled in Golden Gate Park, including **A la Carte, a la Park,** San Francisco's "largest outdoor dining event." This gala gourmet fest, with themed pavilions, showcases the wares of Bay Area restaurants and Sonoma County wineries, the talents of celebrity chefs, and a wide variety of entertainment. It's a benefit for the San Francisco Shakespeare Festival, which offers an annual schedule of free public performances in August. A la Carte, a la Park is usually scheduled in late summer, over the three-day Labor Day weekend. Call (415) 458-1988 for information.

To save money on visits to multiple park attractions, purchase a **Golden Gate Explorer Pass** for $14 at the park office, downtown at the visitors information center at Hallidie Plaza, or at TIX Bay Area in Union Square, tel. (415) 433-7827. For more information about park events and activities (maps are $2.50; other items are free), contact the **San Francisco Recreation and Park Department** office (which is also Golden Gate Park headquarters) in ivy-covered **McLaren Lodge,** 501 Stanyan (at Fulton, on the park's east side), tel. (415) 831-2700, open weekdays 8 a.m.-5 p.m. The park's official website is www.civiccenter.ci.sf.ca.us/recpark/.

Light meals and snacks are available at various concessions or at **Cafe de Young** inside the de Young Museum; at the Academy of Sciences; and at the **Japanese Tea Garden Teahouse** (fortune cookies and tea). There is also great choice in restaurants near the intersection of Ninth Ave. and Irving, or along Haight and Stanyan Streets.

To reach the museums and tea garden via public transportation, board a westbound #5-Fulton bus on Market St., climbing off at Fulton and Eighth Avenue. After 6 p.m. and on Sunday and holidays, take #21-Hayes to Fulton and Sixth. Call (415) 673-MUNI for other routes and schedule information.

ARTFUL PERFORMING ARTS

San Francisco's performing arts scene offers everything from the classics to the contemporary, kitsch, and downright crazed. Find out what's going on by picking up local publications or calling the San Francisco Convention & Visitors Bureau information hotlines (see Useful Information in San Francisco: An Introduction). Tickets for major events and performances are available through the relevant box offices, mentioned below.

Low-income art lovers, or those deciding to "do" the town on a last-minute whim, aren't necessarily out of luck. **TIX Bay Area,** on Stockton St. at Union Square, tel. (415) 433-7827, www.tix.com, offers day-of-performance tickets to local shows at half price. Payment is cash only, no credit card reservations. Along with being a full-service BASS ticket outlet, TIX also handles advance full-price tickets to many Bay Area events. Open Tues.-Sat. noon-7:30 p.m. You can get a catalog for ordering advance tickets at half price by calling **TIX by Mail** at (415) 430-1140. To charge BASS arts and entertainment tickets by phone or to listen to recorded calendar listings, call (415) 478-2277 (BASS). Another helpful information source: KUSF 90.3 FM's **Alternative Music and Entertainment News (AMEN)** information line, tel. (415) 221-2636.

Other ticket box offices include: **City Box Office,** tel. (415) 392-4400, **Entertainment Ticketfinder,** tel. (650) 756-1414 or toll-free (800) 523-1515, and **St. Francis Theatre and Sports Tickets,** a service of the Westin St. Francis Hotel, tel. (415) 362-3500, www.premiertickets.com.

Classic Performing Arts

One of the nation's oldest classical dance companies, the **San Francisco Ballet** has been called "a truly national ballet company" by the *New York Times.* The ballet troupe's regular season, with performances in the Civic Center's War Memorial Opera House, runs Feb.-May, though holiday season performances of the *The Nutcracker* are a long-running San Francisco tradition. For tickets, call (415) 865-2000 or order tickets online at www.sfballet.org. The opera house also hosts visiting performances by The Joffrey Ballet and The Kirov Ballet, among others.

The smaller **Herbst Theatre** inside the War Memorial Veteran Building, 401 Van Ness Ave. (at McAllister), tel. (415) 621-6600, hosts smaller dance and musical productions, including performances by the San Francisco Chamber Symphony and the San Francisco Early Music Society.

The **San Francisco Opera** season runs Sept.-Dec., offering a total of 10 productions with big-name stars. Since this is the heart of the San Francisco social scene, tickets are expensive and hard to come by; call (415) 864-3330. Generally more accessible is the **San Francisco Symphony,** which offers a Sept.-June regular season in Louise M. Davies Hall downtown in the Civic Center, plus July pops concerts. For tickets, call (415) 864-6000. Davies Hall, reopened in 1992 after a two-year, $10 million accoustic renovation, is also a venue for other performances, including some programs of the West's only major independent music conservatory, the **San Francisco Conservatory of Music**—call (415) 759-3475 for tickets. The conservatory's annual Chamber Music West Festival in late May and early June is usually staged at various sites, including Hellman Hall at 19th and Ortega in the Sunset.

San Francisco Theater

Wherever you find it, pick up a free copy of *Stagebill* magazine, for its current and comprehensive show schedules, or check the website at www.stagebill.com. For Broadway shows, the **Curran Theatre,** 445 Geary (between Mason and Taylor), tel. (415) 551-2000 (information), tel. (415) 478-2277 (BASS) for tickets, is the long-running standard, though the **Golden Gate Theatre** at Sixth and Market, the **Orpheum** at Eighth and Market, and the **Marines Memorial Theatre** at Sutter and Mason (same phone numbers as the Curran for all) are other popular mainstream venues for comedies, musicals, and revues. The award-winning **Lamplighters Music Theatre,** tel. (415) 227-4797, specializes in Gilbert and Sullivan musicals and schedules three produc-

tions a year (in August, October, and January) at the Yerba Buena Center, tel. (415) 978-2787.

The repertory **American Conservatory Theater** (ACT), tel. (415) 834-3200 or (415) 749-2228 (box office), performs its big-name-headliner contemporary comedies and dramas in the venerable **Geary Theatre,** 415 Geary (at Mason). Union Square's theater district is also where you'll find **Theatre on the Square,** 450 Post (between Powell and Mason), tel. (415) 433-9500.

San Francisco is also home to a number of small, innovative theaters and theater troupes, including the **Magic Theatre, Cowell Theater,** and **Young Performers Theatre** at Fort Mason and the **Asian American Theatre** in the Richmond District, mentioned in more detail under Fort Mason and The Avenues, respectively. The **Actors Theatre of San Francisco,** 533 Sutter (between Powell and Mason), tel. (415) 296-9179, usually offers unusual plays. Also popular for progressive dramatic theater is SoMa's **Climate Theatre,** 252 Ninth St. (at Folsom), tel. (415) 978-2345. Another innovator in the realm of performance art is **Theater Artaud,** 450 Florida St. (at 17th), tel. (415) 621-7797. **Theatre Rhinoceros,** 2926 16th St. (between Mission and S. Van Ness), tel. (415) 861-5079, is America's oldest gay and lesbian theater company, est. 1978.

The long-running **Eureka Theatre Company,** 215 Jackson (between Front and Battery), tel. (415) 788-7469 (box office and information), is noted for its provocative, politically astute presentations. **Intersection for the Arts,** 446 Valencia St. (between 15th and 16th), tel. (415) 626-2787 (administration) or (415) 626-3311 (box office), the city's oldest alternative arts center, presents everything from experimental dramas to performance and visual art and dance. One-time "new talent" like Robin Williams, Whoopi Goldberg, and Sam Shepard are all Intersection alumni. **George Coates Performance Works,** 110 McAllister (at Leavenworth), tel. (415) 863-8520 (administration) or (415) 863-4130 (box office), offers innovative multimedia theater presentations in a re-purposed neo-Gothic cathedral.

Theater as Circus

Worth seeing whenever the group is in town is the much-loved, always arresting, and far from silent **San Francisco Mime Troupe,** 855 Treat Ave. (between 21st and 22nd), tel. (415) 285-

1717, a decades-old institution true to the classic Greek and Roman tradition of theatrical farce—politically sophisticated street theater noted for its complex simplicity. In addition to boasting actor Peter Coyote and the late rock impressario Bill Graham as organizational alumni, and inspiring the establishment of one-time troupe member Luis Valdez's El Teatro Campesino, the Mime Troupe was repeatedly banned and arrested in its formative years. In 1966, the state Senate Un-American Activities Committee charged the group with the crime of making lewd performances, the same year troupe members were arrested in North Beach for singing Christmas carols without a permit. More recently, the Mime Troupe has won a Tony Award and three Obies.

A tad more family-oriented, "the kind of circus parents might want their kids to run away to," according to NPR's Jane Pauley, is the **Pickle Family Circus,** another exceptional city-based theater troupe, which performs at Fort Mason's Cowell Theatre, tel. (415) 441-3400.

Bizarre cabaret-style **"Beach Blanket Babylon,"** playing at Club Fugazi, 678 Green St. (between Powell and Columbus) in North Beach, tel. (415) 421-4222, is the longest-running musical revue in theatrical history. The story line is always evolving. Snow White, who seems to be seeking love in all the wrong places, encounters characters who strut straight off the front pages of the tabloids.

Theater as Sound
"Eclectic" is the word used most often to describe the Audium, 1616 Bush St. (at Franklin), tel. (415) 771-1616, perhaps the ultimate performance of sound, certainly the only place like this in the world. Some 169 speakers in the sloping walls, coupled with the suspended ceiling and floating floor, all create an unmatched aural experence. Regular performances are on Friday and Saturday nights at 8:30 p.m.; tickets ($10) go on sale at 8 p.m. at the box office, or buy in advance at Tix in Union Square. Children under age 12 not allowed.

MORE ARTFUL, ENTERTAINING SAN FRANCISCO

A selection of entertaining bars, nightclubs, and other worthy diversions is included in The Lay of the Land, which is organized by neighborhood. To keep abreast of the ever-changing arts and entertainment scene, consult local newspapers, especially the calendar sections of the **Bay Guardian** and other local weeklies, and the pink Datebook section of the Sunday **Examiner and Chronicle.**

Artful Art Galleries
The downtown area, especially near Union Square and along lower Grant Ave., is rich with art galleries and arts-related specialty shops. The free **San Francisco Arts Monthly,** available around town and at the visitor information center downtown, includes a complete current listing of special gallery tours, exhibits, and art showrooms. Very useful, too, is **The San Francisco Bay Area Gallery Guide,** tel. (415) 921-1600, which details goings-on at galleries large and small, and provides information about current shows at major Bay Area museums.

Real Food, Real Art
San Francisco's **Real Food Company** delis and stores—at 1001 and 1023 Stanyan St., 2140 and 2164 Polk St., 3939 24th St., and elsewhere in the Bay Area—are the most predictable places to pick up free **San Francisco Open Studios** artists' listings, detailed maps, and resource directories. Or stop by Bay Area bookstores, art supply stores, and selected galleries. The Open Studios concept offers direct-to-you fine arts, plus an opportunity to meet the artists and often see how and where they work. The Bay Area's Open Studios experience, sponsored by California Lawyers for the Arts and local businesses, offers regularly scheduled open-studio days, usually scheduled on consecutive Saturdays and Sundays from late October to mid-November. On these days, more than 500 local artists open their studios or personally share their work with the public. You can come just to schmooze, but these working artists will eat better if you buy. For more information, call (415) 861-9838.

City Comedy
Bay Area Theatresports (BATS), tel. (415) 474-8935, schedules performances in Fort Mason's Bayfront Theater. Their hilarious, improvisational shows are often team efforts, with the

"scripts" for instant plays, movies, and musicals created from audience suggestions.

The hottest yuckspot in town, some say, is **Cobb's Comedy Club** at The Cannery on Fisherman's Wharf, 2801 Leavenworth (at Beach), tel. (415) 928-4320. Another stand-up venue is **Punchline Comedy Club,** 444 Battery (between Washington and Clay), tel. (415) 397-7573.

Playing Pool
Located inside the Rincon Center, **Chalkers Billiard Club,** 101 Spear St. (at Mission), tel. (415) 512-0450, has the feel of a clubby pub with its dark polished wood, pristine pool tables, and workers unwinding after the 9-to-5 grind at nearby Financial District offices. Also gentrified and comfortable even for absolute beginners is **The Great Entertainer,** 975 Bryant (between Seventh and Eighth), tel. (415) 861-8833, once a paint warehouse, now the West Coast's largest pool hall. Most of the tables in the 28,000-square-foot hall are nine feet long. Private suites are available. Also here: snooker, shuffleboard, and Ping-Pong (table tennis) tables.

EVENTFUL SAN FRANCISCO

Even more kaleidoscopic than the city's arts scene, San Francisco events include an almost endless combination of the appropriate, inappropriate, absurd, inspired, and sublime. Museums, theaters, neighborhood groups, and other cultural institutions usually offer their own annual events calendars. Even most shopping centers sponsor a surprising array of entertainment and events. That said, consider the seasonal events selection offered below as merely a sampling, and consult local newspapers for more complete information on what's going on.

Spring Events
In early March, head for the Concourse Exhibition Center and the **Whole Life Expo,** or to **TulipMania** at Pier 39. Later in March, quite the party is the annual **California Music Awards** ceremony in the Civic Auditorium. Around the same time is the huge **San Francisco International Asian American Film Festival.** Expect everything to be Irish and/or green at the city's

annual **St. Patrick's Day Parade** and all-day street party, both events attracting plenty of politicians. Otherwise, people start warming up to the attractions of the great outdoors by attending the *Chronicle's* **Great Outdoors Adventure Fair,** an exposition on everything and anything to do with recreation. One of the funnest runs in the city is the **Houlihan's to Houlihan's 12K,** which crosses the Golden Gate Bridge and finishes with a huge party on Fisherman's Wharf; look for it in late March.

St. Stupid's Day Parade on April 1 is a no-holds-barred celebration of foibles and foolishness. Show up in April with your bonnet for Union Street's annual **Easter Parade.** Japantown's big **Cherry Blossom Festival** usually includes a parade and other cultural festivities, taking place over the course of two weekends in mid-April. And outdoor life comes back to the bay with a bang as both **baseball season** and **yachting season** start up again. The latter's **Opening Day on the Bay** is quite the sight. Starting in late April is the two-week **San Francisco International Film Festival,** featuring more than 100 films and videos from some 30 different countries.

In May, the Mission District hosts two major events: the **Cinco de Mayo Parade & Festival,** a two-day party (with plenty of mariachi music and *folklorico* costumes and dancers) scheduled as close to May 5 as possible, and late May's **Carnaval San Francisco,** featuring an uninhibited parade with samba bands, dancers, floats, and hundreds of thousands of revelers. For more information on both, contact the **Mission Economic & Cultural Association,** 2899 24th St., tel. (415) 826-1401. In mid-May, the whole city turns out for the world's largest footrace, the *San Francisco Examiner* **Bay to Breakers,** when some 100,000 participants, many decked out in hilarious and/or scandalous costumes, hoof it from the Embarcadero out to Ocean Beach. Don't miss this wild, wacky, and wonderfully San Franciscan event.

Summer Events
There's always something going on in summer. The Haight celebrates its long-gone Summer of Love in June with the **Haight Street Fair.** Among the arts, crafts, and other wares, you can probably count on plenty of tie-dyed

POETIC AMUSEMENTS

There's probably only one thing better than reading a good poem in a quiet room by yourself. And that's listening to an impassioned poet reading a poem out loud in a small coffee-scented café full of attentive writers, lawyers, bikers, teachers, computer programmers, divinity students, musicians, secretaries, drug addicts, cooks, and assorted oddball others who all love poetry and are hanging onto every word being juggled by the poet behind the microphone. The only thing better than *that* is to read your own poems at an open-mike poetry reading.

One of the wonderful things about San Francisco and vicinity is that this kind of poetic melee takes place in some café, club, or bookstore almost every night, for those who know where to look. No one revels in the right to free speech like Bay Area denizens, and open poetry readings are as popular as stand-up comedy in many cafés and clubs, with sign-up lists at the door. Bring your own poetry, or just kick back and listen to some amazing musings.

The following suggested venues will get you started. Since schedules for local poetic license programs do change, it's prudent to call or otherwise check it out before setting out. Current open readings and other events are listed in the monthly tabloid *Poetry Flash,* P.O. Box 4172, Berkeley, CA 94704, tel. (510) 525-5476, the Bay Area's definitive poetry review and literary calendar, available free at many bookstores and cafés.

—*Ed Aust*

OPEN-MIKE POETRY READINGS IN SAN FRANCISCO
The Attic, 3336 24th St. (between Mission and Valencia), (415) 643-3376.
Elbo Room, 647 Valencia (at 17th)., tel. (415) 552-7788, Friday at 9 p.m.
Paradise Lounge, 1501 Folsom St. (at 11th) tel. (415) 861-6906, Sunday at 8 p.m. (upstairs).
Keane's 3300 Club, 3300 Mission St. (at 29th), tel. (415) 826-6886, poetry readings on the second and last Tuesdays of each month since 1993.

IN THE EAST BAY
Diesel–A Bookstore, 5433 College (between Lawton and Hudson) in Oakland's Rockridge district, tel. (510) 653-9965, hosts fiction, nonfiction, and poetry readings three times a week.
La Val's Pizza and Subterranean Theatre, 1834 Euclid Ave. (at Hearst) in Berkeley, tel. (510) 843-5617, housed poetry readings and Free Speech Movement gatherings in the 1960s. Poetry readings Tuesdays at 7:30 p.m.

---

items, prism-cut glass, and other hippie-style creations. But everyone's in a street-party mood, so June also features the **North Beach Festival** and the **Union Street Spring Festival Arts and Crafts Fair.** Also in June are the long-running **Ethnic Dance Festival** at the Palace of Fine Arts, the **San Francisco International Lesbian and Gay Film Festival,** and the start of Golden Gate Park's **Stern Grove Midsummer Music Festival,** which offers concerts in the grove on Sundays at 2 p.m. (The festival ends in late August.) Show up, too, for the **Kitemakers Annual Father's Day Kite Festival** on the Marina Green. Usually also late in June, coinciding with the film festival, comes the annual **Lesbian-Gay-Bisexual-Transgender Freedom Day Parade and Celebration,** one huge gay-pride party usually led by Dykes on Bikes and including cross-dressing cowboys (or girls), gay bands and majorettes, cheerleaders, and everyone and everything else. Act Up and other groups also deliver a more serious message—about the rising death toll from AIDS and its (so far) disproportionate impact on the gay community.

In inimitable American style, **Independence Day** (July 4) is celebrated in San Francisco with costumes—prizes for Most Original Uncle Sam and Best Symbol of America—ethnic food, multicultural entertainment, comics, and nighttime fireworks at Crissy Field. Also in July: **Jazz and All That Art on Fillmore,** celebrating the cultural and musical heritage of what was once a largely black neighborhood; the **Midsummer Mozart Festival,** tel. (415) 392-4400 (tickets) or (415) 954-0850 (administration); and the **San Francisco Symphony Pops Concerts,** tel. (415) 864-6000. Golden Gate Park's annual **Summer Festival of Performing Arts** runs into September.

Hot in August is **Comedy Celebration Day** in Golden Gate Park, tel. (415) 777-7120, and the

San Francisco Fair, tel. (415) 703-2729, a flower show in Golden Gate Park. Also in August: Fort Mason's ACC Craft Fair, tel. (415) 896-5060, and the San Francisco Butoh Festival, an ethnic dance fest at Fort Mason, tel. (415) 441-3687. Or head to Japantown for the Nihonmachi Street Fair, tel. (415) 771-9861. In late August or near Labor Day comes the Ringling Brothers Barnum and Bailey Circus at the Cow Palace, tel. (415) 469-6065.

Labor Day weekend brings the big A la Carte, A la Park food and brewfest to Golden Gate Park, tel. (415) 478-2277 (BASS), and kicks off the San Francisco Shakespeare Festival, staged in Golden Gate Park from early September into October.

Autumn Events
In mid-September, look for Chinatown's Autumn Moon Festival, an arts and crafts street fair, tel. (415) 982-6306, and the San Francisco International Art Exposition at Fort Mason, toll-free tel. (877) 278-3247. Also in September: the annual Bay Area Robot Olympics at the Exploratorium, tel. (415) 563-7337; the Mission

District's Festival de las Americas, tel. (415) 826-1401; Opera in the Park, tel. (415) 864-3330; and the San Francisco Blues Festival at Fort Mason, tel. (415) 826-6837 or (415) 478-2277 (BASS), which draws the biggest names in blues. Toward the end of the month, the Folsom Street Fair, tel. (415) 861-3247, offers neighborly entertainment, arts and crafts, food and drink, and more.

In October, the Grand National Livestock Exposition Rodeo and Horse Show comes to the Cow Palace, tel. (415) 469-6065. Bless your pet (or cow or horse) at Grace Cathedral's St. Francis Day service. During Fleet Week, the U.S. Navy puts down the plank for the public and also welcomes ships from around the world. A major cultural blowout around Columbus Day is the Italian Heritage Parade and Festival on Fisherman's Wharf and in North Beach, tel. (415) 989-2220. Also scheduled in October: the German Fest in the Civic Auditorium; the Castro Street Fair, tel. (415) 467-3354; Fort Mason's San Francisco Fall Antiques Show, tel. (415) 546-6661; the annual San Francisco Jazz Festival, tel. (415) 398-

FILM FESTIVALS AND VENUES FOR FILM AFICIONADOS

The San Francisco International Film Festival, tel. (415) 929-5000 (office) or (415) 931-3456 (recorded information), Northern California's longest-running film festival, is scheduled annually, usually from late April into May. This cinematic celebration typically includes 60 or more films from dozens of countries. Call for current program and price information. The city has all sorts of noteworthy festivities focused on film, including the 15-year-old Lesbian & Gay Film Festival, usually held at the Castro Theater in late June, which has apparently survived attacks by Senator Jesse Helms on its National Endowment for the Arts funding.

In San Francisco, going to the movies is always entertaining. If you don't mind the (outdoor) neighborhood horror show, the Strand, 1127 Market (between Seventh and Eighth downtown, near the Civic Center), tel. (415) 431-1259, shows unusual foreign films—sometimes double and triple features—from noon on. Cheap, too.

Classic theaters with friendlier neighborhoods,

these most likely to host foreign, revival, and other film festivals, include the 1922 Castro Theater, 429 Castro St. (near Market), tel. (415) 621-6120, where you get live Wurlitzer music during interludes, Hollywood classics, contemporary films, and clever double bills; and the hip Roxie, 3117 16th St. (near Valencia), tel. (415) 863-1087, www.roxie.com, specializing in independent, oddball, and trendy films, and sometimes showing silent flicks accompanied by organ. At the Haight's Red Victorian Movie House, 1727 Haight St., tel. (415) 668-3994, count on art films, revivals, interesting foreign fare—and California-casual couch-like benches for comfort.

Hole-in-the-wall Artists' Television Access (ATA), 992 Valencia, tel. (415) 824-3890, offers truly underground, experimental, and radical political films from unknown, independent filmmakers. Other good movie theater bets: the Lumiere, 1572 California (at Polk); the Clay, 2261 Fillmore (at Clay); and the Bridge, 3010 Geary Blvd. (at Blake, a few blocks west of Masonic). For schedule information for all three, call (415) 352-0810.

5655; and the **Antique Tribal Art Show and Sale.** To finish off the month in absolutely absurd style, on a weekend near Halloween head for the **Exotic Erotic Ball,** tel. (415) 469-6065. Alternatively, the best Halloween street shows are the Castro's bash (now actually held in the Civic Center) and the Mission District's celebrations of the **Day of the Dead** (and we're not talking Grateful Dead, either).

November events include the **San Francisco Bay Area Book Festival,** tel. (415) 908-2833; the **San Francisco International Auto Show** at Moscone Center, tel. (415) 332-2016; and the start of holiday festivities all over town.

Winter Events
Most December events reflect seasonal traditions. The major traditional arts performances are quite popular, so get tickets well in advance. The **San Francisco Ballet** performs *The Nutcracker,* tel. (415) 865-2000, and the **American Conservatory Theater** presents *A Christmas Carol,* tel. (415) 749-2228. The **Crosby Croon-Alike Contest** takes place at **Pier 39,** tel. (415) 981-7437, with finalists belting out "White Christmas." Be there.

In January, Mac fanatics head for the gargantuan **MacWorld Expo** at the Moscone Center, tel. (415) 974-4000. Mid-month, San Francisco hosts the **Martin Luther King Birthday Celebration,** headquartered at the Yerba Buena Center for the Arts, tel. (415) 771-6300. Also this month comes the **San Francisco Sports and Boat Show** at the Cow Palace, tel. (415) 469-6065, followed by the opening of the **San Francisco Ballet** at War Memorial Opera House, tel. (415) 865-2000.

In February of odd-numbered years, the **California International Antiquarian Book Fair** is held in San Francisco, tel. (415) 551-5190. (When it's not here, it's in Los Angeles.) But the main event, sometimes in January, sometimes in February, is the city's **Chinese New Year Celebration,** complete with parade and throngs of people, a very American tradition. For current information, contact the Chinese Chamber of Commerce, 730 Sacramento St., tel. (415) 982-3000.

On February 14, let your animal passions run wild at the San Francisco Zoo's **Valentine's Day Sex Tour.** The special narrated Safari Train tour will tell you everything you always wanted to know about sex in the animal kingdom. Horny rhinos? Gay wallabees? Lesbian penguins? Why, it's all true. The tour is followed by a champagne and truffles reception where you'll have the chance to get up close and personal with a variety of animals. Reservations required and, because of the risqué subject matter, age 18 and over only. For more information, call (415) 753-7165.

Considerably more subdued, in late February the San Francisco Orchid Society sponsors the annual **Pacific Orchid Exposition** at Fort Mason, tel. (415) 546-9608.

SHOPPING SAN FRANCISCO

Whether the addiction is neighborhood boutique hopping or spending days in major-league malls, San Francisco is a shopper's paradise. To seek something specific, study the current *San Francisco Book* for mainstream shopping destinations. To pursue shopping as social exploration, wander the city's neighborhood commercial districts. (Be sure to take advantage of museum and arts-venue gift shops, which usually feature an unusual array of merchandise. Secondhand and thrift shops can also be surprising. Some suggestions are included in The Lay of the Land.) To shop for one's consumer identity—covering as much ground, and as many shops, as possible without having any particular result in mind—visit the city's mall-like marketplaces.

The uptown **Union Square** area is an upscale shoppers delight. Major San Francisco shopping palaces include the new nine-story **San Francisco Shopping Centre,** tel. (415) 495-5656, a few blocks from Union Square at Fifth and Market, astonishing for its marble and granite elegance as well as its spiral escalators and retractable atrium skylight. Here you'll find J. Crew, Abercrombie & Fitch, Macy's, and Nordstrom. Also in the neighborhood is the **Crocker Galleria,** tel. (415) 393-1505, between Post and Sutter, Kearny and Montgomery, a glass-domed wonder (complete with rooftop gardens) modeled after the Galleria Vittorio Emmanuelle in Milan. Look for a more chi-chi selection here, including Versace and Nicole Miller. Another major downtown commercial attraction is the **Embarcadero Center,** tel. (415) 772-0500, designed by John C. Portman Jr., an eight-block complex (between Clay and Sacramento, Drumm and Battery) with three plaza-style levels and four main buildings plus the Hyatt Regency and Park Hyatt hotels, not to mention five office towers.

The three-square-block **Japan Center,** 1625 Post St. (at Laguna), tel. (415) 922-6776, in the Western Addition's Japantown, designed by Minoru Yamasaki, adds up to about five acres of galleries, shops, restaurants, theaters, hotels, and convention facilities. **Chinatown** is famous for its ethnic commercial attractions, and adjacent **North Beach** also has its share.

But **Fisherman's Wharf,** along the northeastern waterfront, is becoming shopping central. Most famous of the shopping destinations on the Wharf is 45-acre, carnival-crazy **Pier 39,** with more than 100 shops and endless family amusements. A close second is one-time chocolate factory **Ghirardelli Square,** 900 North Point (at Beach), tel. (415) 775-5500, with stylish shops and restaurants, and some great views. **The Cannery,** 2801 Leavenworth (at Beach), tel. (415) 771-3112, one block east of the Hyde St. cable car turnaround, is a brick-and-ivy behemoth. Once the world's largest fruit cannery, the building is now home to collected cafés, restaurants, shops, galleries, a comedy club, a jazz club, and the free Museum of the City of San Francisco (tel. 415-928-0289), which features City Hall's original Goddess of Progress (or at least her head) and a section of a 13th-century Byzantine mosaic ceiling once part of William Randolph Hearst's globetrotting acquisitions program.

The **Anchorage Shopping Center,** 2800 Leavenworth (bounded by Jefferson, Beach, and Jones), tel. (415) 673-7762, is a contemporary, nautical-flavored plaza with daily entertainment and some unusual shops (e.g., Magnet Kingdom and Perfumania). The **Stonestown Galleria,** tel. (415) 759-2626, on Hwy. 1 at Winston Dr. near San Francisco State University and Lake Merced, offers all sorts of sophistication—and the luxury, in San Francisco, of free parking.

CITY SPORTS AND RECREATION

As of April 2000, the **San Francisco Giants** major-league baseball team plays ball on the bay at the city's new 42,000-seat Pacific Bell Park, tel. (415) 468-3700, www.sfgiants.com. (To betray the city's baseball heritage, zip across the bay to the Oakland Coliseum and the Oakland A's games, tel. 510-430-8020, www.oaklandathletics.com.) Still at home at 3Com Park—once known as Candlestick Park—are the **San Francisco 49ers,** NFL footballers made famous by their numerous Super Bowl victories. For 49er tickets and information, call (415) 656-4900 or check www.sf49ers.com.

San Franciscans are big on participatory sports. Some of the city's most eclectic competitive events reflect this fact, including the famous *San Francisco Examiner* **Bay to Breakers** race in May, tel. (415) 777-7770, which attracts

Upscale shopping is just one of the offerings at the Crocker Galleria shopping center.

AISLINN RACE

100,000-plus runners, joggers, and walkers, most wearing quite creative costumes—and occasionally nothing at all. It's a phenomenon that must be experienced to be believed. (Request registration forms well in advance.)

San Francisco's outdoor and other recreational opportunities seem limited only by one's imagination (and income): hot-air ballooning, beachcombing, bicycling, birdwatching, boating, bowling, camping, canoeing, kayaking, hang-gliding, hiking, horseshoes, fishing, golf, tennis, sailing, swimming, surfing, parasailing, rowing, rock climbing, running, windsurfing. Golden Gate National Recreational Area and Golden Gate Park are major community recreation resources.

For a current rundown on sports events and recreational opportunities, or for information on specific activities, consult the helpful folks at the San Francisco Convention & Visitors Bureau (see Useful Information under the first chapter's Just the Facts section).

SAN JOSE CONVENTION AND VISITORS BUREAU

STAYING IN SAN FRANCISCO

San Francisco is an expensive city, for the most part. A first-time visitor's first impression might be that no one is welcome here unless they show up in a Rolls Royce.

Mind you, given prices are for the "standard" room, two persons, one bed, in peak summer season. (Many offer off-season and weekend deals; always ask about specials before booking.) Most hotels also have higher-priced suites, and if you feel the need to drop $500 or $1,000 (or more) per night on a suite, you'll find plenty of places in town that will be more than happy to accommodate you. If you can afford these prices ("tariffs," actually), you'll not be disappointed. And some of the city's four- and five-star hotels also rank among its most historic, survivors—at least in part—of the great 1906 earthquake and fire.

That said, a little looking will uncover plenty of accommodations suitable for the rest of us. San Francisco offers two hostels affiliated with Hostelling International (American Youth Hostels), in addition to other hostels and inexpensive options. Other than the hostels, some dirt-cheap fleabags can be found, but they're often in seedy areas; budget travelers with city savvy, street

smarts, and well-honed self-preservation skills might consider these establishments, but women traveling solo should avoid them. (In the context of truly low-budget accommodations, "European-style" generally means "the bathrooms are in the hallway.")

City-style motels offer another world of possibilities. Some reasonably priced ones are scattered throughout the city, though Lombard St. (west of Van Ness) is the place to go for overwhelming concentrations of motel choice. The city also supports a wide variety of bed and breakfast inns, with ambiences ranging from Haight-Ashbury-style funk to very proper Victoriana.

In general, San Francisco offers great choices in the midrange hotel market, including a number of "boutique" hotels. Many of these attractive and intimate hotels—old-timers and aging grand dames now renovated and redecorated for the modern carriage trade—are well located, near visitor attractions and public transit. Lack of convenient off-street parking is rarely a drawback, since most offer some sort of valet parking arrangement. Very good to exceptional restaurants—and room service—are often as-

RESERVATION SERVICES

If you're unable to make an accommodations choice well in advance, or if you'd rather let someone else do the detail work, contact a local reservations service.

San Francisco Reservations, 22 Second St., Fourth Floor, San Francisco, CA 94105, tel. (415) 227-1500 or toll-free (800) 677-1550, offers a no-fee reservations service for more than 200 hotels, most of these in San Francisco, and keeps current on discounts, specials, and packages. The company offers preferred rates for business travelers at some of the city's finest hotels, including many of the boutiques. With one call, you can also take advantage of their free best-deal airline ticketing and car rental reservations service. Reservation lines are open daily 7 a.m.-11 p.m. If you have access to a computer, you can make reservations (three or more days in advance) through S.F. Reservations' website at www.hotelres.com.

Discount Hotel Rates/California Reservations, 165 Eighth St., Ste. 201, San Francisco, CA 94103, tel. (415) 252-1107 or toll-free (800) 576-0003, also no-fee, represents more than 200 hotels in San Francisco and beyond. Subject to room availability, the firm offers rates at quality hotels for 10-50% less than posted rates.

Bed & Breakfast California, P.O. Box 282910, San Francisco, CA 94128-2910, tel. (650) 696-1690 or toll-free (800) 872-4500, offers referrals to a wide range of California bed and breakfasts—everything from houseboat and home stays to impressive Victorians and country-style inns—especially in San Francisco, the Napa-Sonoma wine country, and the Monterey Peninsula. Rates: $70-200 per night (with two-night minimum). Similar, and often without the mandatory two-night stay, is **Bed and Breakfast San Francisco,** P.O. Box 420009, tel. (415) 899-0060 or toll-free (800) 452-8249, www.bbsf.com.

ducements. Many boutique and fine hotels also offer substantial discounts to business travelers and to members of major "travel-interested" groups, including the American Automobile Association (AAA) and the American Association of Retired People (AARP). The visitor center is located at Benjamin Swig Pavilion on the lower level of Hallidie Plaza at Market and Powell Streets. Open weekdays 9 a.m.-5:30 p.m., Saturday until 3 p.m., Sunday 10 a.m.-2 p.m. Or call (415) 391-2000. You can also call (415) 391-2001 24 hours a day for a recorded message listing daily events and activities.

HOSTELS AND OTHER CHEAP SLEEPS

San Francisco is full of shoestring-priced hostels renting dorm-style bunks for around $12-20 per person per night. Many also have higher-priced private rooms. Some hostels are open to everybody; others, as noted below, are open only to international travelers. Most have group kitchen facilities, laundry facilities, and helpful staff to give you hot tips on seeing the city.

Hostelling International
The **San Francisco Fisherman's Wharf HI-AYH Hostel** is just west of the wharf at Fort Mason, Bldg. 240, tel. (415) 771-3645, fax (415) 771-1468, www.norcalhostels.org. It's a local institution—located on a hill overlooking the bay and occupying part of the city's urban national park, the Golden Gate National Recreation Area. Close to the "Bikecentennial" bike route and the cultural attractions of the Fort Mason complex, the hostel is within an easy stroll of Fisherman's Wharf and Ghirardelli Square, as well as Chinatown and downtown (you could take the cable car).

The hostel itself is one of HI-AYH's largest—and finest—offering a total of 160 beds in clean rooms; one chore a day expected. Popular with all age groups and families, amenities include lots of lounge space, a big kitchen, plenty of food storage, laundry facilities, and pay lockers for baggage. No lockout or curfew. Family rooms are available, as is parking, and it's wheelchair accessible. The ride board here is helpful for travelers without wheels. Guests can also participate in hostel-

sociated with boutique hotels. When travel is slow, most notably in winter, off-season and package deals can make these small hotels (and others) genuine bargains. Do check around before signing in. Also check at the visitors center on Market St., since some establishments offer special coupons and other seasonal in-

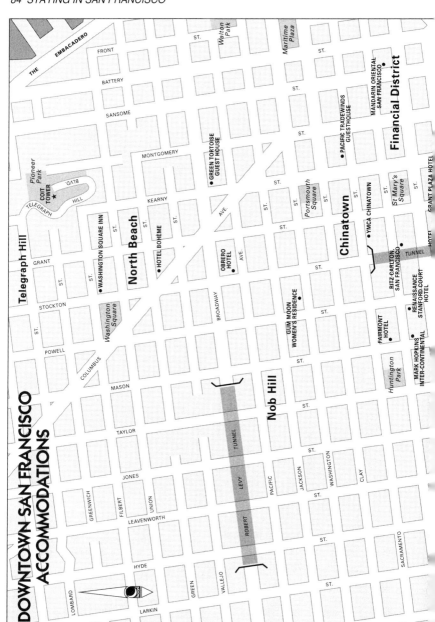

DOWNTOWN SAN FRANCISCO ACCOMMODATIONS

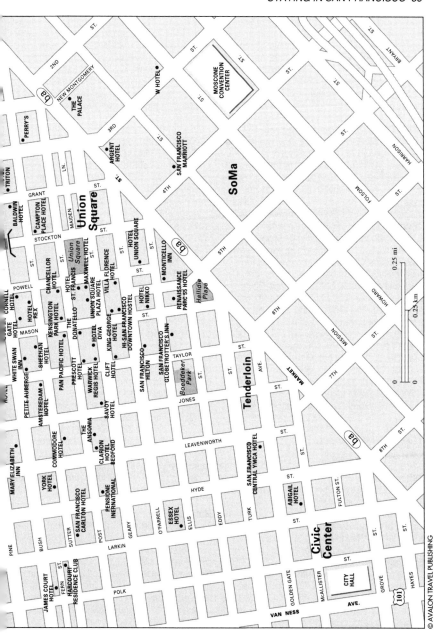

sponsored hikes, tours, and bike rides. Reservations are essential for groups and advisable for others—especially in summer, when this place is jumping. Rates include linen and free breakfast; 14-day maximum, no minimum stay. To reserve by mail, send one night's deposit (address above) at least three weeks in advance; by phone or fax, call at least 48 hours in advance and confirm with a major credit card (Visa, Mastercard).

Near all the downtown and theater district hubbub is the **HI-San Francisco Downtown Hostel,** 312 Mason St. (between Geary and O'Farrell), tel. (415) 788-5604, fax (415) 788-3023, www.hiayh.org, another good choice for budget travelers. This hotel-style hostel offers double and triple rooms—most share a bathroom—and amenities from kitchen to baggage storage and vending machines. Laundry facilities are nearby. The desk is essentially open for check-in 24 hours; no lockout, no curfew, no chores. Family rooms available. Groups welcome, by reservation only, and reservations for summer stays are essential for everyone and should be made at least 30 days in advance. Reserve by phone or fax with Visa or MasterCard. Rates include linens, but bring your own towel. Ask about the best nearby parking.

For membership details and more information about hostelling in the U.S. and abroad, contact: Hostelling International-American Youth Hostels, 733 15th St. NW, Ste. 840, Washington DC 20005, tel. (202) 783-6161, fax (202) 783-6171, www.hiayh.org. For more information on Northern California hostels, contact the **HI-AYH Golden Gate Council,** 425 Divisadero St., Ste. 307, San Francisco, CA 94117, tel. (415) 863-1444 or (415) 701-1320, fax (415) 863-3865, www.norcalhostels.org.

Other Hostels

The excellent **Green Tortoise Guest House,** 494 Broadway, tel. (415) 834-1000, fax (415) 956-4900, www.greentortoise.com, sits on the corner of Broadway and Kearny, where Chinatown runs into North Beach. It offers a kitchen, laundry, sauna, free internet access, and complimentary breakfast.

The **Interclub Globe Hostel,** 10 Hallam Place (south of Market near the Greyhound station, just off Folsom), tel. (415) 431-0540, is a fairly large, lively place with clean four-bed hotel rooms, a private sundeck, community lounge, pool table, café, and laundry room. The Globe is specifically for foreign guests, usually students, but these can also include Americans who present passports with stamps verifying their own international travels. Open 24 hours, no curfew. Also in the area and strictly for international travelers ("operated by students for students" and affiliated with the American Association of International Hostels) are two other SoMa budget outposts: the **European Guest House,** 761 Minna (between Eighth and Ninth Streets), tel. (415) 861-6634, and the affiliated **San Francisco International Student Center,** 1188 Folsom (near BrainWash), tel. (415) 487-1463 or (415) 255-8800, both offering dorm-style accommodations and basic amenities.

North of Market, the **San Francisco Globetrotter's Inn,** 225 Ellis St. (at Mason, one block west of Powell), tel. (415) 346-5786 (or (415) 673-4048 to reach guests), offers daily and weekly rates. In the Chinatown area, the lively **Pacific Tradewinds Guest House,** 680 Sacramento St., tel. (415) 433-7970, is in a prime spot near the Transamerica Pyramid. The hostel offers eight-bed rooms or larger dorm rooms, and rates include free tea and coffee all day, use of a fully equipped kitchen, Internet access, free maps, laundry service, fax service, long-term storage, and (I quote) "an extremely friendly, helpful, and good-looking staff." No curfew. You can make arrangements to stay through their website at www.hostels.com/pt.

A good budget bet in the Mission District is the **San Francisco International Guest House,** 2976 23rd St. (at Harrison), tel. (415) 641-1411, an uncrowded Victorian popular with Europeans. Accommodations include two- to four-bed dorm rooms, as well as four couples rooms; five day minimum stay. It's geared toward longer-term stays and usually full.

Boardinghouses

The **Mary Elizabeth Inn,** 1040 Bush (between Jones and Leavenworth), tel. (415) 673-6768, is a women's residence, part of a mission program sponsored by the United Methodist Church. Tourists are welcome when space is available. Facilities include private rooms (shared baths) with linen service, laundry facilities, a sundeck and solarium, and two meals daily (except Sunday). Weekly rate: $155. An even better bet, though, for a longer visit in San Francisco is the **Harcourt Residence Club,** 1105 Larkin, tel. (415) 673-7720, where a stay includes two meals a day, Sunday brunch, and access to TV. Unlike most other residence hotels, this one attracts international students—a younger clientele. Weekly rates: $150-250 per person. Inexpensive in Chinatown for women only is the **Gum Moon Women's Residence,** 940 Washington (at Stockton), tel. (415) 421-8827.

INEXPENSIVE HOTELS

The large **San Francisco Central YMCA Hotel,** 220 Golden Gate Ave., tel. (415) 885-0460, is in an unappealing area two blocks north of Market at Leavenworth, with adequate rooms for women and men (double locks on all doors), plus a pool, gym, and the city's only indoor track—a plus for runners, since you won't want to run through the neighborhood (for fun, anyway). Room rates include continental breakfast. Inexpensive. Hostel beds are also available, for travelers only. Another "Y" option closer to downtown is the men-only **YMCA Chinatown,** 855 Sacramento St. (between Stockton and Grant), tel. (415) 576-9622.

Close to Nob Hill is the very nice **James Court Hotel,** 1353 Bush St. (between Polk and Larkin), tel. (415) 771-2409, with European-style accommodations and basic amenities plus kitchen. Some rooms have kitchenettes and some have private baths. All have color cable TV and phone. Amenities include complimentary coffee and coin laundry.

Perhaps the epitome of San Francisco's casual, low-cost European-style stays is the **Adelaide Inn,** 5 Isadora Duncan Ct., (in the theater district, off Taylor between Geary and Post), tel. (415) 441-2261. Reservations are advisable for the 18 rooms with shared baths. Rates include continental breakfast. Inexpensive-Moderate. Also in the area, **The Ansonia,** 711 Post, tel. (415) 673-2670, is a real find. This small hotel has a friendly staff, comfortable lobby, nice rooms, a laundry, and breakfast and dinner (except on Sunday). Inexpensive-Moderate (depending upon the bathroom arrangement). Student rates for one month or longer.

MODERATE TO PREMIUM HOTELS

Close to Union Square, the **Gates Hotel,** 140 Ellis (at Cyril Magnin), tel. (415) 781-0430, is cheap and cheerful, though a little rundown, with basic rooms. Inexpensive-Moderate. A budget gem in the Chinatown area, the **Obrero Hotel,** 1208 Stockton, tel. (415) 989-3960, offers just a dozen cheery bed-and-breakfast rooms with bathrooms down the hall. Full breakfast included. Inexpensive-Moderate. Another best bet is the **Grant Plaza Hotel,** 465 Grant Ave. (between Pine and Bush), tel. (415) 434-3883 or toll-free (800) 472-6899, where amenities include private baths with hair dryers, telephones with voice mail, and color TV. Group rates available. Inexpensive-Moderate. Unpretentious and reasonably priced (private bathrooms) is the **Union Square Plaza Hotel,** 432 Geary (between Powell and Mason), tel. (415) 776-7585. Expensive.

A few blocks north of the Civic Center between Hyde and Larkin, in a borderline bad neighborhood, is the justifiably popular **Essex Hotel,** 684 Ellis St., tel. (415) 474-4664 or toll-free (800) 443-7739 in California, (800) 453-7739 from elsewhere in the country. The hotel offers small rooms with private baths and telephones; some have TV. Free coffee. It's especially popular in summer—when rates are slightly higher—with foreign tourists, particularly Germans. Moderate-Expensive. Weekly rates, too.

Noteworthy for its antiques, comfort, and fresh flowers, is the small **Golden Gate Hotel,** 775 Bush St. (between Powell and Mason), tel. (415) 392-3702 or toll-free (800) 835-1118. Sixteen of the rooms have private bath; the other seven, with shared bath, are less expensive. Rates include complimentary breakfast and afternoon tea. Moderate-Expensive. **Pensione International,** 875 Post St., tel. (415) 775-3344, lies at the gentrifying edge of the Tenderloin just east of Hyde St. and offers attractive rooms with either shared or private bath. Breakfast included. Moderate-Expensive.

Located right across from the Chinatown gate just off Union Square, the bright and comfortable **Baldwin Hotel,** 321 Grant Ave. (between Sutter and Bush), tel. (415) 781-2220 or toll-free (800) 622-5394, www.baldwinhotel.com, offers comfortable, newly renovated guest rooms with

TV and telephones with modem hookups. Expensive-Premium.

A relative of the Phoenix Inn, the new **Abigail Hotel,** 246 McAllister St., tel. (415) 861-9728 or toll-free (800) 243-6510, www.sf trips.com, offers spruce British-style charm and antiques, even down comforters, all just a hop, skip, and a jump from City Hall, the Civic Auditorium, and nearby arts venues. The onsite vegan restaurant, **Millennium,** is purportedly superb. Discounts for artists, government employees, and groups; other deals when the town slows down. Weekly and monthly rates also available. Continental breakfast included. Expensive-Premium.

Styled after a 1920s luxury liner, the **Commodore Hotel,** 825 Sutter St., tel. (415) 923-6800 or toll-free (800) 338-6848, www.sf trips.com, is a fun place to stay downtown. All of the rooms are spacious, with modern bathrooms and data ports on the phones. Downstairs, the **Titanic Café** serves California-style breakfast and lunch, and the Commodore's **Red Room** is a plush cocktail lounge decorated with rich red velvets, pearlized vinyl, and red tile. Expensive-Premium.

Nearby, and also between the theater district and Nob Hill, the newly refurbished 1909 **Amsterdam Hotel,** 749 Taylor St. (between Bush and Sutter), tel. (415) 673-3277 or toll-free (800) 637-3444, features an attractive Victorian lobby and clean, comfortable, spacious rooms, all with contemporary private bathrooms. All rooms have color cable TV, radio, and direct-dial phones. Rates include complimentary breakfast. Expensive-Premium.

Near Union Square, the **Sheehan Hotel,** 620 Sutter St. (at Mason), tel. (415) 775-6500 or toll-free (800) 848-1529 in the U.S. and Canada, is a real find—a surprisingly elegant take on economical downtown accommodations. Rooms have cable TV and phones; some have private baths, others have European-style shared baths (these the bargains). Other facilities include an Olympic-size lap pool, a fitness and exercise room, and a downstairs tearoom and wine bar. The hotel is close to shopping, art, BART, and other public transportation. Discount parking is available. Rates include continental breakfast, and children under 12 stay free with parent(s). Moderate-Premium.

Quite charming, between Union Square and Nob Hill, is the **Cornell Hotel,** 715 Bush St. (at Powell), tel. (415) 421-3154 or toll-free (800) 232-9698, where rates include breakfast and all rooms are nonsmoking. Expensive-Premium.

BOUTIQUE HOTELS

San Francisco's bouquet of European-style boutique hotels is becoming so large that it's impossible to fit the flowers in any one container. In addition to those mentioned above, the following sampling offers an idea of the wide variety available. Most of the city's intimate and stylish small hotels are included in the annual San Francisco Convention & Visitors Bureau Lodging Guide, listed among all other accommodations options, by area, and not otherwise distinguished from more mainstream hostelries. Two clues to spotting a possible "boutique": the number of rooms (usually 75 to 150, rarely over 200) and prices in the Premium or Luxury category.

Near Union Square and Nob Hill

The 111-room **Hotel Diva,** 440 Geary (between Mason and Taylor, right across from the Curran and Geary Theaters), tel. (415) 885-0200 or toll-free (800) 553-1900, is a chrome-faced contemporary Italian classic, awarded "Best Hotel Design" honors by *Interiors* magazine. Special features include a complete business center—with computers, modems, you name it—daily newspaper, complimentary breakfast delivered to your door, meeting facilities, and a 24-hour fitness center. Monday through Friday, Diva offers complimentary limousine service to downtown. Premium-Luxury ($159-199 for standard rooms, $179-219 suites).

Cable cars roll right by the six-floor **Hotel Union Square,** 114 Powell St., tel. (415) 397-3000 or toll-free (800) 553-1900, one of the city's original boutiques, with an art deco lobby and 131 rooms decorated in a blend of contemporary California and old-brick San Francisco. Multiple amenities, including continental breakfast and on-site parking. Wonderful rooftop suites with gardens. Premium.

The one-time Elks Lodge #3 is now the 87-room **Kensington Park Hotel,** 450 Post St., tel. (415) 788-6400 or toll-free (800) 553-1900, just steps from Union Square. Its parlor lobby still sports the original handpainted Gothic ceiling and warm Queen Anne floral decor. Guests enjoy all the amenities, including financial district limo service, a fitness center, complimentary continental breakfast, and afternoon tea and sherry. Premium-Luxury ($175-205). (Inquire about hotel/theater packages, since Theatre On The Square is also located here.)

The century-old **King George Hotel,** 334 Mason (at Geary), www.kinggeorge.com, is a cozy and charming stop near Geary St. theaters and Union Square. Breakfast and afternoon tea served daily in the traditional English **Windsor Tearoom.** Ask about seasonal discounts and other specials, with rates as low as $85. Moderate-Premium.

Fairly reasonable, near the theater scene, is the cheerful and colorful **Clarion Hotel Bedford,** 761 Post St., tel. (415) 673-6040 or toll-free (800) 252-7466, a 17-story 1929 hotel featuring florals and pastels. There's a café adjacent, but don't miss the tiny mahogany-paneled Wedgwood Bar just off the lobby, decorated with china gifts from Lord Wedgwood. Luxury ($179-199). Another good choice in the vicinity is the restored art deco **Maxwell Hotel,** 386 Geary, tel. (415) 986-2000, or toll-free (888) 734-6299. Luxury (rates run $155-205, though specials can drive the price as low as $119). Also close to the theaters is the 1913 **Savoy Hotel,** 580 Geary, tel. (415) 441-2700 or toll-free (800) 227-4223, a taste of French provincial with period engravings, imported furnishings, and goose down featherbeds and pillows. Amenities include complimentary afternoon sherry and tea. Premium-Luxury ($149-229). Downstairs is the Brasserie Savoy.

Closer to Nob Hill and Chinatown is the ninefloor **Hotel Juliana,** 590 Bush St., tel. (415) 392-2540 or toll-free (800) 372-8800 in California, (800) 328-3880 elsewhere in the United States. The 107 rooms and suites have in-room coffee makers, hair dryers, and irons and ironing boards. Other amenities include complimentary evening wine, morning limo service to the Financial District (just a few blocks away), and the on-site **Oritalia** restaurant (MediterrAsian). Premium-Luxury (singles and doubles $179, suites $235; great deals in the low season).

Also within an easy stroll of Nob Hill: the elegant art deco **York Hotel,** 940 Sutter St., tel. (415) 885-6800 or toll-free (800) 808-9675 in the U.S. and Canada, used as the setting for Alfred Hitchcock's *Vertigo.* The York offers the usual three-star comforts, including limousine service and complimentary breakfast. Expensive-Premium.

The **Villa Florence Hotel,** 225 Powell St., tel. (415) 397-7700 or toll-free (888) 501-4909 in California, (800) 553-4411 elsewhere in the U.S., www.villaflorence.com, features a 16th-century Tuscany/Italian Renaissance theme, and American-style European ambience. The colorful and comfortable guest rooms feature soundproofed walls and windows—a good idea above the cable cars and so close to Union Square—as well as in-room coffeemakers and all basic amenities. The hotel has a beauty salon and features the adjacent (and outstanding) NorCal-NorItal **Kuleto's Restaurant** and antipasto bar, tel. (415) 397-7720. Premium-Luxury ($155-215).

For an all-American historical theme, consider the **Monticello Inn,** 127 Ellis (between Powell and Cyril Magnin), tel. (415) 392-8800 or toll-free (800) 669-7777, www.monticelloinn.com. Its cool colonial-style lobby holds Chippendale reproductions and a wood-burning fireplace. Rooms feature early-American decor, soundproofed walls and windows, refrigerators, honor bars, phones with data ports and voice mail, and other amenities. Complimentary continental breakfast is served in the lobby. Premium-Luxury ($115-175). The inn's adjacent **Puccini & Pinetti,** tel. (415) 392-5500, is a highly regarded Cal-Italian restaurant well patronized by theatergoers.

Between Union Square and Nob Hill is **Hotel Rex,** 562 Sutter (between Powell and Mason), tel. (415) 433-4434 or toll-free (800) 433-4434, www.sftrips.com, furnished in 1930s style and "dedicated to the arts and literary world." Rates include a complimentary evening glass of wine. Premium-Luxury (as high as $250). Also reasonable by boutique hotel standards is the **San Francisco Carlton Hotel,** 1075 Sutter (at Larkin), tel. (415) 673-0242 or toll-free (800) 922-7586, www.carltonhotel.com, placed on Condé Nast Traveler's 1999 Gold List and offering 165 comfortable rooms with Queen Anne-style chairs and pleasant decor, as well as the on-site Oak Room Grille. Expensive-Luxury ($115-175).

Moving into San Francisco's trend-setting strata, the gleeful **Hotel Triton,** 342 Grant Ave., tel. (415) 394-0500 or toll-free (800) 433-6611, is

SOME HIP SAN FRANCISCO STAYS

Every city has its style, reflected in how things appear, of course, but mostly in how they feel. The following establishments offer just a sample of that inimitable San Francisco attitude.

The Phoenix Inn at 601 Eddy St. (on the corner of Eddy and Larkin at the edge of the Tenderloin), tel. (415) 776-1380 or toll-free (800) 248-9466, www.sftrips.com, is more than just a 1950s motel resurrected with flamingo pink and turquoise paint. It's a subtle see-and-be-seen art scene, first attracting rock 'n' roll stars and now attracting almost everybody—*the* place in San Francisco to spy on members of the cultural elite. This is, for example, the only place Sonic Youth ever stays in San Francisco. Just-plain-famous folks like Keanu Reaves and Ben Harper can also be spied from time to time. Like the trendy, on-site California-style restaurant, **Backflip**, even the heated swimming pool here is famous, due to its Francis Forlenza mural, "My Fifteen Minutes—Tumbling Waves," the center of a big state-sponsored stink over whether it violated health and safety codes (since public pool bottoms are supposed to be white). "That's how it is up at Eddy and Larkin, where the limos are always parkin'," according to the inn's complimentary *Phoenix Fun Book,* a cartoon-style coloring book history illustrated by *Bay Guardian* artist Lloyd Dangle. (Also as a service for guests, the Phoenix sporadically publishes its own hippest-of-the-hip guide to San Francisco, *Beyond Fisherman's Wharf.*)

Accommodations at the Phoenix—the inn named for the city's mythic ability to rise from its own ashes,

as after the fiery 1906 earthquake—are glass-fronted, uncluttered, pool-facing '50s motel rooms upscaled to ultramodern, yet not particularly ostentatious, with handmade bamboo furniture, tropical plants, and original local art on the walls. Phoenix services include complimentary continental breakfast (room service also available), the "Phoenix Movie Channel" on in-room cable—with 15 different made-in-San Francisco movies (plus a film library with 20 "band on the road" films)—and a complete massage service, including Swedish, Esalen, Shiatsu, even poolside massage. In addition to concierge services, the Phoenix also offers blackout curtains, an on-call voice doctor (for lead vocalists with scratchy throats), and free VIP passes to SoMa's underground dance clubs. Regular rates: $89-109, and $139 for each of the three suites, including the Tour Manager Suites. Ask about deals, including the "special winter rate" for regular customers (subject to availability), with the fourth night free.

Awesomely hip, too, is the playful **Hotel Triton** on Grant, in the heart of the city's downtown gallery district. The one-time Beverly Plaza Hotel just across from the Chinatown Gateway has been reimagined and reinvented by Bill Klimpton, the man who started the boutique hotel trend in town in 1980. The Triton's artsy ambience is startling and entertaining, boldly announcing itself in the lobby with sculpted purple, teal, and gold columns, odd tassle-headed, gold brocade "dervish" chairs, and mythic Neptunian imagery on the walls. Rooms are comfortable and contemporary, with custom-

---

the talk of the town—and other towns as well—attracting celebrities galore as well as comparisons to New York's Paramount and Royalton Hotels. (For more information, see special topic Some Hip San Francisco Stays.)

The city has more classical class, of course. The four-star **Prescott Hotel,** 545 Post St. (between Taylor and Mason), tel. (415) 563-0303 or toll-free (800) 283-7322, www.prescotthotel.com, elegantly combines earthy Americana—most notable in the lobby—with the feel of a British men's club. Rooms and suites come complete with paisley motif, overstuffed furniture, and every imaginable amenity—from honor bar and terry robes to shoe shines and evening wine and cheeses. Not

to mention room service courtesy of Wolfgang Puck's downstairs **Postrio** restaurant, where hotel guests also receive preferred dining reservations

(if rooms are also reserved well in advance). Services for guests on the Executive Club Level include express check-in (and check-out), continental breakfast, hors d'oeuvres from Postrio,

designed geometric mahogany furniture, sponge-painted or diamond-patterned walls, original artwork by Chris Kidd, and unusual tilework in the bathrooms. Each guest room reflects one of three basic configurations: a king-size bed with camelback upholstered headboards, similar double beds, or oversized daybeds that double as a couch. Imaginative guest suites include the kaleidoscopic J. Garcia suite, furnished with swirls of colorful fabrics and a self-portrait of Jerry next to the bed. All rooms include soundproof windows, same-day valet/laundry service, room service, color TV with remote (also cable and movie channels), in-room fax, voice mail, and two-line phones with long cords and dataports. Basic rates: $159-179, $229-305 for deluxe rooms and suites. A nice feature of this and other Klimpton-owned hotels, too, is the fully stocked honor bar—unusual in that items are quite reasonably priced. For more information or reservations, contact: Hotel Triton, 342 Grant Ave., San Francisco, CA 94108, tel. (415) 394-0500 or toll-free (800) 433-6611, www.hotel-tritonsf.com.

Affordable style is apparent and available at other small San Francisco hotels, including Klimpton's Prescott Hotel, home to Wolfgang Puck's Postrio Restaurant. But there's nothing else in town quite like Haight-Ashbury's **Red Victorian Bed and Breakfast Inn,** a genuine blast from San Francisco's past. This 1904 survivor is red, all right, and it's a bed and breakfast—but except for the architecture, it's not very Victorian. The style is early-to-late Summer of Love. Downstairs is the Global Village Bazaar, a New Age shopper's paradise. (The Global Family

also offers a coffee house, computer networking services, meditation room, and gallery of meditative art with calligraphic paintings to help you program yourself, subliminally and otherwise, with proper consciousness.) Everything is casual and *very cool*—just two blocks from Golden Gate Park and its many attractions.

Upstairs, the Red Victorian's 18 guest rooms range from modest to decadent, with sinks in all rooms; some have private baths, others share. (If you stay in a room that shares the Aquarium Bathroom, you'll be able to answer the question: "What happens to the goldfish when you flush the toilet?") The Summer of Love Room features genuine '60s posters on the walls and a tie-dyed canopy over the bed. The Peace Room has an unusual skylight, though the Skylight Room beats the band for exotica. Or get back to nature in the Japanese Tea Garden Room, the Conservatory, or the Redwood Forest Room. Expanded continental breakfast (with granola and fresh bakery selections) and afternoon popcorn hour are included in the rates, which range from $75-120 (with specials if you stay over three days, two-night minimum on weekends). Spanish, German, and French spoken. No smoking, no pets, and leave your angst outside on the sidewalk. Well-behaved children under parental supervision are welcome. Make reservations for a summer stay well in advance. For more information, contact: The Red Victorian Bed and Breakfast Inn, 1665 Haight St., San Francisco, CA 94117, tel. (415) 864-1978, www.redvic.com.

personal concierge service, and even stationary bicycles and rowers delivered to your room on request. Luxury ($185-215, suites run $235-255).

Among other exceptional small hostelries in the vicinity of Union Square is the wheelchair-accessible, 80-room **Warwick Regis Hotel,** 490 Geary St., tel. (415) 928-7900 or toll-free (800) 827-3447 in the U.S. and Canada, www.warwickregis.com, furnished with French and English antiques and offering exceptional service. Amenities include hair dryers and small refrigerators in every room, plus cable TV, complimentary morning newspaper, and on-site café and bar. Premium-Luxury ($135-205). Another best bet, and a bargain for the quality, is the

Chancellor Hotel, 433 Powell (on Union Square), tel. (415) 362-2004 or toll-free (800) 428-4748, www.chancellorhotel.com, offering elegant rooms within walking distance of just about everything. (Or hop the cable car.) Expensive-Luxury ($100-230). Truly exceptional is **The Donatello,** 501 Post St. (at Mason, a block west of Union Square), tel. (415) 441-7100 or toll-free (800) 227-3184 in the U.S. and Canada, noteworthy for its four-star amenities and its restaurant, **Zingari** (tel. 415-885-8850). Luxury ($189-210). Quite refined, too, with the feel of a fine residential hotel, is **Campton Place Hotel,** 340 Stockton St. (just north of Union Square), tel. (415) 781-5555 or toll-free (800) 235-4300 in

California, (800) 426-3135 in U.S. and Canada. The hotel has all the amenities, including the superb, critically acclaimed (and AAA five diamond) **Campton Place Restaurant** featuring impeccable contemporary American cuisine (tel. 415-955-5555). Luxury ($230-345).

Other Areas

North of Market at the edge of the Financial District is the **Galleria Park Hotel,** 191 Sutter (between Montgomery and Kearny), tel. (415) 781-3060 or toll-free (800) 792-9639, www.galleriapark.com, its striking art nouveau lobby with crystal skylight still somehow overshadowed by the curvaceous, equally original sculpted fireplace. Amenities include attractive rooms with soundproofed windows and walls, meeting facilities, on-site parking, a rooftop park and jogging track, and athletic club access. Dine at adjacent **Perry's** restaurant. Luxury ($169-325).

The Embarcadero YMCA south of Market near the Ferry Building now shares the waterfront building with the **Harbor Court Hotel,** 165 Steuart St. (at Mission), tel. (415) 882-1300 or toll-free (800) 346-0555, www.harborcourthotel.com, a fairly phenomenal transformation at the edge of the financial district and a perfect setup for business travelers. The building's Florentine exterior has been beautifully preserved, as have the building's original arches, columns, and vaulted ceilings. Inside, the theme is oversized, Old World creature comfort. The plush rooms are rich with amenities, including TV, radio, direct-dial phones with extra-long cords, and complimentary beverages. The penthouse features a Louis XVI-style bed and 18-foot ceilings. Business travelers will appreciate the hotel's business center, financial district limo service, and same-day valet laundry service. And to work off the stress of that business meeting, head right next door to the renovated multilevel YMCA, where recreational facilities include basketball courts, aerobics classes, an Olympic-size pool, whirlpool, steam room, dry sauna, and even stationary bicycles with a view. Rates include complimentary continental breakfast and valet parking. Luxury ($220 for a Bay view room, $205 Courtyard room, specials as low as $175). Affiliated Victorian saloon-style Harry Denton's Bar & Grill here has predictably good food and becomes a lively dance club/bar scene after 10 p.m.

Adjacent and also worthwhile is the **Hotel Griffon,** 155 Steuart St. (at Mission), tel. (415) 495-2100 or toll-free (800) 321-2201 in the U.S. and Canada, www.hotelgriffon.com, with amenities like continental breakfast, complimentary morning newspaper, and a fitness center. Luxury ($220-270).

Two blocks from Pier 39 at Fisherman's Wharf, the **Tuscan Inn,** 425 North Point, tel. (415) 561-1100 or toll-free (800) 648-4626, though part of the Best Western hotel chain, has been reinvented by hotelier Bill Kimpton. The hotel features an Italianate lobby with fireplace, a central garden court, and 221 rooms and suites with modern amenities. Rates include morning coffee, tea, and biscotti, and a daily wine hour by the lobby fireplace. Premium-Luxury ($118-228). Just off the lobby is a convenient Italian trattoria, Cafe Pescatore, specializing in fresh fish and seafood, pastas, and pizzas (baked in a wood-burning oven) at lunch and dinner. Open for breakfast also.

Near Civic Center cultural attractions is the exceptional small **Inn at the Opera,** 333 Fulton, tel. (415) 863-8400 or toll-free (800) 325-2708, featuring complimentary breakfast and morning newspaper, in-room cookies and apples, free shoeshine service, available limousine service, and an excellent on-site restaurant, **Ovation.** The guest list often includes big-name theater people. Rooms were immaculately refurbished in 1999. Premium-Luxury (singles $140, doubles $180).

In Pacific Heights, west of Van Ness and south of Lombard, the **Sherman House,** 2160 Green St. (between Fillmore and Webster), tel. (415) 563-3600, is among the city's finest small, exclusive hotels. Once the mansion of Leander Sherman, it now attracts inordinate percentages of celebrities and stars. The ambience here, including the intimate dining room, exudes 19th-century French opulence. Luxury ($305-415). In the same neighborhood is a somewhat cheaper option for a "boutique stay": the **Laurel Inn,** 444 Presidio Avenue (at California), tel. (415) 567-8467 or toll-free (800) 552-8735, www.thelaurelinn.com. Comfortable if a bit trendy—in 1960s' style—and within walking distance of the Presidio, the Laurel features 49 rooms, eighteen with kitchenettes. Ask about their pet-friendly policy. Premium ($120-150).

TOP OF THE LINE HOTELS

In addition to the fine hotels mentioned above, San Francisco offers an impressive selection of large, four- and five-star superdeluxe hotels. The air in these establishments is rarefied indeed. (Sometimes the airs, too.) Many, however, do offer seasonal specials. Business-oriented hotels often feature lower weekend rates.

The Ritz

Peek into **The Ritz-Carlton, San Francisco,** 600 Stockton (between California and Pine), tel. (415) 296-7465 or toll-free (800) 241-3333, www.ritzcarlton.com, to see what a great facelift an old lady can get for $140 million. Quite impressive. And many consider the hotel's Dining Room at The Ritz-Carlton among the city's finest eateries. (For more information, see special topic Puttin' on the Ritz.) Luxury (singles and doubles run $335-385, suites $525-3,500).

The Palace

Equally awesome—and another popular destination these days for City Guides and other walking tours—is that grande dame of San Francisco hostelries, the recently renovated and resplendent 1909 Sheraton Palace Hotel, 2 New Montgomery St. (downtown at Market), tel. (415) 512-1111 or toll-free (800) 325-3535, www.sfpalace.com. Wander in, under the metal grillwork awning at the New Montgomery entrance, across the polished marble sunburst on the foyer floor, and sit a spell in the lobby to appreciate the more subtle aspects of this $150 million renovation. Then mosey into the central Garden Court restaurant. The wonderful lighting here is provided, during the day, by the (cleaned and restored) 1800s atrium skylight, one of the world's largest leaded-glass creations; some 70,000 panes of glass arch over the entire room. It's a best bet for Sunday brunch. Note, too, the 10 (yes, 10) 700-pound crystal chandeliers. The Pied Piper Bar, with its famous Maxfield Parrish mural, is a Palace fixture, and adjoins **Maxfield's**

PUTTIN' ON THE RITZ

Serious visiting fans of San Francisco, at least those with serious cash, tend to equate their long-running romance with a stay on Nob Hill, home base for most of the city's ritzier hotels. And what could be ritzier than the Ritz?

The Ritz-Carlton, San Francisco, 600 Stockton at California St., tel. (415) 296-7465 or toll-free (800) 241-3333, www.ritzcarlton.com, is a local landmark, San Francisco's finest remaining example of neoclassical architecture. At the financial district's former western edge, and hailed in 1909 as a "temple of commerce," until 1973 the building served as West Coast headquarters for the Metropolitan Life Insurance Company. Expanded and revised five times since, San Francisco's Ritz has been open for business as a hotel only since 1991. After painstaking restoration (four years and $140 million worth), this nine-story grande dame still offers some odd architectural homage to its past. Witness the terra-cotta tableau over the entrance: the angelic allegorical figure ("Insurance") is protecting the American family. (Ponder the meaning of the lion's heads and winged hourglasses on your own.)

The Ritz offers a total of 336 rooms and suites, most with grand views. Amenities on the top two floors ("The Ritz-Carlton Club") include private lounge, continuous complimentary meals, and Dom Perignon and Beluga caviar every evening. All rooms, however, feature Italian marble bathrooms, in-room safes, and every modern comfort, plus access to the fitness center (indoor swimming pool, whirlpool, training room, separate men's and women's steam rooms and saunas, massage, and more). Services include the usual long list plus morning newspaper, child care, VCR and video library, car rental, and multilingual staff. Rates run $335-385 for rooms, $525-3,500 for suites. (The Ritz-Carlton's "Summer Escape" package, when available, includes a deluxe guest room, continental breakfast, valet parking, and unlimited use of the fitness center.) The Ritz-Carlton also provides full conference facilities. **The Courtyard** restaurant here offers the city's only alfresco dining in a hotel setting—like eating breakfast, lunch, or dinner on someone else's well-tended garden patio. (Come on Sunday for brunch—and jazz.) Adjacent, indoors, is somewhat casual **The Restaurant.** More formal, serving neoclassical cuisine, is **The Dining Room.**

restaurant. Tours of the hotel are available; call for schedules and information.

In addition to plush accommodations (rooms still have high ceilings), the Palace offers complete conference and meeting facilities, a business center, and a rooftop fitness center. The swimming pool up there, under a modern vaulted skylight, is especially enjoyable at sunset; spa services include a poolside whirlpool and dry sauna. Luxury (rooms $255-320, suites $760-2,800).

The St. Francis

Another beloved San Francisco institution is the Westin St. Francis Hotel, 335 Powell St. (between Post and Geary, directly across from Union Square), tel. (415) 397-7000 or toll-free (800) 228-3000, www.westin.com, a recently restored landmark recognized by the National Trust for Historic Preservation as one of the Historic Hotels of America. When the first St. Francis opened in 1849 at Clay and Dupont (Grant), it was considered the only hostelry at which ladies were safe, and was also celebrated as the first "to introduce bedsheets to the city." But San Francisco's finest was destroyed by fire four years later. By the early 1900s, reincarnation was imminent when a group of local businessmen declared their intention to rebuild the St. Francis as "a caravansary worthy of standing at the threshhold of the Occident, representative of California hospitality." No expense was spared on the stylish 12-story hotel overlooking Union Square—partially opened but still under construction when the April 18, 1906, earthquake and fire hit town. Damaged but not destroyed, the restored St. Francis opened in November 1907; over the entrance was an electrically lighted image of a phoenix rising from the city's ashes. Successfully resurrected, the elegant and innovative hotel attracted royalty, international political and military leaders, theatrical stars, and literati.

But even simpler folk have long been informed, entertained, and welcomed by the St. Francis. People keep an eye on the number of unfurled flags in front of the St. Francis, for example, knowing that these herald the nationalities of visiting dignitaries. And every long-time San Franciscan knows that any shiny old coins in their pockets most likely came from the St. Francis; the hotel's long-standing practice of washing coins—to prevent them from soiling ladies' white

gloves—continues to this day. Meeting friends "under the Clock" means the Magneta Clock in the hotel's Powell St. lobby, this "master clock" from Saxony a fixture since the early 1900s.

Both the Tower and Powell St. lobbies were freshened up by 1991 restorations. Highlights include three 40-foot trompe l'oeil murals by Carlo Marchiori depicting turn-of-the-century San Francisco, new inlaid marble floors and central carpet, and gold-leaf laminate applied to the ornate woodwork in the Powell St. lobby. Restoration of the original building's Colusa sandstone facade was finished in 1997.

After additions and renovations, the St. Francis today offers 1,200 luxury guest rooms and suites (request a suite brochure if you hanker to stay in the General MacArthur suite, the Queen Elizabeth II suite, or the Ron and Nancy Reagan suite), plus fitness and full meeting and conference facilities, a 1,500-square-foot ballroom, five restaurants (including elegant Victor's atop the St. Francis Tower), shopping arcade, valet parking. Luxury (rooms $255-320, suites $760-2,800).

Others Downtown

The **Clift Hotel,** 495 Geary St. (at Taylor), tel. (415) 775-4700 or toll-free (800) 652-5438, www.clifthotel.com, is a five-star midsize hotel offering every imaginable comfort and service, including free Financial District limo service, transportation to and from the airport (for a fee), and a good on-site restaurant. Luxury ($240-1,260).

Also within easy reach of downtown doings is the sleek, modern, four-star **Pan Pacific Hotel,** 500 Post St. (at Mason, one block west of Union Square), tel. (415) 771-8600, toll-free (800) 533-6465 or (800) 327-8585, www.panpac.com. The business-oriented Pan Pacific offers three phones with call waiting in each room, personal computers delivered to your room upon request, notary public and business services, and Rolls Royce shuttle service to the Financial District. It's also luxurious; bathrooms, for example, feature floor-to-ceiling Breccia marble, artwork, a mini-screen TV, and a telephone. Luxury ($199-309). "The Pampering Weekend" special starts at $139 and includes breakfast in your room or at the third-floor **Pacific** restaurant (California-fusion cuisine), tel. (415) 929-2087.

Other worthy downtown possibilities include the contemporary Japanese-style **Hotel Nikko,** 222

Mason, tel. (415) 394-1111 or toll-free (800) 645-5687, www.nikkohotels.com, which boasts a glass-enclosed rooftop pool (Luxury—$195-255); the **San Francisco Hilton,** 333 O'Farrell (at Mason), tel. (415) 771-1400 or toll-free (800) 445-8667, www.hilton.com, the city's largest with almost 2,000 rooms and suites (Luxury—$185-205); and the 1,000-room **Renaissance Parc 55 Hotel,** 55 Cyril Magnin St. (Market at Fifth), tel. (415) 392-8000 or toll-free (800) 697-3103. (Luxury—$205-285, though inquire about special offers).

The exquisite **Mandarin Oriental San Francisco,** 222 Sansome, tel. (415) 276-9888, (415) 885-0999, or toll-free (800) 622-0404, www.mandarin-oriental.com, is housed in the top 11 floors of the California First Interstate Building in the financial district. The 160 rooms boast great views (even from the bathrooms) and all the amenities, including wonderful **Silks** restaurant, tel. (415) 986-2020. Luxury (rooms $295-520, suites $800-1,650). The **Hyatt Regency San Francisco,** 5 Embarcadero Center (Market and California), tel. (415) 788-1234 or toll-free (800) 233-1234, www.hyatt.com, is famous for its 17-story lobby, atrium, and rotating rooftop restaurant, **The Equinox.** Luxury (standard rooms, with city view, $255-285; deluxe rooms, with bay view, $285-315). There are Hyatts all over San Francisco, including the nearby Park Hyatt on Battery—home of the outstanding Park Grill, tel. (415) 296-2933—plus those at Union Square, Fisherman's Wharf, and out at the airport in Burlingame; a toll-free call can reserve a room at any and all.

Other comfortable hotel choices near the financial district and the booming new media companies south of Market include the superstylish, granite-faced **W Hotel,** 181 Third St. (at Howard), tel. (415) 777-5300 or toll-free (877) 946-8357, www.whotels.com, which is as sleek as its next-door neighbor, the San Francisco Museum of Modern Art. This business-oriented hotel also offers boutique touches: plush down comforters and Aveda bath products in all rooms. Downstairs, the XYZ restaurant and bar serves creative fusion cuisine. Luxury (starting at $175). Also in the area are the **San Francisco Marriott,** 55 Fourth St., tel. (415) 896-1600 or toll-free (800) 228-9290, www.marriott.com, south of Market and just north of the Moscone Convention Center (Luxury—$199-295); and the nearby **Argent Hotel,** 50 Third St., tel. (415) 974-6400 or toll-free (877) 222-6699, www.destinationtravel.com (Luxury—starting at $220).

Nob Hill

Some of the city's finest hotels cluster atop Nob Hill. Since judgment always depends upon personal taste, despite official ratings it's all but impossible to say which is "the best." Take your pick.

Across from Grace Cathedral and Huntington Park, the **Huntington Hotel,** 1075 California St. (at Taylor), tel. (415) 474-5400 or toll-free (800) 652-1539 in California, (800) 227-4683 from elsewhere in the U.S., www.huntingtonhotel.com, is the last surviving family-owned fine hotel in the neighborhood. It's a beauty, a destination in and of itself. Every room and suite (one-time residential apartments) has been individually designed and decorated, and every service is a personal gesture. Stop in just to appreciate the elegant lobby restoration. Dark and clubby, and open daily for breakfast, lunch, and dinner, the **Big Four Restaurant** off the lobby pays pleasant homage to the good ol' days of Wild West railroad barons—and often serves wild game entrées along with tamer continental contemporary cuisine. Luxury ($190-260).

Top-of-the-line, too, is the romantic, turn-of-the-century **Fairmont Hotel,** 950 Mason St. (at California), tel. (415) 772-5000 or toll-free (800) 527-4727, www.fairmont.com, noted for its genuine grandeur and grace. The Fairmont offers 596 rooms (small to large) and suites, all expected amenities, and several on-site restaurants. For a panoramic Bay Area view at Sunday brunch, the place to go is the hotel's **Crown Room** atop the hotel's Tower section. Locally loved, too, however, are the hotel's **Mason's,** for steak and seafood (also open for breakfast), and the Tiki-inspired **Tonga Room,** which specializes in Chinese and Polynesian cuisine and features a simulated tropical rainstorm every half hour. The Fairmont also offers full conference and business facilities (20 meeting rooms) and the Nob Hill Club (extra fee) for fitness enthusiasts. Luxury ($229 and up).

The five-star **Renaissance Stanford Court Hotel,** 905 California St. (at Powell), tel. (415) 989-3500 or toll-free (800) 468-3571, www.renaissancehotels.com, boasts a 120-foot-long, sepia-toned lobby mural honoring San Francisco's historic diversity. On the west wall, for example, are panels depicting the hotel's predecessor, the original Leland Stanford Mansion, with railroad barons and other wealthy Nob Hill nabobs on one side, Victorian-era African Americans on the other. Other panels depict the long-running economic exploitation of California places and peoples, from Russian whaling and fur trading, redwood logging, and the California gold rush (with Native Americans and the Chinese looking on) to the 1906 earthquake and fire framed by the construction of the transcontinental railroad and California's Latinization, as represented by Mission Dolores. Stop in and see it; this is indeed the story of Northern California, if perhaps a bit romanticized.

The hotel itself is romantic, recognized by the National Trust for Historic Preservation as one of the Historic Hotels of America. The Stanford Court features a decidedly European ambience, from the carriage entrance (with beaux arts fountain and stained-glass dome) to guest rooms decked out in 19th-century artwork, antiques, and reproductions (not to mention modern comforts like heated towel racks in the marble bathrooms and dictionaries on the writing desks). Opulent touches in the lobby include Baccarat chandeliers, Carrara marble floor, oriental carpets, original artwork, and an 1806 antique grandfather clock once owned by Napoleon Bonaparte. Guest services include complimentary stretch limo service, both for business and pleasure. Luxury ($235-315). Even if you don't stay, consider a meal (breakfast, lunch, and dinner daily, plus weekend brunch) at the hotel's Mediterranean-inspired restaurant, **Fournou's Ovens,** tel. (415) 989-1910 for reservations, considered one of San Francisco's best.

Don't forget the Mark Hopkins Hotel, now the **Mark Hopkins Inter-Continental,** 1 Nob Hill (California and Mason), tel. (415) 392-3434 or toll-free (800) 327-0200, www.interconti.com, another refined Old California old-timer. Hobnobbing with the best of them atop Nob Hill, the Mark Hopkins features 391 elegant guest rooms (many with great views) and all the amenities, not to mention the fabled **Top of the Mark** sky room, still San Francisco's favorite sky-high romantic bar scene. The French-California **Nob Hill Restaurant** is open daily for breakfast, lunch, and dinner. Luxury ($220-340).

CITY-STYLE BED AND BREAKFASTS

With most of San Francisco's European-style and boutique hotels offering breakfast and other homey touches, and many of the city's bed and breakfasts offering standard hotel services (like concierge, bellman, valet/laundry, and room service), it's truly difficult to understand the difference.

The eight-room **Chateau Tivoli** townhouse, 1057 Steiner St., tel. (415) 776-5462 or toll-free (800) 228-1647, is an 1892 Queen Anne landmark with an astounding visual presence. "Colorful" just doesn't do justice as a description of this Alamo Square painted lady. The Tivoli's eccentric exterior architectural style is electrified by 18 historic colors of paint, plus gold leaf. Painstaking restoration is apparent inside, too, from the very Victorian, period-furnished parlors to exquisite, individually decorated guest rooms, each reflecting at least a portion of the city's unusual social history. (Imagine, under one roof: Enrico Caruso, Aimee Crocker, Isadora Duncan, Joaquin Miller, Jack London, opera singer Luisa Tettrazini, and Mark Twain. Somehow, it is imaginable, since the mansion was once the residence of the city's pre-earthquake Tivoli Opera.) Chateau Tivoli offers nine rooms and suites, all but two rooms with private baths, two with fireplaces. Premium-Luxury ($110-250).

One-time home to Archbishop Patrick Riordan, the **Archbishop's Mansion,** 1000 Fulton St. (at Steiner), tel. (415) 563-7872 or toll-free (800) 543-5820, is also exquisitely restored, offering comfortable rooms and suites in a French Victorian mood. Some rooms have fireplaces and in-room spas, and all have phones and TV. Continental breakfast. Luxury ($159-419).

Also close to the Civic Center arts scene is the **Inn San Francisco,** 943 S. Van Ness Ave., tel. (415) 641-0188 or toll-free (800) 359-0913, www.innsf.com, a huge, renovated 1872 Italianate Victorian with 21 guest rooms, double parlors, and a sun deck. The five bargain rooms here share two bathrooms, but most rooms feature private baths. All include TV, radio, telephone, and refrigerator; some have a hot tub or in-room spa tub; and two also have a fireplace and balcony. Expensive-Luxury ($85-235). Another Victorian option, this one near Alamo

SAN FRANCISCO CONVENTION AND VISITORS BUREAU/CAROL SIMOWITZ

You'll find a number of bed-and-breakfast inns near historic Alamo Square.

Square, is the **Grove Inn,** 890 Grove St., tel. (415) 929-0780, a restored Italianate Victorian with 19 rooms (some share baths). Off-street parking available for a small fee. Complimentary breakfast. Expensive-Premium. The **Alamo Square Inn,** 719 Scott St., tel. (415) 922-2055 or toll-free (800) 345-9888, www.alamoinn.com, is another neighborhood possibility, offering rooms and suites in an 1895 Queen Anne and an 1896 Tudor Revival. Expensive-Premium.

Petite Auberge, 863 Bush St. (near Nob Hill and Union Square), tel. (415) 928-6000, is an elegant French country inn right downtown, featuring Pierre Deux fabrics, terra-cotta tile, oak furniture, and lace curtains. All 26 guest rooms here have private bathrooms; 16 have fireplaces. The "Petite Suite" has its own entrance and deck, a king-size bed, fireplace, and jacuzzi. Premium-Luxury ($110-225). Two doors down is the affiliated **White Swan Inn,** 845 Bush, tel. (415) 775-1755, with parlor, library, and 26 rooms (private baths, fireplaces, wet bars) dec-

orated with English-style decorum, from the mahogany antiques and rich fabrics to floral-print wallpapers. Premium-Luxury ($145-250). Both these inns serve full breakfast (with the morning paper), afternoon tea, and homemade cookies, and provide little amenities like thick terry bathrobes. All rooms have TV and telephone.

Close to the Presidio and Fort Mason in Cow Hollow is the **Edward II Inn,** 3155 Scott St. (at Lombard), tel. (415) 922-3000 or toll-free (800) 473-2846, an English-style country hotel and pub offering 24 rooms and six suites, all with color TV and phone, some with shared bathrooms. The suites have in-room whirlpool baths. A complimentary continental breakfast is served. Moderate-Expensive.

Peaceful and pleasant amid the hubbub of North Beach is the stylish and artsy 15-room **Hotel Bohème,** 444 Columbus Ave., tel. (415) 433-9111, offering continental charm all the way to breakfast, which is served either indoors or out on the patio. On-site restaurant, too. Premium (a good deal). Also in North Beach is the French country **Washington Square Inn,** 1660 Stockton St., tel. (415) 981-4220 or toll-free (800) 388-0220, featuring 15 rooms (most with private bath), continental breakfast, and afternoon tea. Premium-Luxury ($125-210).

Near Lafayette Park in Pacific Heights and something of a cause célèbre is **The Mansions,** 2220 Sacramento St., tel. (415) 929-9444 or toll-free (800) 826-9398, www.themansions.com, an elegant bed-and-breakfast-style hotel composed of two adjacent historic mansions filled with art. The 28 rooms and suites here are opulent and feature telephones, private bathrooms, and numerous amenities. Stroll the Bufano sculpture gardens, play billiards, or attend nightly music concerts or magic shows. Full breakfast is served every morning, in the dining area or in your room, and dinners are also available. Premium-Luxury ($139-250).

Not a B&B per se, but providing as intimate a lodging experience as you'll get, **Dockside Boat & Bed,** Pier 39, tel. (415) 392-5526 or toll-free (800) 436-2574, www.boatandbed.com, contracts a stable of luxury yachts, both motor and sail, on which guests can spend the night. Luxury ($165-270).

SAN FRANCISCO CONVENTION AND VISITORS BUREAU/DAWN STRANNE

EATING IN SAN FRANCISCO

San Franciscans love to eat. For a true San Franciscan, eating—and eating well—competes for first place among life's purest pleasures, right up there with the arts, exercising, and earning money. (There may be a few others.) Finding new and novel neighborhood eateries, and knowing which among the many fine dining establishments are currently at the top of the trendsetters' culinary A-list, are points of pride for long-time residents. Fortunately, San Franciscans also enjoy sharing information and opinions—including their restaurant preferences. So the best way to find out where to eat, and why, is simply to ask. The following listings should help fine-food aficionados get started, and will certainly keep everyone else from starving.

UNION SQUARE AND NOB HILL

A well-kept secret, perhaps downtown's best breakfast spot, is **Dottie's True Blue Cafe,** 522 Jones St., tel. (415) 885-2767, a genuine all-American coffee shop serving every imaginable American standard plus new cuisine, such as (at lunch) grilled eggplant sandwiches. Open daily for breakfast and lunch only, 7 a.m.-2 p.m. But those in the know say you haven't "done" the city until you've ordered breakfast—specifically, the 18 Swedish pancakes—at **Sears Fine Foods,** 439 Powell (at Post), tel. (415) 986-1160, a funky, friendly old-time San Francisco café.

Another area classic, if for other reasons, is **John's Grill,** 63 Ellis (just off Powell), tel. (415) 986-3274 or (415) 986-0069, with a neat neon sign outside and *Maltese Falcon* memorabilia just about everywhere inside. (In the book, this is where Sam Spade ate his lamb chops.) Named a National Literary Landmark by the Friends of Libraries, USA, this informal eatery ode to Dashiell Hammett serves good continental-style American fare, plus large helpings of Hammett hero worship, especially upstairs in Hammett's Den and the Maltese Falcon Room. Open Mon.-Sat. for lunch and dinner; Sunday for dinner only. Live jazz nightly.

For excellent seafood, dive into the French provincial **Brasserie Savoy** at the Savoy Hotel, 580 Geary St. (at Jones), tel. (415) 441-8080, open for breakfast (until noon), dinner, and late supper. Gallic stodgy? *Mais, non!* How about a

COCKTAIL TIME

Sometimes you just need to cast out the flannel shirt and Dr. Martens and join what used to be known as the "jet set" to toast the high life. The following establishments offer a sample of that old San Francisco sparkle.

Entering the magnificent art-deco **Redwood Room,** 495 Geary St. (at Taylor) at the Clift Hotel, tel. (415) 775-4700, in the heart of the theater district and just two blocks from bustling Union Square, makes you feel like you've been transported to an earlier era. Romantic lighting, gleaming redwood walls, and a baby grand appeal to WASPy types and businesspeople in search of a quiet drink. And the drinks, especially martinis, are top-notch.

The **Tonga Room** at 950 Mason St. (between California and Sacramento), tel. (415) 772-5278, opened its exotic doors in 1945 inside the Fairmont Hotel—the lobby recognizable by American TV addicts as the one in the short-lived series *Hotel*—to bring the Pacific Islander theme to San Francisco. Polynesian decor and thatch-roofed huts surround a deep blue lake, where simulated tropical rainstorms hit every half hour. The lethal Bora Bora Horror tops the list of intriguing frozen cocktails, combining rum, banana liqueur, and Grand Marnier with a huge slice of pineapple. Rum also features in the Hurricane, lava bowl, and the Zombie. Happy hour offers the most economical visit possible. Normally pricey drinks cost $5, and you can graze on a buffet of edible treats (egg rolls, pot stickers, and dim sum) while listening to the house band's forgettable elevator music.

The drinkery at the **Top of the Mark,** 999 California St. (at Mason), tel. (415) 392-3434, is the city's most famous view lounge, an ideal place to take friends and dazzle them with the lights of San Francisco. Large windows take in a panorama of San Francisco's landmarks, from the Twin Peaks Tower to the Transamerica Pyramid and the Golden Gate Bridge. There's live music every night, and given the ritzy setting, a $7-10 cover charge doesn't seem all that steep. Classic cocktails—Manhattans, sidecars, and Martinis–are the libations of choice. The bar food is upscale and excellently prepared, with selections ranging from a Mediterranean platter to Beluga caviar.

The word "cocktail" practically whispers from behind the ruby red silk curtains at the glamorous **Starlight Room** at 450 Powell St. (between Post and Sutter), tel. (415) 395-8595, perched on the 21st floor of the 1928 Sir Francis Drake Hotel. Polished mahogany fixtures, luxurious furnishings, and a 360-degree view of the city make the Starlight Room one of the nicest cocktail experiences going. The spacious bar embraces the retro swing theme, and a mahogany dance floor and live music by Harry Denton's Starlight Orchestra attract young swing fans and older couples from out on the town. Light supper options range from pan-roasted crab cakes to oysters on the half-shell. All of this dazzle is surprisingly affordable, with a small evening cover charge and cocktails from $7-10.

—Pat Reilly

"Lobster Martini?" Or a fish soup described as "haunting" by one local food writer (perhaps she had one too many Lobster Martinis?).

Farallon, 450 Post (near Powell), tel. (415) 956-6969, might be *the* place in town for seafood. And the unique Pat Kuleto-designed interior might make you feel like you're under the sea, in an octopus's garden, perhaps. Look for such intriguing specialties as truffled mashed potatoes with crab and sea urchin sauce, or ginger-steamed salmon. Open for lunch Mon.-Sat. and for dinner nightly.

Two blocks from Union Square, **Oritalia,** 586 Bush St. (at Stockton), tel. (415) 782-8122, offers an eclectic menu mixing Asian, American, and Mediterranean cuisine. Try the signature tuna tartare on sticky rice cakes, perhaps, or the potato gnocchi with Maine lobster and asparagus. Open daily for dinner.

Puccini & Pinetti, 129 Ellis (at Cyril Magnin), tel. (415) 392-5500, is a beautifully designed Cal-Italian restaurant popular with theater crowds. Menu highlights include bruschetta with arugula and roasted garlic, smoked salmon pizzas, and risotto with charred leeks and wild mushrooms. Prices are surprisingly reasonable—most entrées run $10-15. Open for lunch and dinner.

Worth searching for downtown is **Cafe Claude,** 7 Claude Ln. (between Grant and Kearny, Bush and Sutter, just off Bush), tel. (415)

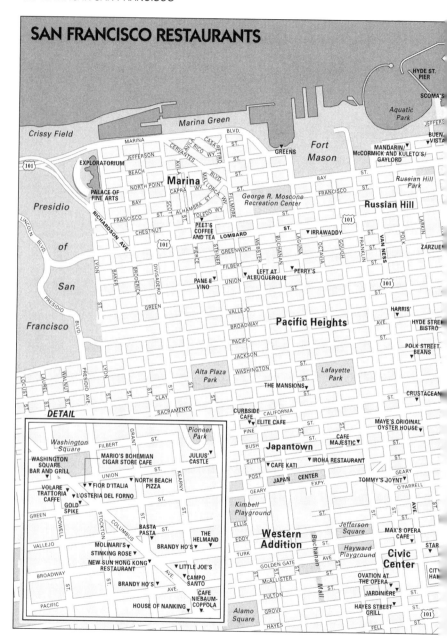

SAN FRANCISCO RESTAURANTS

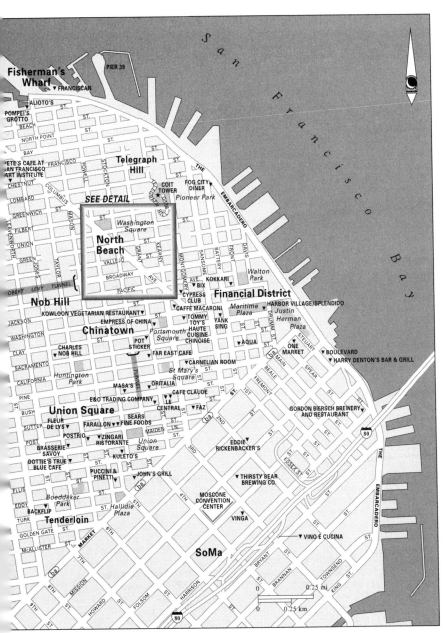

San Francisco Bay

Fisherman's Wharf
FRANCISCAN
PIER 39
ALIOTO'S
POMPEI'S GROTTO
PETE'S CAFE AT SAN FRANCISCO ART INSTITUTE

Telegraph Hill

COIT TOWER
FOG CITY DINER
Pioneer Park

SEE DETAIL
Washington Square
North Beach
VALLEJO

Nob Hill

KOKKARI
Walton Park
BIX
CYPRESS CLUB
Financial District
CAFFE MACARONI
HARBOR VILLAGE/SPLENDIDO
Maritime Plaza
Justin Herman Plaza
KOWLOON VEGETARIAN RESTAURANT
EMPRESS OF CHINA
TOMMY TOY'S HAUTE CUISINE CHINOISE
YANK SING
Chinatown
Portsmouth Square
POT STICKER
AQUA
ONE MARKET
BOULEVARD
HARRY DENTON'S BAR & GRILL
FAR EAST CAFE
CARNELIAN ROOM
St Mary's Square
MASA'S
ORITALIA
GORDON BIERSCH BREWERY AND RESTAURANT
E&O TRADING COMPANY
CAFE CLAUDE
LE CENTRAL
FAZ
Union Square
FLEUR DE LYS
FARALLON
SEARS FINE FOODS
POSTRIO
ZINGARI RISTORANTE
Union Square
EDDIE RICKENBACKER'S
BRASSERIE SAVOY
KULETO'S
DOTTIE'S TRUE BLUE CAFE
PUCCINI & PINETTI
JOHN'S GRILL
THIRSTY BEAR BREWING CO.
Boeddeker Park
MOSCONE CONVENTION CENTER
BACKFLIP
St Hallidie Plaza
Tenderloin
VINGA
VINO E CUCINA
SoMa

Huntington Park

0 0.25 mi
0 0.25 km

392-3505, an uncanny incarnation of a genuine French café, from the paper table covers to the café au lait served in bowls. Good food, plus live jazz four nights a week.

A good choice downtown for pasta is **Kuleto's**, 221 Powell St., tel. (415) 397-7720, a comfortable trattoria-style Italian restaurant and bar at the Villa Florence Hotel. It's popular for power lunching and dinner, and it's also open for peaceful, pleasant breakfasts.

Better yet, though, is **Zingari Ristorante**, 501 Post St. (at Mason, in the Donatello hotel), tel. (415) 885-8850, justifiably famous for its Northern Italian regional dishes. This premiere San Francisco restaurant, where the separate dining rooms are small and intimate, and dressing up is de rigueur, puts on a show as good as, or better than, almost anything else in the neighborhood.

People should at least pop into Wolfgang Puck's **Postrio**, 545 Post St. (at Mason, inside the Prescott Hotel), tel. (415) 776-7825, www.postrio.com, to appreciate the exquisite ribbon-patterned dining room designs by Pat Kuleto. The food here is exceptional, with most entrées representing Puck's interpretations of San Francisco classics. Since the restaurant is open for breakfast, lunch, and dinner, try Hangtown fry and some house-made pastries at breakfast, perhaps a pizza fresh from the woodburning oven or Dungeness crab with spicy curry risotto at lunch. Dinner is an adventure. Great desserts. Make reservations well in advance, or hope for a cancellation.

Famous among local foodies, not to mention its long-standing national and international fan club, is **Masa's**, 648 Bush St. (at the Hotel Vintage Court), tel. (415) 989-7154, one of the city's finest dinner restaurants and considered by many to be the best French restaurant in the United States. Masa's serves French cuisine with a fresh California regional touch and a Spanish aesthetic. Reservations accepted three weeks in advance. Very expensive.

Fleur de Lys, 777 Sutter (between Jones and Taylor), tel. (415) 673-7779, is another local legend—a fine French restaurant that also transcends the traditional. Nothing is too heavy or overdone. Everything is elegant and expensive. Open Mon.-Sat. for dinner. Reservations. Also on Sutter is the **E&O Trading Company,** 314 Sutter (between Stockton and Grant), tel. (415) 693-0303, which serves up Pacific Rim cuisine with flavors borrowed from all over Southeast Asia: small plates include Naan breads, satays, and Vietnamese rice paper rolls. The Dragon Bar offers tropical cocktails like Mai Tais and Singapore Slings, as well as house-made microbrews. An odd combination, perhaps, but it seems to work.

On Nob Hill, **Charles Nob Hill,** 1250 Jones St., tel. (415) 771-5400, is a neighborhood French restaurant featuring specialties like Hudson Valley foie gras and Sonoma duck. Open for dinner Tues.-Saturday. Some of the city's finest hotels, on Nob Hill and elsewhere, also serve some of the city's finest food.

THE FINANCIAL DISTRICT AND EMBARCADERO

One of the hottest haute spots for young refugees from the Financial District is the casual **Gordon Biersch Brewery and Restaurant,** 2 Harrison St., tel. (415) 243-8246, along the Embarcadero in the shadow of the Bay Bridge. The German-style lagers here are certainly a draw—three styles (Pilsner to Bavarian dark) are created on the premises—as is the surprisingly good food, which is far from the usual brewpub grub. Open from 11 a.m. daily. (Gordon Biersch also has outposts in Palo Alto and San Jose.)

Harry Denton's Bar & Grill, 161 Steuart St. (across from Rincon Center, inside the Harbor Court Hotel), tel. (415) 882-1333, is a great bar, restaurant (hearty American cuisine), and club, usually crowded as a sardine can after 5 p.m. The food is excellent. To hold a conversation, sink into a booth in the narrow dining room above the bar scene; to take in the great scenery, head for the back room (which doubles as a dance floor Thurs.-Sat. nights). Harry Denton's is open weekdays for lunch and nightly for dinner. Nearby **Boulevard,** 1 Mission St. (at Steuart), (415) 543-6084, is a Franco-American bistro serving American classics—ribs, pork chops, mashed 'taters—in an art nouveau atmosphere. Nice views. Open for lunch weekdays and dinner nightly. Also overlooking the Embarcadero is **One Market,** 1 Market St., tel. (415) 777-5577, featuring the best of seasonal fresh California ingredients in its upscale American specialties. Extensive wine list. Open for lunch weekdays and dinner Mon.-Saturday.

Art deco **Faz,** 161 Sutter (between Montgomery and Kearny), tel. (415) 362-0404, is an unstuffy but upscale place for pizza, pasta, and Mediterranean cuisine located in the Crocker Galleria shopping center. In the seafood swim of things, **Aqua,** 252 California St., tel. (415) 956-9662, is making a global splash among well-heeled foodies nationwide. Entrées include basil-grilled lobster, lobster potato gnocchi, and black-mussel soufflé. Open weekdays for lunch, Mon.-Sat. for dinner. **Le Central,** 453 Bush St., tel. (415) 391-2233, is a New York-style Parisian bistro and another power-lunching place par excellence.

At **Delancey Street Restaurant,** 600 Embarcadero, tel. (415) 512-5179, the restaurant staff is comprised of Delancey's drug, alcohol, and crime rehabilitees. The daily changing menu at this radical chic, sociopolitically progressive place is ethnic American—everything from matzo ball soup to pot roast. And there's a great view of Alcatraz from the outdoor dining area. Open for lunch, afternoon tea, and dinner.

On the 52nd floor of the Bank of America building, the **Carnelian Room,** 555 California St. (between Kearny and Montgomery), tel. (415) 433-7500, is the closest you'll get to dining in an airplane above the city. On a clear night, you can see all the way to Detroit. The menu is upscale American, with specialties including Dungeness crab cakes, rack of lamb, and Grand Marnier soufflé. **Yank Sing,** 427 Battery, tel. (415) 781-1111, is popular with the Financial District crowd and noteworthy for the shrimp dumplings in the shapes of goldfish and rabbits. (There's another Yank Sing at 49 Stevenson St. between First and Second Streets, tel. 415-541-4949.)

A good choice for Cantonese food is Hong Kong-style **Harbor Village,** 4 Embarcadero Center (at the corner of Clay and Drumm), tel. (415) 781-8833, serving everything from dim sum to Imperial banquets. Open daily for lunch and dinner. Straight upstairs (on the Promenade level), behind those old olive-wood doors, is splendid **Splendido,** tel. (415) 982-3222, a contemporary Mediterranean-style retreat for Italian-food fanatics. Everything here is fresh and house-made, from the breads and seafood soups to the pastas and unusual pizzas. Exceptional entrées include grilled swordfish and guinea hens roasted in the restaurant's wood-burning oven. Good wine list; save

some space for dessert. Open for lunch and dinner daily; the bar serves appetizers until closing (midnight). Alfresco dining available in summer.

CIVIC CENTER AND VICINITY

Backflip, 601 Eddy (near Larkin), tel. (415) 771-3547, serves up California cuisine in an aquatically inspired setting that sits poolside at the Phoenix Hotel, another beacon of style in the seedy Tenderloin. Fountains and lots of blue have you thinking "fish" from the get-go, and sure enough, seafood is the specialty here. At night, the house turns into a nightclub with DJ dancing.

Tommy's Joynt, 1101 Geary (at Van Ness), tel. (415) 775-4216, is a neighborhood institution—a hofbrau-style bar and grill boasting bright paint, a bizarre bunch of bric-a-brac, beers from just about everywhere, and a noteworthy pastrami sandwich. Farther north along Polk Gulch (roughly paralleling fairly level Polk St., from Post to Broadway) are abundant cafés, coffeehouses, and avant-garde junque and clothing shops. Worthwhile eateries include **Polk Street Beans,** 1733 Polk (at Clay), tel. (415) 776-9292, a funky Eurostyle coffeehouse serving good soups and sandwiches, and **Maye's Original Oyster House,** 1233 Polk, tel. (415) 474-7674, a remarkably reasonable Italian-style seafood restaurant that's been in business in San Francisco since 1867.

Tucked inside the Inn at the Opera, **Ovation at the Opera,** 333 Fulton St. (between Gough and Franklin), tel. (415) 305-8842 or (415) 553-8100, is a class act noted as much for its romantic charms as its fine French-Continental cuisine—a fitting finale for opera fans who have plenty of cash left to fan (this place is on the expensive side). Open nightly for dinner (until 10:30 or 11 p.m. Friday and Saturday nights).

Max's Opera Cafe, 601 Van Ness, tel. (415) 771-7300, also pitches itself to the neighborhood's more theatrical standards. Like Max's enterprises elsewhere, you can count on being served huge helpings of tantalizing all-American standards. At least at dinner, you can also count on the wait staff bursting into song—maybe opera, maybe a Broadway show tune. Open daily for lunch and dinner, until late (1 a.m.) on Friday and Saturday nights for the post-theater crowds.

Also by the Opera House is the elegant and superlative **Jardinière,** 300 Grove St. (at Franklin), tel. (415) 861-5555, a French restaurant created by the city's top restaurant designer and one of its top chefs. Open for lunch weekdays and for dinner nightly (late-night menu available after 10:30 p.m.).

The **Hayes Street Grill,** 320 Hayes (at Franklin), tel. (415) 863-5545, is a busy bistro serving some of the best seafood in town. Open weekdays for lunch, Mon.-Sat. for dinner.

Sometimes more like a moveable feast for fashion, judging from all the suits and suited skirts, the **Zuni Cafe,** 1658 Market (at Gough), tel. (415) 552-2522, is an immensely popular restaurant and watering hole noted for its Italian-French country fare in a Southwestern ambience. (Expensive.) Still yuppie central, even after all these years, is somewhat immodest, barn-sized **Stars,** 555 Golden Gate Ave. (between Van Ness and Polk), tel. (415) 861-7827. It's strictly reservations-only beyond the bar.

At Chelsea Square, **Crustacean,** 1475 Polk St. (at California), tel. (415) 776-2722, is another one of those cutting-edge eateries enjoyable for ambience as well as actual eats. This place serves exceptional Euro-Asian cuisine (specialty: roast crab) and looks like a fantasy home to those particularly crunchy critters, with underwater murals and giant seahorses, not to mention handblown glass fixtures and a 17-foot wave sculpture. Open for dinners only, nightly after 5 p.m.; valet parking, full bar, extensive wine list. Reservations preferred.

Near Japan Center, **Cafe Kati,** 1963 Sutter (near Fillmore), tel. (415) 775-7313, is one of those casual neighborhood places serving surprisingly good food. **Iroha Restaurant,** 1728 Buchanan (at Post), tel. (415) 922-0321, is a great inexpensive stop for noodles and Japanese standards.

CHINATOWN

To find the best restaurants in Chinatown, go where the Chinese go. Some of these places may look a bit shabby, at least on the outside, and may not take reservations—or credit cards.

But since the prices at small family-run enterprises are remarkably low, don't fret about leaving that plastic at home.

Very popular, and always packed, the **House of Nanking,** 919 Kearny (between Jackson and Columbus), tel. (415) 421-1429, has a great location at the foot of Chinatown on the North Beach border. At this tiny restaurant, diners often sit elbow to elbow, but the excellent food and reasonable prices make it well worth the wait.

For spicy Mandarin and the best pot stickers in town, try the **Pot Sticker,** 150 Waverly Place, tel. (415) 397-9985, open daily for lunch and dinner. Another Hunan hot spot is **Brandy Ho's,** 217 Columbus (at Pacific), tel. (415) 788-7527, and also at 450 Broadway (at Kearny), tel. (415) 362-6268, open daily from noon to midnight.

A great choice for Cantonese, the **Far East Cafe,** 631 Grant Ave., tel. (415) 982-3245, is a dark place lit by Chinese lanterns. Another possibility is the tiny turn-of-the-century **Hang Ah Tea Room,** 1 Pagoda Place (off Sacramento St.), tel. (415) 982-5686, specializing in Cantonese entrées and lunchtime dim sum. Inexpensive and locally infamous, due largely to the rude waiter routine of Edsel Ford Wong (now deceased), is three-story **Sam Woh,** 813 Washington St. (at Grant), tel. (415) 982-0596, where you can get good noodles, jook (rice gruel), and Chinese-style doughnuts (for dunking in your gruel).

Empress of China, 838 Grant Ave. (between Washington and Clay), tel. (415) 434-1345, offers a wide-ranging Chinese menu, elegant atmosphere, and great views of Chinatown and Telegraph Hill. They've been in business for three decades, so you know they're doing something right. Open daily for lunch and dinner.

Vegetarians will appreciate **Kowloon Vegetarian Restaurant,** 909 Grant Ave., tel. (415) 362-9888, which serves more than 80 meatless selections, including 20 types of vegetarian dim sum and entrées like sweet and sour or curried (faux) pork (with soybean and gluten substituting for meat). Open daily 9 a.m.-9 p.m.

Great Eastern Restaurant, 649 Jackson (between Grant and Kearny), tel. (415) 986-2500, is a relaxed family-style place serving good food at great prices. A best bet here is the fixed-price seafood banquet.

JACKSON SQUARE, NORTH BEACH, AND RUSSIAN HILL

In and Around Jackson Square

"Like the Flintstones on acid," one local food fan says of the almost indescribable style of the **Cypress Club,** 500 Jackson St. (at Montgomery), tel. (415) 296-8555. This popular restaurant near the Financial District is named after the nightclub in Raymond Chandler's *The Big Sleep.* Snide types say: "Très L.A." Others have called doing lunch or dinner here "like sitting under a table" (those huge columns could be table legs) or "like going to a very expensive, very garish, catered carnival." You enter through a copper door, then push past the blood-red velvet speakeasy curtain. Curvaceous copper sectional "pillows," something like overblown landscaping berms, frame the dining room and separate the booths. At table, you sink into plush burgundy mohair seats or pull up a clunky chair, then relax under the familiarity of the WPA-style Bay Area mural wrapping the walls near the ceiling. (Finally, something seems familiar.) Then you notice the odd polka-dotted light fixtures. If the atmosphere is stimulating, so is the food—simple French cuisine reinvented with fresh local ingredients. Matching the decor, desserts are tantalizing "architectural constructs." The wine list is remarkable—and safe, since the 14,000-bottle wine cellar is downstairs in an earthquake-proof room. The Cypress Club is open daily for dinner, Mon.-Sat. for lunch, and Sunday for brunch.

If that's not enough otherworldly ambience, head around the corner and down an alley to **Bix,** 56 Gold St. (between Jackson and Pacific, Montgomery and Sansome), tel. (415) 433-6300, a small supper club and bar with the feel of a 1940s-style film noir hideout. At Kearny and Columbus, you'll find movie-magnate-turned-winemaker Francis Ford Coppola's **Cafe Niebaum-Coppola,** 916 Kearny St., tel. (415) 291-1700, which offers an Italian menu and a good wine bar (serving, among other selections, Coppola's own vintages).

One of the country's best Greek restaurants is **Kokkari,** 200 Jackson St. (at Front), tel. (415) 981-0983. Open weekdays for lunch and Mon.-Sat. for dinner. While in the Montgomery-Washington Tower, **Tommy Toy's Haute Cuisine Chinoise,** 655 Montgomery St. (between Washington and Clay), tel. (415) 397-4888, serves up classical Chinese cuisine with traditional French touches, called "Frenchinoise" by Tommy Toy himself. The restaurant itself is impressive enough; it's patterned after the reading room of the Empress Dowager of the Ching Dynasty, and the rich decor includes priceless Asian art and antiques. Open for dinner nightly and for lunch on weekdays; reservations always advisable.

North Beach Proper

Farther north in North Beach proper, you'll find an almost endless selection of cafés and restaurants. Historically, this is the perfect out-of-the-way area to eat, drink good coffee, or just while away the hours. These days, North Beach is a somewhat odd blend of San Francisco's Beat-era bohemian nostalgia, new-world Asian attitudes, and other ethnic culinary accents. An example of the "new" North Beach: the **New Sun Hong Kong Restaurant,** 606 Broadway (at the sometimes-harmonic, very cosmopolitan cultural convergence of Grant, Broadway, and Columbus), tel. (415) 956-3338. Outside, marking the building, is a three-story-tall mural depicting the North Beach jazz tradition. But this is a very Chinatown eatery, open from early morning to late at night and specializing in hot pots and earthy, homey, San Francisco-style Chinese fare.

Also here are some of old San Francisco's most traditional traditions. The **Washington Square Bar and Grill,** 1707 Powell St. (at Union), tel. (415) 982-8123, is an immensely popular social stopoff for the city's cognoscenti—a place that also serves outstanding food with your conversation. The live jazz, too, is often worth writing home about. The venerable **Fior D'Italia,** 601 Union St. (at Stockton), tel. (415) 986-1886, established in 1886, is legendary for its ambience—including the Tony Bennett Room and the Godfather Room—and its historic ability to attract highbrow Italians from around the globe.

"Follow your nose" to the **Stinking Rose,** 325 Columbus (between Broadway and Vallejo), tel. (415) 781-7673, an exceptionally popular Italian restaurant where all the food is heavily doused in garlic. For exceptional food with a more elevated perspective, a dress-up restaurant on Telegraph Hill is appropriately romantic: **Julius' Castle,** 1541 Montgomery St. (north of Union), tel. (415) 392-2222, for French and Italian, and beautiful views of the city. Not that far away (along the Embarcadero), renowned for its fine food and flair, is the one and only **Fog City Diner,** 1300 Battery St. (at Lombard), tel. (415) 982-2000. Though this is the original gourmet grazing pasture, Fog City has its imitators around the world.

But the real North Beach is elsewhere. **Campo Santo,** 240 Columbus Ave. (between Pacific and Broadway), tel. (415) 433-9623, is yet another cultural change-up: Latin American kitsch kicking up its heels with campy Day of the Dead decor. The food is lively, too, from mahimahi tacos to crab quesadillas. Open Mon.-Sat. from lunchtime through dinner (until 10 p.m.). For genuine neighborhood tradition, head to stand-up **Molinari's,** 373 Columbus (between Broadway and Green), tel. (415) 421-2337, a fixture since 1907. It's a good deli stop for fresh pastas, homemade sauces, hearty sandwiches, and tasty sweet treats. Or stop off for a meatball sandwich or cappuccino at landmark **Mario's Bohemian Cigar Store Cafe,** 566 Columbus (near Washington Square), tel. (415) 362-0536. The inexpensive sandwiches, frittata, and cannelloni here are the main menu attraction, but folks also come to sip cappuccino or Campari while watching the world whirl by, or while watching each other watching. Sorry, they don't sell cigars.

"Rain or shine, there's always a line" at very-San Francisco **Little Joe's,** 523 Broadway (between Kearny and Columbus), tel. (415) 433-4343, a boisterous bistro where the Italian food is authentic, the atmosphere happy, and everyone hale and hearty. The open kitchen is another main attraction. For faster service, belly up to a counter stool and watch the chefs at work. Classic, too, especially with the lots-of-food-for-little-money set, is the casual **Basta Pasta,** 1268 Grant Ave., tel. (415) 434-2248, featur-

ing veal, fresh fish, and perfect calzones fresh out of the wood-burning oven.

Volare Trattoria Caffe, 561 Columbus (between Union and Green), tel. (415) 362-2774, offers superb Sicilian cuisine—try the exceptional calimari in tomato-garlic sauce. Owner Giovanni Zocca plants himself outside on Friday and Saturday nights and sings the restaurant's theme tune, "Volare, volare, volare, ho ho ho." The prohibition-era **Gold Spike,** 527 Columbus (near Green), tel. (415) 986-9747, also serves wonderful Italian fare. (Friday is crab cioppino night.) Just up the street is **L'Osteria del Forno,** 519 Columbus, tel. (415) 982-1124, a tiny storefront trattoria with six tables. This place is a great budget bet for its wonderful Italian flatbread sandwiches.

For pizza, the place to go is **North Beach Pizza,** 1499 Grant (at Union), tel. (415) 433-2444, where there's always a line, and it's always worth standing in. Heading down toward the Financial District, **Caffe Macaroni,** 59 Columbus (between Washington and Jackson), tel. (415) 956-9737, is also a true blue—well, red, white, and green—pasta house in the Tuscany tradition: intimate, aromatic, and friendly.

Exceptional for Afghan fare is **The Helmand,** 430 Broadway (between Keany and Montgomery), tel. (415) 362-0641. Here linguistics majors can enjoy ordering such dishes as *dwopiaza, bowlani,* and *sabzi challow.* Most entrées are oriented around lamb and beef, but vegetarian entrées are available and are separated out on the menu, making for easy selection.

Russian Hill

Zarzuela, 2000 Hyde St. (at Union, right on the Hyde/Powell cable-car route), tel. (415) 346-0800, offers its eponymous signature dish—a seafood stew—and other Spanish delicacies, including paella and assorted tapas. Open for dinner Tues.-Saturday. Another neighborhood possibility is the **Hyde Street Bistro,** 1521 Hyde St. (between Jackson and Pacific), tel. (415) 292-4415, one of those sophisticated little places where San Franciscans hide out during tourist season. It's quiet, not too trendy, and serves good French cuisine. Appreciate the breadsticks.

Ristorante Milano, 1448 Pacific Ave. (between Hyde and Larkin), tel. (415) 673-2961, is a happy, hopping little Italian restaurant with pastas—do try the lasagna—fresh fish, and sometimes surprising specials.

Not far away and a real deal for foodies who don't care one whit about the frills is **Pete's Cafe at San Francisco Art Institute,** 800 Chestnut St. (at Jones), tel. (415) 749-4567, where you can get a great lunch for $5 or less, along with one of the city's best bay views. The atmosphere is arty and existential, with paper plates and plastic utensils just to remind you that this is for students. Everything is fresh and wholesome: Southwestern black bean/vegetable stew, white bean and escarole soup, even house-roasted turkey sandwiches. Good breakfasts, too. Open in summer Mon.-Fri. 9 a.m.-2 p.m., and during the school year Mon.-Fri. 8 a.m.-9 p.m., Saturday 9 a.m.-2 p.m. (hours can vary; it's best to call ahead).

FISHERMAN'S WHARF AND GHIRARDELLI SQUARE

Fisherman's Wharf is both tourist central and seafood central. Most locals wouldn't be caught dead eating at one of the Wharf's many seafood restaurants—but that doesn't mean the food isn't good here. Pick of the litter is probably **Scoma's,** on Pier 47 (walk down the pier from the intersection of Jefferson and Jones Streets), tel. (415) 771-4383. It's just off the beaten path (on the lightly pummeled path) and therefore a tad quieter and more relaxing than the others—or at least it seems so. The others would include: **A. Sabella's,** 2766 Taylor St. (at Jefferson), tel. (415) 771-4416; **Alioto's,** 8 Fisherman's Wharf (at Jefferson), tel. (415) 673-0183; the **Franciscan,** Pier 43¹/₂, The Embarcadero, tel. (415) 362-7733; **Pompei's Grotto,** 340 Jefferson St. (near Jones), tel. (415) 776-9265; and a large number of places at Pier 39. You can get a decent bowl of clam chowder and a slab of sourdough bread at any of them.

Ghirardelli Square, 900 North Point (at Larkin), though technically part of the same Fisherman's Wharf tourist area, houses some fine restaurants patronized by locals even in broad daylight. The **Mandarin,** tel. (415) 673-8812, was the city's first truly palatial Chinese restaurant and the first to serve up spicy Szechuan and Hunan dishes. The food here is still great. Stop by at lunch for off-the-menu dim sum (including green onion pie, spring rolls with yellow chives, and sesame shrimp rolls), served 11:30 a.m.-3:30 p.m. daily, or come later for dinner. You won't go wrong for seafood at **McCormick and Kuleto's,** tel. (415) 929-1730, which features its own Crab Cake Lounge and 30 to 50 fresh specialties every day. Another much-loved Ghirardelli Square eatery is **Gaylord,** tel. (415) 771-8822, serving astounding Northern Indian specialties with a side of East Indies decor.

Elsewhere in the area, the Victorian-style **Buena Vista,** 2675 Hyde St. (at Beach), tel. (415) 474-5044, is notorious as the tourist bar that introduced Irish coffee. It's a great spot to share a table for breakfast or light lunch, and the waterfront views are almost free.

PACIFIC HEIGHTS, THE FILLMORE, AND THE MARINA DISTRICT

Perhaps San Francisco's most famous, most fabulous vegetarian restaurant is **Greens,** at Building A, Fort Mason (enter at Buchanan and Marina), tel. (415) 771-6222, where the hearty fare proves for all time that meat is an unnecessary ingredient for fine dining—and where the views are plenty appetizing, too. Open for lunch and dinner Tues.-Sat., and for brunch on Sunday; reservations always advised. The bakery counter is open Tues.-Sun. from 10 a.m. to midor late afternoon.

Left at Albuquerque, 2140 Union St. (at Fillmore in Cow Hollow), tel. (415) 749-6700, offers Southwestern ambience and an energetic, dining-and-drinking clientele. Modern-day Malcolm Lowrys could spend the rest of their tormented days here, sampling from among 100-plus types of tequila. (Stick with the 100% blue agave reposados.) Good food, too. Open daily for lunch and dinner.

For coffee and tasty pastries, an outpost of that Berkeley intellectual original **Peet's Coffee and Tea** is at 2156 Chestnut (between Pierce and Steiner), tel. (415) 931-8302. **Pane e Vino,** 3011 Steiner St. (at Union), tel. (415) 346-2111, is a justifiably popular neighborhood trattoria that's unpretentious and unwavering in its dedication to serving up grand, deceptively simple pastas. If you tire of privacy, head over to **Perry's,** 1944 Union (between Buchanan and Laguna), tel. (415) 922-9022, one of the city's ultimate see-and-be-seen scenes and a great burger stop.

Irrawaddy, 1769 Lombard St. (between Octavia and Laguna), tel. (415) 931-2830, is a good spot for Burmese cuisine. **Curbside Cafe,** 2417 California, tel. (415) 929-9030, specializes in flavorful delights from all over—France, Morocco, Mexico, and the Caribbean (the crab cakes are justifiably famous). **Lhasa Moon,** 2420 Lombard (at Scott), tel. (415) 674-9898, offers excellent, authentic Tibetan cuisine Thurs.-Fri. for lunch, and Tues.-Sun. for dinner.

Elite Cafe, 2049 Fillmore (between Pine and California), tel. (415) 346-8668, is a clubby pub serving Cajun and Creole food in a dark, handsome room. It's somehow appropriate to the neighborhood. **The Mansions,** 2220 Sacramento (between Laguna and Buchanan), tel. (415) 929-9444, serves wonderful food in a Victorian dining room, complete with unusual entertainment. Be sure to reserve in advance.

For people of modest means planning a special night out, **Chateau Suzanne,** 1449 Lombard, tel. (415) 771-9326, is a good choice, serving healthy and absolutely elegant French-Chinese entrées. Open Tues.-Sat. for dinner only; reservations advised.

Close to Japantown and adjacent to the Majestic Hotel (a one-time family mansion), the **Cafe Majestic,** 1500 Sutter St. (at Gough), tel. (415) 776-6400, is widely regarded as one of San Francisco's most romantic restaurants.The setting radiates old-world charm: ornate Edwardian decor, pale green and apricot decor with potted palms. It's sedate, yet far from stuffy and serves plentiful breakfasts on weekdays and brunch on weekends. Listen to a live classical pianist Fri.-Sat. nights and at Sunday brunch. Lunch is served Tues.-Fri., dinner nightly. Reservations are wise.

East of Pacific Heights (in Pacific Depths?), right on the stretch of Hwy. 101 that surface-streets its way through the city en route to the Golden Gate Bridge, is **Harris',** 2100 Van Ness Ave. (at Pacific), tel. (415) 673-1888, the city's best steakhouse, and unabashedly so. This is the place to come for a martini and a steak: T-

GHIRADELLI SQUARE

Tourist district it may be, but Ghirardelli Square houses some fine restaurants.

bones, ribeyes, and filet mignon all star on a beefy menu. Open for dinner daily.

THE RICHMOND, SEACLIFF, THE SUNSET

A fixture in the midst of the Golden Gate National Recreation Area and a favorite hangout at the edge of the continent, the current incarnation of the **Cliff House,** 1090 Point Lobos Ave. (at Upper Great Hwy.), tel. (415) 386-3330, is also a decent place to eat. Sunsets are superb, the seafood sublime. As close to fancy as it gets here is **Upstairs at the Cliff House,** an Old San Francisco-style dining room. Decidedly more casual at this cliff-hanging complex are both the **Seafood and Beverage Company** and the **Phineas T. Barnacle** pub.

Heading south down the beachfront, on the opposite side of Great Hwy. is the **Beach Chalet Brewery and Restaurant,** 1000 Great Hwy. (between Fulton and Lincoln), tel. (415) 386-

8439. This delightful renovation, upstairs (above a visitor center and City Store outlet) in the old 1925 Willis Polk-designed building, features wall-to-wall windows looking out on the surf (a great spot to watch the sunset), as well as creative California cuisine and a long list of housemade microbrews. The atmosphere is casual—don't come in your bathing suit, but you won't need the dinner jacket—and the service is friendly. Open daily for lunch and dinner.

Moving inland, exceptional ethnic fare is a specialty of Richmond District restaurants. The 100-plus eateries lining Clement St.—among them Asian, South American, Mexican, Italian, and even Russian restaurants and delis—are representative of the district's culinary and cultural mix.

Notable in the city's "new Chinatown," the modern **Fountain Court,** 354 Clement St. (at Fifth Ave.), tel. (415) 668-1100, is a wonderful, inexpensive stop for northern-style dim sum and other Shanghai specialties. One of the few San Francisco restaurants serving spicy, sweet Singapore-style fare is **Straits Cafe,** 3300 Geary (at Parker), tel. (415) 668-1783, a light, airy, white-walled rendition complete with interior palm trees. For delicious (and cheap) Taiwanese food, head to the **Taiwan Restaurant,** 445 Clement (at Sixth), tel. (415) 387-1789, which serves great dumplings.

Good for Indonesian fare is **Jakarta,** 615 Balboa St. (between Seventh and Eighth Avenues), tel. (415) 387-5225, another airy and bright place featuring an extensive menu of unusually well-done dishes, plus an eye-catching array of artifacts, musical instruments, and shadow puppets. Some say that the romantic **Khan Toke Thai House,** 5937 Geary (at 23rd Ave.), tel. (415) 668-6654, is San Francisco's best Southeast Asian restaurant (and a good deal). Open daily for dinner only, reservations accepted. Another reliable neighborhood choice is **Bangkok Cafe,** 2845 Geary (at Collins), tel. (415) 346-8821.

For the whole Moroccan experience, including a belly dancer on some nights, try **El Mansour,** 3121 Clement (near 32nd Ave.), tel. (415) 751-2312. A bit more grand, **Kasra Persian & Mediterranean Cuisine,** 349 Clement (at Fifth Ave.), tel. (415) 752-1101, is a very good choice for all kinds of shish kabobs.

Tiny, welcoming **Cafe Maisonnette,** 315 Eighth Ave., tel. (415) 387-7992, specializes in country-French cuisine. People rave about the rack of lamb. Monthly changing menu. **Café Riggio,** 4112 Geary (between Fifth and Sixth Avenues), tel. (415) 221-2114, is much appreciated for its antipasti, world-class calamari, and homemade cannoli for dessert.

Clement Street Bar & Grill, 708 Clement (at Eighth Ave.), tel. (415) 386-2200, serves a mostly American menu featuring vegetarian fare, grilled seafood, and California-style pastas. Farther up Geary toward the beach, **Bill's Place,** 2315 Clement (between 24th and 25th Avenues), tel. (415) 221-5262, is an eclectic burger joint with presidential portraits on the walls and a Japanese-style garden. The culinary creations here are named in honor of local celebrities. Guess what you get when you order a Carol Doda burger: two beefy patties with an olive sticking out smack dab in the middle of each. **Tia Margarita,** 300 19th Ave. (at Clement), tel. (415) 752-9274, is a long-running family café serving American-style Mexican food.

Things are more than a bit gentrified in Presidio Heights. Just a few blocks south of the Presidio is the **Magic Flute Garden Ristorante,** 3673 Sacramento (between Locust and Spruce), tel. (415) 922-1225, which offers Italian and other continental specialties in a sunny French country atmosphere. Folks also sing the praises of nearby **Tuba Garden,** 3634 Sacramento (between Locust and Spruce), tel. (415) 921-8822, a cozy Victorian open just for lunch and brunch, serving up Belgian waffles, homemade blintzes, and eggs Benedict.

Out at the edge of the Sunset District, assemble everything for a memorable picnic from the delis and shops along Taraval. Or check out the diverse ethnic neighborhood eateries. **Leon's Bar-BQ,** in an oceanside shack at 2800 Sloat Blvd. (at 46th Ave.), tel. (415) 681-3071, is a great stop for chicken and ribs. (Leon's has outposts in the Fillmore and at Fisherman's Wharf.) **Brother's Pizza,** 3627 Taraval (near 46th Ave.), tel. (415) 753-6004, isn't much to look at, but the pizzas (try the pesto special), pastas, and calzone overcome that first impression in a big hurry. The colorful, always crowded **Casa Aguila,** 1240 Noriega (between 19th and 20th Avenues), tel. (415) 661-5593, specializes in authentic Mexican fare from Cuernavaca and offers lots of food for the money. **El Toreador Fonda Mejicana,** 50 W. Portal (between Ulloa and Vicente), tel. (415) 566-2673, is a homey place serving traditional Central and Southern Mexican food. Just down the way on the buzzing West Portal retail strip, **Cafe for All Seasons,** 150 W. Portal (between Vicente and 14th Ave.), tel. (415) 665-0900, is a popular stop for hungry shoppers. The California-American menu emphasizes light pastas, grilled fish, and big salads.

HAIGHT-ASHBURY AND VICINITY

On any afternoon, most of the restaurants and cafés lining the Haight will be filled to the gills with young hipsters chowing down on brunch specials or self-medicating with food to cure party-related hangovers.

Campy as all get out, what with those murals and all, **Cha Cha Cha,** 1805 Haight St. (at Shrader), tel. (415) 386-5758, is just a hop or skip from Golden Gate Park. A hip tapas bar, it features unforgettable entrées such as grilled chicken paillard in mustard sauce, shrimp in spicy Cajun sauce, and New Zealand mussels in marinara. It's one of the most popular places around, so it's sometimes hard to find a place to park yourself.

Love the Haight: you can fill up at hippie-ish prices (cheap!) at several places that serve all-day breakfasts or pizza by the slice. For monstrously generous omelettes and a hearty side of potatoes, slide on into **All You Knead,** 1466 Haight (between Ashbury and Masonic), tel. (415) 552-4550. You'll get just that. Always popular for pizza is **Cybelle's,** with two neighborhood outlets: one at 1535 Haight St. (near Ashbury), tel. (415) 552-4200; the other at 203 Parnassus (at Stanyan), tel. (415) 665-8088. When East Coast transplants get homesick, they escape to **Escape from New York Pizza,** 1737 Haight (between Cole and Shrader), tel. (415) 668-5577. (There's another Escape at 508 Castro, at 18th, tel. 415-252-1515.)

In the Haight's heyday, **Magnolia Pub & Brewery,** 1398 Haight (at Masonic), tel. (415) 864-7468, was occupied by the Drugstore Café and later by Magnolia Thunderpussy's, a way-cool dessert-delivery business. The place has retained much of its bohemian charm with colorful murals and sweeping psychedelic signs out front. The menu offers a twist on traditional pub fare—mussels steamed in India Pale Ale, mushroom risotto cakes, along with regular old burgers and house-cut fries. The formidable house-made beer list includes Pale Ales, Porters, and more offbeat selections like the Old Thunderpussy Barleywine, a tribute to the brewpub's most famous tenant.

The area referred to as "the lower Haight" is an avant-garde enclave sandwiched between seedy Western Addition and the Webster St. public housing, with nary a tourist attraction in sight. Without the homeless, runaways, and drug dealers notable in the upper Haight, this several-block area has become a fairly happy haven for

THE SAN FRANCISCO FOOD? IT'S SOURDOUGH BREAD

As mentioned elsewhere, if only in passing, San Francisco has a long roster of culinary inventions—from the all-American Chinese fortune cookie (invented in the Japanese Tea Garden) and "Italian" fish stew, or cioppino, to hangtown fry and peach melba. But nothing is more San Francisco in the food department than sourdough French bread, a much-loved local specialty. Dating from gold-rush days, when yeasts and shortenings were scarce, breads were leavened by fermented "starters" of flour, water, and other live ingredients, this bacteria-enhanced souring ingredient then added in small amounts to bread dough. With each new batch of bread, some dough was pinched and put aside as the next generation of leavening. And on and on, down through time. Since sourdough bread connoisseurs believe that a good starter, and the bread line it creates, can only improve with age, a bakery's most prized asset is its own unique variety. It's no surprise, then, that during the great San Francisco earthquake and fire of 1906, many of the city's bakers risked their lives to rescue their starters. Such heroic acts are directly responsible for the time-honored tastes of the city's best breads.

artists and low-end wannabes, as well as the cafés, bars, and restaurants they inhabit. (Great people-watching.) **Kate's Kitchen,** 471 Haight (at Fillmore) tel. (415) 626-3984, is a small storefront diner where the emphasis is on down-home American food like buttermilk pancakes and scallion-cheese biscuits. A bit more boisterous, with sunny-day sidewalk tables, is the **Horse Shoe Coffee House,** 566 Haight (between Fillmore and Steiner), tel. (415) 626-8852, which also offers high-octane coffee and Internet access.

Most of the neighborhood's bars serve fairly decent food during the day and into the evening; try **Mad Dog in the Fog,** 530 Haight (between Steiner and Fillmore), tel. (415) 626-7279, a rowdy English-style pub, or just across the street, painfully hip **Noc Noc,** 557 Haight, tel. (415) 861-5811. Particularly off the wall, in the spirit of the neighborhood, is **Spaghetti Western,** 576 Haight, tel. (415) 864-8461, an earring-heavy reinterpretation of our collective cowboy heritage. Lots of food for the money.

THE MISSION DISTRICT
AND THE CASTRO

The Mission District is known for its open-air markets. One of the best is **La Victoria Mexican Bakery & Grocery,** 2937 24th St. (at Alabama), tel. (415) 550-9292. Buy some homemade tamales, fruit, and a few *churros* (Mexican sugar-dipped doughnuts) and have a feast at the children's park (between Bryant and York on 24th) while studying the murals. Other ethnic bakeries worth poking into for impromptu picnic fixings include **Pan Lido Salvadoreno,** 3147 22nd St. (at Capp), tel. (415) 282-3350, and **Pan Lido Bakery,** 5216 Mission (at Niagra), tel. (415) 333-2140. An ethnic change-up, serving great sandwiches, is **Lucca Ravioli Company,** 1100 Valencia (at 22nd St.), tel. (415) 647-5581.

Among the Mission's inexpensive neighborhood joints is the justifiably famous **Taqueria Can-Cun,** 2288 Mission (at 19th), tel. (415) 252-9560, which serves jumbo-size veggie burritos, handmade tortilla chips, and scorching salsa. There are two other locations: 10 blocks south on Mission (near Valencia) and at Sixth and Market. **Fina Estampa,** 2374 Mission St. (between 19th and 20th), tel. (415) 824-4437, is a nondescript

Peruvian outpost featuring exceptional seafood, chicken, and beef entrées (humongous portions) and good service. At **La Rondalla,** 901 Valencia (at 20th), tel. (415) 647-7474, mariachi bands play while you eat. At **Pancho Villa Taqueria,** 3071 16th (between Mission and Valencia), tel. (415) 864-8840, you'll be hard-pressed to find anything over seven bucks. And the portions are huge, including the grand dinner plates of grilled shrimp. At **Los Jarritos,** 901 S. Van Ness Ave. (at 20th), tel. (415) 648-8383, the "little jars" add color to an already colorful menu of Jalisco specialties.

The line between the Mission and Castro Districts, like distinct geographical and sociopolitical divisions elsewhere in the city, is often blurred. **Pozole,** 2337 Market St., tel. (415) 626-2666, has an almost religious south-of-the-border folk feel, what with the candlelit shrines, skull masks, and festive colors. But the food here isn't a literal cultural interpretation—especially comforting when one recalls that *pozole* originally was human flesh specially prepared as fight fuel for Aztec warriors.

The **Flying Saucer,** 1000 Guerrero (at 22nd), tel. (415) 641-9955, where the daily-changing menu is beamed over onto the wall, is a happy landing for mostly French culinary creativity— like an interplanetary marriage between Berkeley's Chez Panisse and the Zuni Cafe in a neighborhood burger stand. Three nightly seatings.

One more stop along the Mission's restaurant row (Valencia between 16th and 24th Streets) is the bustling **Slanted Door,** 584 Valencia (at 17th), tel. (415) 861-8032, where the food is healthy, eclectic, and surprisingly reasonable. People flock from all over the city, so make a reservation or be prepared to wait. Menu changes weekly. Another popular spot for Vietnamese is **Saigon Saigon,** 1132 Valencia (at 22nd), tel. (415) 206-9635, serving an astounding array of dishes, from majestic rolls and barbecued quail to Buddha's delight (vegetarian). Open for lunch on weekdays, for dinner nightly.

Both restaurant and tapas bar, **Esperpento,** 3295 22nd St. (at Valencia), tel. (415) 282-8867, is a great place for delectable Catalonian entrées, as well as tasty and sophisticated Spanish finger foods. Fairly inexpensive. Open Mon.-Sat. for lunch and dinner. **Cafe Nidal,** 2491 Mission (at 18th), tel. (415) 285-4334, is a long-standing neighborhood stop for falafels and other inexpensive Middle Eastern specialties. **Cafe Istanbul,** 525 Valencia (between 16th and 17th), tel. (415) 863-8854, occasionally has belly dancers.

A neighborhood classic in the retro diner genre is **Boogaloos,** 3296 22nd St. (at Valencia), tel. (415) 824-3211, famous for huge breakfasts, slacker crowds, and its signature dish, the Temple o' Spuds. **Cafe Ethiopia,** 878 Valencia (at 20th), tel. (415) 285-2728, offers all the usual espresso drinks plus Ethiopian cuisine, including poultry, beef, and vegetarian dishes from mild to spicy hot. Hugely popular and excellent value for the money, **Ti Couz,** 3108 16th St. (at Valencia), tel. (415) 252-7373, specializes in crepes—stuffed with everything from spinach to salmon to berries.

For real cheap eats in the Castro, head to **Hot 'n' Hunky,** 4039 18th St., tel. (415) 621-6365, for locally famous burgers and renowned French fries, not to mention excessive neon and Marilyn Monroe memorabilia. Very Castro is **Cafe Flore,** 2298 Market St. (at Noe), tel. (415) 621-8579, a popular gay hangout and café serving up omelettes and crepes, salads and good sandwiches, and current information about what's going on in the neighborhood. (Great for people-watching, especially out on the plant-populated patio.)

Missed by most tourists but popular for brunch is the **Patio Cafe,** 531 Castro (near 18th), tel. (415) 621-4640, a romantic hideaway where diners sit outside in a sunny, glass-domed patio sheltered from the wind. Another popular Castro destination is the **Bagdad Cafe,** 2295 Market St. (at 16th), tel. (415) 621-4434, offering a healthy take on American-style fare, plus great salads. Nearby, and wonderful for succulent seafood, is the **Anchor Oyster Bar,** 579 Castro (between 18th and 19th), tel. (415) 431-3990.

It's Tops, 1801 Market (at McCoppin), tel. (415) 431-6395, looks like a classic American greasy spoon—the decor hasn't changed since 1945—but the surprise is just how good the pancakes and other breakfast selections are. **Sparky's 24-Hour Diner,** 242 Church St. (between Market and 15th), tel. (415) 626-8666, got lost somewhere in the 1950s, style-wise, but the breakfast omelettes, burgers, and salads are certainly up to modern expectations.

The atmosphere at suave, contemporary **2223 Market** (at Noe), tel. (415) 431-0692, is cozy,

and the food is down-home American. Excellent garlic mashed potatoes and onion rings.

SOUTH OF MARKET (SoMa)

San Francisco's answer to New York City's SoHo, the South of Market area, or SoMa, is post-hippie, post-hip, post-just about everything. Anything goes. Reality here ranges from street-people chic and chichi supper clubs to only-those-in-the-know-know-where-it's-at dance clubs. An exploration of the neighborhood reveals the same stunning cultural contrast as those encampments of the homeless in front of the White House. Many areas here are considered unsafe after dark—stay with a group.

The burgers at **Eddie Rickenbacker's,** 133 Second St., tel. (415) 543-3498, are considered by connoisseurs to be close to the best, though other good bets at Eddie's include the salads, soups, and fish dishes.

Head toward the bay down second to reach the delightful South Park neighborhood, home to photo studios and shops serving the multimedia and advertising industries, as well as trendy coffeehouses, restaurants, and the postage-stamp-size greensward of South Park itself (bordered by Bryant and Brannan, Second and Third). The design-and-dine crowd is attracted in spades by South Park's **Infusion,** 555 Second St. (at Brannan), tel. (415) 543-2282, a busy, chic restaurant beloved for its innovative, spicy menu and fruit-infused vodka drinks. **Ristorante Ecco,** 101 South Park, tel. (415) 495-3291, is a trattoria-style California/Italian place with yellow sponge-painted walls; it's popular with the young professional crowd. Great desserts. Straight across the park is Ecco's slightly older sibling, the **South Park Cafe,** 108 South Park, tel. (415) 495-7275, an intimate French-style bistro whipping up espresso and croissants in the morning and more elaborate creations at lunch and dinner. Open daily.

After exploring Moscone Center and Yerba Buena Gardens, drop in for a cold one at **Thirsty Bear Brewing Co.,** 661 Howard (at Third), tel. (415) 974-0905, where you can enjoy one of the seven housemade microbrews and outstanding Spanish and Catalan dishes. Marked by the huge tomato hanging outside, no-fuss **Vino e Cucina,** 489 Third St. (at

Bryant), tel. (415) 543-6962, offers fine Italian cuisine scene, including pastas, pizzas, and unusual specials. Down a block, **Vinga,** 320 Third St., tel. (415) 546-3131, specializes in Catalan cuisine, including six different kinds of paella. Exceptional **Fringale,** 570 Fourth St. (between Bryant and Brannan), tel. (415) 543-0573, is a bright and contemporary French/American bistro serving excellent food at remarkably reasonable prices—a place well worth looking for. Open for lunch weekdays and for dinner Mon.-Saturday.

Continuing southwest through the district, you'll find good and pretty cheap, fast-as-your-laundry-cycle fare at **BrainWash,** 1122 Folsom (between Seventh and Eighth), tel. (415) 861-3663 (see the special topic Clean Up Your Act at Brain-Wash). It's by one of the area's sociocultural flagships, **Julie's Supper Club,** 1123 Folsom, tel. (415) 861-0707, a restaurant and nightclub/bar known for its combination of space-age-meets-the-'50s supper-club style and Old West saloon atmosphere. Not to mention the famous martinis.

For spice and great atmosphere, **India Garden,** 1261 Folsom (at Ninth), tel. (415) 626-2798, is well worth poking into for wonderful nans (flat-breads) and *kulchas* baked in a tandoor oven.

Although most folks come for the fresh-brewed beer, the **Twenty Tank Brewery,** 316 11th St. (at Folsom), tel. (415) 255-9455, also serves respectable bar food. You can fill up on a plate of nachos, a tasty sandwich, or a bowl of chili—and almost nothing's over five bucks. For those stirred to the soul by the world burger beat, the top stop is **Hamburger Mary's,** 1582 Folsom (at 12th), tel. (415) 626-1985 (reservations) or (415) 626-5767 (information), a cleaned-up bikers' bar easily mistaken for a downhome junque store. For deliciously spicy Thai food at bargain prices, you won't go wrong at **Manora's Thai Cuisine,** 1600 Folsom (at 12th), tel. (415) 861-6224, with a menu featuring well-prepared seafood and curries. Night owls like to come here before hitting the nearby clubs.

Also a possibility (if only for the great view of the railroad tracks) is **42 Degrees,** 235 16th St. (at Illinois, along the waterfront in China Basin), tel. (415) 777-5558, serving "nouvelle Mediterranean" food. The menu offers cuisine from southern France, Italy, Spain, and Greece—all regions at 42° north latitude. This is one of the trendiest spots around, so sometimes you wait awhile. Open weekdays for lunch and Wed.-Sat. for dinner.

BEYOND SAN FRANCISCO

"Everything in life is somewhere else, and you get there in a car," writer E.B. White once observed. And so it is, for the most part, once outside San Francisco with one's sights set on the wilds, scrambling through the urban and suburban fringe surrounding the bay. Worth exploring in its almost endless urbanism, the Bay Area also has its own wildness and wayside pleasures. As White also said: "I would feel more optimistic about a bright future for man if he spent less time proving that he can outwit Nature and more time tasting her sweetness and respecting her seniority." The San Francisco Bay Area offers ample opportunity for both.

THE PENINSULA

Sticking out into the Golden Gate like an aristocratic nose is the city and county of San Francisco, the northern tip of the San Francisco Peninsula. South of the city along the San Mateo County coastline is **Daly City,** its hillside neighborhoods almost immediately recognizable as the inspiration for Malvina Reynolds's "Little Boxes" lyrics: "And they're all made out of ticky tacky and they all look just the same." Smaller communities, including **Pacifica** and **Half Moon Bay,** pop up alongside the string of state beaches that continue down the coast as far as the northern elephant seal refuge at Año Nuevo. Just inland from the coast near San Andreas

Lake is Sweeney Ridge, a small nugget among the parks collected into the Bay Area's Golden Gate National Recreation Area.

South of the city along the shores of San Francisco Bay are **Brisbane** (which merges with Daly City) and undeveloped San Bruno Mountain County Park. Continuing south, you'll pass a stretch of the San Francisco Bay National Wildlife Refuge and a slew of bayside communities stretching into

See color map of the San Francisco Bay Area at front of book.

Santa Clara County. A bit farther is the heart of high-tech Silicon Valley, its suburbs spreading out like printed circuits from hard-driving **San Jose.**

South from San Francisco along the peninsula's inland spine is **Colma,** an incorporated city inside Daly City where the dead outnumber the living by more than 2,000 to one, due to Colma's cemetery industry. Among the city of the dead's most famous residents are gunfighter Wyatt Earp, riveted-blue-jeans creator Levi Strauss, sculptor Benjamin Bufano, and baseball batting champ Lefty O'Doul (whose gravestone lists his statistics and this comment: "He was here at a good time and had a good time while he was here.")

After the one-time dairy town of **Millbrae** comes down-to-the-bayshore **Burlingame** (the West's first community dedicated to the country club lifestyle) and very highbrow Hillsborough, founded in 1851 by a deserter from the British Navy, just north of **San Mateo.** San Mateo spreads into **Belmont,** which collides with **San Carlos** and the outskirts of **Redwood City,** named for its brisk business, historically, as a redwood-lumber port. **Atherton,** nearby **Menlo Park,** and economically depressed **East Palo Alto** all stand in the intellectual shadow of **Palo Alto,** home of California's prestigious Stanford University and the contentious Hoover Institution.

SAN MATEO COASTLINE: FROM PACIFICA SOUTH

The unstable wave-whipped coast south of San Francisco is all buff-colored bluffs and sandy beaches faced with rough rocks. Often foggy in summer, the coastline in winter is crowded with bird- and whalewatchers. But from late summer into autumn, the weather is usually good and the crowds mimimal, making this the perfect time for a superb escape. Though wetsuit-clad surfers brave the snarling swells even in gale-force winds, swimming is dangerous even on serene sunny days due to treacherous undertows. Many of the region's beaches are officially accessible as state beaches or local beach parks; others are state-owned and undeveloped, or privately owned. Almost 20 miles of this 51-mile-long coastline are included as part of the San Mateo Coast State Beaches, starting with

Daly City's **Thornton Beach** (popular for fishing and picnicking) in the north and ending with tiny **Bean Hollow State Beach** just north of Año Nuevo in the south. Though campgrounds are available inland, seaside public camping is possible only at Half Moon Bay State Beach, tel. (650) 726-8820. For more information, call **San Mateo State Beaches,** (650) 726-8819. For more information on public-transit access to the San Mateo coast, call SamTrans toll-free at (800) 660-4287.

Pacifica: California's Fog Capital
The self-proclaimed Fog Capital of California, Pacifica is sometimes a dreary place. But the locals make up for the opaque skies with *attitude*. Come here in late September for the annual **Pacific Coast Fog Fest,** which features a Fog Calling Contest (almost everyone's a winner), the Phileas Fogg Balloon Races, high-octane alcoholic "fogcutters" (if drinking, *don't* drive off into the fog), plus a fog fashion show. When the weather's sunny, the town offers superb coastal views. And good food abounds here—fog or shine. For more information on the town or the Fog Fest, call the **Pacifica Chamber of Commerce** at (650) 355-4122.

At **Sharp Park State Beach** along Beach Blvd. (reached from Hwy. 1 via Paloma Ave., Clarendon Rd., or streets in between) is the **Pacifica Pier,** popular for fishing and winter whalewatching. Migrating gray whales are attracted to the abundant plankton at the end of the community's sewage outfall pipe (the treatment plant is the building with the Spanish arches). Some old salts here say the great grays swim so close to the pier you can smell the fish on their breath.

Farther south is sort-of-secluded **Rockaway Beach,** a striking black-sand beach in a small rectangular cove where the coast has backed away from the rocky bluffs. Hotels and restaurants cluster beyond the rock-reinforced parking lot.

South from Pacifica
Long and narrow **Montara State Beach** offers hiking and rock-and-sand beachcombing. The state's tiny **Gray Whale Cove Beach** here is a concession-operated clothing-optional beach, open for all-over tans only to those 18 and over; for information, call (650) 728-5336. Just south of

Montara proper is the cypress-strewn **Moss Beach** area, named for the delicate sea mosses that drape shoreline rocks at low tide.

Best for exploration Nov.-Jan. are the 30 acres of tidepools at the **James V. Fitzgerald Marine Reserve** (open daily from sunrise to sunset), which stretches south from Montara Point to Pillar Point and Princeton-by-the-Sea. At high tide, the Fitzgerald Reserve looks like any old sandy beach with a low shelf of black rocks emerging along the shore, but when the ocean rolls back, these broad rock terraces and their impressive tidepools are exposed. For area state park information, call (415) 330-6300; for information on low-tide prime time at the Fitzgerald Reserve, call (650) 728-3584; for more about docent-led guided tours of the reserve, call Coyote Point Museum, (650) 342-7755.

Nearby, along Hwy. 1 in Montara, are **McNee Ranch State Park** and Montara Mountain, with hiking trails and great views of the Pacific. Next south is **El Granada,** an unremarkable town except for the remarkable music showcased by the **Bach Dancing & Dynamite Society,** 311 Mirada Rd. (technically in Miramar), tel. (650) 726-4143, the longest-running venue for jazz greats in the Bay Area. Begun in 1958 when jazz fanatic Pete Douglas started letting jazz musicians hang out at his house and jam, public concerts blast off every Sunday (except around Christmas and New Year's) in a baroque beatnik beachhouse. The family lives downstairs; upstairs at "the Bach" is the concert hall and deck, though guests are free to amble down to the beach and back at all times. Admission isn't charged, but a contribution of $10-15 or so is the usual going rate for Sunday concerts. The Dancing & Dynamite Society has become so popular that Friday night candlelight dinner concerts cosponsored by local businesses or other supporters are also offered (reservations and advance payment required). For a small fee, anyone can join the society and receive a newsletter and calendar of coming attractions.

South Coast Accommodations

Inexpensive and incredibly pleasant for a coast overnight is **HI-AYH Point Montara Lighthouse Hostel,** on Hwy. 1 at 16th St., Montara, tel. (650) 728-7177. It's quite popular, so reservations (by mail only) are advisable. Dorm-style bunks, and couple and family rooms are available in the wheelchair-accessible annex. Bud-

the popular Point Montara Lighthouse Hostel

get. Also, motels—not many are inexpensive—pop up here and there along the coast.

The charming **Goose and Turrets Bed and Breakfast,** 835 George St., Montara, tel. (650) 728-5451, fax (650) 728-0141, is a huge 1908 Italian-style seaside villa that dates back to the Bay Area's early bohemian days, when the adventurous and/or artistic rode the Ocean Shore Railroad from San Francisco to the arts colony and beach here. The five guest rooms are just part of the pleasure of this 6,000-square-foot home, which features great windows on its west wall. All rooms have private bathrooms and little luxuries; three rooms have fireplaces, German down comforters, and English towel warmers. French spoken; e-mail the Goose and Turrets at rhmgt@montara.com, and find them on the web at www.montara.com/goose.html. Breakfast is a four-course feast; tea and treats are served in the afternoon. Expensive-Premium.

The English-style **Seal Cove Inn,** 221 Cypress Ave., Moss Beach, tel. (650) 728-4114, is another find—an elegant and romantic inn overlooking the Fitzgerald Marine Reserve. The 10 guest rooms here each feature a wood-burning fireplace, refrigerator, TV, and ocean views; some have a private deck. For small group meetings, there's even a conference room. Luxury.

South Coast Fare

Traditional in Moss Beach is the straightforward Italian fare at **Dan's Place,** on Virginia Ave. overlooking the Fitzgerald Reserve, tel. (650) 728-3343; open for lunch and dinner. The old **Moss Beach Distillery** in Moss Beach, 140 Beach Way (at Ocean), tel. (650) 728-5595, is now a romantic cliffside restaurant, very good for seafood, ribs, lamb, and veal. Open for lunch and dinner. **Barbara's Fish Trap,** 281 Capistrano Rd. in Princeton-by-the-Sea, tel. (650) 728-7049, open daily for lunch and dinner, offers great Half Moon Bay views, fishnet kitsch decor, and fish selections that are a cut above the usual. Try the garlic prawns.

HALF MOON BAY

Known until the turn of the century as Spanishtown, Half Moon Bay was a farm community settled by Italians and Portuguese, and specializing in artichokes and Brussels sprouts. Down and out during the early 1900s, things picked up during Prohibition when the area became a safe harbor for Canadian rumrunners. Fast becoming a fashionable Bay Area residential suburb, Half Moon Bay is famous for its pumpkins and offers a rustic Main St. with shops, restaurants, and inns, plus pseudo-Cape Cod cluster developments along Highway 1. In 1999, Half Moon Bay's commercial ship-to-shore radiotelegraph station, the nation's last, tapped out its final Morse code transmission. Just a few miles south of Half Moon Bay off Pillar Point and legendary among extreme surfers is **Mavericks,** home of the world's baddest wave. When surf's up here, during wild winter storms, Mavericks creates mean and icy 35-foot waves—mean enough to break bones and boards.

Nearby **Burleigh Murray Ranch State Park** is still largely undeveloped, but the former 1,300-acre dairy ranch is now open to the public for day use. You can take a hike up the old ranch road, which winds up through sycamores and alders along Mill Creek. About a mile from the trailhead is the ranch's most notable feature, the only known example of an English bank barn in California. This century-old structure relied on simple but ingenious design, utilizing slope ("bank") and gravity to feed livestock most efficiently. Especially for those who can't remember even the basics of farm life, other outbuildings also deserve a peek. To get here, turn east on Higgins-Purisima Rd. from Hwy. 1 just south of Half Moon Bay. It's about two miles to the parking area (marked, on the left).

A Portuguese **Chamarita** parade and barbecue are held here seven weeks after Easter. Over the July 4th weekend, the community's **Coastside County Fair and Rodeo** takes place. But the biggest annual event in these parts is the popular **Half Moon Bay Art and Pumpkin Festival** in October, where pumpkin-carving and pumpkin pie-eating contests as well as the Great Pumpkin Parade take center stage. For a complete list of area events and other information, contact the **Half Moon Bay/Coastside Chamber of Commerce,** 520 Kelly Ave., Half Moon Bay, CA 94019, tel. (650) 726-5202 or (650) 726-8380.

Practical Half Moon Bay

At **Half Moon Bay State Beach** campground (open year-round, hot showers and all), reservations are usually required March-Oct. to guarantee a tent or RV campsite. Unreserved space is often available on nonweekend autumn days. For reservations, call **ReserveAmerica,** toll-free (800) 444-7275.

Motels in Half Moon Bay tend to be on the pricey side. A nice midrange choice is **Harbor View Inn,** 51 Alhambra Ave. (four miles north of town in El Granada), tel. (650) 726-2329. Expensive. The upscale **Half Moon Bay Lodge,** 2400 S. Hwy. 1 (about 2.5 miles south of the Hwy. 92 junction), tel. (650) 726-9000, has a pool, jacuzzi, fitness center, some rooms with fireplaces and some with golf course views. Luxury.

The in thing in Half Moon Bay is inns, many of which offer reduced midweek rates. Much loved is the **Mill Rose Inn** bed and breakfast, 615 Mill St. (in "old town"), tel. (650) 726-7673, (650) 726-8750, or toll-free (800) 829-1794, a romantic Victorian with frills like fireplaces, a spa, English gardens, and excellent breakfasts. Luxury. Another local favorite is the restored **San Benito House** country inn, 356 Main St., tel. (650) 726-3425, with 12 rooms on the upper floor (two share a bath), plus a sauna, redwood deck with flowers and firepit, and a downstairs restaurant and saloon. Moderate-Premium. The **Old Thyme Inn,** 779 Main St., tel. (650) 726-1616 or toll-free (800) 720-4277, has some rooms with two-person whirlpools. For special occasions or extra privacy, book the Garden Suite, which features a private entrance. The atmosphere here is very English, in a casually elegant style. Rooms are individually decorated, and some feature fireplaces and/or in-room whirlpool tubs. Especially delightful for gardeners is the herb garden here, boasting more than 80 varieties (true aficionados are allowed to take cuttings). Expect such treats as homemade scones and marmalade, or possibly even French cherry flan. Expensive-Luxury.

Another historic local favorite is the **Zaballa House,** 324 Main St. (right next door to the San Benito House), tel. (650) 726-9123. It's Half Moon Bay's oldest surviving building (circa 1859) and now features nine standard guest rooms and three private-entrance suites, all with private bath. Several rooms have two-person whirlpool tubs and/or fireplaces. Ask about the "resident ghost" in Room 6. Expensive-Luxury.

The contemporary **Cypress Inn,** 407 Mirada Rd. (three miles north of Hwy. 92, just off Hwy. 1; exit at Medio Ave.), Miramar, tel. (650) 726-6002 or toll-free (800) 832-3224, is right on the beach and just a few doors down from the Bach Dynamite & Dancing Society. The inn's motto is "in celebration of nature and folk art," and the distinctive rooms—each with an ocean view and private deck, fireplace, and luxurious private bath—do live up to it, whether you stay in the Rain, Wind, Sea, Sky, Star, Sun, or Moon rooms. For a special treat, head up into the Clouds (the penthouse). Gourmet breakfasts, afternoon tea, winetasting, and hors d'oeuvres included. Massage is available by appointment. Luxury. North of Half Moon Bay, **Pillar Point Inn** 380 Capistrano Rd., El Granada, tel. (650) 728-7377, overlooks the harbor in Princeton-by-the-Sea. All rooms have fireplaces and other modern amenities. Luxury.

The **Half Moon Bay Bakery,** 514 Main, tel. (650) 726-4841, is also a stop on the local historic walking tour. The bakery still uses its original 19th-century brick oven and offers sandwiches, salads, and pastries over the counter. Other popular eateries include the **Pasta Moon** café, 315 Main St., tel. (650) 726-5125, and the **San Benito House** restaurant, 356 Main (at Mill), tel. (650) 726-3425, noted for its French and Northern Italian country cuisine at dinner. Simpler but excellent lunches (including sandwich selections on homemade breads) also served. Open Thurs.-Sun. only; excellent Sunday brunch. Call for reservations.

FROM SAN GREGORIO SOUTH

On the coast just west of tiny San Gregorio is **San Gregorio State Beach,** with the area's characteristic bluffs, a mile-long sandy beach, and a sandbar at the mouth of San Gregorio Creek. San Gregorio proper is little more than a spot in the road, but the back-roads route via Stage Rd. from here to Pescadero is pastoral and peaceful.

Inland Pescadero ("Fishing Place") was named for the creek's once-teeming trout, not for any fishing traditions on the part of the town's Portuguese settlers. Both **Pomponio** and

Pescadero State Beaches offer small estuaries for same-named creeks. The 584-acre **Pescadero Marsh Natural Preserve** is a successful blue heron rookery, as well as a feeding and nesting area for more than 200 other bird species. (To birdwatch—best in winter—park at **Pescadero State Beach** near the bridge and walk via the Sequoia Audubon Trail, which starts below the bridge.) Rocky-shored **Bean Hollow State Beach,** a half-mile hike in, is better for tidepooling than beachcombing, though it has picnic tables and a short stretch of sand.

For a longer coast walk, head south to the **Año Nuevo** reserve. (Año Nuevo Point was named by Vizcaíno and crew shortly after New Year's Day in 1602.) The rare northern elephant seals who clamber ashore here are an item only in winter and spring, but stop here any time of year for a picnic and a stroll along Año Nuevo's three-mile-long beach.

Coastal Accommodations

The cheap place to stay in the area is **AYH Pigeon Point Lighthouse Hostel,** five miles south of the turnoff to Pescadero and just off Hwy. 1 via Pigeon Point Rd., tel. (650) 879-0633. The hostel's basic but adequate facilities include bunk and family rooms, plus an on-the-cliffs hot tub. Good tidepooling nearby. Budget. Reservations are usually essential.

If the hostel is full, the campground at **Butano State Park,** tel. (650) 879-2040, probably will be too—at least on Fridays, Saturdays, and holidays May-September. Reached from Pescadero via Cloverdale Rd. (or from near Gazos Beach via Gazos Creek Rd.), the park offers 21 family campsites, 19 walk-in sites, and a handful of backcountry trail camps. During the high season, reserve main campsites through **ReserveAmerica,** toll-free tel. (800) 444-7275. The rest of the year, it's usually first-come, first-camped.

The deluxe place to camp in the area is **Costanoa Lodge and Camp,** 2001 Rossi Rd., Pescadero, tel. (650) 879-1100, a "boutique campground" and lodge built by Joie de Vivre Hotels, the San Francisco boutique-hotels specialist. Look for furnished tent cabins, as well as traditional cabins and a 40-room lodge, on this 40-acre spread. Moderate-Luxury.

Hard to beat for an overnight in Pescadero are the six cottages at **Estancia del Mar,** 460 Pigeon Point Rd., tel. (650) 879-1500, fax (650) 712-8688, e-mail: estanciadm@aol.com. Located 500 yards from the surf, each attractive cottage sleeps four and includes custom-tiled bathroom, fully equipped kitchen, wood-burning stove, and stereo/CD player/radio and VCR. Linens and towels are provided. Kids and pets welcome. Luxury, with multinight discounts.

Another option is the Spanish-style **Rancho San Gregorio** bed and breakfast, 5086 La Honda Rd., San Gregorio, tel. (650) 747-0810 or (650) 747-0722, a best bet featuring just four attractive rooms (three have woodstoves; all have private baths). Many of the veggies and fruits served at breakfast are home-grown. Great hiking nearby. Expensive-Premium. Or head south along the coast. About nine miles north of Santa Cruz, the **New Davenport Bed and Breakfast Inn,** 31 Davenport Ave. (Hwy. 1), tel. (831) 425-1818, (831) 426-4122, or toll-free (800) 870-1817, is a colorful ocean-view hideaway (rooms above the restaurant) with artist owners and beach access. Moderate-Premium.

Coastal Fare

In Pescadero, down-home **Duarte's Tavern,** 202 Stage Rd., tel. (650) 879-0464, is most noted for its artichoke soup and delicious olallieberry pie, not to mention the ever-changing fresh fish specials scrawled across the menu chalkboard. Open daily for breakfast, lunch, and dinner; reservations wise (especially in summer) for dinner and Sunday brunch. Near Pescadero is **Phipps Ranch,** where berries, dried beans, baby lettuce, squash, and other local produce are available in season. (San Mateo County's *Coastside Harvest Trails* map lists other regional produce stands.)

Down the coast toward Santa Cruz, the **New Davenport Cash Store & Restaurant,** tel. (831) 426-4122, is a store, arts and crafts gallery, and inexpensive eatery with healthy food (whole grains, salads, soups) in the Americanized Mexican tradition. Great desserts. Bed-and-breakfast rooms upstairs.

OTHER SAN MATEO PARKS: NORTH

San Bruno Mountain County Park exists because the lupine-loving mission blue butterflies were wiped out elsewhere in the Bay Area. Their last remaining habitat (on one east-facing slope) is now protected from development. San Bruno is a great almost-in-the-city hiking park also fine for picnics. Its trails are most enjoyable during the spring wildflower bloom, but the views are fabulous on any unfoggy day. Bay Area Mountain Watch and Friends of Endangered Species offer free group walks to prime butterfly-viewing spots and ancient Native American village sites.

To get here from San Francisco, head south on the Bayshore Freeway (Hwy. 101), take the Cow Palace-Brisbane exit, and follow Bayshore Blvd. past Geneva Ave. to Guadalupe Road. Turn right at Guadalupe and climb to the saddle, then turn left at the park sign and follow Radio Rd. uphill all the way; park near the telecommunications towers. For more information about San Bruno Mountain and other county parks, contact: **San Mateo County Parks and Recreation,** 590 Hamilton St., Redwood City, CA 94063, tel. (650) 363-4020.

Down the bayshore, **Coyote Point County Park,** 1701 Coyote Point Dr., tel. (650) 573-2592, is popular for fishing, sailboarding, swimming, and picnicking. Entrance fee. The park is also home to the **Coyote Point Museum for Environmental Education,** 1651 Coyote Point Dr., tel. (650) 342-7755, one of the best environmental science centers in the Bay Area. The museum houses superb educational displays, including a bay ecosystems exhibit and the world's largest bee tube. Special events are scheduled year-round. Open Tues.-Sat. 10 a.m.-5 p.m., Sunday noon-5 p.m.; small admission. If you've got some time and bikes on board, start from Coyote Point or the parking lot near the San Mateo Fishing Pier (at the eastern end of Hillsdale Blvd.) to explore the eight-mile **Bayfront Path,** a paved bicycling and walking trail that heads south along the bay, meanders through area sloughs, then loops back to (and through) Foster City and Marina Lagoon. Leave early to avoid afternoon winds, and pack a picnic if you'll be making a day of it. For a map of this and other bikeways in the area, call the **San Mateo Department of Public Works,** tel. (650) 363-4100. To the northwest, where Skyline Blvd. branches off from scenic I-280, is **Junipero Serra County Park,** 1801 Crystal Springs Ave., San Bruno, tel. (650) 589-5708, with hiking and nature trails, playgrounds, picnicking, and great views.

Sweeney Ridge, just east of Hwy. 1 near Pacifica, and south of Sharp County Park, is a fairly new segment of the Bay Area's extensive Golden Gate National Recreation Area. The ridge offers great hiking and 360-degree views of San Francisco Bay and the Pacific—the same vantage point that Gaspar de Portolá stumbled upon during his expedition to find Monterey Bay in 1769. From the Pacific coast side, the GGNRA trailhead up to Sweeney Ridge is near the Shelldance Bromeliad Nursery at 2000 Cabrillo Hwy. (Hwy. 1), on the left facing the hill. From the east, hike in from the trailhead just off Sneath Ln. from Skyline Boulevard. (However you arrive, wear good hiking boots or shoes and bring a sweater or jacket.) For more information, call the GGNRA information line at (650) 556-0560.

Narrow San Andreas Lake and Crystal Springs Reservoir mark the route taken by the discouraged Gaspar de Portolá expedition of 1769 (which he described as "that small company of persons, or rather say skeletons, who had been spared by scurvy, hunger, and thirst"). The lakes also mark the route of the San Andreas Fault. Due to chain-link fences and the hum of the freeway, modern-day adventurers will be disappointed with a hike along the San Andreas Trail, but the connecting Crystal Springs Riding and Hiking Trail to the south is worthwhile.

Worth it, too, is a moment of reverent reflection at the **Pulgas Water Temple** at the reservoir's south end just off Canada Rd., a monument to the elusive and liquid god of California progress. This circular Greek-style classic designed by architect Willis Polk marks the spot where the once-wild waters from behind Hetch Hetchy Dam in Yosemite are taken into custody by the San Francisco Water Department, originally established by gold-rush czar William Bourn in the 1860s as part of his Spring Valley Water Works. The old company is also enshrined here, near the two major reservoirs it built to provide water for up-and-coming San Francisco.

Also off Canada Rd. is Bourn's 17-acre **Filoli Mansion,** one of several mansions he built as temples to his wealth. This one was named from a condensation of his personal motto: FIght, LOve, LIfe. (Nighttime soap opera fans of a certain age will recognize Filoli as Blake Carrington's *Dynasty* mansion.) Also a creation of

San Francisco architect Willis Polk, the mansion is filled with priceless furnishings from around the world. Almost more impressive, though, are Bourn's acres of formal gardens—at their best on a sunny spring day. The mansion and grounds are open mid-February through mid-November; moderate admission fee. Children under age 12 not allowed (and no one allowed even in the gift shop without reservations). Tours are offered by Friends of Filoli. For more information about tours and to make reservations, call (650) 364-2880.

South of Lower Crystal Springs Reservoir are two distinct parks connected via trails. **Huddart County Park,** 1100 Kings Mountain Rd., Woodside, tel. (650) 851-0326, comprises almost 1,000 acres of cool canyons with second-growth redwoods, Douglas firs, and foothill oaks. It offers a short trail system with ties to the Crystal Springs Trail to the north and the Skyline Trail to the south. The Skyline Trail leads two miles to **Wunderlich County Park,** 4040 Woodside Rd., Woodside, tel. (650) 851-0326, which has its own 25-mile trail system. To get to Huddart, take Hwy. 84 west to Kings Mountain Rd. in Woodside (stop off at the historic Woodside Store) and continue along Kings Mountain for two miles. From Wunderlich, the Skyline Trail continues south to the hamlet of Sky Londa. Across the Junipero Serra Freeway (I-280) is **Edgewood County Park and Natural Preserve,** Edge-

wood Rd. at Old Stage Rd., tel. (650) 368-6283, a wonderful patch of open space threaded with trails and bright with blossoming wildflowers from spring into summer.

OTHER SAN MATEO PARKS: SOUTH

Five miles inland from Año Nuevo State Reserve is **Butano State Park,** tel. (650) 879-2040, which offers 20 miles of excellent if strenuous hikes among redwoods, plus picnicking, camping, and summer campfire programs. Another worthy redwoods destination is **San Mateo Memorial County Park,** 9500 Pescadero Rd. (eight miles east of Pescadero), tel. (650) 879-0238, which features a nature museum, 200-foot-tall virgin trees, creek swimming, camping, and trails connecting with surrounding local and state parks. Adjacent **Pescadero Creek County Park** (same address and phone) includes the steelhead trout stream's upper watersheds—6,000 acres of excellent hiking. (The Old Haul Rd. and Pomponio Trails link Pescadero to nearby Memorial and Portola Parks.)

Just to the north outside La Honda (though the entrance is off Pescadero Rd.) is 867-acre **Sam McDonald County Park** (same address and phone as San Mateo Memorial and Pescadero Creek Parks), offering rolling grasslands and redwoods, trails interconnecting with Pescadero Park, and a Sierra Club hiker's hut for

Redwood groves, along with beaches, are typical of the peninsula.

overnights (to reserve, call the Loma Prieta chapter of the Sierra Club at 650-390-8411). To the southeast via Alpine Rd. and Portola State Park Rd. is La Honda's **Portola State Park,** tel. (650) 948-9098, comprised of rugged redwood terrain between Butano and Skyline Ridges. Here you'll find backcountry hiking, a short nature trail, a museum and visitor center, picnicking, and year-round camping. Campsite reservations are usually necessary April-Sept.; call **ReserveAmerica** toll-free at (800) 444-7275 (reserve the trail camp through park headquarters).

The **Midpeninsula Regional Open Space District,** 330 Distel Circle, Los Altos, CA 94022, tel. (650) 691-1200, administers other parkland in San Mateo and Santa Clara Counties—primarily preserves and limited-use areas perfect for hikers seeking even more seclusion. Among these: Purisima Creek Redwoods, southeast of Half Moon Bay; Mount El Sereno, south of Saratoga; the Long Ridge Preserve near Big Basin; and the rugged chaparral Sierra Azul-Limekiln Canyon Area near Lexington Reservoir. Contact the district's office for more information and maps.

For detailed information about regional sights, restaurants, and lodging, contact any of the following chambers of commerce: the **San Mateo County Convention and Visitors Bureau,** 111 Anza Blvd., Ste. 410, Burlingame, CA 94010, tel. (650) 348-7600; the **Burlingame Chamber of Commerce,** 290 California Dr., Burlingame, CA 94010, tel. (650) 344-1735; the **San Carlos Chamber of Commerce,** 1560 Laurel St., San Carlos, CA 94070, tel. (650) 593-1068; and the **Belmont Chamber of Commerce,** 1070 Sixth Ave., Ste. 102, Belmont, CA 94002, tel. (650) 595-8696.

PALO ALTO

Characteristic of the San Francisco region, most Peninsula and South Bay communities offer up culture in surprising, usually delightful ways. In Palo Alto, hometown of Stanford University, cultural creativity is concentrated and always accessible—making this a choice destination when climbing down out of the hills. This is the place, after all, where the Silicon Valley computer revolution started—where, in the 1930s, Bill Hewlett and Dave Packard, founders of modern-day Hewlett-Packard, started their spare-time tinkering with electronic bells, whistles, and other gadgetry in a garage on Addison Avenue. (Their first creation was the audio oscillator, a sound-enhancing system first used by Walt Disney in *Fantasia,* which catapulted the inventive duo into the corporate big leagues.)

The northernmost city in Santa Clara County, Palo Alto is not a typical tourist destination, which is in itself a major attraction for those tired of prepackaged community charm. For more information, including a current listing of member restaurants and accommodations, contact the **Palo Alto Chamber of Commerce,** 325 Forest Ave., tel. (650) 324-3121. For local public transportation options, depending on which way you're heading, contact: **Caltrain** (Caltrans), which serves the peninsula and San Francisco, toll-free tel. (800) 660-4287; **San Mateo County Transit** (SamTrans), tel. (650) 508-6219, (650) 508-6200 or toll-free (800) 660-4287; or **Santa Clara County Transit,** tel. (408) 321-2300.

STANFORD UNIVERSITY

Once known as The Farm, the 9,000-acre campus of modern-day Stanford University was formerly Leland Stanford's Palo Alto stock farm, his spacious spread for thoroughbred racehorses. Some people now refer to Stanford as The Idea Farm, since this is the place that spawned birth-control pills, gene splicing, heart transplants, the IQ test, the laser, the microprocessor, music synthesizers, and napalm—among other breakthroughs of the civilized world. Royalties from on-campus inventiveness earn private Stanford University millions of dollars each year.

Though Stanford has a renowned medical school, a respected law school, and top-drawer departments in the sciences, most famous here is the Hoover Institution on War, Revolution, and Peace, which started out in 1919 to delineate and demonstrate "the evils of Karl Marx" with an original collection of five million World War I-related documents contributed by 40 governments. Though less stridently since the fall of the Berlin Wall, critics of the Hoover Institution, both on-campus and off, suggest that the organization has become too ideological—tainting Stanford University's otherwise legitimate claims to intellectual objectivity—to stay on campus in the hallowed Hoover Tower and should establish headquarters elsewhere.

Next most famous on campus: the run-amok Stanford University Marching Band, a self-perpetuating autocracy still blamed by embarrassed alumni for "the Play" in 1982, when winning Stanford lost The Big Game to arch nemesis UC Berkeley across the bay with just four seconds remaining. When not getting trampled by football players for being in the wrong place at the wrong time, the Stanford band never marches (members say they don't know how) but instead swarms onto the field during half time and jostles into formations like Gumby's head, Ronald Reagan's nose, Jimmy Carter's hemorrhoids, the Death Star from Star Wars, and more mundane symbols like chainsaws and computers.

Seeing and Doing Stanford

The sprawling Spanish-style campus, designed by famed landscape architect Frederick Law Olmstead (designer of New York City's Central Park), is much too large to tour on foot; use a bike or the free Marguerite Shuttle. A good place to start is the campus quadrangle, where between-class undergraduate students mill around (some perhaps still proudly wearing T-shirts announcing the student body's unofficial motto: Work, Study, Get Rich). Before arriving, get a campus map and other Internet information at www.stanford.edu; once arrived, try the second floor of the Tresidder Student Union, tel. (650) 723-4311. For special event tickets, call (650) 725-2787.

For a fairly comprehensive one-hour general campus walking tour, contact **Stanford University Guide and Visitor Service,** Building 170, Stanford, CA 94305, tel. (650) 723-2560. The student-guided tours are offered daily, except holidays and quarter breaks. (Tours leave from the Serra St. quadrangle entrance.) For a tour of the **Hoover Observation Tower and Archives** (small fee), call (650) 723-2053. Finely focused tours of the **Stanford Linear Accelerator Center,** home of the quark, are led by graduate students; call (650) 926-3300 or (650) 926-2204 for information and appointments. For unguided good times, try the hiking trails through the campus's wooded west end—or, for birdwatching, head out to the **Baylands Nature Preserve** outside Palo Alto at the end of Embarcadero Rd., tel. (650) 329-2506.

Ten years after the 1989 Loma Prieta Earthquake closed down the Stanford Art Museum, it has been expanded and reopened as the **Iris & B. Gerald Cantor Center for the Visual Arts,** Museum Way and Lomita Dr., tel. (650) 723-4177, www.stanford.edu/dept/ccva. New wings have been added to the seismically restored original 1890s building, for a total of 27 galleries. The museum's exhibits range from ancient to contemporary times and roam the globe, from the ancient Mediterranean to Africa, America, Asia, and Oceania. The Cantor center is also home to the world's second largest collection of Rodin works, after only the Musée Rodin in Paris. Outside in the sculpture garden are *The Gates of Hell, Adam and Eve,* and 18 others, and inside are two Rodin galleries. The museum is open Wed.-Sun. 11 a.m.-5 p.m. (until 8 p.m. on Thursday). Admission is free.

That brawling bad boy of American letters is showcased in the Stanford Library's **Charles D. Field Collection of Ernest Hemingway,** which includes first editions, translations, stories and poems, published and unpublished letters, and galley proofs. (While a student at Stanford, another American literary lion—double-dropout **John Steinbeck**—got a "C" in freshman English. He later said college was a waste of time.)

OTHER AREA SIGHTS

Palo Alto-Stanford (PASt) Heritage, tel. (650) 299-8878, offers guided one-hour walking tours of Palo Alto, either downtown or "Professorville." Both areas are included on the National Register of Historic Districts. Usually departing on Saturdays at 10 or 11 a.m., the downtown tour covers Ramona St. and architectural gems like William Weeks's Cardinal Hotel and Birge Clark's shops, plus Spanish colonial revival courtyards by Pedro de Lemos. The 1932 U.S. post office at 380 Hamilton was the first to sidestep the formal federal style. Professorville describes the collection of historic homes bordered by Addison, Cowper, Embarcadero, and Emerson, characterized by brown shingle-style houses built between the 1890s and 1920s. A standout is Bernard Maybeck's Sunbonnet House at 1061 Bryant.

Other Palo Alto community attractions include the **Cultural Center,** 1313 Newell Rd., tel. (650) 329-2366, a de facto art museum with child- and family-oriented features as well as rotating exhibits and performances, and the **Junior Museum,** 1451 Middlefield Rd., tel. (650) 329-2111, the nation's first children's museum, this one emphasizing science and the arts. More children's "firsts" here: the **Children's Theatre,** 1305 Middlefield Rd., tel. (650) 329-2216, a theatrical arts program started in 1932 with youngsters doing it all, from the writing and staging to lighting, sound, and set design, and the nearby public **Children's Library,** 1276 Harriet St., tel. (650) 329-2134, which includes 18,000 books plus an adjacent "Secret Garden," a favorite for storytellers.

It's also fun to just stroll around downtown. Especially along University and Hamilton Avenues, notice the town's nine surreal outdoor murals by Greg Brown. Some of Palo Alto's best attractions are its bookstores, from **Megabooks,** 444 University Ave., tel. (650) 326-4730 (good used books) and the **Stanford Bookstore** just down the street at 135 University, tel. (650) 614-0280, to **Chimæra Books and Records,** 165 University, tel. (650) 327-1122, noted for its great selection of new and used poetry. **Bell's Books,** 536 Emerson, tel. (650) 323-7822, is a Palo Alto classic—a time-honored book emporium stacked floor to ceiling with both new and used volumes. **Printers Inc.,**

Printers Inc. Bookstore

310 California Ave., tel. (650) 327-6500, is a café and bookstore all in one.

Did you know that the number of Barbie dolls sold in the United States since 1959 is at least five times greater than the number of Americans born since then? That obscure 1991 *Harper's Magazine* statistic surely comes as no surprise to fans. The history of Barbie and cohorts is as much about American conceptions of the feminine ideal, and fashion, as it is about dolls. Palo Alto was once (and will be again?) home to the **Barbie Doll Hall of Fame,** a 20,000-piece private shrine to American cultural value of human physical perfection as symbolized by plastic Ken, Barbie, Skipper, and related dolls manufactured by Mattel Toys. Mattel purchased the collection and has yet to reopen its version of the Hall of Fame. For current information, call (650) 326-5841.

Near Palo Alto, Menlo Park is home to the West Coast lifestyle-establishing institution of *Sunset* magazine, 80 Willow Rd. (at Middlefield), tel. (650) 321-3600. The gorgeous gardens at *Sunset* are open to the public weekdays 8:30 a.m.- 4:30 p.m. Also in Menlo Park is the **U.S. Geological Survey map center,** 345 Middlefield Rd., tel. (650) 329-4390. For earthquake infor-

mation, call the survey office at (650) 329-4025 or visit their website at quake.wr.usgs.gov.

PRACTICAL PALO ALTO

Area Accommodations
Southwest of town in Los Altos Hills is the wonderful **HI-AYH Hidden Villa Ranch Hostel,** 26870 Moody Rd., tel. (650) 949-8648, a woodsy and rustic ranch-style cabin setup on 1,600 acres but open only Sept.-May. Budget. (Popular, so call ahead.) Also available—and not that far for those with a car—is the **AYH Sanborn Park Hostel** in Saratoga (see San Jose and Vicinity).

Though some distance away, in Burlingame north of Palo Alto, unusual and unusually enjoyable is a stay at the tranquil **Mercy Center,** 2300 Adeline Ave., tel. (650) 340-7474, an ecumenical retreat run by the Sisters of Mercy. Individuals can stay in rooms when space is available. Silence is the rule. The center is popular for group retreats, so call ahead to check current rates and make reservations.

In Palo Alto proper, ever-faithful **Motel 6,** 4301 El Camino Real, tel. (650) 949-0833, is almost always full—call well in advance for reservations. This one is pricey by Motel 6 standards. Moderate. Other motels abound along El Camino Real. The **Country Inn Motel,** 4345 El Camino Real, tel. (650) 948-9154, is among the most reasonable (Moderate), though there's also **Townhouse Inn,** 4164 El Camino Real, tel. (650) 493-4492 (Expensive). Also good midrange choices include the **Coronet Motel,** 2455 El Camino Real, tel. (650) 326-1081 (Moderate), and the very nice **Sky Ranch Inn,** 4234 El Camino Real (across from the Hyatt), tel. (650) 493-7221 (Moderate-Expensive). The **Hyatt Rickeys,** 4219 El Camino Real, tel. (650) 493-8000 or toll-free (800) 532-1496, has all the usual Hyatt amenities. Luxury. (Rooms are cheapest on Friday and Saturday nights.) A better bargain, usually, is the **Creekside Inn,** 3400 El Camino Real, tel. (650) 493-2411 or toll-free (800) 492-7335. Premium-Luxury.

Top-drawer accommodations close to campus include the **Sheraton Palo Alto,** 625 El Camino Real, tel. (650) 328-2800 or toll-free (800) 325-3535 (Luxury), and **Stanford Terrace Inn,** 531 Stanford Ave., tel. (650) 857-0333 (Luxury). The exquisite **Garden Court Hotel** is downtown at 520 Cowper St., tel. (650) 322-9000. Luxury.

Homier and usually more reasonable is **Cowper Inn** bed and breakfast, 705 Cowper St., tel. (650) 327-4475, which offers 14 rooms in a turn-of-the-century Victorian within walking distance of downtown and the university. Nice continental breakfast. Two rooms with shared bath (Moderate; others Premium). Quite reasonable, too, is **Hotel California,** a bed-and-breakfast establishment at 2431 Ash St., tel. (650) 322-7666. Moderate. The **Victorian on Lytton,** 555 Lytton Ave., tel. (650) 322-8555, is an elegant Victorian, circa 1895, with an English country garden, 10 guest rooms, in-room continental breakfast service, and afternoon tea and cookies, port, and sherry. Luxury. Also serving up a taste of history, minus most of the frills, is downtown Palo Alto's historic **Cardinal Hotel,** 235 Hamilton Ave., tel. (650) 323-5101, with rooms with shared or private bath. Even if you don't stay, do stop by for a look—noting in particular the automobile included in the exterior terra-cotta, a very unusual artistic flourish. Rates vary widely, from Moderate to Luxury.

For more information about accommodations and restaurants in the greater Palo Alto area, contact either the **Menlo Park Chamber of Commerce,** 1100 Merrill St., Menlo Park, CA 94025, tel. (650) 325-2818, or the **Los Altos Chamber of Commerce,** 321 University Ave., Los Altos, CA 94022, tel. (650) 948-1455.

Inexpensive Student-Style Fare

The University Ave. area offers a generous choice in fairly cheap eats. For gourmet pizza, including cornmeal crusts and dozens of topping choices, head to **Vicolo Pizzeria,** 473 University Ave. (at Cowper), tel. (650) 324-4877, where you can even buy by the slice. Open daily for lunch and dinner. Chili pepper lights brighten **Andale Taqueria,** 209 University, tel. (650) 323-2939, which specializes in California-fresh Mexican: mesquite-grilled chicken, low-fat black beans and fresh tamales. Even healthier is **The Good Earth,** 185 University, tel. (650) 321-9449, a natural foods franchise with good earthy muffins, omelettes, and breakfast shakes served until 11 a.m. At lunch and beyond, expect burgers (vegetarian, turkey, or beef) and tasty sandwiches (like the Key Largo

shrimp), homemade soups and salads, fresh fish specials, and hearty entrées like walnut mushroom au gratin and Malaysian cashew chicken. Good desserts, too.

A little farther afield is one of two local **Hobee's,** 4224 El Camino Real, tel. (650) 856-6124, locally famous for its coffeecake, omelettes, burgers, sandwiches, and such. No reservations, so prepare to wait. (The other Hobee's is at the Town & Country Village shopping center on El Camino Real, tel. 650-327-4111.) In Mountain View, **Frankie, Johnnie, and Luigi Too,** 939 W. El Camino Real, tel. (650) 967-5384, is popular for pizza.

More Expensive Fare

Spago Palo Alto, 265 Lytton Ave., tel. (650) 833-1000, is the Northern California outpost of Wolfgang Puck's celebrated L.A. eatery. Look for the same intriguing approach—anything from gourmet minipizzas to Chinese-style duck. Open for lunch weekdays only and for dinner daily. For an interesting Victorian-Industrial ambience and excellent Mediterranean-influenced cuisine, try **Zibibbo,** 430 Kipling Ave., tel. (650) 328-6722, which sports a wood-fired grill and lots of alfresco seating. New Orleans Cajun and Creole cookin' is the specialty at **NOLA,** 535 Ramona St. (between University and Hamilton), tel. (650) 328-2722, open weekdays for lunch, nightly for dinner.

Here as elsewhere, **Il Fornaio,** 520 Cowper St. (inside the Garden Court Hotel), tel. (650) 853-3888, is a chic California-style franchise born at a baker's school in Milan and noted for its good breakfasts and Northern Italian specialties. Always a good bet for a bit of that Northern Italian ambience is the venerable **Osteria,** 247 Hamilton Ave., tel. (650) 328-5700, one of the area's best trattorias. **L'Amie Donia,** 530 Bryant St., tel. (650) 323-7614, serves outstanding rustic French-American cuisine from an open kitchen where you can watch the action. Open Tues.-Sat. for dinner.

Astounding portions of good American food are served with a song (at least at dinner) at the local outpost of **Max's Opera Cafe,** 711 Stanford Shopping Center (180 El Camino Real), tel. (650) 323-6297. (In nice weather, head for a patio table.) A prime stop for meat eaters is **MacArthur Park,** 27 University Ave., tel. (650) 321-9990, where oak- and mesquite-grilled meats, fowl, and fish are served in a historic building. **Gordon Biersch Brewery,** 640 Emerson St., tel. (650) 323-7723, is a brewery/restaurant ("brewpub" doesn't quite fit) serving ethnically interesting variations on the California cuisine theme. Good for French food is New Orleans-style **Chantilly II,** 530 Ramona, tel. (650) 321-4080. For elegant and upscale California cuisine with a Vietnamese flair, head for Los Altos and **Beausejour,** 170 State St., tel. (650) 948-1382.

Surrounding communities also offer some excellent fine-dining choices. In Mountain View, **Amber India,** 2290 El Camino Real, tel. (650) 968-7511, ranks as one of the Bay Area's finest Indian resataurants, with food and decor both thoroughly authentic. Open for lunch and dinner daily. **Chef Chu's,** 1067 N. San Antonio Rd. (at El Camino Real) in Los Altos, tel. (650) 948-2696, serves Chinese food, with Mandarin cuisine a specialty. Very organic, in the innovative California cuisine category, is the amusingly translated **Flea Street Cafe,** 3607 Alameda de las Pulgas (near Santa Cruz Ave.) in Menlo Park, tel. (650) 854-1226, worth a special trip for Sunday brunch. Also in Menlo Park, **Left Bank,** 635 Santa Cruz Ave., tel. (650) 473-6543, serves "casual" French cuisine inspired by *grand-mère.* Look for specialties such as bouillabaisse, or perhaps snails in polenta with Roquefort sauce. Open for lunch and dinner daily. Great atmosphere. For Thai food, not far away is **Siam Garden,** 1143 Crane St. (between Oak Grove and Santa Cruz Ave.), tel. (650) 853-1143. **Carpaccio,** 1120 Crane, tel. (650) 322-1211, is Northern Italian, in a California kind of way, from the exceptional entrées right down to the oak-oven pizzas.

For fine Spanish dining, don your formal dining duds and head to the ritzy Portola Valley suburbs and the spectacular **Iberia Restaurant,** 190 Ladera-Alpine Rd., tel. (650) 854-1746, where the Sunday brunch is superb.

Eventful, Entertaining Palo Alto

For a university town, Palo Alto is somewhat straight-laced—more spit-polished than scruffy— but there's life here nonetheless. Pick up the free local *Intermission* weekly around town for its calendar section and reviews of upcoming events. Another good source of information, particularly for university events, is the *Stanford Daily,* which lists events daily and provides a comprehensive look at what's coming up in its "Friday Daily" section. Even better for what's happening is the *Stanford Weekly.*

In May, the **Palo Alto Film Festival** showcases the work of Bay Area filmmakers. Local **TheatreWorks,** tel. (650) 463-1950 (administration) or (650) 903-6000 (box office), is one of the Bay Area's best repertory theater companies, with performances usually staged in the **Mountain View Center for the Performing Arts,** 500 Castro, tel. (650) 903-6000. Though movie theaters abound, particularly enjoyable are the offbeat flicks shown at **Stanford Theatre,** 221 University Ave., tel. (650) 324-3700, a nonprofit enterprise dedicated to the memory of Hollywood's "golden age." The theater is famous for its classics double features. (Come early or stay late to appreciate a performance on the "Mighty Wurlitzer" pipe organ.) Admission is $6 adults, $4 seniors, $3 youths.

Being a college town, Palo Alto and environs has its fair share of bars and nightclubs. A bit different, for those on the prowl, is Menlo Park's **British Banker's Club,** 1090 El Camino Real, tel. (650) 327-8769, a convincing Edwardian bar with 25-foot ceilings, stained glass, and library books. More traditional is the **Rose and Crown,** 547 Emerson, tel. (650) 327-7673, a small and friendly place where locals have staked out their seats at the small bar and like to play darts.

SAN JOSE AND VICINITY

Once thickly forested in oaks, the vast Santa Clara Valley was quickly converted to farmland by the early settlers. Even within recent memory, the valley was one continuous orchard of almonds, apples, apricots, peaches, cherries, pears, and prunes where blossom snow fell from February into April. Now unofficially known as Silicon Valley—in honor of the computer chip and its attendant industry—these fertile soils today grow houses, office buildings, and shopping malls—all tied together by frightening freeways.

Sunny San Jose, more or less in the middle of it all, though aptly described as "all edges in search of a center," is the biggest city in Northern California. Though such a sprawling suburban enclave doesn't feel like a city, it is—with lively, sophisticated arts and entertainment and other attractions. San Jose, in fact, was California's first city—not counting mission settlements and other early outposts of empire—and was the state's first capital following American territorial occupation. What is now **San Jose State University** was California's first normal school, the only one in the state for many years.

Though others in the Bay Area taunt San Jose for its all-too-contemporary concrete and its apparent lack of community, the area has many merits—one being a good sense of humor. While Palo Alto enshrines the memory of Ernest Hemingway, and Oakland honors its native-born Gertrude Stein, San Jose honors the badly written novel. Launched by professor Scott Rice, San Jose State University's Bulwer-Lytton ("It was a dark and stormy night . . .") Fiction Contest attracts 10,000 or more entries each year for its Worst Possible Opening Sentence competition. Among earlier entries: "She was like the driven snow beneath the galoshes of my lust" (Larry Bennett, Chicago) and "We'd made it through yet another nuclear winter and the lawn had just trapped and eaten its first robin" (Kyle J. Spiller, Garden Grove). The contest's 1999 Purple Prose Award winner, by David Hirsch of Seattle, describes a phenomenon he no doubt knows well: "Rain—violent torrents of it, rain like fetid water from a God-sized pot of pasta strained through a sky-wide collander, rain as Noah knew it, flaying the shuddering trees, whipping the white-capped waters, violating the sodden firmament, purging purity and filth alike from the land, rain without mercy, without surcease, incontinent rain, turning to intermittent showers overnight with partial clearing Tuesday."

For an anthology of the best of the contest's worst writing, look for Penguin's *It Was a Dark and Stormy Night: The Final Conflict.*

DOWNTOWN SAN JOSE

Tired of being mocked for years as the city without a heart, San Jose is determined to obtain both heart and soul. Typical of the Bay Area gentrification trend, the city's decrepit downtown—more or less defined as the plaza area near San Carlos and Market Streets—is being swept clean of derelicts and the otherwise down-and-out. Nowadays, new office buildings, hotels, and cleaned-up urban shopping and residential neighborhoods are taking the place of flophouses and run-down liquor stores.

As a friendly destination for families and businessfolk alike, the new downtown San Jose is astounding. The unofficial and striking centerpiece is the towering 541-room **Fairmont Hotel,** part of the city's Silicon Valley Financial Complex, which also includes a 17-story office tower, an apartment complex, and a retail pavilion. Market Street's **Plaza de César Chávez,** the original center of the Pueblo of San Jose, is almost like the Fairmont's private front lawn, with walkways, benches, and a dancing-water fountain. Not far away, at Market St. and Viola Ave., is the city's downtown **San Jose McEnery Convention Center,** a 425,000-square-foot, $140 million project that augments existing convention facilities and the **Center for Performing Arts.** Other hotels surrounding the Convention Center—including the Crowne Plaza San Jose, the San Jose Hilton and Towers, and the refurbished historic Hotel De Anza and Hyatt Sainte Claire—help make the area attractive to conventioneers. Families and other travelers will enjoy downtown's variety of museums—including the **Tech Museum of Innovation,** the **Children's Discovery Museum of San Jose,** and the **San Jose Museum of Art.** Nearby **San Jose State**

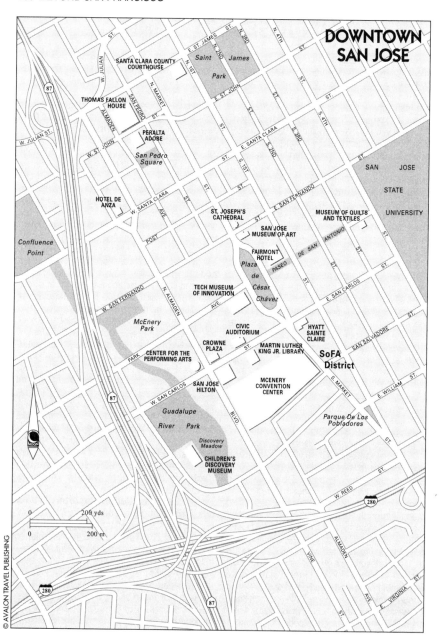

University, between E. San Fernando and E. San Salvador Streets at S. Fourth St., is home to the unique **Center for Beethoven Studies and Museum.** Not far away is San Jose's artsy **SoFA** neighborhood, a blend of galleries, small theaters, and coffee joints located in the South of First (Street) Area.

Still under development these days is **Guadalupe River Park,** a three-mile stretch of parks, gardens, jogging trails, and recreational facilities that will one day connect directly to San Jose International Airport. The park runs by downtown's **San Jose Arena,** a major sports facility that is home to the immensely popular National Hockey League team, the San Jose Sharks. Next to the Arena, on Arena Green, is a carousel featuring several custom-designed animals (including a shark for the hockey team).

To make it easy to get around once you've arrived in central San Jose, the downtown transit mall is a centralized stop for public buses—including the vintage trolleys that ply an around-downtown route—and a light rail system that runs all the way to Great America.

San Jose Museum of Art

Tucked in next to the newly restored St. Joseph Cathedral right downtown on the plaza, the San Jose Museum of Art, 110 S. Market St. (at San Fernando St.), San Jose, CA 95113, tel. (408) 294-2787, is a sparkling touch of tradition hitched to the avant-garde art world. The striking dark Romanesque main building, built in 1892 as a post office, later became the San Jose City Library. Since 1971, it has been San Jose's public home for the arts. In 1991, with the addition of an ultramodern, 45,000-square-foot, $14 million annex, the museum took a giant step into the big-time art world. It's now able to attract major traveling exhibits, concentrating on contemporary and culturally diverse regional, national, and international visual arts. The museum's permanent collection emphasizes modern and American paintings, sculpture, drawings, and photographs. It includes works by David Best, Richard Diebenkorn, Sam Francis, Rupert Garcia, Robert Hudson, Nathan Oliveira, and many others.

The museum also sponsors an active public education program—from art classes, lectures, and symposia to art and art history instruction in the public schools—and features a fine book and gift shop. Museum hours are Tues.-Sun. 10 a.m.-5 p.m. (until 8 p.m. on Thursday). It may be open at other times as well, for special events. The book/gift shop is open Mon.-Sat. 10 a.m.-7 p.m., Sunday noon-5 p.m. Admission to the museum is $6 adults, $3 seniors/students/ages 6-17, free for children age 5 and under, and free for everyone on the first Thursday of each month. Free guided docent tours are offered daily at 12:30 and 2:30 p.m., and are also scheduled at other times. Spanish- and Vietnamese-speaking docents are available, as are free audiotape tours in English, Spanish, and Vietnamese. Visit the museum on the web at www.sjmusart.org.

Tech Museum of Innovation

People visiting San Jose often ask how to find Silicon Valley, that mythic destination where California has worked its high-tech, silicon-chip magic since the 1960s. The exact directions are difficult to give. Silicon Valley is a phenomenon, more than any precise place—though that "place," to the extent it can be located on a map, is indeed here, in the general vicinity of the Santa Clara Valley. If one really wants to see the result of computer-related creativity, entrepreneurial drive, innovation, unrelenting competitiveness, and massive amounts of venture capital, one can easily find Silicon Valley. The facile facelessness of the area's contemporary industrial parks is as much a part of San Jose's integrated circuitry as its freeway system.

A better place to "see" Silicon Valley, in the end, is at the community's technology museum. Everyone knows a purported "children's museum" is a smashing success when grown-ups practically knock each other over trying to get their hands on the exhibits. San Jose's exciting Tech Museum of Innovation, 201 S. Market St. (at Park), tel. (408) 795-6100 or (408) 294-8324, www.thetech.org, is just that kind of place.

The museum's new 132,000-square-foot building houses five galleries—Innovation, Exploration, Communication, Life Tech, and "Center of the Edge"—all filled with interactive exhibits. You can design a roller coaster, pilot a robot sub, experience a simulated earthquake, look at an ultrasound image of your hand, or experience the huge, wrap-around Hackworth IMAX Dome Theater and its 14,000-watt sound system. This is without a doubt the Mother of All Interactive Museums.

The gift shop is also entertaining, stocking an impressive selection of educational toys and oddities, like jewelry made with real chips and light-emitting diodes. The Tech Museum is open daily 10 a.m.-6 p.m. in summer, and Tues.-Sun. (and Monday holidays) 10 a.m.-5 p.m. the rest of the year; closed on Easter, Thanksgiving, Christmas, and New Year's Day. Admission to either the galleries or the IMAX theater is $8 general, $7 seniors, $6 kids 3-12. Combination tickets good for both cost $14/$13/$11, respectively. Discounts available for groups of 12 or more.

To "help fight scientific illiteracy," which is the purpose of the Tech Museum, become a Tech Member. For membership information, call (408) 795-6107.

Children's Discovery Museum

The concept is enough to terrorize parents and babysitters, but the fact is, there are no rules at the Children's Discovery Museum of San Jose, a shocking purple presence in the southern section of Guadalupe River Park. Open since 1990, this is a learning and discovery center for children, families, and schools, based on the premise that children need a place where they can be children without undue interference. Three particular themes—connections, community, and creativity—drive the action here. Children can run the lights and sirens on police cars, for example, and clamber all over firetrucks, or slide down a culvert to "Underground," to explore sewers and termite colonies. They can write letters and send them anywhere in the museum via the U.S. Post Office, or experiment with pneumatic tubes, telecommunications devices, and ham radio. They can try their hand at banking, play doctor or dentist, and move water with pumps and valves. Always popular are Apple Computer's "Around the World, Around the Corner" multicultural exhibit, and Steve Wozniak's "Jesse's Clubhouse." In good weather, adventures and games are often available outside, too. And the museum of-

There are no rules at the Children's Discovery Museum.

fers a full calendar of special events year-round.

The Children's Discovery Museum is close to downtown at 180 Woz Way, which can be reached via the Guadalupe Parkway (Hwy. 87) between I-280 and Hwy. 101, then Auzerais Street. Call (408) 298-5437 for current hours and special activities. The museum's regular hours are Tues.-Sat. 10 a.m.-5 p.m., Sunday noon-5 p.m. Admission is $6 adults, $5 seniors, $4 children (age 2 and younger free).

San Jose Museum of Quilts and Textiles

Unusual downtown is the San Jose Museum of Quilts and Textiles, 110 Paseo de San Antonio, tel. (408) 971-0323, which features galleries of historic and contemporary samples of the fabric arts, in addition to special rotating shows by individual artists. The museum is open Tues.-Sun. 10 a.m.-5 p.m. (Thursday until 8 p.m.); admission is $4 general, $3 seniors and students, under age 13 free, and free for everyone on the first Thursday of each month.

MORE SAN JOSE ADVENTURES

Winchester Mystery House

Though somewhat expensive for voyeuristic time travel, at least once in a lifetime everyone should visit the beautifully bizarre **Winchester Mystery House,** 525 S. Winchester Blvd. (west of downtown, at Hwy. 17 and I-280), tel. (408) 247-2101. A six-acre monument to one woman's obsession, built up from eight rooms by Sarah L. Winchester and now a state historic monument, this labyrinth of crooked corridors, doors opening into space, and stairs leading nowhere includes 40 stairways, some 2,000 doors and trapdoors in strange places, and 10,000 or so windows. (Though only 160 rooms survive, 750 interconnecting chambers once testified to Winchester's industriousness.)

A sudden widow and heir to the Winchester firearms fortune, the lady of the house was convinced by a medium that she was cursed by her "blood money" and the spirits of all those shot by Winchester rifles, but that she would never die as long as she kept up her construction work. So Sarah Winchester spent $5.5 million of the family fortune to create and re-create her Gothic Victorian, working feverishly for 38 years straight. But death eventually came knocking on her door anyway, and the around-the-clock racket of workers' hammers and saws finally ceased.

At least, that's the official version of the story, the one that draws the crowds to this amazing mansion. But others, including her personal attorney, recall Sarah Winchester as quite sane, a clearheaded businesswoman who actively managed her vast holdings and estate. According to a 1923 *San Jose Mercury News* interview with Roy F. Leib, Winchester reconstructed the house "due to her desire to provide accommodations for her many relatives who she thought would come to California to visit her." And she stopped work on the house long before her death; according to Leib's records, she hired no more carpenters after the 1906 earthquake. The wild stories about Winchester's eccentricities, Leib suggested, grew out of her extreme reclusiveness, which may have been related to severe arthritis and limb deformities.

In any event, the lady of the house was quite a woman. People tend to focus on Sarah Winchester's craziness, but—once here—it's hard not to be impressed by her creativity and craft as an impromptu architect.

The estate is open daily except Christmas. In summer, it opens at 9 a.m., with the last tour departing at 7 p.m.; reduced hours the rest of the year. The Estate Tour costs $13.95 general, $10.95 seniors, $7.95 children ages 6-12. The Behind the Scenes Tour costs $10.95 adults, $9.95 seniors. A combined tour costs $21.95 general, $18.95 seniors. Children under 12 are not permitted on the Behind the Scenes or combined tours.

An immensely popular area attraction is the Rosicrucian Egyptian Museum.

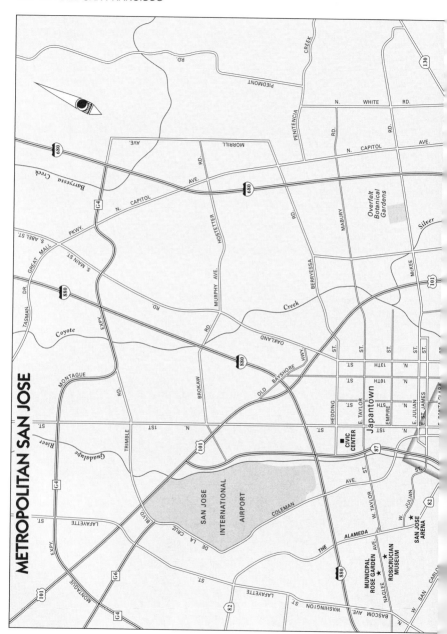

METROPOLITAN SAN JOSE

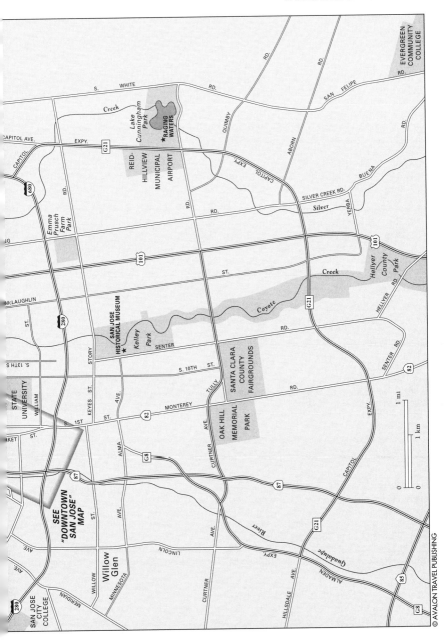

Rosicrucian Museum

A very worthwhile destination and San Jose's most popular tourist attraction is the Rosicrucian Egyptian Museum, 1342 Naglee Ave. (at Park Ave.), tel. (408) 947-3635, a temple of possibilities (in the California tradition) set up in a parklike setting open to all. The Egyptian Museum includes outdoor statuary and the largest collection of Assyrian, Babylonian, and Egyptian artifacts in the western U.S.: amulets and charms, mummies, musical instruments, a life-sized walk-through replica of a pyramid tomb (guided tours every half hour), and other artifacts in the mystical mode. Also here is the **Rosicrucian Planetarium,** built in 1936, which has been closed for major repairs; call to inquire about its reopening date.

The museum is open in summer Tues.-Sun. 10 a.m.-5 p.m. (until 8 p.m. on Thursday); the rest of the year, open daily 10 a.m.-5 p.m. Museum admission is $7 adults, $5 seniors and students (with ID), $3.50 children ages 6-15, free for children under age 6.

Kelley Park and San Jose Historical Museum

One of a string of parks developed (and being developed) along San Jose's past-trashed Guadalupe River is 156-acre Kelley Park, 635 Phelan Ave., tel. (408) 297-0778, which offers some special pleasures, including the **Japanese Friendship Garden,** 1500 Senter Rd., tel. (408) 277-2757, six acres of serenity created around small lakes complete with koi, strong-swimming ornamental carp representing the male principle.

Also well worth some time here is the small San Jose Historical Museum, 1600 Senter Rd., tel. (408) 287-2290, a full-scale village of historic buildings and replicas. Next to A.P. Giannini's first Bank of Italy (now Bank of America) branch office and looming above all else is a half-scale reconstruction of one of old San Jose's "Eiffel Towers." After a priest at St. Ignatius College invented arc lighting in 1881, San Jose latched onto the idea and constructed four 327-foot-tall light towers to illuminate the entire downtown district. The system worked—so well, in fact, that the entire sky was lit up at night and surrounding farmers complained that their livestock couldn't sleep and became confused and crotchety. But, way off in Paris, Alexander Eiffel heard

about the towers' design and found his way to San Jose to study them.

In addition to historic homes, hotels, businesses, and fundraising concessions, the 16-acre outdoor museum also includes a Trolley Barn, where in-progress restoration of the city's trolleys can be observed, also the starting point for short trolley rides around "downtown." Inside the elegant Pacific Hotel, displays document the history and culture of the area's native Ohlone people. Fascinating, too, is the new replica of the 1888 Ng Shing Gung Chinese Temple, or the "Temple of Five Sages," once located at Taylor and Sixth Streets (the site of today's Fairmont Hotel) and central to San Jose's Chinatown. Original temple furnishings and other displays tell the story of the Chinese in Santa Clara Valley. Representing a more recent historical era, the 1927 Associated Gasoline Station is a classic. For a deeper sense of life in the Santa Clara Valley prior to freeways and suburban development, stop by the Stevens Ranch Fruit Barn and take in the "Passing Farms: Enduring Values" exhibit.

The museum is open Mon.-Fri. 9 a.m.-5 p.m., Sat.-Sun. noon-5 p.m. Admission is $6 general, $5 seniors, and $4 children 5-17. Tours are available every day but Monday. Ask about membership in the nonprofit San Jose Historical Museum Association, which supports the preservation of Santa Clara Valley's heritage.

At the opposite end of Kelley Park is **Happy Hollow Park and Zoo,** 1300 Senter Rd., tel. (408) 295-8383, great fun for the kiddos with more than 150 animals, as well as playgrounds and rides. Small admission fee.

Kelley Park and all of its attractions are managed and maintained by the San Jose Parks and Recreation Department. They maintain a well-designed website at www.serve.com/sjhistory/ where you'll find a map of the park, information on current events, and driving directions. There are two nominal-cost public parking lots off Senter Rd. between Phelan and Keyes/Story Roads.

Peralta Adobe and Fallon House

Two historic buildings make up this minipark at San Pedro and W. St. John Streets, tel. (408) 993-8182. The Peralta Adobe was built in 1797 and is the city's oldest surviving building. The Fallon House is an 1855 Victorian that was home to early San Jose mayor Thomas Fallon. Each is furnished in the style of its period. A gift shop offers books, postcards, souvenirs, and gifts. Guided tours are offered Tues.-Sun. noon-3:30 p.m.; $6 adults, $5 seniors, $4 children 6-17.

ADVENTURES NEAR SAN JOSE

Well worth a look-see in nearby Milpitas is the unique, free **Wall of Garbage Recycling Museum** at the Browning-Ferris Recyclery, 1601 Dixon Landing Rd., tel. (408) 262-1401. (Take the Dixon Landing Rd. West exit from I-880 and follow the garbage trucks.) The 100-foot-long, 20-foot-high "wall" represents the amount of trash discarded by the entire United States every second, by Santa Clara County in three minutes, and by one person in about six years—empty beer cans, half-eaten food, disposable diapers, plastic foam cups and containers, egg cartons, plastic bags, paint thinner cans, old shoes, and broken toys and appliances. This museum is about as real as they get. (Despite the overwhelming odds, the garbage on display is not malodorous, since it's all been sterilized or preserved.) Other museum displays show how metals can be separated for recycling by an electromagnet; how garbage dumps can produce methane gas; and other aspects of refuse recycling. Children, and sometimes adults, especially appreciate the recycling trivia shared by the museum—including the fact that every recycled can saves enough energy to power a TV set for three years, and that the average car interior contains 60 pounds of recycled paper. The Recyclery is open Tues.-Fri. 9 a.m.-5 p.m., Saturday 7:30 a.m.-4 p.m. Free (guided tours available).

If the kids are overly distressed by life in the real world, perhaps they can be distracted for a time by the waterslides and pools at **Raging Waters** at Lake Cunningham Regional Park east of I-680 on Tully Rd. off Capitol Expressway. The 14-acre theme park has more than 30 waterslides in a tropical atmosphere. Admission is $21.99 general; $17.99 seniors over 60 and kids under 42 inches tall; $3 off after 3 p.m.; under 3 free. Call (408) 654-5450 for more information.

Top gun wannabes swoop down on **Fightertown USA** just off Hwy. 101 in Mountain View, 1625 N. Shoreline Blvd., tel. (650) 254-7325, www.caladventures.com/fightertown, a virtual reality adventure complete with ersatz jet simulators, aircraft carriers, ready rooms, flight checks, and officers' clubs.

Alviso Environmental Education Center
Just north of San Jose proper is tiny Alviso, an officially nonexistent city of 1,600 or so (plus chickens and stray dogs) technically incorporated into San Jose but actually at home on 11 square miles of bayside swampland. Fairly new here is the Environmental Education Center of the San Francisco Bay National Wildlife Refuge (at the southern tip of the bay and reached via Hwy. 237, then Taylor St. and Grand Blvd.), tel. (408) 262-5513, a solar-powered building plus trail complex dedicated to educating the public about the bay environment. The building itself is designed for classroom use, but the self-guided Alviso Slough Trail is available for marsh exploration and birdwatching. For more information, contact the San Francisco Bay National Wildlife Refuge, 1 Marshlands Rd. in Fremont (P.O. Box 524, Newark, CA 94560), tel. (510) 792-0222.

Ames Research Center and Great America
Two miles and a time warp away is NASA's space-age Ames Research Center at Mountain View's Moffett Field, tel. (650) 604-6497, reservations necessary. Facilities include the world's largest wind tunnel and—more modern and certainly appropriate to Silicon Valley—computer-simulated aircraft-safety test facilities. Tours are free; call for current information.

Several miles north of San Jose (via Hwy. 101) in Santa Clara is **Paramount's Great America,** tel. (408) 988-1776 (recorded information), www.pgathrills.com, one of the nation's largest family-style amusement parks, with more than 100 rides—some considerably more thrilling than the traditional roller coaster—plus kiddie diversions of all types, live entertainment, shops, and restaurants. Attractions at this 100-acre complex include eight roller coasters (among them Vortex—a stand-up coaster—Whitewater Falls, and Invertigo), KidZville for the younger set, and the IMAX Pictorium Theater (extra charge). Open daily from Memorial Day weekend to Labor Day, otherwise weekends only from late March through May and early September to mid-October. Admission is $32.99 general,

$21.99 seniors, $19.50 children ages 3-6 or under 48 inches tall. Group rates and season passes are available; ask about ticket specials. Parking is $6 per vehicle.

Santa Clara is also home to well-respected Santa Clara University, on the site of the original but long-gone Mission Santa Clara.

Los Gatos and Saratoga Sights

Nearby Los Gatos and Saratoga are picturesque upscale communities tucked into the forested hills west of San Jose. Both of these one-time logging towns are now noted for their turn-of-the-century architecture and sophisticated downtown shopping districts. In Los Gatos, particularly worthwhile are the **Forbes Mill History Museum,** 75 Church St. (off Main), tel. (408) 395-7375, and, for movie buffs, the **Los Gatos Cinema,** 41 N. Santa Cruz Ave., tel. (408) 395-0203, which runs many foreign and art films. Stop for some good joe and baked goods at the Los Gatos Coffee Roasting Company at 101 W. Main, tel. (408) 354-3263, to fortify yourself before heading on to Saratoga—because if you go to Saratoga, you might as well go hiking in the redwoods. Unusual gardens seem to be the signature of Saratoga, an affluent foothill town southwest of San Jose and the starting point for the very scenic Hwy. 9 route up to Saratoga Gap and Skyline Blvd., then on past undeveloped Castle Rock State Park and the backdoor entrance to Big Basin Redwoods.

In Saratoga proper, near city hall, is world-class **Saso Herb Gardens,** 14625 Fruitvale Ave., tel. (408) 867-2135, possibly the most complete herb collection in the country, a stunning display of some 1,000 living herbs complete with educational displays. The herbally correct astrological garden is also a fascination. In April and August an open house is held, though organized tours can be arranged. Visitors are otherwise welcome to wander around on their own. Call for current hours. Free.

Saratoga's **Hakone Japanese Gardens** city park, nearby at 21000 Big Basin Way, tel. (408) 741-4994, is considered the finest of its type outside Japan, a 17th-century-style Zen garden: monochromatic, simple, and symbolically powerful. Open weekdays 10 a.m.-5 p.m., weekends and hoildays 11 a.m.-5 p.m. Parking fee $5 per car, except on the first Tuesday of each month.

Still in Saratoga, **Villa Montalvo,** 15400 Montalvo Rd., tel. (408) 961-5800, is a monument to wealth, one of California's last ostentatious country estates. Built for one-time U.S. senator and three-time San Francisco mayor James Phelan, patron of artists and writers, the villa is now an artists-in-residence hall plus gallery, book shop, and gift shop surrounded by terraced gardens with nearby arboretum and bird sanctuary. Various concerts and other cultural events are offered regularly at the villa gallery and in the one-time carriage house (now a theater). The 175-acre arboretum is open weekdays 8 a.m.-5 p.m., weekends and holidays 9 a.m.-5 p.m.; admission is free.

Lick Observatory and Fremont Peak State Park

On the western peak of Mount Hamilton to the east of San Jose and reached from downtown via Hwy. 130 (the Alum Rock Ave. extension of E. Santa Clara St., which connects with adventurous Mt. Hamilton Rd.) is **Lick Observatory,** tel. (408) 274-5061, which has been casting its 36-inch telescopic eye skyward since 1888. The telescope was named for its eccentric gold rush-millionaire benefactor James Lick, who was convinced there was life on the moon. At the time that it was dedicated as part of UC Berkeley's research facilities, the Lick telescope was the world's most powerful and the only one on the planet staffed permanently. Nowadays, the Lick Observatory is administered by UC Santa Cruz, and additional telescopes (including the 120-inch Shane Telescope, built in the 1950s and one of the world's most productive) have been added to this mountaintop astronomy enclave.

Excepting major holidays, the observatory opens to the public Mon.-Fri. 12:30-5 p.m., Sat.-Sun. 10 a.m.-5 p.m. Fifteen-minute tours are offered every half hour, starting half an hour after opening and ending at 4:30 p.m. From spring through fall, free stargazing programs are conducted one or two nights a week (usually Friday and/or Saturday); for reservations (required far in advance), call the UCSC box office at (831) 459-2159. Also ask about concerts and other special events at the observatory.

Also fun for astronomy buffs—considerably farther away, at **Fremont Peak State Park** south of San Juan Bautista—is the 30-inch homemade

Kevin Medlock telescope, available to the public for the actual eyes-on experience of stargazing on most new-moon or quarter-moon Saturday nights, March-Oct., weather permitting. No reservations required. Call (831) 623-2465 or (831) 623-4255 for information. Medlock, a mechanical engineer at the Lawrence Berkeley Laboratory, scrounged up the necessary materials ($2,000 worth) for this project, an amazing accomplishment in itself.

Mission San Jose

Well north of San Jose via I-680, then Mission Blvd. (Hwy. 238) is beautiful Mission San Jose at Mission and Washington Boulevards in Fremont, tel. (510) 657-1797, open daily 10 a.m.-5 p.m. for self-guided tours (slide shows on the hour, in the museum). Painstakingly restored at a cost of $5 million, then reopened to the public in 1985, Mission San Jose was once the center of a great cattle-ranching enterprise—a successful Spanish outpost noted also for its Ohlone Indian orchestra. Very evocative, worth a stop. Wheelchair accessible and free, though donations are appreciated. Group tours available by advance reservation.

Hikes near San Jose

South of downtown San Jose is **Almaden Quicksilver County Park,** 21785 Almaden Rd., tel. (408) 268-8220. The old New Almaden Mine here was once the largest U.S. mercury mine. These days, there's a small museum open Thurs.-Sun. as well as 23 miles of old mining roads now converted to trails. No dogs allowed. For more information on Almaden and other county parks, call (408) 358-3741. Off Alum Rock Ave. (Hwy. 130) is **Joseph D. Grant County Park,** 18405 Mt. Hamilton Rd., tel. (408) 274-6121, a former cattle ranch now offering camping and heavenly hiking, with 40 miles of trails—especially enjoyable in spring when wildflowers are in bloom.

Southeast of San Jose and reached via Hwy. 101 and E. Dunne Ave. (follow it to the end) is undeveloped **Henry W. Coe State Park,** California's second largest, with 67,000 acres of oak woodlands and pines, wildflowers, spectacular views, and the best spring and fall backpacking in the Bay Area. The Pine Ridge Museum here is also worthwhile. Family campsites and back-packing campsites (no showers or hookups) are

available by reservation through ReserveAmerica, toll-free tel. (800) 444-7275; $8 per night, or $3 per night per person for the backcountry sites. Day-use fee: $5. For more information, contact Henry W. Coe State Park, P.O. Box 846, Morgan Hill, CA 95038, tel. (408) 779-2728.

West of Saratoga in Cupertino, **Stevens Creek County Park,** 11401 Stevens Canyon Rd., tel. (408) 867-3654, includes a popular recreation lake as well as picnicking and hiking trails that interconnect with the Fremont Older Open Space Preserve to the east and adjacent Pichetti Ranch to the west. The **Sanborn-Skyline County Park** southwest of Saratoga and Los Gatos along Skyline Blvd. offers some walk-in camping, hikes, and a tie-in (at the park's north end) to the Skyline-to-the-Sea Trail, which slips down through Castle Rock State Park, then follows Hwy. 9 into Big Basin Redwoods State Park before reaching the Pacific Ocean. Also here: the AYH Sanborn Park Hostel (see below).

PRACTICAL SAN JOSE

For more information about food and lodgings in the San Jose area, as well as area wineries and other diversions, contact the excellent **San Jose Convention & Visitors Bureau,** downtown at 333 W. San Carlos St., Ste. 1000, San Jose, CA 95110, tel. (408) 295-9600, toll-free (800) 800-7522 or (888) 726-5673, www.san-jose.org. The visitors bureau also sponsors three Visitor Information Centers, one in the lobby of the San Jose McEnery Convention Center (tel. 408-977-0900), the others inside Terminal C and the new Terminal A at the San Jose International Airport.

In addition to brochures and listings of major area attractions, the visitors bureau also offers a useful annual *Travel & Meeting Planner* and the *Official Visitors Guide to San Jose* (both free). Also available here: the *San Jose History Walk* brochure, the *Historic Trolley Rider's Guide,* the *Downtown Public Art and Gallery Guide,* and the Santa Clara Valley Wine Growers Association brochure. To get a sense of the depth and breadth of the local multicultural arts, entertainment, and community celebration scene, also request a current calendar of events—there's always something going on.

For current San Jose events, call the **F.Y.I. Events Line** at (408) 295-2265.

For information about nearby communities, contact the **Santa Clara Chamber of Commerce/Convention and Visitors Bureau,** 1850 Warburton Ave., Santa Clara, CA 95052, tel. (408) 244-9660 or (408) 244-8244; the **Saratoga Chamber of Commerce,** 20460 Saratoga-Los Gatos Rd., Saratoga, CA 95071, tel. (408) 867-0753; or the **Los Gatos Chamber of Commerce,** 333 N. Santa Cruz Ave., Los Gatos, CA 95030, tel. (408) 354-9300.

As befits the megalopolis it has become, the San Jose area is fairly serious about its public transportation. In addition to the downtown historic trolleys (summers only) and the light rail transit system that runs from South San Jose/Almaden to North San Jose and Santa Clara, the local **Santa Clara Valley Transportation Authority (VTA),** tel. (408) 321-2300 or toll-free (800) 894-9908, also operates a fleet of mass transit buses that travel all over San Jose and connect with other public transportation. The trolleys are primarily a downtown district convenience and entertainment, running along light rail tracks in the immediate vicinity of downtown attractions. Visitors can get farther on the commuter-oriented light rail—to Great America, and even to the San Jose International Airport from downtown. Buses and/or CalTrain and Amtrak connections can get you almost anywhere.

Get oriented to local public transit with a system map and a variety of other easily available publications, including the *Bus and Light Rail Rider's Guide,* the *Light Rail Schedule,* and the *Guide to Park and Ride.* Try the visitors bureau, which usually carries most of them, or stop by the **Transportation Information Center** downtown at 2 N. First St., open Mon.- Fri. 8 a.m.-6 p.m., Saturday 9 a.m.-3 p.m. Otherwise, for information on bus and light rail operations, including fares and schedules, call (408) 321-2300 between 5:30 a.m. and 10 p.m. weekdays, 7:30 a.m.-6 p.m. weekends. (From the 415 or 650 area codes, call toll-free 800-894-9908.) Information is posted on the Transportation Information Center's website at www.vta.org. For information on **AC Transit** bus connections to Fremont, call (510) 839-2882; call (510) 441-2278 for information on **BART** mass transit service connections in Fremont. For **SamTrans** bus service in-

formation, in San Mateo County up the peninsula, call toll-free (800) 660-4287.

Train transportation to and from the area, already a very viable option due to Amtrak's new routes through San Jose, will be even better now that the historic **Cahill Street Station,** an Italian Renaissance Revival building circa 1935, has been restored and refurbished as a full-fledged transit center. The station is currently used by both Amtrak and the 47-mile Caltrain, a freeway-commuter train service between San Jose and San Francisco. For information on **Caltrain** service, call toll-free (800) 660-4287 or visit Caltrain's website at www.transitinfo.org/Caltrain. For **Amtrak** route and schedule information, call toll-free (800) 872-7245.

San Jose Area Stays: Inexpensive and Moderate

Best bet on the low-cost end is out a ways: the **HI-AYH Sanborn Park Hostel,** 15808 Sanborn Rd., Saratoga, CA 95070, tel. (408) 741-0166, featuring the wonderful old redwood Welchhurst hunting lodge, listed on the National Register of Historic Places, and surrounding cabins. A plush place by hostel standards, Sanborn Park Hostel offers a fireplace-cozy lounge, dining room, and modern kitchen complete with three refrigerators, range, and microwave. Family room available. Budget. Popular in summer, reservations advised.

Close to downtown San Jose, rooms at **San Jose State University** are available in summer, tel. (408) 924-6180. **Motel 6,** 2560 Fontaine Rd. (off Hwy. 101, the Bayshore Freeway), tel. (408) 270-3131, is fairly close to everything. Moderate. There's another Motel 6 near the airport, reasonably accessible to downtown, at 2081 N. First St., tel. (408) 436-8180 (Moderate), and a third in Campbell at 1240 Camden Ave., tel. (408) 371-8870 (Moderate). For reservations at any Motel 6, call toll-free (800) 466-8356.

Also off the Bayshore is the **Best Western Gateway Inn,** 2585 Seaboard Ave., tel. (408) 435-8800 or toll-free (800) 437-7855. Premium. Downtown is the **Ramada Limited,** 455 S. Second St. (east off Hwy. 82), tel. (408) 298-3500 or toll-free (800) 350-1113, with sauna, whirlpool, pool. Moderate-Expensive. The **Best Western San Jose Lodge** is at 1440 N. First St., tel. (408) 453-7750 or toll-free (800) 528-1234. Moderate. For more low and moderately priced accommo-

San Jose's Fairmont Hotel is the unofficial centerpiece of downtown redevelopment.

dations choices, and/or suggestions on places to stay in a specific area of San Jose and vicinity, contact local visitors bureaus (see above.)

Fine Downtown Hotels

An immense presence towering over San Jose's newly redeveloped downtown plaza, the **Fairmont Hotel,** 170 S. Market St., tel. (408) 998-1900 or toll-free (800) 527-4727, is a 541-room study in elegance and sophistication. San Jose's Fairmont, one of five in the world-class luxury chain, features comfortable rooms and every imaginable amenity, and is central to just about everything. There's a 58-foot rooftop pool on the Cabana Level with restaurant service and a complete fitness center below—exercise room with Nautilus, both men's and women's saunas, steam rooms, and massage. Restaurants here include the excellent **Grill on the Alley,** serving steaks, chops, and seafood (reservations suggested); **Pagoda** for Cantonese cuisine; and the more casual, all-Amer-

ican **Fountain Restaurant.** Underground valet parking. Luxury.

The queen of San Jose's original hotels, the historic **Sainte Claire,** now the Hyatt Sainte Claire, 302 S. Market St. (at San Carlos St., downtown), tel. (408) 885-1234 or toll-free (800) 492-8822, has been immaculately restored into a state-of-the-art luxury hotel with every amenity and fine European-style service. This relatively small hotel has 170 rooms, including 17 suites, and offers services such as in-room safes and valet parking. Especially attractive is the newly restored interior courtyard, with exceptional Spanish tile work, circa 1927, by local artist Albert Solon. The Sainte Claire is also home to an outpost of **Il Fornaio** restaurant, noted for its Northern Italian specialties and wonderful bakery items. Luxury.

Another long-time local beauty, the 1931 art deco **Hotel De Anza,** 233 W. Santa Clara St., tel. (408) 286-1000 or toll-free tel. (800) 843-3700, has also recently been redone—a national historic landmark and a 10-story study in elegance with a deco-esque bar, the **Hedley Club,** and Northern Italian restaurant, **La Pastaia** (tel. 408-286-8686). Luxury.

The 17-story **San Jose Hilton and Towers** nearby at 300 Almaden Blvd., tel. (408) 287-2100 or toll-free (800) 445-8667, is next to the convention center. Amenities here include health club, spa, private pool, restaurant, and bar. Luxury. Also in the neighborhood: **Crowne Plaza—Downtown San Jose,** 282 Almaden Blvd., tel. (408) 998-0400 or toll-free (800) 465-4329, with all the usual amenities and pool. Premium.

Out near the airport are some other top-of-the-line choices, including the French provincial **Radisson Plaza Hotel,** 1471 N. Fourth St., tel. (408) 452-0200 or toll-free (800) 333-3333, with some great weekend bargain rates (Luxury); the **Doubletree San Jose,** 2050 Gateway Place, tel. (408) 453-4000 or toll-free (800) 222-8733 (Luxury); and the **Hyatt San Jose,** 1740 N. First St., tel. (408) 993-1234 or toll-free (800) 233-1234 (Luxury).

Area Inns, Bed and Breakfasts

One of Saratoga's hidden attractions is the **Inn at Saratoga,** 20645 Fourth St., tel. (408) 867-5020 or toll-free (800) 338-5020 for reservations. This exclusive, romantic European-style retreat was named 1992's "Best Little Hotel in Northern California" in *San Francisco Focus* Magazine's travel writers poll, a distinction easy for anyone to appreciate. The inn's 46 guest rooms and suites, some with double whirlpool baths, all overlook Saratoga Creek. Luxury. Special retreat packages with a welcome gift, continental breakfast, afternoon refreshments, and access to the Los Gatos Athletic Club (exercise facilities, pool, spa, the works) are available.

Back in San Jose, the **Hensley House,** 456 N. Third St. (at Hensley), tel. (408) 298-3537 or toll-free (800) 498-3537, is a statuesque 1884 Queen Anne Victorian with elegant dark wood decor, crystal chandeliers, and nine comfortable guest rooms with queen-size beds and private bathrooms. Wonderful gourmet breakfast. Premium-Luxury.

To commune with the memory of Maxfield Parrish, stroll through English gardens, and feast on real (and real good) food, plan on a stay at the **Briar Rose,** 897 E. Jackson St., tel. (408) 279-5999, an 1875 farmhouse-style Victorian with six rooms, full breakfast. Expensive-Premium.

Inexpensive San Jose Fare

A shining star in San Jose's small downtown Japantown district, lively **Gombei** 193 E. Jackson St. (Jackson and Fifth St.), tel. (408) 279-4311, is well worth seeking out, for the specials and noodle dishes as much as the ambience. Open for lunch and dinner, closed Sunday. Also downtown and a bit more expensive is **Thepthai,** 23 N. Market (between Santa Clara and St. John), tel. (408) 292-7515, open daily at lunch and dinner for Thai specialties, especially good for fried tofu dishes. Another option for Thai food is the **House of Siam,** 55 S. Market St., tel. (408) 279-5668.

A place worth hunting for, if you've got the time, is unpretentious **Chez Sovan,** next to a gas station at 923 Old Oakland Rd. (13th St. and Oakland), tel. (408) 287-7619, a decrepit diner-style joint serving exeptional Cambodian fare. All-American **Bini's Bar and Grill,** 665 N. Sixth St., tel. (408) 279-9996 or (408) 292-9770, is the place for burgers, fries, and homemade pies.

Otherwise, central San Jose holds plenty of inexpensive choices. (With a small appetite, some of the places listed below, under Pricier Fare, may also fit into the budget category.) For the

real McCoy in Mexican food, head for **Tacos al Pastor,** 400 S. Bascom Ave., tel. (408) 275-1619. **Original Joe's,** 301 S. First St., tel. (408) 292-7030, is famous for its "Joe's Special" sandwich of scrambled eggs, spinach, and ground beef. The **Red Sea,** 684 N. First St., tel. (408) 993-1990, serves Ethiopian food.

Pricier San Jose Area Fare

Brewpub fans: **Gordon Biersch Brewery Restaurant** is an upscale place in an alley downtown between First and Second Streets, 33 E. San Fernando St., tel. (408) 294-6785, where in good weather you can quaff a few of the namesake German-style brews out on the patio. The food's not bad, either. (Gordon Biersch also has outposts in Palo Alto, San Francisco, and beyond.) Some people prefer the area's other notable brewpub, boisterous **Tied House Cafe and Brewery of San Jose,** 65 N. San Pedro St., tel. (408) 295-2739, with eight beers on tap and an American-style pubhouse menu. (Vegetarian dishes, too.) Chic for sushi and such is **California Sushi and Grill,** 1 E. San Fernando, tel. (408) 297-1847 (there's another at 2050 Gateway Place, tel. 408-436-1754).

The city's most genuine steak house and rib joint is **Henry's World Famous Hi-Life,** 301 W. St. John St. (at Almaden Blvd.), tel. (408) 295-5414, a no-frills thrill from the Formica tables and paper placemats to the rhythm and blues on the jukebox. For German food, try **Germania Restaurant at the Hochburg,** 261 N. Second St. (at Julian), tel. (408) 295-4484, or **Teske's Germania,** 255 N. First St., tel. (408) 292-0291.

Eulipia, 374 S. First St. (between San Salvador and San Carlos), tel. (408) 280-6161, is chic yet casual, one of the South Bay's best for California cuisine at lunch and dinner. Longtime local legend **Paolo's** is now home downtown at 333 W. San Carlos St., tel. (408) 294-2558, across from the Center for Performing Arts, and noted for its contemporary turn on Italian classics. Open for lunch weekdays, for dinner nightly except Sunday. Also good for upscale Italian fare is **Bella Mia,** 58 S. First St. downtown, tel. (408) 280-1993.

San Jose suffers no shortage of fine French restaurants. Inside an old hotel overlooking a creek, **La Forêt,** 21747 Bertram Rd., tel. (408) 997-3458, is an exceptional French restaurant specializing in seafood and wild game entrées.

Other good choices for French cuisine include **Gervais Restaurant Français,** 1798 Park Ave., tel. (408) 275-8631, open for lunch Tues.-Fri. and for dinner Tues.-Sat.; **Le Papillon,** 410 Saratoga Ave. (at Kiely Blvd.), tel. (408) 296-3730, open for lunch weekdays and for dinner daily; and **Rue de Paris,** 19 N. Market St. downtown, tel. (408) 298-0704, open for lunch weekdays and for dinner Mon.-Saturday. For other top-of-the-line choices, consider also the best hotels. But the general consensus is that the area's best restaurant is another local institution. In the four-star category, **Emile's,** 545 S. Second St., tel. (408) 289-1960, is famous for its very expensive Swiss and French fare and classically romantic ambience.

Surrounding communities, including Campbell, Santa Clara, and upscale Saratoga, also have their culinary claims to fame. In Saratoga, for example, top fine-dining selections include the **Plumed Horse,** 14555 Big Basin Way, tel. (408) 867-4711, for French country; the exceptional French **Le Mouton Noir,** 14560 Big Basin Way, tel. (408) 867-7017, housed in a classy Victorian; and **Sent Sovi,** 14583 Big Basin Way, tel. (408) 867-3110, for superb contemporary French cuisine that earned the restaurant a place on the *San Francisco Chronicle*'s "Top 100 Bay Area Restaurants" list. Casual and contemporary in nearby Los Gatos: **Cats Restaurant,** 17533 Santa Cruz Hwy., tel. (408) 354-4020, a roadhouse with good dinners Tues.-Sun. and live music Tues.-Saturday. For current regional restaurant reviews, pick up a Friday edition of the *San Jose Mercury News.*

OAKLAND

Since the job description requires them to say what needs to be said, writers tend to offend. Gertrude Stein, for example, apparently insulted her hometown until the end of time when she described Oakland with the statement "There is no there there"—most likely a lament for the city she no longer recognized. But Oakland later proved Stein wrong by erecting a sculpture to *There,* right downtown on City Square at 13th and Broadway where everyone can see it.

Long bad-rapped as crime-riddled and somehow inherently less deserving than adjacent Berkeley or San Francisco across the bay, Oakland has come a long way, with a booming economy, downtown redevelopment and neighborhood gentrification, and both a thriving port industry and waterfront district to prove it. In many ways, Oakland has become one with Berkeley, with some neighborhoods defined most strongly by shared cultural associations. And the city has become a respectable neighbor to San Francisco, that relationship integrated by accessibility. But Oakland still struggles with its own contradictions. It was the birthplace of the Black Power movement but also home base for the Hell's Angels. It's home to the World Series-winning Oakland A's but also home to one of the most troubled public school systems in the nation. The class distinctions here are obvious; Oakland houses its immigrants and low-income residents in the flatlands while those with money and power live up in the hills. There's definitely a there here, for those who can afford it.

The city was shaken to its roots by the October 1989 Bay Area earthquake, which collapsed a section of the Bay Bridge and flattened a double-decker section of the Nimitz Freeway (I-880) in the flatlands. No sooner had the city made peace with that disaster than another struck; in October 1991, wildfires raged through the Oakland hills, killing 22 people, torching entire neighborhoods at a cost of some $2 billion, and stripping hills of the luxuriant growth so typical of the area. Though wildflowers and other sturdy survivors sprang back to life with the next spring's rains, these naked neighborhoods have been slow to rebuild. Times have been tough in many areas of Oakland.

And yet, Oakland abides. Blessed with fair weather year-round, excellent health-care services, a generally robust economy, and a good public transportation system, Oakland ranked 24th in *Money* magazine's 1997 survey of the best U.S. places to live. Even political life here seems destined to wake up: in January 1999, new urban visionary and former California governor Jerry Brown was sworn in as Oakland's mayor.

SEEING AND DOING OAKLAND

Downtown and the Waterfront

Water seems to be Oakland's most prominent natural feature. Right downtown, wishbone-shaped **Lake Merritt** is an unusual urban lake—actually an enclosed saltwater tidal basin. Merritt's **Lakeside Park** includes delightful gardens (spectacular chrysanthemums in the fall); the **Rotary Nature Center and Wildlife Refuge,** 552 Bellevue Ave. (at Perkins), tel. (510) 238-3739, a fine nature center and bird sanctuary featuring Buckminster Fuller's first public geodesic dome (now a flight cage); and **Children's Fairyland,** the original inspiration for all the world's theme parks (including Disneyland). Well-heeled hopeless romantics will want to avail themselves of **Gondola Servizio,** 568 Bellevue Ave., tel. (510) 663-6603, a company offering gondola rides on the lake (from $55 per couple). Or, stroll down the trail through Channel Park on the lake's bayside, an area noted for its decent city-style birdwatching. Despite the beads remaining in its 1925 necklace of lights and its relative proximity to downtown, Lake Merritt is not safe to stroll at night.

Preservation Park, 13th St. at Martin Luther King Jr. Way (near the City Center), tel. (510) 874-7580, is worth a wander for lovers of Victoriana. A re-creation of a 19th-century Oakland neighborhood, the park is home for 16 old Victorians that had been slated for demolition. The old homes are being developed as office space.

For some architectural appreciation and a close-up look at old and new Oakland, take a walking tour with the **Oakland Heritage Alliance,** 1418 Lakeside Dr., tel. (510) 763-9218. The organization offers various Oakland tours, including an Art Deco tour, for a small fee—call for a descriptive brochure and to make reservations.

On the waterfront where Jack London once toted cargo is **Jack London Square,** a collection of shops and restaurants the twice-defeated Socialist candidate for Oakland mayor probably would have ignored. (Take a peek into Jack London's Yukon Cabin and maybe quaff a couple at the classic **Heinhold's First & Last Chance Saloon,** 56 Jack London Square, tel. 510-839-6761.) What a shame, for locals and visitors alike, that so many ignore nearby Jack London Village. It's a mystery why anyone would prefer San Francisco's Pier 39, for example, considering the quality of these shops and businesses housed in a former warehouse district. Here you'll find the **Ebony Museum of Art,** 30 Jack London Square, tel. (510) 763-0745, a museum and gift shop dedicated to African-American art, and adjacent **Samuel's Gallery,** tel. (510) 452-2059, which holds one of the nation's largest collections of African-American posters, original prints, cards, and graphics.

In summer, Jack London Square (at the foot of Alice St. and Broadway) is the launch point for free tours of the thriving Port of Oakland; for reservations and information, call (510) 272-1188. It's also home port (at the foot of Broadway) for the **Jack London Water Taxi,** tel. (510) 839-7572, which can putt you over to Alameda or just take you on a cruise around the estuary. Other good port-activity vantage points include the foot of Clay St. and Portview Park at the end of Seventh Street. Or head seaward by car over the Bay Bridge to Treasure Island, created to accommodate the 1939 Golden Gate International Exposition and later used as a naval base.

More Oakland Sights

A walk up 10th St. from the Oakland Museum leads straight into thriving **Chinatown** (though "Asiatown" is actually more accurate) east of Broadway, its wide streets packed with authentic restaurants and shops but surprisingly few tourist traps. Aside from regional parks offering hiking and recreation (see below), the park in Oakland is **Knowland Park and Zoo,** 9777 Golf

There is a there here.

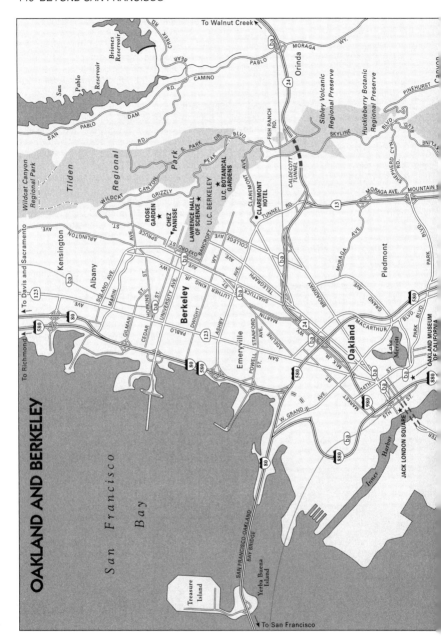

OAKLAND AND BERKELEY

© AVALON TRAVEL PUBLISHING

OAKLAND MUSEUM OF CALIFORNIA

On Lake Merritt's harbor side is the jewel of downtown Oakland, the renowned Oakland Museum of California, 1000 Oak St. (at 10th, one block from the Lake Merritt BART Station), tel. (510) 238-2200 or toll-free (888) 625-6873. Actually three separate museums under one roof, the Oakland Museum creatively examines California art, history, and the natural sciences, suggesting how all are interrelated. Altogether, this is probably the finest regional museum in the country.

The first stop is actually a stroll through the "Walk Across California" exhibit in the first-floor Hall of California Ecology, which displays the state's eight major life zones in varying levels of detail in a west-to-east "walk" across the state. For warm-ups, spend a few minutes at the massive relief map (with push-button "table of contents" overlays) and watch the astounding five-minute John Korty film, *California Fast Flight,* for ground-level views of the state.

If the Smithsonian Institution is the nation's attic, then the Oakland Museum's Cowell Hall of California History is California's. The happy historical clutter on the second floor includes the whimsical 20th-century "Story of California: A People and Their Dreams," displaying everything from old automobiles and Apple computers to Mickey Mouse memorabilia and Country Joe McDonald's guitar. The museum's third level, devoted to California art and artists, offers a chronological collection of paintings, photography, pottery, and other artistic endeavors. The museum's central courtyard includes multilevel lawns and a sculpture garden.

The museum is open Wed.-Sat. 10 a.m.-5 p.m. (until 9 p.m. on the first Friday of every month), Sunday noon-5 p.m.; admission is $6 adults, $4 seniors and students, free on the second Sunday of every month. Parking is available beneath the museum. Call or check the museum's website, www.museumca.org, for current information on special exhibits.

Links Rd. (off I-580, at 98th St.), tel. (510) 632-9523; admission $6.50 general, $3.50 seniors and children 2-14, plus $3 per auto. With more time to nose around, visit the campuses of **California College of Arts and Crafts,** 5212 Broadway (at College), tel. (510) 594-3600, one of the oldest art colleges in the nation, and well-respected **Mills College,** 5000 MacArthur Blvd., tel. (510) 430-2255, the only independent all-women's college west of the Mississippi. Many of the buildings at Mills were designed by famed architect Julia Morgan.

The **Western Aerospace Museum,** 8260 Boeing St. (off Earheart Rd., North Field, Oakland International Airport), tel. (510) 638-7100, offers exhibits of aircraft, aviation artifacts, and historical photos with a local emphasis. Open Tues.-Sun. 10 a.m.-4 p.m.; admission $6 general, $2 kids 12 and under. The **Museum of Children's Art (MOCHA),** 560 Second St. (at Clay), tel. (510) 465-8770, is a gallery and studio for young prodigies and wannabes. Open Mon.-Sat. 10 a.m.-5 p.m., Sunday noon-5 p.m.

The **African-American Museum and Library at Oakland,** tel. (510) 597-5053, houses some 20,000 photos and more than 200 original manuscripts relating to the African-American community in Northern California since 1850. The museum is currently closed, pending a move into new quarters. Reopening is scheduled for late spring 2000. Call for current information.

Oakland Outdoors: Into the Hills

In the hills behind Oakland is large **Anthony Chabot Regional Park,** most noted for large Lake Chabot, a peaceful and popular spot for fishing and boating (rentals only). No swimming is allowed, since it's classified as an emergency local water supply. On weekends April-Sept., take the *Lake Chabot Queen* ferry (small fee) to points around the lake. Other attractions include picnic areas, archery and rifle ranges, and a golf course. The vast backyard of this 4,700-acre park holds some hidden attractions, including a blue heron rookery and remnants of an old Chinese village. You can also camp here: 73 eucalyptus-shaded sites above Lake Chabot (including 35 walk-in sites), hot showers, flush toilets, group camping also available; $21 for RV camping, $15 for tenting. To get here, take Castro Valley Blvd. east off I-580, then turn north onto Lake Chabot Boulevard. To reserve camping and picnic sites, call (510) 562-2267.

Adjacent to Chabot Park on the north, mushroom-shaped **Redwood Regional Park** offers 1,800 acres of redwood serenity and forest meadows and creeks—wonderful hiking. To get here, take Hwy. 13 to the Redwood Rd. exit, then take Redwood uphill beyond Skyline for two miles to the main entrance.

West of Redwood Regional Park, smaller **Joaquin Miller Park** was named for the irascible writer who once lived on 80 acres here and hoped to establish an artists' colony. At the park's entrance, on the corner of Sanborn Dr. and Joaquin Miller Rd., you can see Miller's small home, The Abbey. Here he wrote his masterwork, "Columbus," which was equated with the Gettysburg Address before the poet's literary reputation was eclipsed by the passage of time. You can tip your hat to the house, but you can't go in. Farther up Sanborn is a ranger station where you can appreciate a small display about Joaquin Miller and pick up a park brochure and map. The most lasting homage to the poet are the redwood trees here, planted by Miller and now integral to the park, which is said to be the world's only urban redwood forest. (Along with whiskey, women, and poetry, trees were a passion of Joaquin Miller's.)

Joaquin Miller Park will also soon be home to the huge, 80-some-thousand-square-foot **Chabot Observatory and Science Center,** which will boast several large telescopes, a 270-seat planetarium, a Challenger Center space mission simulation, an OMNIMAX-type domed-screen theater, and three exhibition halls hosting permanent and traveling exhibits focusing on the natural and physical sciences. The grand opening is scheduled for spring 2000. For more information, call (510) 530-3480. Other facilities at the park include picnic grounds and an amphitheater. To get here from Hwy. 13, take the Joaquin Miller Rd. exit.

Nearly surrounded by Redwood and Joaquin Miller Parks is lush **Roberts Regional Recreation Area** off Skyline Blvd., which offers more hiking among the redwoods, as well as picnicking, baseball and volleyball, an outdoor dance floor, and a heated swimming pool equipped with a hoist to assist the disabled in and out of the water.

Just north of this multipark complex, in the hills behind Piedmont, are the wild surprises of

Huckleberry Botanic Regional Preserve. Though the eucalyptus and logged-over redwoods here testify to the area's disturbance over time, most of the shrubs in this rare-plant community are natives—thriving in the park's unusually protective microclimate. Spring comes early every year, attracting hummingbirds, and autumn comes early too, with still more birds flocking in to harvest berries and nuts. The preserve's narrow path can be almost invisible amid the thickets, yet offers some scenic overviews in spots; more views are gained by looping back on the East Bay Skyline National Trail.

Farther north is **Robert Sibley Volcanic Regional Preserve,** actually the remnants of what was once the East Bay's dominant volcano. Exploring otherwise unimpressive Round Top Peak here is a favorite pastime for amateur and professional geologists alike. To find out why, follow the self-guided trail.

For more information about regional parks here and in nearby Berkeley, call the East Bay Regional Park District office at (510) 635-0135.

Bayshore Parks near Oakland

A few areas along San Francisco and San Pablo Bays offer some respite from modern reality. In Alameda, **Crab Cove Marine Reserve,** McKay near Central, tel. (510) 521-6887, offers a nice beach and a visitor center with marine biology exhibits. And while you're in the area, head out to the former Alameda Naval Air Station to view the **USS Hornet,** a World War II-era aircraft carrier now serving as a museum; open daily 10 a.m.-6 p.m. in summer, 10 a.m.-5 p.m. the rest of the year.

Along the eastern edge of the South Bay, the **Don Edwards San Francisco Bay National Wildlife Refuge,** 1 Marshlands Rd., Fremont, tel. (510) 792-0222, usually yields good birdwatching throughout its protected marshes and mudflats. The refuge was renamed in recognition of Congressman Don Edwards' 25-year effort to protect sensitive wetlands in southern San Francisco Bay. Trailheads are located at Alviso (see Adventures near San Jose, above), at nearby Coyote Hills Regional Park, and at the visitors center at the end of the Newark Slough (reached via Thornton Rd.) parallel to the Dumbarton Bridge toll plaza. The refuge is open for day use only (free).

An intriguing if downcast monument to the past here is the 1876 ghost town of Drawbridge near the modern bridge. Once a popular bird-hunting resort (where rotating bridges across Coyote Creek and Warm Springs Slough permitted Southern Pacific trains to pass), Drawbridge died a slow death as both marshland and birds disappeared—the latter partly due to "market hunting," which involved loading and firing cannons with nails and shot to kill 1,000 birds or more with one attack. Today the old townsite is accessible only on docent-led guided tours, usually offered May-Oct., Saturday at 10 a.m. Call for reservations.

In the midst of semi-industrial Fremont is an unusual Victorian-era farm park, the only one of its kind in the northstate. **Ardenwood Historical Farm,** 34600 Ardenwood Blvd. (off Hwy. 84), tel. (510) 796-0663, is a 200-acre remnant of a major mid-1800s ranch. The highlight here is historic Patterson House mansion, which has been restored by the East Bay Regional Park District to its original, upper-class ambience and features picket fences, period furnishings, and period-clothed character actors. Small admission fee. To get here: from I-880 take the Hwy. 84 (Decoto Rd./Dumbarton Bridge) exit, then exit at Newark Blvd. and follow Ardenwood/Newark north to the park's entrance.

The bulk of the land once encompassed by the old ranch now makes up nearby **Coyote Hills Regional Park,** noted for its own living-history program—one that re-creates the daily life of the Ohlone people who lived in these salt-marsh grasslands ("Old Ways" workshops are also offered). For more information on ranger-led tours to area shell mounds and other archaeological sights, including a reconstructed Ohlone village, stop by the Coyote Hills Visitor Center, 8000 Patterson Rd. in Fremont, open daily 10 a.m.-5 p.m., or call (510) 795-9385. Coyote Hills Regional Park is also a good place to start a creekside trek along the Alameda Creek Bicycle Path, the longest (12 mile) paved bike trail in the East Bay. Pick up trail and park maps at the visitor center.

Farther north, undeveloped **Hayward Regional Shoreline** (in two separate sections along the bay just north of Hwy. 92) is not particularly appealing—but will be one day, because this is the largest salt-marsh restoration project underway on the West Coast. Though it's much more difficult to reestablish what was so easily destroyed through diking and other diversions of nature, the birds are already coming back.

North of San Pablo and jutting into San Pablo Bay is 2,000-acre **Point Pinole Regional Shoreline,** an area once dedicated to manufacturing dynamite—which explains why there has been no development here—and now an amazement: several miles of pristine bay frontage and salt marshes sheltering rare birds, meadows, and peace.

PRACTICAL OAKLAND

Staying in Oakland

Though San Francisco offers a wider range of accommodations options, Oakland has its share of nice digs; for a complete listing, contact the **Oakland Convention and Visitors Bureau,** toll-free (800) 262-5526, or the **Oakland Chamber of Commerce,** 475 14th St., tel. (510) 874-4800. Camping at Lake Chabot is always an option (see above).

Best Western Inn at The Square, 233 Broadway (near the entrance to Jack London Square), tel. (510) 452-4565 or toll-free (800) 780-7234, offers a pool, sauna, and parking garage. Premium. Just north of Jack London Square is **Waterfront Plaza Hotel,** 10 Washington St., tel. (510) 836-3800 or toll-free (800) 729-3638. Luxury.

Hampton Inn, 8465 Enterprise Way (a few miles south of downtown, off I-880 and Hegenberger Rd.), tel. (510) 632-8900 or toll-free (800) 426-7866, offers the usual amenities plus whirlpool and airport transportation. Expensive. The **Marriott Oakland,** 1001 Broadway, tel. (510) 451-4000 or toll-free (800) 228-9290, is near the Convention Center and has rooms with a view. Luxury.

Special Oakland Stays

The **Washington Inn,** 495 10th St. (between Broadway and Washington, just across from the Oakland Convention Center), tel. (510) 452-1776, is an intimate 1913 hotel restored to its turn-of-the-century self, yet with all the modern amenities, including a business center for corporate roadies and a great little bar and restaurant downstairs. Good value in the Expensive price category. Also appealing in downtown Oakland is the 1927 art deco **Clarion Suites—Lake Merritt Hotel,** 1800 Madison, tel. (510) 832-2300 or toll-free (800) 933-4683, which has been restored to its original elegance. The deluxe and apartment-style suites feature modern amenities like in-room coffee makers, microwaves, and dataport phone connections, not to mention the plush appointments. Aside from basic business services, the Lake Merritt offers complimentary limo service to the downtown financial district in the a.m., after continental breakfast downstairs. If at all possible, get a room facing the lake. Given all the amenities and service, the rates constitute a great bayside bargain. Premium-Luxury.

Quite special in Oakland is the fabled **Claremont Resort and Spa,** 41 Tunnel Rd. (in the hills at Ashby and Domingo Avenues), tel. (510) 843-3000 or toll-free (800) 551-7266. The elegant white-as-a-handkerchief grand dame is built in the 1915 chateau style, offering well-manicured grounds and luxury accommodations with all the frills: heated pools, saunas, whirlpools, 10 tennis courts, and—for an extra charge—a health club, massage, steam room, and restaurant. People often come just for the pampering offered by the Claremont's exceptional spa. Luxury.

Also unique in the vicinity of Oakland is **East Brother Light Station Bed and Breakfast,** tel. (415) 233-2385, www.bcg.net/brother, which sits on a tiny island just north of the I-580 Richmond-San Rafael Bridge. It's accessible only by boat and offers accommodations plus dinner and breakfast Thurs.-Sunday. Definitely different; reservations necessary well in advance. Luxury.

In Alameda, bed-and-breakfast choices include the **Garratt Mansion,** 900 Union St., tel. (510) 521-4779 (Moderate-Premium), and **Webster House,** 1238 Versailles Ave., tel. (510) 523-9697, an 1854 Gothic revival and the oldest house on the island. Rates include afternoon tea for two and a full breakfast. Expensive-Luxury. Another option is the restored 1887 **Krusi Mansion,** 2033 Central Ave., tel. (510) 864-2300 (Premium). If you're heading south, consider **Lord Bradley's Inn,** 43344 Mission Blvd. in Fremont, tel. (510) 490-0520, an Early California-style B&B adjacent to Mission San Jose. Good value. Expensive-Premium.

Chinatown-Area Fare

For exotic food supplies, head to Oakland's Chinatown, centered between Clay and Webster, and Seventh and Ninth Streets; everything here is generally cheaper than in San Francisco. Come on Friday mornings, 8 a.m.-2 p.m., for the **Old Oakland Certified Farmers' Market,** tel. (510) 745-7100, Alameda County's largest. Other farmers' markets in town include **Grand Lake Certified Farmers' Market,** Saturday 9 a.m.-1 p.m. at Grand Ave. and Lake Park Way, toll-free tel. (800) 897-3276, and **Jack London Square Certified Farmers' Market,** Sunday 10

Chinatown in Oakland is nontouristy–and offers unusual produce as well as good inexpensive restaurants.

a.m.-2 p.m. at Broadway and Embarcadero, toll-free tel. (800) 949-3276. Otherwise, **G.B. Ratto & Company International Grocers,** 821 Washington (at Ninth), tel. (510) 832-6503, features an appetizing and eclectic collection of predominantly Italian wines and foods, from barrels of smoked fish to exotic cheeses and salamis and open crates of imported pastas, as well as an unpretentious restaurant serving lunch (sandwiches, salads, daily specials) and, on Friday nights, dining and opera singing; call ahead for reservations. Similar in some respects is the **Housewives Market** at Ninth and Clay, tel. (510) 444-4396, an indoor country market with separate specialized grocers selling everything from eggs and sausages to Asian vegetables and fish.

Some of the most reasonable restaurants around are either in Chinatown or nearby. Among these, **Jade Villa,** 800 Broadway (at Eighth St.), tel. (510) 839-1688, serves varied and very good dim sum during the day, Cantonese fare at night. **Pho 84,** 354 17th St., tel. (510) 832-1338, is an Asian-style stop serving rich beef broth with noodles (and just about anything else you choose to add), chicken or crab combination soups, and daily specials (second location at 416 13th St., tel. 510-832-1499). The tidy **Gulf Coast Grill & Bar,** 736 Washington (at Eighth), tel. (510) 836-3663, serves wonderful Southern-style specialties and oysters on the half shell; fabulous but pricey. **Oakland Seafood Restaurant,** 307 10th St., tel. (510) 893-3388, serves inexpensive yet refined seafood specialties and attracts a largely Chinese clientele.

Inexpensive Food Here and There
Bright blue **Mama's Royal Cafe,** 4012 Broadway, tel. (510) 547-7600, is a true neighborhood restaurant with an astounding breakfast menu. **Ann's Cafe,** 3401 Fruitvale Ave., tel. (510) 531-9861, sits in a grim setting under the I-580 freeway, but the simple lunch counter setup serves exceptional omelettes (be prepared to stand in line); closed weekends. **Taqueria Morelia: Talk of the Town,** 4481 International Blvd., tel. (510) 535-6030, is a good choice for burritos and quesadillas.

Over in Rockridge, **Isobune,** 5897 College Ave., tel. (510) 601-1424, offers diners the opportunity to sit at the bar and pick from sushi floating by on little boats. For award-winning

Chicago-style pizza, try **Zachary's,** 5801 College Ave., tel. (510) 655-6385. Reservations or a wait in line are usually necessary.

Zza's Trattoria, 552 Grand Ave., tel. (510) 839-9124, is always packed and always cheerful. The daunting line streaming down the sidewalk is testimony to the popularity of the pizzas and exceptional yet inexpensive entrées here. Another pizza hot spot is **Pizza Rustica,** 5422 College Ave., tel. (510) 654-1601, serving pizzas traditional-style as well as California-style (with cornbread crusts), and specializing in the exotic—like Cuban and Thai pizzas. The **Rockridge Cafe,** 5492 College Ave., tel. (510) 653-1567, is an all-American hip diner beset by fans at breakfast, lunch, and dinner; it's great for burgers (on whole wheat buns) and real food of all persuasions. **Asmara,** 5020 Telegraph, tel. (510) 547-5100, is the place to go for East African fare.

At Jack London Square, **Everett & Jones,** 126 Broadway (at Second), tel. (510) 336-7021, serves up some mean barbecue, along with plentiful rations of blues and beer.

More Expensive Oakland Fare
For "Louisiana Fancyfine" food, head to the visually astounding and somehow spiritually supercharged **Gingerbread House,** 741 Fifth St., tel. (510) 444-7373, a chocolate-brown building dressed up like a fairy tale from the bayou and serving up Cajun/Creole specialties like iron pot jambalaya, cherry duck, sauteed quail, and catfish étouffée. Reservations essential.

Oliveto, 5655 College Ave., tel. (510) 547-5356, specializes in creative Mediterranean fare, especially Northern Italian. It's the ultimate in authentic; open for lunch weekdays and for dinner daily. **La Creme de la Creme,** 5362 College Ave., tel. (510) 420-8822, is noted for its country French and Italian menu. The homey **Bay Wolf Cafe & Restaurant,** 3853 Piedmont, tel. (510) 655-6004, resembles Berkeley's Chez Panisse and is known for its fine Mediterranean-style dishes and California cuisine, served here long before anyone thought to call it that. Reservations wise. One of the Bay Area's best French restaurants is **La Brasserie,** 542 Grand Ave. (near Lake Merritt), tel. (510) 444-8746.

In Emeryville, **Hong Kong East Ocean Seafood Restaurant,** 3199 Powell St. (at the end of the Emeryville Marina), tel. (510) 655-

3388, serves views of the Bay Bridge, exceptional seafood and vegetable dishes, and dim sum. Also well worth seeking out in Emeryville is **Bucci's,** 6121 Hollis (between 59th and 61st), tel. (510) 547-4725, which has an upscale brick-and-glass warehouse ambience and very good Cal-Italian fare.

Eventful Oakland

February, Black History Month, would be a particularly good time to sign on for **The Black Panther Legacy Tour,** offered every Saturday year-round, noon-2:30 p.m. The Dr. Huey P. Newton Foundation offers a guided historical tour of 18 Oakland sites that were significant to the Black Panther Party. Tour fee is $20 adults, $15 children 14 and under. For information, call (510) 986-0660. Also see what's showing at the monthly **Black Filmmakers Hall of Fame,** tel. (510) 465-0804, www.blackfilmmakershall.org.

Usually starting in March or April, narrated bay history cruises are offered onboard the **Presidential Yacht** *Potomac,* Franklin Delano Roosevelt's "Floating White House." For details and advance reservations (advised), call (510) 839-7533. Come in mid-May for the **Annual Wildflower Show** at the Oakland Museum, tel. (510) 238-2200, which offers a very full year-round calendar of events as well as changing exhibits. The annual **Open Studios** tour of East Bay artists studios is scheduled in early June; for details, call (510) 763-4361. Come in August for **Picnic in** the Park—**Jazz in the Meadow** at the Oakland Zoo in Knowland Park, tel. (510) 632-9525, and to the **Enduring Arts Festival** at Dunsmuir House & Gardens, tel. (510) 615-5555.

Not to be missed in September: **Blues and Art on the Bay** and the **Oakland Blues and Heritage Festival,** both held at deFremery Park in West Oakland, tel. (510) 836-2227. In mid-September, celebrate **Italian Festa** at Jack London Square, tel. (510) 814-6000. The free **Community Dance Day** in October, tel. (510) 451-1230, includes celebrations of African dance, jazz, hip hop, and the samba. The **Annual Black Cowboys Parade and Festival,** tel. (510) 531-7583, celebrates the considerable contributions of the black cowboy in America.

From just after Thanksgiving to early January, don't miss the mile-long holiday **ZooLights at the Oakland Zoo,** in Knowland Park—a "megawatt menagerie" of some 90 characters created from 90,000 lights. December events include the **Annual Lighted Yacht Parade** at Jack London Square, and the ongoing **Christmas at Dunsmuir** traditions at historic Dunsmuir House, tel. (510) 615-5555. All month, the **Oakland Ballet** performs the *Nutcracker* at the Paramount.

For an inexpensive thrill anytime, have a drink atop Oakland's world at the **Marriott Oakland,** downtown at 1001 Broadway, where it costs nothing extra to drink in the nighttime views of San Francisco across the bay.

The Oakland Ballet is one of the gems of the American dance scene.

For more detailed arts and events information, contact the **City of Oakland, Visitor Marketing,** tel. (510) 238-2935, or try the city website: oaklandnet.com.

Entertaining Oakland

If you're around during baseball season (April-Sept.), head to the Oakland Coliseum to take in an **Oakland A's baseball** game; call (510) 638-0500 for information and tickets. You can also visit the Athletics' official website at www.oaklandathletics.com. Or, from October to April, take in a **Golden State Warriors basketball** game; call (510) 986-2222 for information, or (510) 762-2277 for tickets. At **Golden Gate Fields Racetrack,** 1100 Eastshore Hwy. in Albany, tel. (510) 559-7300, thoroughbred races take place Nov.-Jan. and April-June, and pari-mutuel wagering is offered on races at other tracks year-round.

For other happenings and events, pick up local newspapers—including the *Bay Guardian* and the *Express,* both of which feature comprehensive calendar listings and worthwhile arts and entertainment coverage.

Oakland is famous for its nightclubs; jazz and blues are the town's mainstays but also popular are the reggae and salsa scenes. **Eli's Mile High Club,** 3629 Martin Luther King Jr. Way, tel. (510) 655-6661, is the well-advertised historic heart of Oakland's homestyle blues but also honors the Mississippi blues tradition. (Eli's is not exactly in a tourist-oriented part of town; one local wag observed that if you come sporting a shiny set of wheels, you can be sure someone else will re-park it across town and dismantle it for you.) **Yoshi's,** 510 Embarcadero West in Jack London Square, tel. (510) 238-9200, combines a Japanese restaurant with eclectic jazz. For information on other blues venues and special events, contact the **Bay Area Blues Society,** tel. (510) 836-2227.

Traditional performing-arts groups in the city include the **Oakland Ballet,** tel. (510) 452-9288, which usually performs in the astounding 1931 art deco **Paramount Theatre of the Arts,** 2025 Broadway, tel. (510) 893-2300. Also well worth: the **Oakland Lyric Opera** (not to be confused with the defunct Oakland Opera), tel. (510) 531-4231, and the **Oakland Symphony,** tel. (510) 446-1992.

Movie buffs, head to the restored Egyptian-style art deco **Grand Lake Theatre,** 3200 Grand Ave., tel. (510) 452-3556. On weekends, the theater presents live organ music. The Paramount Theatre of the Arts (see above) also hosts regular film series; call for current information.

If Oakland proper is having a sleepy night, head west to adjacent Emeryville, in the shadow of the Bay Bridge. Neighborhood diversions here include **First Place Sports Bar and Billiards,** 5900 Hollis St. (at 59th), tel. (510) 658-5821, an upscale pool hall inside an old tractor factory, with a café and dart boards; open daily at noon. Or head to **Oaks Club Room,** 4097 San Pablo Ave., tel. (510) 653-4456, a 24-hour card club (Pai Gow, Hold-Em, Pan, Low-Ball) with hofbrau and grill.

Oakland Information and Transportation

The **Oakland Community and Economic Development Agency,** 250 Frank Ogawa Plaza, Oakland, CA 94612, tel. (510) 839-9000 or toll-free (800) 262-5526, publishes the slick annual *Destination Oakland,* a fairly comprehensive listing of where to go, eat, and sleep; it's also helpful with other information. The visitors bureau also publishes two newsletter-like tabloids: *Oakland Travel Monthly,* most useful for travelers; and *Oakland Monthly.* Worth the price wherever you find it is *Oakland—A Guide to the Cultural, Architectural, Environmental, and Historic Assets of the City,* a detailed map-style guide to the city's major (and minor) attractions. Walk-in **visitor centers** are located in Jack London Square at Broadway and Embarcadero (in the same building with Barnes & Noble), at the **Oakland City Store,** 14th and Broadway, and at the **Oakland Black Chamber Convention & Visitor Center,** 117 Broadway, tel. (510) 444-5741.

The main traffic artery between San Francisco and Oakland is I-80 over the San Francisco-Oakland Bay Bridge. The bridge is nightmarishly crowded most of the time, as are all of the highways surrounding either end of the span. To avoid the traffic, use public transit. Oakland is well served by **Bay Area Rapid Transit (BART),** tel. (510) 465-2278, the high-speed intercity train system that runs 4 a.m.-midnight; fare depending upon destination. Call for fare and connecting bus service information; fare charts are also posted at each BART station.

If BART doesn't do it, try **AC Transit** buses, tel. (510) 817-1717 or (510) 891-4777, which operate in and around Oakland daily; routes are covered every six to eight minutes during peak hours (6-9 a.m. and 4-6 p.m.), every 15 minutes between "peaks," and every 30-40 minutes after 6 p.m.

If the idea of trying to drive across the Bay Bridge in bumper-to-bumper traffic doesn't thrill you, consider taking a ferry to San Francisco and back. The Blue & Gold Fleet's **Alameda-Oakland Ferry** provides service from Jack London Square and Alameda to San Francisco's Ferry Building and Pier 41; for schedules and information, call (510) 522-3300.

Travelers can also get to and from Oakland via **Greyhound,** 2103 San Pablo Ave. (at 21st St.), tel. (510) 834-3213, though the depot north of downtown is in a questionably safe neighborhood; doors are open 5:30 a.m.-midnight. **Amtrak** is in Jack London Square at 245 Second St., tel. (510) 238-4306 or toll-free (800) 872-7245 for general information and reservations; if you're coming into Oakland via Amtrak and aiming for Oakland International Airport, get off at the Richmond train station (which is adjacent to BART), then take BART to the Coliseum Station and catch the airport shuttle. BART buses leave the Fremont Line's Coliseum BART Station for the airport south of town every 10 minutes; call (510) 465-2278 for information.

Now there's even more of the Bay Area to see from the train window. Oakland is connected to the state's capital via Amtrak **Capitol** trains, a system initiated by Amtrak but now managed by the Capitol Corridor Joint Powers Authority and operated by the Bay Area Rapid Transit District. Each day, six trains connect Oakland and Emeryville with Sacramento, passing through Richmond, Martinez, Fairfield, and Davis on the way. From Oakland, "feeder" bus links continue on to destinations including San Francisco, Hayward, Fremont, and San Jose. Call toll-free (800) 872-7245—or check the website, www.Amtrak.com—to verify current schedule and fare information. Fares were still remarkably reasonable, at last report, at $30 roundtrip for the Oakland-Sacramento trip. For more information on Amtrak's "Capitol Corridor" train service, write to the Capitol Corridor Joint Powers Authority, 800 Madison St., P.O. Box 12688, Oakland, CA 94604-2688. Make advance reservations through Amtrak or your travel agent—or take your chance on a space-available trip; Amtrak station agents accept cash and major credit cards.

Oakland International Airport at Doolittle and Airport Dr. on the bay south of Oakland, tel. (510) 577-4000, is efficient, well run, and preferred by many over San Francisco International due to its usually on-time flights. To reach downtown San Francisco or North Bay counties from the Oakland airport, take the BART bus directly from the airport to San Francisco, or hop on the **Oakland-Alameda County Airporter,** tel. (510) 444-4404.

BERKELEY

Berkeley is too casually dismissed as "Berserkley" or the "People's Republic of Berkeley," epithets deriding fairly recent historical trends. Berkeley, after all, was named for evangelist Bishop Berkeley of Ireland, who crossed the great waters to save wild America from itself with the cry: "Westward, the course of empire takes its way." The course of empire in Berkeley, however, veered off to the left. That trend began in the 1930s, was sparked anew in the '60s with Mario Savio and the Free Speech Movement, and ignited during years of anti-Vietnam War protests and activism on behalf of minorities, women, the politically downtrodden worldwide, and the beleaguered environment. Still the star at the city's center, the prestigious University of California at Berkeley has become the somewhat reluctant mother ship in the ever-expanding universe of ideas swirling around it.

SEEING AND DOING BERKELEY

The University of California

Despite the existence of many other campuses in the University of California system, UC Berkeley—by virtue of its history and preeminence—is the one often referred to simply as "Cal." Despite town-gown tensions, most everything in Berkeley radiates from the Frederick Law Olmsted-designed campus. Before wandering around this sprawling 1,232-acre institution, get oriented at the **visitors information center** in University Hall Room 101, 2200 University Ave. (at Oxford St.), tel. (510) 642-5215. The center offers maps and pamphlets for self-guided tours in addition to other information. Or take a guided tour, also offered through the visitors center.

Behind Sather Gate is Sproul Plaza, where Mario Savio and others spoke out against university policies in the 1964 genesis of the Free Speech Movement. Fronting the plaza is Sather Tower, still known as the Campanile, which holds 61 fully chromatic carillon bells that are usually played weekdays just before 8 a.m., at noon, and at 6 p.m.; the bells can be heard from almost anywhere on campus. (To watch the bell players at work, take a ride to the top.)

To soak up some of the university's powerfully impersonal seriousness, spend time in any of its 25 libraries, a total information collection second only in size and prestige to Harvard's. The **Bancroft Library,** tel. (510) 642-3781 or (510) 642-6481, is the most immediately impressive; its stacks are open to the public, and its excellent exhibits change frequently. Also worth a stop: the **UC Earth Sciences Building,** home of the Berkeley Seismographic Station, the Museum of Paleontology (tel. 510-642-1821), and the Museum of Geology (tel. 510-642-4330); and the **Phoebe Apperson Hearst Museum of Anthropology** in Kroeber Hall, once known as the Lowie Museum of Anthropology (tel. 510-643-7648), which boasts the finest collection of anthropological artifacts in the western United States, including many of A.L. Kroeber's contributions.

Another on-campus monument to the memory of William Randolph Hearst and clan is the **Hearst Memorial Mining Building.** Also donated by Hearst: UC's gorgeous outdoor **Greek Theatre,** tel. (510) 642-0527. The **University Art Museum,** 2626 Bancroft Way, tel. (510) 642-0808, also runs the **Pacific Film Archives,** 2625 Durant Ave., tel. (510) 642-1124 or (510) 642-1412, a cinema collection with screenings of oldies but goodies. The films are presented on campus at the PFA theater, Bancroft at Bowditch (tickets available at either the theater or the Durant Ave. box office).

Modest **Le Conte Hall** on campus has been the birthplace of some of the university's most

striking achievements: physical and nuclear science breakthroughs that have changed the course of history. The university was already internationally renowned as a leader in the field of physics by 1939, when Ernest Lawrence won the Nobel Prize for inventing the cyclotron. By 1941, as a result of cyclotron experiments by Glenn Seaborg and others, plutonium had been discovered. In that same year, Lawrence, Edward Teller, and J. Robert Oppenheimer began planning the development of the atomic bomb, at the behest of the U.S. government. For development and testing, that project was transferred from Berkeley to New Mexico—the world saw the result in 1945 when the first A-bombs were dropped on Nagasaki and Hiroshima—the swan song of World War II and the birth of our brave new world.

The exceptional **Lawrence Hall of Science** on Centennial Dr. (at Grizzly Peak), tel. (510) 642-5132 or (510) 642-5133, pays postmodern homage. A top contender for the title of Northern California's best science museum, Lawrence Hall holds hands-on exhibits (and the opportunity to try some freestyle physics experiments in the Wizard's Lab) and includes Holt Planetarium. Outside are fabulous giant wind chimes and a Stonehenge-style "solar observatory." Open daily 10 a.m.-5 p.m. Admission is $6 general, $4 seniors, $2 children 3-6. Nearby, on UC's eastern fringe, is the Strawberry Canyon **UC Botanical Garden,** 200 Centennial Dr. (above Memorial Stadium), tel. (510) 643-2755. The garden's 30 acres of native plants and exotics include some 17,000 species, one of the world's biggest and best botanic collections. Open daily 9 a.m.-7 p.m. in summer, 9 a.m.-5 p.m. the rest of the year. Small admission, free on Thursday. Free guided tours are offered on weekends. Pleasant picnicking. Across the way is the university's **Mather Redwood Grove,** open daily.

More Berkeley Sights

If you plan to be here awhile, an invaluable resource is a copy of *Berkeley Inside/Out,* by Don Pitcher and Malcolm Margolin; it's currently out of print but is readily available at used bookstores in the Bay Area. Berkeley's northside, with its burgeoning bookstores and high-tech trendiness, attracts mostly the university crowd these days. More famous during its Free Speech heyday and later anti-war riots is the Telegraph Ave. and Durant area south of the university. From Dwight Way to Bancroft, it's one busy blur of bookstores, boutiques, cheap clothing shops, record shops, ethnic restaurants, and fast-food stops—plus street people and street vendors, Berkeley's version of a year-round carnival. One wag has called Telegraph Ave. "a theme park with no theme"—an astute observation about much of California.

Since the area has also been inundated on weekends by bored teenagers and the drug dealers and other unsavories who prey upon them, cleaning up the area has become a new community rallying cry. The notorious **People's Park,** on Haste just off Telegraph, is owned by the university but hasn't yet been repossessed from the homeless. A rallying point for community self-determination since the 1960s and '70s, today the area is primarily a refuge for dealers and lost souls. The park seems destined to have no genuine purpose in the community—which may, after all, be its purpose. Among the incredible numbers of bookstores in the area, **Cody's,** 2454 Telegraph (at Haste), tel. (510) 845-7852, has been a haven for poetry (readings once a week) and prose since the days of the Beats.

Bookstores are almost as necessary to maintaining community consciousness as coffee. Older hipsters may remember **Moe's,** 2476 Telegraph, tel. (510) 849-2087, from the film *The Graduate.* The store holds four floors of used books, including antiquarian and art sections. Literature and art lovers should also meander through **Shakespeare and Company,** 2499 Telegraph, tel. (510) 841-8916, and, if you're in the Gourmet Ghetto, **Black Oak Books,** 1491 Shattuck, tel. (510) 486-0698 or (510) 486-0699, where they actually hope you'll sit down and start reading. Popular contemporary authors, from Ursula K. Le Guin and Toni Morrison to Salman Rushdie, are often on the guest lecture circuit here. **University Press Books,** 2430 Bancroft Way, tel. (510) 548-0585, carries the largest selection of university press regional titles in the West.

Berkeley Outdoors

Back up in the Berkeley Hills, **Tilden Regional Park** and adjacent **Wildcat Canyon Regional**

Park are the area's major parks. The trend at Tilden over the years has been toward recreational development, so this is the place for getting away from it all city-style: swimming in Lake Anza and sunning on the artificial beach; picnicking with family and friends; stopping off at Little Farm and riding the miniature train, merry-go-round, and ponies with the kiddies; or playing tennis or 18 holes at the golf course.

Tilden Park's popular **Native Plant Botanic Garden** (not to be confused with the university's), tel. (510) 841-8732, shelters 1,500 varieties of native California plants and wildflowers. Open 10 a.m.-5 p.m. daily, with free tours offered on weekends June-August. The park's Environmental Education Center, tel. (510) 525-2233, is a good stop for trail brochures and other park information, as well as the starting point for a self-guided nature walk around little Jewel Lake on the Wildcat border. Though Tilden has some trails, for full-tilt hiking, Wildcat Canyon is preferable—no paved roads and not many hikers or runners on its fire roads, which contour through grazing lands and foothill forests.

Right in town on the southeast side of the university is **Claremont Canyon Regional Preserve,** consisting of 200 steep, secluded acres suitable for deer-path wandering. **Indian Rock Park** on Indian Rock Ave. at Shattuck is popular with practicing rock climbers. But for just smelling the roses, stop by **Berkeley Rose Garden** on Euclid Ave. at Eunice, tel. (510) 644-6530, open May-September.

STAYING IN BERKELEY

Since Berkeley residents have a hard time both finding a place to live then affording it once they do, visitors shouldn't complain. If none of the following places suit you, pick up a more complete list of local accommodations at the visitors bureau (information below).

Berkeley Hotels and Motels
A good deal on the cheap end, for men only (age 18 and older), is the **YMCA,** 2001 Allston Way (at Milvia), tel. (510) 848-6800. Budget-Inexpensive.

Golden Bear Motel, 1620 San Pablo Ave., tel. (510) 525-6770, is quite nice and quite reasonable. Moderate. **Berkeley Ramada Inn** is at 920

University Ave., tel. (510) 849-1121. Moderate. **Hotel Durant,** 2600 Durant Ave., tel. (510) 845-8981 or toll-free (800) 238-7268, is just a block from the university; pay parking, but airport transportation is provided. Expensive. Close to campus, too, is the stunning pink **Flamingo Motel,** 1761 University Ave., tel. (510) 841-4242, a 1950s-style wonder with the basics plus in-room coffee. Moderate. If you want to get away from it all, or be near the water, consider the Berkeley **Marina Radisson,** 200 Marina Blvd. (take the University Ave. exit and head west), tel. (510) 548-7920, where some rooms have a view. Expensive-Premium.

The **French Hotel,** 1538 Shattuck Ave., tel. (510) 548-9930, is right across the street from Chez Panisse, smack dab in the center of Berkeley's food lover's zone—a consideration if you become too satiated to move. This small European-style hotel sits right above its own café, a popular coffee-and-pastries hangout, so the wonderful aroma of freshly ground coffee wafts right up the stairs. (Room service is available, but you can also go downstairs for some latte and join the Berkeleyites out on the sidewalk.) Rooms are airy and contemporary, and complimentary continental breakfast is a genuine pleasure. But once you park your stuff, parking your car can be a problem; ask the concierge for suggestions. Expensive.

Berkeley Bed-and-Breakfast Inns
For help in locating and reserving a bed-and-breakfast stay, contact either **Bed & Breakfast Accommodations in Berkeley,** tel. (510) 548-7556, or **B&B California,** tel. (650) 696-1690. For a comfortable stay in Berkeley's brown-shingled neighborhoods, residential style, try **Hillegass House,** 2438 Hillegass Ave., tel. (510) 548-5517, just two blocks from Telegraph Ave. yet quite quiet. It offers four rooms and a large continental breakfast featuring specialties from nearby Nabalom Bakery. Expensive. An expanding local institution is **Gramma's Rose Garden Inn,** 2740 Telegraph Ave., tel. (510) 549-2145, now offering a total of 40 rooms in two huge old homes—a turn-of-the-century Tudor-style mansion and the Victorian next door—plus a cottage, carriage house, and garden house. English gardens in back. Rooms in the Fay House have striking stained-glass windows and pristine hardwood floors; those in the carriage and garden

houses have fireplaces. Guests can expect a basket of apples in their room. Coffee and cookies are available all day; complimentary wine and cheese are served in the evening. Expensive-Luxury.

Julia Morgan's Moorish "little castle" is the 1927 **Berkeley City Club,** 2315 Durant Ave. (between Ellsworth and Dana), tel. (510) 848-7800, fax (510) 848-5900, originally a posh women's club with grand public areas. The pool, fitness facilities, and on-site restaurant are open only to club members and bed-and-breakfast guests. The 40 guest rooms here are fairly small and modestly appointed, with private bathrooms. Expensive-Luxury, buffet breakfast included.

EATING IN BERKELEY

The Shattuck Ave. and Walnut St. area between Rose and Virginia Streets is known as Berkeley's Gourmet Ghetto (or Gourmet Gulch) in wry recognition of the fine delis, food shops, gelato stops, and upscale restaurants so prominent here—a phenomenon started by the internationally renowned Chez Panisse. The entire neighborhood offers poor parking possibilities but wonderful opportunities for trend-watching. And the trend has spread far beyond its original geographical limits—onto University and San Pablo Avenues, along Fourth St., even onto Telegraph Ave.—hence the far-flung listings below. For truly inexpensive food, head south toward Telegraph, though bargains can be found in and around the fringes of Berkeley's Gourmet Ghetto.

Student-Style Fare

The **Blue Nile,** 2525 Telegraph, tel. (510) 540-6777, offers good Ethiopian food, both vegetarian and meat entrées. **Blondie's Pizza,** 2340 Telegraph, tel. (510) 548-1129, is a local institution for good pizza available by the slice. **Mario's La Fiesta,** 2444 Telegraph, tel. (510) 540-9123, serves excellent, inexpensive Mexican food (and has lines inside and out at rush hours).

For authentic Chicago-style pizza, head to **Zachary's Chicago Pizza,** 1853 Solano, tel. (510) 525-5950 (there's another at 5801 College Ave. in Oakland, tel. 510-655-6385). Great for inexpensive real food in West Berkeley, from apple-cornmeal pancakes to hearty sandwiches, is **Westside Bakery Cafe,** 2570 Ninth St., tel. (510) 845-4852, open daily for breakfast and lunch. Good for lunch anytime is **Panini,** 2115 Allston Way (at Shattuck, in Trumpet Vine Court), tel. (510) 849-0405, which offers fresh gourmet everything in sometimes exotic combinations.

The **Berkeley Thai House,** 2511 Channing Way (near Telegraph), tel. (510) 843-7352, has reasonable choices at lunch and dinner. **Long Life Vegi House,** 2129 University Ave. (at Shattuck), tel. (510) 845-6072, serves vegetarian Chinese food (even potstickers) and brown rice. **Pasand Madras,** 2286 Shattuck (at Bancroft), tel. (510) 549-2559, serves excellent Indian food, with dinners as cheap as $5. **Party Sushi,** 1776 Shattuck Ave. (at Francisco), tel. (510) 841-1776, is great for exotic California-style sushi. Near Rockridge, **La. Bayou,** 3278 Adeline, tel. (510) 594-9302, is worth checking out for its heaping portions of down-home Cajun and Creole cuisine at low prices, open Tues.-Sat. for lunch and dinner.

Berkeley's Gourmet Ghetto: On Shattuck Avenue

Along Shattuck, the true heart of Berkeley's upscale Gourmet Ghetto, is **Chez Panisse,** 1517 Shattuck, tel. (510) 548-5525 for dinner reservations, tel. (510) 548-5049 for café information. Alice Waters's excellent and expensive but relaxed restaurant in a wood-frame house was the unassuming epicenter of California's culinary earthquake. Dinners (downstairs) are fixed-price, with a daily changing menu; reservations a must. Café fare is served upstairs from the central open kitchen with brick ovens—little pizzas and other simple fare in an amiable atmosphere. (No reservations.) Open for dinner Mon.-Saturday.

Cesar, 1515 Shattuck, tel. (510) 883-0222, is an upscale gourmet tapas bar with a casual country ambience; the big, family-style tables encourage you to strike up a conversation with your fellow diners, perhaps over a glass of sangria. Open daily from 3 p.m. **Poulet,** 1685 Shattuck, tel. (510) 845-5932, is famous for its chicken specialties and organic and low-cholesterol chicken choices. Another worthy stop on Shattuck's gourmet trail is the collectively run **Cheese Board,** 1512 Shattuck, tel. (510) 549-3055, which specializes in handmade bread, cheese,

BERKELEY COFFEE STOPS

Coffeehouses and coffee stops are popular in Berkeley. **Peet's Coffee,** 2124 Vine St. (at Walnut, a block off Shattuck), tel. (510) 841-0564, is a much-loved local institution, with caffeine addicts buzzing like bees outside on the sidewalk. (Peet's has several other locations around town and elsewhere in the Bay Area.) Peet's fans will be happy to know they can order fresh coffee direct, from anywhere in California at least, by calling toll-free (800) 999-2132. **Sufficient Grounds,** 2431 Durant (just off Telegraph), tel. (510) 841-3969, offers good coffees, croissants and such, and Berkeley atmosphere. The neighborhood classic, though, is **Caffe Mediterraneum,** 2475 Telegraph, tel. (510) 549-1128. Among Berkeley's other coffee house hangouts: very hip **Cafe Milano,** 2522 Bancroft, tel. (510) 644-3100, and **Espresso Roma,** 2960 College Ave. (at Ashby), tel. (510) 644-3773, a see-and-be-seen stop for the intelligentsia.

and gourmet pizza. A little farther up the street, next to Black Oak Books, **Saul's Restaurant & Deli,** 1475 Shattuck, tel. (510) 848-3354, serves fresh bagels, lox, and deli sandwiches.

On Hopkins Street

Gourmet grazing is also available along Hopkins St., between Monterey and McGee, where you'll find **Made To Order,** 1576 Hopkins, tel. (510) 524-7552, a neighborhood deli with handmade sausages and at least 30 kinds of olive oil; and **Magnani Poultry,** 1586 Hopkins, tel. (510) 528-6370, where you'll find those famous free-range chickens and even more unusual fowl, as well as rabbits. For fresh fish, almost next door is **Monterey Fish Co.,** 1582 Hopkins, tel. (510) 525-5600. The **Monterey Market,** 1550 Hopkins, tel. (510) 526-6042, carries some organically grown local and exotic produce. And don't even walk down this street unless you stop at **Hopkins Street Bakery,** 1584 Hopkins, tel. (510) 526-8188, noted for its widely varied and unusual breads as well as decadent sweet treats. Chocolate cookie lovers, pick up a dozen Freak Outs.

On Fourth Street and Gilman Street

Locally mythic is **O Chame,** 1830 Fourth St., tel. (510) 841-8783, a Japanese-style wayside inn with a rustic interior. The fare here reflects Tai-

wanese Buddhist-Taoist culinary influences, as well as Japan's Kansei and Kaiseki cuisine. The fixed-price menu at dinner allows patrons to choose delicacies from various categories. For lunch, select an entrée—or buy a bento box lunch from the cart outside. Microbrews, both Japanese and American, are served. Open Mon.-Sat. for lunch and dinner. Nearby, contemporary **Cafe Rouge,** 1782 Fourth St., tel. (510) 525-1440, offers rotisserie chicken, steaks, oysters, and more—all with French and Italian finesse. Open for lunch daily and for dinner Tues.-Sunday. For that red vinyl-and-white-Formica ambience, complete with jukebox, try **Bette's Oceanview Diner,** 1807-A Fourth St., tel. (510) 644-3230, which serves thick milkshakes and other all-American standards.

At **Lalime's Cafe,** 1329 Gilman St., tel. (510) 527-9838, the nightly changing menu may include chicken, beef, pork, and fresh fish, but people have been known to make a meal of the appetizer selections alone. Down the street, **Pyramid Brewery & Alehouse,** 901 Gilman, tel. (510) 528-9880, is the large brewing concern's Berkeley brewpub, though "pub" seems a drastic understatement for the cavernous "nouveau-warehouse" brewery/restaurant. Good beer, and gourmet pub grub. Open for lunch and dinner daily.

Eating in Other Neighborhoods

Cafe Fanny, 1603 San Pablo Ave., tel. (510) 524-5447, is another of Alice Waters's progeny, wonderful for breakfast and simple lunches. The casual layout includes just a counter and a bench or two. Next door is another Alice Waters enterprise, the **Acme Bread Company,** 1601 San Pablo, which makes the best bread around. Popular for burgers and simple suppers is **Christopher's Nothing Fancy Cafe,** 1019 San Pablo Ave., tel. (510) 526-1185.

For good Thai food, head to **Plearn Thai Cuisine,** 2050 University Ave., tel. (510) 841-2148, or **Siam,** 1181 University, tel. (510) 548-3278. **Kensington Circus,** 389 Colusa, tel. (510) 524-8814, is a pub known for its hearty fish-and-chip suppers. Tiny **À La Carte,** 1453 Dwight Way (in west Berkeley), tel. (510) 548-2322, serves superb traditional French fare. Open Wed.-Sun. for dinner; reservations recommended. **Mazzini,** 2826 Telegraph Ave., tel. (510) 848-5599, offers the food and ambience of Tuscany for lunch and dinner daily.

The main transport link between Berkeley-Oakland and San Francisco is the Bay Bridge (viewed from Yerba Buena Island).

Rivoli, 1539 Solano, tel. (510) 526-2542, is a Mediterranean favorite for its rustic cuisine, bright atmosphere, and good service. Open for dinner daily.

PRACTICAL BERKELEY

Artful, Entertaining Berkeley

Count on the **University Art Museum,** 2626 Bancroft (on campus), tel. (510) 642-0808, for some unusual, and unusually brave, special exhibits. Also noteworthy in Berkeley is the **Judah L. Magnes Museum,** 2911 Russell St. (at Pine), tel. (510) 549-6950, the West's largest Jewish cultural museum, with a Holocaust exhibit in addition to modern Jewish art and special exhibits. The lovely redwood and fir **Julia Morgan Theater,** 2640 College Ave., tel. (510) 845-8542, considered its namesake's masterpiece, is a prime venue for local productions, including jazz, kids' shows, and chamber music. Best known for nonuniversity theater, one of the state's finest repertory companies is the **Berkeley Repertory Theater,** tel. (510) 845-

4700. For the latest in dance, plays, and performance art by black artists, find out what's playing with the **Black Repertory Group,** 3201 Adeline, tel. (510) 652-2120. **UC Theater,** 2036 University, tel. (510) 843-6267, shows nightly changing revival films, and count on the **Pacific Film Archives,** 2625 Durant, tel. (510) 642-1412, for classics as well as avant-garde and underground movies.

Call the Berkeley Convention & Visitors Bureau 24-hour hot line at (510) 549-8710 for a recorded update on current activities and events. For information about local galleries and current arts and entertainment events on campus and off, pick up the UC Berkeley *Daily Californian* student paper, the free weekly *Express* (usually available in book and record shops), and the slick and reliable *East Bay Monthly* magazine, tel. (510) 658-9811.

Definitely different is sake tasting at **Takara Sake USA,** 708 Addison, tel. (510) 540-8250, which brews exceptional sake from Sacramento Valley rice and Sierra Nevada water; open to visitors noon-6 p.m. daily. During the afternoon at least, before the place becomes standing-room-only, the **Triple Rock Brewery and Alehouse,** 1920 Shattuck, tel. (510) 843-2739, is a hotspot for beer lovers. Shuffleboard out back, roof garden. Less fratty is **Bison Brewery,** 2598 Telegraph, tel. (510) 841-7734, which experiments with the genre. Try some sagebrush ale.

Ashkenaz, 1317 San Pablo, tel. (510) 525-5054, is a folk-dance cooperative with folk, reggae, and world beat, while **Freight and Salvage,** 1111 Addison St., tel. (510) 548-1761, is the Euro-style folkie hangout. For blues, head to **Blake's** downstairs at 2367 Telegraph, tel. (510) 848-0886, or **Pasand Lounge,** 2284 Shattuck, tel. (510) 848-0260. The **Starry Plough,** 3101 Shattuck Ave., tel. (510) 841-2082, is an Irish-style pub with darts, a good selection of beers, and live music most nights.

Since every day in Berkeley is an event, organized activities per se aren't really the point here. One significant Berkeley event, though, is the **California Shakespeare Festival,** formerly the Berkeley Shakespeare Festival, usually held outdoors in Orinda from mid-June through mid-October (dress warmly). For information, call the festival at (510) 548-9666 (box office) or 548-3422 (administration).

Berkeley Information and Transportation

For basic Berkeley information, contact the **Berkeley Convention and Visitors Bureau,** 2015 Center St., tel. (510) 549-7040 or toll-free (800) 847-4823, www.berkeleycvb.com, though budget travelers will find the **Council on International Education Exhange,** 2486 Channing Way (at Telegraph), tel. (510) 848-8604, much more helpful. AC Transit buses and BART serve the community, though Oakland is closest and most convenient for Amtrak and Greyhound travelers. For more transit information, see Oakland, above. For other information and options on public transportation, cycling, and otherwise just getting around, contact **Berkeley TRIP,** 2033 Center St., tel. (510) 644-7665. There are ride boards in the Student Union building on the UC Berkeley campus.

EAST BAY OUTBACK

The eastern expanse of the Bay Area is best known for its Berkeley-Oakland metropolis and surrounding suburban communities. But natural areas in the East Bay's outback offer snippets of silence and serenity in the midst of suburban sprawl, and an occasional glimpse of life as it once was in these hilly former farmlands. Many of the East Bay's treasures are collected into the East Bay Regional Park District, which includes some 60,000 acres of parklands.

For brochures, maps, and other information about the major East Bay parks—including current information on the system's ever-expanding interconnecting trail system—call the district office at (510) 635-0135; for picnicking and camping reservations, call (510) 562-2267. For help in figuring out public transit routes to parks, call Bay Area Rapid Transit (BART), tel. (510) 464-6000, and AC Transit, tel. (510) 817-1717 or (510) 891-4777.

A beautifully written "personal guide" to the East Bay's regional parks, the perfect hiking companion, is *The East Bay Out* by Malcolm Margolin, available from Heyday Books.

EAST BAY PARKS

Briones Regional Park

More than 5,000 semiwilderness acres between Lafayette and Martinez, Briones Regional Park offers wonderful hiking up hillsides, down valleys, and across meadows, past everything from wildflowers and waterfalls to valley oaks and vistas of the bay and Mount Diablo. When temperatures and leaves fall and autumn winds whisk away the haze, you can even see the Sierra Nevada from the Briones Crest Trail. Grazing cattle and deer are fairly abundant year-round, but in the spring newts are more noticeable. Included in the park are the John Muir Nature Area, small lakes, 45 miles of trails, and an archery range.

To get there from Lafayette, take Happy Valley Rd. north from Hwy. 24 and turn right on Bear Creek Rd., or, farther east, take Pleasant Hill Rd. north from Hwy. 24 (access off Pleasant Hill Road). From Martinez, take Alhambra Valley Rd. south from Hwy. 4 and turn left on Reliez Valley Road.

For more information, contact the park office, 5361 Alhambra Valley Rd., Martinez, tel. (925) 370-3020.

Las Trampas Regional Wilderness

More than 3,000 acres of wilderness just west of Danville—home to mountain lions, wildcats, skunks, foxes, weasels, and golden eagles—Las Trampas Regional Wilderness offers heavenly hikes and great views, particularly from Las Trampas Ridge. The developed Little Hills Ranch area near the park's entrance offers picnic areas, a swimming pool, playground, stables (horse rentals available; call 925-838-7546), and a stocked fishing hole. To get here: from I-680 south of Danville, take Crow Canyon Rd., then Bollinger Canyon Rd. into the park. For more information, call East Bay Regional Parks at (925) 837-3145.

Black Diamond Mines Regional Preserve

One way to beat the heat in summer is by heading underground for a stroll through the cool sandstone caverns deep within the six-level Hazel-Atlas Mine—part of the former Mount Diablo coal-mining district (the state's largest) and later, prime underground fields for harvesting high-grade silica sand. Included as part of the Black Diamond Mines Regional Preserve, the mine is open for two-hour tours by advance reservations only. For safety reasons, children under age 7 are not allowed. For more information, call (925) 757-2620; for tour reservations, call East Bay Parks headquarters in Oakland at (510) 562-2267 or (510) 562-7275. To contemplate the generally short life spans of miners—too often killed in cave-ins, explosions, or by silicosis—wander through the nearby Rose Hill Cemetery. To get here: from Hwy. 4 in Antioch, head six miles south via Somersville Road.

Morgan Territory Regional Preserve

A fascinating feature on these remote eastern ridgetops beyond Mount Diablo, as elsewhere throughout the East Bay (on Mission Peak in Fremont, near Vollmer Peak in Tilden Park, and

Mount Diablo's stone
Summit Building, now a
visitor center, under a rare
blanket of snow

CALIFORNIA DEPARTMENT OF PARKS AND RECREATION

MOUNT DIABLO STATE PARK

When early explorers and settlers first started groping toward California's great bay, they set their course by Mount Diablo's conical presence, and the peak itself was the base point for the U.S. government's first territorial surveys in 1851. Then—and on a clear day now, usually after a winter storm—views from Mount Diablo (elevation 3,849 feet) are spectacular: the Farallon Islands to the west, Mount Lassen to the north, even (with binoculars) Half Dome in Yosemite to the southeast. Mythic home of Eagle and Coyote to the Miwok, the mountain has rugged terrain and wicked winds that led settlers to believe it was haunted. According to a tale told to the state legislature by Mariano Vallejo in 1850, the mountain's name resulted from some linguistic confusion; local native people believed that their victory over Spanish troops in an early 1800s skirmish was due to assistance from the mountain's "spirit," which the Spanish incorrectly translated as "devil" (diablo).

Mount Diablo State Park is a wonder, one which some half-million people enjoy each year. Peak experiences here include the view from the summit, the Mitchell Canyon hike to the summit (the park has a total of 50 miles of trails), rock climbing, fabulous spring wildflower displays, and Fossil Ridge (don't touch). Mountain bikers may ride unpaved roads to the west of North Gate and South Gate Roads. A wonderful visitor center occupies the beautiful 1939 stone Summit Building built by the WPA.

Diablo is open daily 8 a.m. to sunset, when both gates close. The day-use fee is $5, but when area fire danger is extremely high, the park may be closed for all uses. Three year-round campgrounds with water and flush toilets but no showers are often available on a first-come basis, but can be reserved in advance through ReserveAmerica, toll-free tel. (800) 444-7275. Remote walk-in environmental campgrounds are available only Oct.-May due to high fire danger; bring your own water. No alcohol is permitted in Mount Diablo State Park (due to drunk-driving incidents and other disasters). For more information, contact: Mount Diablo State Park, 96 Mitchell Canyon Rd., Clayton, CA 94517, tel. (925) 837-2525 (information) or (925) 673-2893 (administration).

on Round Top Peak in the Oakland Hills), are squat stone walls with no traceable history. Someone obviously went to considerable trouble to build them, hauling large stones up the mountainside, but the walls have no apparent practical value and follow no known property lines. Rumor has it that they predate the Spanish and even native populations, and were possibly built by early Chinese explorers as astronomical markers.

Even today, the park's 4,147 acres are mysterious, remote, quiet, and almost inaccessible due to the wild one-lane road winding up the mountain. For those looking for solitude, here it is. Also here: a few picnic tables (pack out your trash), rusting farm equipment, and fruit trees from the land's one-time ranch status. To get here: from I-580 north of Livermore, head north on N. Livermore Ave. to the end, turn left onto Manning Rd., then turn right at Morgan Territory Road. For more information, call (925) 757-2620 or (510) 562-7275.

Other Regional Parks

Ohlone Regional Wilderness encompasses some 7,000 acres of wild high ridges on the south end of Alameda County, accessible only via the Sunol Regional Wilderness to the west or the Del Valle Regional Recreation Area to the north. Backpackers generally have the place to themselves, following old roads over ridges and through meadowlands, then camping at one of several backcountry sites. The peak experience here is a day hike (starting 10 miles in from either entrance) to the top of Rose Peak—a brutal climb for heavily laden backpackers. Rewards from the summit include top-of-the-world views of the Santa Clara Valley, San Francisco Bay, and Mount Diablo.

Sunol Regional Wilderness, tel. (925) 862-2244, also features oak woods and remoteness as well as developed family picnic facilities, and backpack and walk-in camping. To get here: from the I-680/Hwy. 84 interchange take Calaveras Rd. to Geary Rd. and continue to the end.

Del Valle Regional Recreation Area, tel. (925) 373-0332, is popular for swimming and windsurfing on Lake Del Valle, as well as picnicking and camping around the shore. Particularly worthwhile is a spring hike to Murietta Falls, a fairly rugged 12.5-mile roundtrip (pack a lunch and carry water, plenty of it); park at the south end of the reservoir, where the trail begins as an old fire road. Access to Del Valle is via Arroyo Dr., south of Hwy. 84 in Livermore.

For more information on all these parks, call the **East Bay Regional Park** headquarters at (510) 562-7275.

OUTBACK COMMUNITIES

Benicia: Camel Town

Just north of the Benicia-Martinez Bridge via I-780 lies Benicia, the one-time capital of California. The town is proud of its "firsts," though some seem stretched in significance. Benicia had the state's first chamber of commerce, law school, fire department, and public school (so far, so good)—but also the first steamboat built by Americans in California, the first railroad ferry west of the Mississippi, and the first recorded marriage in Solano County.

Take a quick tour of the town's historic architecture (most buildings aren't open to the public) and stop at the restored **Benicia Capitol State Historic Park,** 115 W. G St. (at First St.), tel. (707) 745-3385, which preserves the 1852 brick building that housed the California Senate, Assembly, and Treasury for 13 months in 1853-54. Also part of the park is the 1850s Fischer-Hanlon House next door, which holds Victorian-era furnishings and displays of period clothing. Admission to the park is free.

Benicia's **Camel Barn Museum,** 2024 Camel Rd. (in the town's one-time military arsenal complex, now an industrial park), tel. (707) 745-5435, is named for a short-lived 1860s experiment—using camels to transport military supplies across the Southwest. The cranky creatures were once stabled here, but the barn is now home to local memorabilia. Open Wed.-Sun. 1-4 p.m.; small admission.

The **Benicia Fire Museum,** 900 E. Second St. (at E. J St.), tel. (707) 745-1688, holds displays of rare firefighting equipment and a collection of historical photos. It's open on the first and third Saturday of each month, noon-4 p.m., or by appointment.

Benicia proper is experiencing an art-community boom and overall revitalization, with interesting cafés and shops popping up everywhere. Try breakfast, lunch, or dinner at Benicia's **Union Hotel,** 401 First St., tel. (707) 746-0105, noted for its creative (and fairly reasonable) California-style cuisine and nice hotel rooms. Just northwest of town along the strait (off I-780) is **Benicia State Recreation Area,** tel. (707) 648-1911, popular for fishing, hiking, and picnicking. Day-use fee is $2 per vehicle—but be prepared for the automatic gates, which take only dollar bills or quarters.

Martinez: Martinis, Joe DiMaggio, and John Muir

Martinez, on the other end of the Benicia bridge, was settled by Italian fishing families and is historic home to both the martini and New York Yankee baseball great Joe DiMaggio. A modern-day attraction is the **John Muir House National Historic Site,** 4202 Alhambra Ave., tel. (925) 228-8860, which preserves the naturalist's 1882 Victorian home and grounds. Home to Muir and his wife during the last 24 years of his life, this is where he did most of his conservation writing. In addition to becoming an astute businessman, orchardist, inventor, pioneer of factory automation, patron of the arts, and magazine editor, the indefatigable Scot explored California and Alaska, established the U.S. Forest Service and five national parks, and co-founded the Sierra Club.

The house holds many of Muir's books and writings, along with exhibits chronicling his amazing influence. In mid-December, come for Christmas carols and Victorian tea. Also on the grounds is the **Martinez Adobe,** the 1844 home of Don Vincente Martinez, part of the old Rancho Las Juntas. Muir House is open Wed.-Sun. (except major holidays) 10 a.m.- 4:30 p.m.; small admission.

Also in the area is the **Carquinez Strait Regional Shoreline Park,** a 969-acre tract good for birdwatching, biking, and hiking. It's reached via Hwy. 4 (from I-80), then McEwen Rd. and Carquinez Scenic Drive. After a short hike down to Port Costa, backtrack to 344-acre **Martinez Regional Shoreline Park,** on N. Court St. (north of Ferry St.), for more views and usually fresh air (and wind). The park has a marina, fishing pier, playground and ball fields, a picnic area, par course, and numerous other recreation facilities. For more information on regional parks, call East Bay Regional Parks headquarters at (510) 562-7275.

Crockett

Crockett is most famous for the C&H sugar refinery here, but it's also something of an artsy-industrial enclave, like a smokestack-style Sausalito. Under the Carquinez Bridge, on the pilings, is **Nantuck-**

et Restaurant, 501 Port St., tel. (510) 787-2233, a good seafood place with views of the bridge's underbelly and the nearby sugar refinery.

Danville: Eugene O'Neill Cometh

Worthwhile in Danville is a stop at **Eugene O'Neill's Tao House National Historic Site,** a two-story Spanish-style home and national historic landmark where O'Neill wrote some of his last plays, including *The Iceman Cometh, Long Day's Journey into Night,* and **A Moon for the Misbegotten.** Two tours per day are offered Wed.-Sun. at 10 a.m. and 12:30 p.m., with buses leaving from downtown Danville. Every spring, in the restored barn, the acclaimed **Playwright's Theatre** performs works by O'Neill and playwrights he influenced. Call (925) 838-0249 for more information and advance reservations (required) or visit them online at www.nps.gov/euon.

Also in Danville, the opulent **Blackhawk Automotive Museum,** 3700 Blackhawk Plaza Circle, tel. (925) 736-2277, is a showcase for a $100 million collection of classic cars, including: the 1924 torpedo-shaped Tulipwood Hispano Suiza built for Andre Dubonnet of French aperitif fame; Clark Gable's 1935 Deusenberg convertible; and Rudolph Valentino's 1926 Isotta Fraschini. The ground floor of the museum holds an **Automotive Art Gallery.** Open Wed.-Sun. 10 a.m.-5 p.m.; admission is $8 adults, $5 seniors and students, free for children 6 and under. Free guided tours offered weekends at 2 p.m. To get here: from I-680, exit at Crow Canyon Rd. 10 miles south of Walnut Creek, head east to Camino Tassajara, then turn right and look for the sign—and the mall.

If you get hungry out here in the hinterlands, the expensive, shiny, and automobile-oriented **Blackhawk Grille,** 3540 Blackhawk Plaza Circle (at the other end of the mall), tel. (925) 736-4295, serves exceptional and eclectic food. Other good choices in the area, generally less pricey: **Bridges,** 44 Church St., tel. (925) 820-7200, with an impressive East-West menu, and inexpensive **La Ultima** in downtown Danville, 455 Hartz Ave., tel. (925) 838-9705, serving genuine New Mexican specialties rarely found in California.

Livermore Valley: Star Wars and Wineries

Pleasanton seems to be the face of California's

future: corporate business parks mixed with back-yard barbecues. But the surrounding hills provide some great hiking opportunities, particularly at 1,800-acre **Pleasanton Hills Regional Park** (exit I-680 at Sunol Blvd., head west on Castlewood Dr., then north on Foothill Road). If you're exploring the area and need a place to stay, try **Evergreen,** 9104 Longview Dr., tel. (925) 426-0901, a contemporary B&B up in the hills. Each of the four rooms has a private bath, telephone, TV, and refrigerator. Premium-Luxury.

Livermore is home of **Lawrence Livermore National Laboratory,** 7000 East Ave. (follow the signs), tel. (925) 423-3272 (visitor center), (925) 422-4599 (public affairs), or (925) 422-1100 (main operator), which was developing the X-ray laser for the U.S. "Star Wars" defense system before the world changed. The visitor center here is open to the public daily, with scientific displays and videos of atomic test sites and the lab's underground linear accelerator. Tours of the top-secret research and development facilities are not available. One thing no one here will probably discuss is the fact that this is a Superfund toxic waste site (with a 50-year cleanup time frame) and that lab employees have a melanoma cancer rate about five times the national average.

If the lab gives you the willies, you can stop to pray at the town's lovingly handcrafted **Hindu Shiva-Vishnu Temple,** 1232 Arrowhead Ave., tel. (925) 449-6255. Unique because it combines the stylistic traditions of both northern and southern India, the temple is an architectural anachronism here amid Livermore's tract homes.

The surrounding Livermore Valley, home of the Livermore Rodeo every June, is noted for its wineries—some of the oldest in the state. The historic Cresta Blanca vineyard has been resurrected as **Wente Vineyards,** 5050 Arroyo Rd., tel. (925) 456-2400, which offers a restaurant open daily for lunch and dinner. Also in the neighborhood: **Concannon Vineyards,** 4590 Tesla Rd., tel. (925) 456-2500; award-winning **Fenestra Winery,** 83 E. Vallecitos Rd., tel. (925) 447-5246, which offers limited winetasting in summer, otherwise only quarterly by invitation (call for information); and the traditional **Wente Estate Winery,** 5565 Tesla Rd., tel. (925) 456-2300, where picnicking is possible on the grounds.

A wine-related stop in the area is **Ravenswood Historic Site,** 2647 Arroyo Rd. (south of Superior), tel. (925) 373-5708, an early winery estate open to the public only on free guided tours given by costumed docents on the second Sunday of each month. Two Victorian homes preside over 33 acres of apple orchards and vineyards; one of the old Vics is filled with period furniture and functions as a museum.

Beyond Livermore on the way to Tracy via I-580 is the Altamont Pass area, open foothill grazing land best known for the thousands of wind turbines in the power-generating "wind farms" here—an alternative energy source with the nasty negative side effect of chopping airborne birds into bits.

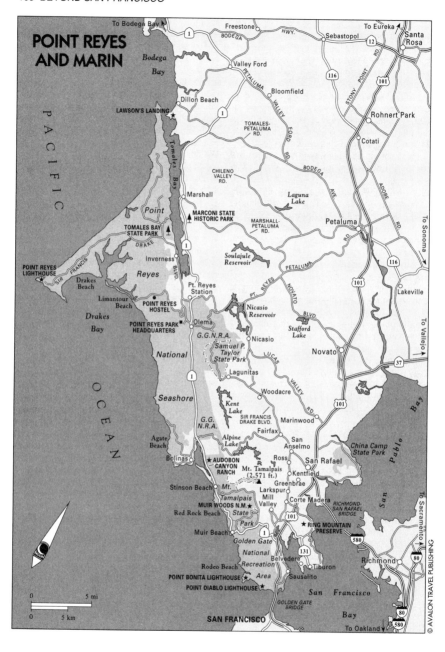

POINT REYES AND MARIN

POINT REYES NATIONAL SEASHORE

Some 65,000 acres of fog-shrouded lagoons, lowland marshes, sandy beaches, coastal dunes, and ridgetop forests, Point Reyes National Seashore also features windy headlands and steep, unstable, colorful cliffs, populations of tule elk and grazing cattle, and a wonderful lighthouse all too popular for winter whalewatching. A dramatically dislocated triangular wedge of land with its apex jutting out into the Pacific Ocean, Point Reyes is also land in motion: this is earthquake country. Separated from mainland Marin County by slitlike Tomales Bay, the Point Reyes Peninsula is also sliced off at about the same spot by the San Andreas Fault. When that fault shook loose in 1906—instantly thrusting the peninsula 16 feet farther north—the city of San Francisco came tumbling down.

Geologists were long baffled by the fact that the craggy granite outcroppings of Point Reyes were identical to rock formations in the Tehachapi Mountains some 310 miles south. But the theory of plate tectonics and continental drift provided the answer. The Point Reyes Peninsula rides high on the eastern edge of the Pacific Plate, which moves about three inches to the northwest each year, grinding against the slower-moving North American Plate. The two meet in the high-stress, many-faulted rift zone of the Olema Valley, an undefined line "visible" in landforms and weather patterns. In summer, for example, fog may chill the coastal headlands and beaches while the sun shines east of Inverness Ridge.

Seasonally, dogs are specifically restricted at Point Reyes—and people must also restrain themselves—because the northern elephant seals have returned to area beaches and established a breeding colony. To protect the elephant seals during the winter breeding and pupping season, no dogs are allowed on South Beach and beaches to the south Nov.-April. Only leashed dogs are allowed on North Beach, Kehoe Beach, and the southern part of Limantour Beach. Contact the park office for current details.

To be fully informed about what's going on in and around Point Reyes while visiting, a good free companion is the quarterly tabloid **Coastal Traveler,** published by the area's Pulitzer Prize-winning *Point Reyes Light* newspaper and available at area shops and businesses. For advance or additional information, contact the **West Marin Chamber of Commerce,** P.O. Box 1045, Point Reyes Station, CA 94956, tel. (415) 663-9232.

SEEING AND DOING POINT REYES

Get oriented at the park's barnlike **Bear Valley Visitor Center,** tel. (415) 663-1092, just off Bear Valley Rd. (off Hwy. 1 near Olema), which, in addition to natural history and fine arts exhibits, includes a seismograph for monitoring the earth's movements. Near the picnic tables at the visitor center is the short **Earthquake Trail** loop (wheelchair accessible), which demonstrates the San Andreas seismic drama, from sag ponds and shifts in natural boundary lines to the old Shafter Ranch barn, a corner of which slid off its foundations during the 1906 San Francisco earthquake. Also near the Bear Valley Visitor Center are the short, self-guided **Woodpecker Nature Trail;** the **Morgan Horse Ranch,** where the Park Service breeds and trains its mounts; and **Kule Loklo,** an architectural re-creation of a Coast Miwok community. (When Sir Francis Drake purportedly arrived at Point Reyes in the late 1500s, he found more than 100 such villages on the peninsula.) The best time to see Kule Loklo is during July's Annual Native American Celebration, when this outdoor exhibit, complete with sweathouse, thatched and redwood bark

Peak whalewatching season runs from late December to January

THE MYSTERY OF SIR FRANCIS DRAKE

Though named by Sebastián Vizcaíno in 1603 while he was passing the rocky headlands on the 12th day of Christmas, or the Feast of the Three Kings, Point Reyes was actually explored earlier by the privateer Sir Francis Drake. Tired of pursuing Spanish ships around the world, he beached the *Pelican* (later known as the *Golden Hinde*) and came ashore at "a fit and convenient harbour" somewhere in California in June 1579. Naming the land Nova Albion, here he made repairs, rested his tired crew, and claimed the area for Queen Elizabeth I with "a plate of brasse, fast nailed to a great and firme post." This much most historians agree on. The rest of the story is contentious at best.

Where exactly did Drake land? Since the main estuary at Point Reyes is named after Drake, as is the bay, the simple answer is that he came ashore here, some 20 nautical miles north of San Francisco. But some contend that Drake actually landed at Bolinas Lagoon or explored San Francisco Bay and landed near Point San Quentin or Novato, near an old Olompali village site where a 1567 English silver sixpence was discovered in 1974. A more recent quest for remnants of Drake's visitation centers on Bodega Bay. Others say he stumbled ashore on Goleta Beach near Santa Barbara, where five cast-iron British cannons similar to those missing from the *Golden Hinde* were unearthed in the 1980s. But 70 pieces of antique Ming porcelain have been found near Point Reyes—proof enough, say true believers of the Point Reyes theory, since four chests of Chinese porcelain, which Drake stole from the Spanish, never arrived in England. (Unbelievers counter that the porcelain washed ashore instead from the wreckage of the *San Agustin* off Drakes Bay.)

Other related questions remain unanswered. Is the infamous brass plate found on a beach near Point San Quentin in 1936 genuine or a clever forgery? After years of controversy, in the 1970s the British Museum declared the corroded placard an "undoubted fake" despite the olde English ring of its language, and metallurgists say the plate is no more than 100 years old. (To judge for yourself, the brass plate is on permanent display at UC Berkeley's Bancroft Library.)

What became of Drake's journal, which supposedly documented this journey as well as Drake's discovery of the Northwest Passage? What happened to the gold, gems, and silver Drake stole from the Spanish ship *Cacafuego* and others, estimated in today's currency values as worth $50 million? Some say no treasure was buried along the California coast, that Drake would have jettisoned cannons, china, and other goods instead to lighten his ship's load. Drake, they say, took all his loot back to England, where he and his crew became millionaires, and the queen retired some of the national debt and started the East India Company. Others, however, are still looking.

---

dwellings, and dancing lodge, comes to life with Miwok basketmakers, wood- and stonecarvers, and native singing and dancing.

Limantour Estero near Drakes Estero and Drakes Beach is great for birdwatching; **McClures Beach** is best for tidepooling; and both **North Beach** and **South Beach** north of Point Reyes proper offer good beachcombing but treacherous swimming. Protected **Drakes Beach** and **Limantour Beach** along the crescent of Drakes Bay are safe for swimming.

For astounding views when the fog lifts above the ship graveyard offshore, head out to Point Reyes proper and the **Point Reyes Lighthouse and Visitor Center,** tel. (415) 669-1534 (open daily 9 a.m.-5 p.m. during whalewatching season, more limited hours at other times). The Chimney Rock Trail is wonderful for spring and summer wildflowers and, if you head west, is also a roundabout way to reach the lighthouse. On all Point Reyes hikes, carry water, wear proper walking shoes, and dress for sudden, unpredictable weather changes.

To experience the sound and fury of Coast Creek hurling itself into the Pacific via the "sea tunnel" at the **Arch Rock Overlook**, dress warmly, wear raingear and slip-proof shoes, and come (via the popular Bear Valley Trail) during a storm. For safety's sake, stay well back from the spectacle, and don't attempt to walk through the tunnel under any circumstances—though people often do in calm weather.

To make the most of a full moon at Point Reyes, head to the **Wildcat Beach Overlook** via the Bear Valley Trail from the visitor center, then south via the Coast Trail to the area overlooking the beach, **Alamere Falls** (most spectacular after heavy rains), and the southern stretch of Drakes Bay. An alternate route to Alamere Falls, about one mile south of Wildcat Camp, is via the Palomarin Trail from Bolinas or the Five Brooks Trail. For the best panoramic vista of Drakes Bay, take the Bear Valley, Sky, then Woodward Valley Trails to the bay (alternatively, take the Coast Trail from Coast Camp to the Woodward Valley Trail), then climb up the small hill overlooking the bay, just northwest of the trail.

The **Randall Spur Trail,** created by the Civilian Conservation Corps, connects the Bolinas Ridge Trail with the various Inverness Ridge and Olema Valley trails—making Point Reyes's southern stretches more accessible for day hikers. Worth a stop on the way to the Palomarin trailhead in south Point Reyes is the **Point Reyes Bird Observatory,** tel. (415) 868-1221, established in 1965 as the first bird observatory in the country. Though it's a full-fledged research facility, the Palomarin observatory is open to the public, with educational classes (call ahead for information), interpretive exhibits, and a nature trail. To get here by car, take the unmarked turnoff to Bolinas (near highway marker 17.00 at the north end of Bolinas Lagoon), continue two miles or so to Mesa Rd., then turn right and continue four miles to the observatory's bird-banding station.

These days, visitors can also horse around in Point Reyes, thanks to guided tours offered by **Five Brooks Ranch,** tel. (415) 663-1570, www.fivebrooks.com. The two-hour Fir Top Trail Ride is $50 per person, though one-hour and six-hours ride, overnight pack trips, and brief pony rides for the kids are also available.

Point Reyes Whalewatching

Whalewatching, particularly fine from the lighthouse, is immensely popular at Point Reyes and best from about Christmas through January, when whales pass from one to five miles offshore. (Come on a weekday to avoid the crowds.) A hundred or more whale sightings per day is fairly typical here, though a 307-step descent to the lighthouse must be negotiated first. You'll also get good views from the platform at the top of the stairs. The parking lot at the Point Reyes Lighthouse is fairly small, so in peak season, whalewatchers will have to park at Drakes Beach near the park entrance and take a shuttle bus to the lighthouse; the fee is $2.50 general, kids 12 and under free. National Park Service naturalists provide whale facts and whalewatching tips in January from 10 a.m.-4 p.m. daily, both at the lighthouse and the small information center near the viewing platform. For more information about Point Reyes whalewatching, including the complete shuttle schedule and special naturalist programs, call (415) 663-1092 or (415) 669-1534. The lighthouse is open to the public for self-guided and ranger-led tours Thurs.-Monday. Otherwise, the Point Reyes Lighthouse Visitor Center is open 10 a.m.-5 p.m., and the steps down to the lighthouse open 10 a.m.-4:30 p.m. (closed in the event of high winds). Since hours may change, call to verify before setting out.

Not far from the lighthouse is the **Point Reyes Historic Lifeboat Station,** established in 1889 with a "surfcar" (like a tiny submarine) pulled through the surf on a cable, hand-pulled surfboats, and a Lyle gun and breeches buoy. The facility is open infrequently and is available for educational programs on marine biology and maritime history. For more information, call (415) 663-1092.

Point Reyes Information

For information about Point Reyes, including current trail maps, and to obtain permits for

THE FARALLON ISLANDS

Visible from Point Reyes on a clear day are the Farallon Islands to the southwest. Protected as the Farallon National Wildlife Refuge, the largest seabird rookery south of Alaska, these islands are one of the five most ecologically productive marine environments on earth and now part of an international UNESCO Biosphere Reserve. Some 948 square nautical miles of ocean from Bodega Head to Rocky Point are included in the Gulf of the Farallones National Marine Sanctuary. These rugged granite islands 27 miles west of San Francisco are actually the above-sea-level presence of the Farallones Escarpment, which parallels the coast from the tip of Point Reyes to south of the Golden Gate. The natural but rare phenomenon of upwelling around the islands, with warm offshore winds drawing cold, nutrient-rich ocean water to the surface in spring, creates the phenomenal algae and plankton populations that support the feeding frenzies and breeding successes of animals farther up the food chain.

But during recent centuries, life has been almost undone at the Farallones. In the 1800s, "eggers" exploited the rookeries here to provide miners and San Franciscans with fresh eggs at breakfast. The islands have also survived assaults from sealers, whalers, gill netters, bombers, ocean oil slicks, and radioactive waste dumping.

In the summer, more than 250,000 breeding birds—from tufted puffins and petrels to auklets and murres—consider the Farallones home. Seals (including the once-almost-extinct northern elephant seal) and sea lions also breed here, and gray and humpback whales as well as northern fur seals are often spotted in the area. The nonprofit, member-supported **Point Reyes Bird Observatory,** 4990 Shoreline Hwy. (Hwy. 1), Stinson Beach, CA 94970, tel. (415) 868-1221, staffs a scientific study center at the Farallones (in addition to its center at Point Reyes), but otherwise people are not allowed on the islands—though the Oceanic Society (see North Bay Diversions below) sponsors educational expeditions around the Farallon Islands June-Nov. and during the winter whalewatching season. (Bring binoculars.) The public is welcome, however, at the Point Reyes Bird Observatory's Palomarin Field Station, tel. (415) 868-0655, at the end of Mesa Rd. near Bolinas, to observe bird banding. The station is open daily May-Nov. and on Wednesday, Saturday, and Sunday the rest of the year; call for hours and to make reservations for groups of five or more people.

For more information about the Farallon Islands and the surrounding marine sanctuary, contact: Gulf of the Farallones National Marine Sanctuary, tel. (415) 561-6622.

---

camping and backpacking, stop by any of the park's three visitor centers: **Bear Valley Visitor Center** at the park's Bear Valley entrance; **Kenneth C. Patrick Visitor Center** at Drakes Beach; or **Point Reyes Lighthouse Visitor Center.** Or contact: Point Reyes National Seashore, Point Reyes, CA 94956, tel. (415) 663-1092.

For information about the year-round schedule of excellent classes and field seminars held at Point Reyes (most offered for credit through Dominican College, some offered cooperatively through the Elderhostel program), contact: **Point Reyes Field Seminars,** Point Reyes, CA 94956, tel. (415) 663-1200, and ask for the current seminar catalog.

A very good guidebook to the area is *Point Reyes—Secret Places & Magic Moments* by Phil Arnot. Also by Arnot (and Elvira Monroe):

Exploring Point Reyes: A Guide to Point Reyes National Seashore.

For information about what's going on in Point Reyes and surrounding communities, pick up a copy of the Pulitzer Prize-winning *Point Reyes Light,* which made a name for itself with investigative reporting on the area's former Synanon cult. For information about area practicalities, see Staying in Western Marin and Eating Well in Western Marin below.

GOLDEN GATE NATIONAL RECREATION AREA AND VICINITY

Beginning immediately adjacent to Point Reyes near Olema is the Golden Gate National Recreation Area (GGNRA), which wraps itself around various state and local parks inland, then extends southeast across the Marin Headlands and the Golden Gate Bridge to include the Presidio and a thin coastal strip running south to Fort Funston. The GGNRA also includes two notable tourist attractions in San Francisco Bay: Angel Island and Alcatraz. Most notable is the dramatic natural beauty of the Marin Headlands—sea-chiseled chilly cliffs, protected valleys, and grassy wind-combed hills rich with wildlife and wildflowers, all opening out to the bay and the Pacific Ocean. Protected at first by the Nature Conservancy until coming under national management in 1972, the vast Marin Headlands feature trails for days of good hiking and backpacking (stop by headquarters for a current trail map). Backcountry and group camps are scattered across the area.

Aside from the GGNRA's natural beauty, here also is historic scenery, from the 1877 Point Bonita Lighthouse to four military installations—Forts Barry, Cronkhite, Baker, and Funston—that protected the Bay Area beginning in the 1870s and continuing through World War II.

For more information about the GGNRA, contact: **Golden Gate National Recreation Area,** Building 201, Fort Mason, San Francisco, CA 94123, tel. (415) 556-0560. Or stop for maps and other information at the **Marin Headlands GGNRA Visitor Center** at Fort Barry (near Rodeo Lagoon and Fort Cronkhite), tel. (415) 331-1540, open daily 8:30 a.m.-4:30 p.m.; or the **Muir Woods Visitor Center** at Muir Woods, tel. (415) 388-2595 or (415) 388-2596. Pick up trail maps and events calendars, and ask about backcountry camping at the visitor centers.

Several guidebooks published by the nonprofit Golden Gate National Parks Association (tel. 415-561-3000 or 415-657-2757) are well worth buying—including the 96-page *Park Guide* ($9.95), which covers every feature of the recreation area.

Hawk Hill

For views of the Golden Gate Bridge, San Francisco Bay, and the San Francisco skyline—not to mention exceptional birding opportunities—head to Hawk Hill (abandoned Battery 129, reached via Conzelman Rd.) on the north side of the Golden Gate above the bridge. Come in the fall (with binoculars and fog-worthy clothing) to appreciate the incredible numbers of birds of prey congregating here—100 or more each day representing 20 or so species. In spring, bring your kite. Any time of year, this is a great vantage point for watching huge cargo ships and other vessels make their way through the Golden Gate. For more information, call the Marin Headlands Visitor Center at Fort Barry, tel. (415) 331-1540.

Point Bonita Lighthouse

The Point Bonita Lighthouse (call 415-331-1540 for hours and tour information) was one of the first lighthouses ever built on the West Coast and is still operating. Technically, though, this isn't really a lighthouse—there's no house, just the French-import 1855 Fresnel lens with protective glass, walls, and roof, with gargoyle-like American eagles guarding the light. Getting here is as thrilling as being here—meandering along the half-mile footpath to the rocky point through hand-dug tunnels and across the swaying footbridge, in the middle of nowhere yet in full view of San Francisco. Especially enjoyable are the sunset and full-moon tours conducted by GGNRA rangers. The tours and admission to the lighthouse are free.

To get to the lighthouse, follow the signs to Fort Baker/Fort Cronkhite/Fort Barry from Alexander Ave. just off the north end of the Golden Gate Bridge, then turn left at Field Rd. and continue, following the signs. (For seaside barbecues, head to the picnic area at Battery Wallace near Point Bonita.) For more information about American lighthouses, contact the **U.S. Lighthouse Society,** 244 Kearny, Fifth Floor, San Francisco, CA 94108, tel. (415) 362-7255.

Fort Barry

Just north of Point Bonita, Fort Barry includes an intact 1950s missile launch site and underground bunkers not usually open to the public; one of the bunkers is still home to a Nike Hercules missile. "Guardians of the Gate" military-history tours, offered twice-monthly by park personnel, tel. (415) 331-1540, include the various batteries in the area and end at the Nike site.

Also at Fort Barry: an **AYH youth hostel,** Building 941, tel. (415) 331-2777; the **Headlands Center for the Arts,** Bldg. 144, tel. (415) 331-2787, which explores the relationship of art and the environment (studio space for artists is provided, and public programs include lectures, installations, exhibits, and performances); and the **Marin Headlands Visitor Center,** tel. (415) 331-1540, open to the public 8:30 a.m.-4:30 p.m. daily and offering hands-on natural science exhibits, and educational and historical displays.

Fort Cronkhite

Just north of the Visitor Center is Fort Cronkhite, home of the **California Marine Mammal Center,** 1044 Fort Cronkhite (just above Cronkhite Beach), Sausalito, CA 94965-2610, tel. (415) 289-7325. Established in 1975, this hospital for wild animals returns its "patients," once fit, to their native marine environments. The center, with more than 400 active volunteers and popular hands-on environmental education programs for children, is open to the public daily 10 a.m.-4 p.m. Wheelchair accessible. (New members and financial contributions always welcome.) Also at Fort Cronkhite: the **Pacific Environment and Resources Center,** tel. (415) 332-8200, which offers teacher training, special elementary and secondary school programs, and exhibits on local and global environmental issues.

Other Marin GGNRA Sights

The hands-on **Bay Area Discovery Museum** at East Fort Baker, tel. (415) 487-4398, is designed for children ages 2-12 and their families. It offers a great variety of special programs year-round—"In the Dream Time" children's art workshops, for example. Open Wed.-Sun. 10 a.m.-5 p.m. Two miles north of Muir Beach is the **Slide Ranch** demonstration farm and family-oriented environmental education center, 2025 Hwy. 1, tel. (415) 381-6155, which offers special events (such as "Family Farm Day") year-round. Reservations are required for all events.

Alcatraz: "The Rock"

Part of the GGNRA is infamous Alcatraz, one-time military outpost, then island prison and federal hellhole—"The Rock"—for hard-core criminals. Among the notorious bad guys incarcerated here were mobsters Al Capone, "Machine Gun" Kelley, and Mickey Cohen, not to mention Robert Stroud, the "Birdman of Alcatraz"—who, despite the romance of his popular myth, never kept birds on The Rock. Closed in the 1960s,

then occupied for two years by Native Americans who hoped to reacquire the property for a cultural heritage center, Alcatraz Island and its prison facilities are now open for tours; see Touring the Real Rock in the Delights and Diversions chapter. Ferries operated by the Blue & Gold Fleet at San Francisco's Pier 39, tel. (415) 773-1188 (recorded schedule) or (415) 705-5555 (information and advance ticket purchase), shuttle visitors out to The Rock and back. For general information, call the GGNRA office in San Francisco, tel. (415) 556-0560.

Tomales Bay State Park

Among the half-moon beaches and secret coves along the steep cliffs and shores of Tomales Bay are those protected within fragments of Tomales Bay State Park. One section is just north of Inverness, via Pierce Point Rd. off Sir Francis Drake Blvd., and others are scattered along Hwy. 1 north of Point Reyes Station on the east side of the bay. One of the prime picnic spots at Tomales Bay is **Heart's Desire Beach,** popular for family picnicking and swimming, and usually empty on weekdays (parking $5 per vehicle). The warm, usually sunny, and surf-free inland beaches here are the main attraction, but hiking the forested eastern slope of Inverness Ridge is also worth it—especially in early spring, when trees, young ferns, and wildflowers burst forth from their winter dormancy. Unique is the park's fine virgin forest of Bishop pines. Walk-in campsites are available. For views and a great hiking trail, get directions to Inverness Ridge from Tomales Bay State Park personnel. The southern grasslands section of Tomales Bay, now included in the GGNRA after the federal purchase of the 250-acre Martinelli Ranch, is prime turf for hiking (best in March for wildflowers) and birdwatching. The trailhead and parking area is just off Hwy. 1, about 1.5 miles north of Point Reyes Station.

Along the eastern edge of Tomales Bay, the **Marconi Conference Center,** 18500 Hwy. 1, Marshall, CA 94940, tel. (415) 663-9020, occupies the 1914 Marconi Hotel once owned by Guglielmo Marconi, inventor of the wireless. This one-time communications center facility—taken over by the U.S. Navy during World War I, later operated by RCA, and more recently home to the much-praised then pilloried Synanon alcohol and drug abuse program—is now a state-owned conference center operated on the model of Asilomar on the Monterey Peninsula.

For more information about the park, contact: Tomales Bay State Park, HCR 62, Inverness, CA 94937, tel. (415) 669-1140.

Samuel P. Taylor State Park

East of Point Reyes National Seashore and hemmed in by the Golden Gate National Recreation Area is Samuel P. Taylor State Park, 2,600 acres of redwoods, mixed forests, and upcountry chaparral reached via Sir Francis Drake Boulevard. The park offers an extensive hiking and horseback trail system, a paved bicycle path running east-west, no-frills camping (including hiker/biker camps), picnicking, and swimming. For more information, contact: Samuel P. Taylor State Park, 8889 Sir Francis Drake Blvd., P.O. Box 251, Lagunitas, CA 94938, tel. (415) 488-9897 or (415) 893-1580.

East of Samuel Taylor near Nicasio is the vast Skywalker Ranch owned by Lucasfilms and George Lucas, film- and mythmaker in the tradition of mythologist Joseph Campbell and his Hero With a Thousand Faces. The public is not welcome. (And for the record, Lucas Valley Rd., connecting Nicasio and Marinwood, was named long before Lucas bought property here.) Lucasfilms is also destined to inhabit parts of San Francisco's Presidio within the GGNRA.

Bolinas Lagoon and Audubon Canyon Ranch

Well worth a visit is the Bolinas Lagoon, as serene as a Japanese nature print, especially in spring, when only the breeze or an occasional waterfowl fracas ruffles the glassy blue smoothness of this long mirror of water surrounded by a crescent-moon sandspit. Reflected above is wooded Bolinas Ridge, the northwestern extension of Mount Tamalpais. In autumn, the lagoon is much busier, temporary home to thousands of waterfowl migrating south along the Pacific Flyway as well as the salmon offshore waiting for a ferocious winter storm to break open a pathway through the sandbars blocking their migratory path. At minus tide any time of year, the surf side of the sandspit offers good beachcombing.

Facing out into the Bolinas Lagoon several miles north of Stinson Beach is the Audubon Canyon Ranch, a protected canyon offering a safe haven and rookery for great blue herons and common egrets in particular, though more than 50 other species of water birds arrive here each year. By quietly climbing up the canyon slopes during the March-July nesting season, visitors can look down into egret and heron nests high atop the redwoods in Schwartz Grove and observe the day-to-day life of parent birds and their young. Other hiking trails lead to other discoveries; picnic facilities also available.

The white Victorian farmhouse here serves as ranch headquarters and bookstore/visitor center, and participants in weekend seminar programs bed down in the bunkhouse, which features wind-powered toilets (God's truth) and solar-heated water. (Bring your own bedding, food, and other necessities.) The ranch is wheelchair accessible and generally open to the public mid-March through mid-July only on weekends and holidays, 10 a.m.-4 p.m., admission free, though donations are always appreciated. Large groups can make tour arrangements for weekdays, though the ranch is always closed Mondays. For more information, contact: Audubon Canyon Ranch, 4900 Shoreline Hwy. (Hwy. 1), Stinson Beach, CA 94970, tel. (415) 868-9244.

Mount Tamalpais State Park

Though the park also stretches downslope to the sea, take in the views of Marin County, San Francisco Bay, and the Pacific Ocean from the highest points of Mount Tamalpais. This long-loved mountain isn't particularly tall (elevation 2,600 feet), but even when foggy mists swirl everywhere below, the sun usually shines atop Mount Tam. And the state park here has it all·redwoods and ferns, hillsides thick with wildflowers, 200 miles of hiking trails with spectacular views (plus access to Muir Woods), beaches and headlands, also camping and picnicking. The best way to get here is via Hwy. 1, then via the Panoramic Hwy., winding up past Pan Toll Ranger Station and park headquarters (stop for information and a map) to near the summit. From the parking lot, it's a quarter-mile hike up a steep dirt road to the fire lookout on top of Mount Tam.

The best way to explore Mount Tamalpais is on foot. Take the loop trail around the top. For the more ambitious, head downslope to the sea and the busy public beaches at Stinson Beach, still noted for its annual Dipsea Race held on the last Sunday in August, a tradition since 1904. Rugged cross-country runners cross the still more rugged terrain from Mill Valley to the sea at Stinson Beach; the last stretch down the footpath is known as the Dipsea Trail. Or hike into the park from Marin Municipal Water District lands on the east (for information, call the Sky Oaks Ranger Station in Fairfax, tel. 415-459-5267) and head upslope, via the Cataract Trail from just off Bolinas Rd. outside of Fairfax and past Alpine Lake—something of a steep climb but worth it for the waterfalls, most dramatic in winter and early spring but sublime for pool-sitting in summer.

Via the Matt Davis Trail, or the Bootjack Camp or Pan Toll Ranger Station routes, hike to the charming old (1904) **West Point Inn,** 1000 Panoramic Hwy., tel. (415) 388-9955, for a glass of lemonade and a rest in the porch shade. Four miles away is the **Tourist Club,** 30 Ridge Ave., tel. (415) 388-9987, a 1912 chalet where overnight stays are available only to members and their families, but hikers arriving via the Sun, Redwood, or Panoramic Trails can get snacks, cold imported beer, sodas, and juices. (To cheat for the beer, park at the end of Ridge Ave., which intersects the Panoramic Hwy., and hike the quarter-mile down the driveway.) Open daily, great views of Muir Woods from the deck. More accessible for a picnic or snack stop (bring your own) is Mount Tam's Greek-style **Mountain Theater,** a 5,000-seat outdoor amphitheater on Ridgecrest Blvd., the site each spring of a major musical stage production.

Mount Tamalpais State Park (admission free, though parking may cost you) is open daily from 7 a.m. to sunset. Limited primitive camping and other accommodations are available (see Staying in Western Marin, below). For more information, contact park headquarters at 801 Panoramic Hwy., Mill Valley, CA 94941, tel. (415) 388-2070. For current information on Mount Tam's Mountain Theater productions, contact the **Mountain Play Association,** 177 E. Blithedale, Mill Valley, CA 94941, tel. (415) 383-1100 or (415) 383-0155.

Muir Woods National Monument

Muir Woods is peaceful and serene but quite a popular place—not necessarily the best desti-

nation for getting away from them all. Lush redwood canyon country surrounds Redwood Creek within the boundaries of Mount Tamalpais State Park, with a short trail system meandering alongside the stream, up to the ridgetops, and into the monument's main Cathedral and Bohemian redwood groves. For an easy, introductory stroll, the Muir Woods Nature Trail wanders through the flatlands, identifying the characteristic trees and shrubs. Fascinating at Muir Woods, the first national monument in the U.S., are the dawn redwood from China and the park's albino redwood, the shoots from this freak of nature completely chlorophyll-free. But to avoid the crowds imported in all those tour buses clogging the parking lot, get away from the visitor center and the trails near the parking lot. Muir Woods is open daily 8 a.m.-sunset, $2 day-use fee, no picnicking or camping. No dogs. For more information, contact: Muir Woods National Monument, Mill Valley, CA 94941, tel. (415) 388-2595 or (415) 388-2596.

STAYING IN WESTERN MARIN

Point Reyes Hostel
Best bet for noncamping budget travelers is **HI-AYH Point Reyes Hostel** on Limantour Rd., P.O. Box 247, Point Reyes Station, CA 94956, tel. (415) 663-8811. Pluses here include the well-equipped kitchen (get food on the way). Advance reservations advisable, particularly on weekends. To get here: from Point Reyes Station, take Seashore west from Hwy. 1, then follow Bear Valley Rd. to Limantour Rd. and continue

POINT REYES HOSTEL
in the Pt. Reyes National Seashore

on Limantour for six miles. Budget. For information on getting to Point Reyes on public transit, call the hostel or Golden Gate Transit, tel.

(415) 923-2000. The hostel's office hours are 7:30-9:30 a.m. and 4:30-9:30 p.m. daily. Considerably closer to urban Marin but also an excellent choice is the hostel within the Golden Gate National Recreation Area. For information, see Staying in Eastern Marin, below.

Point Reyes Camping
So popular that each has a one-day limit, the four primitive walk-in campgrounds at Point Reyes National Seashore are perfect for backpackers, since each is within an easy day's hike of the main trailhead and each other. Call (415) 663-1092 for information; permits required (available at park headquarters on Bear Valley Rd. just west of Olema). Stop, too, for maps and wilderness permits. The office is open weekdays 9 a.m.-5 p.m., weekends 8 a.m.-5 p.m.

Popular Coast Camp is most easily accessible from the parking lot at the end of Limantour Rd. and makes a good base for exploring the Limantour Estero and Sculptured Beach. Wildcat Camp is a group camp popular with Boy Scouts and others in Point Reyes's lake district (best swimming in Bass and Crystal Lakes). Glen Camp is tucked into the hills between Wildcat Camp and Bear Valley, and Sky Camp, perched on the western slopes of Mount Wittenberg, looks down over Drakes Bay and Point Reyes.

Other area camping options include the backpack and group camps of GGNRA, tel. (415) 331-1540; the state campground at Samuel P. Taylor State Park, tel. (415) 488-9897; and the 18 primitive campsites plus backpack camps and group camp at Mount Tamalpais State Park, tel. (415) 388-2070.

Steep Ravine: A Rustic and Inexpensive Stay
The state's quite reasonable **Steep Ravine Environmental Cabins** on Rocky Point in Mount Tamalpais State Park, looking out to sea from near Stinson Beach, are small redwood-rustic homes-away-from-home with just the basics: platform beds (bring your own sleeping bag and pad), woodstoves, separate restrooms with pit toilets. But such a deal: $30 per cabin per night (each sleeps five) and an almost-private beach below in a spectacularly romantic setting. Before the state wrested custody of these marvelous cabins from the pow-

erful Bay Area politicians and other clout-encumbered citizens who held long-term leases, photographer Dorothea Lange wrote about staying here in *To a Cabin,* co-authored by Margaretta K. Mitchell. Even the walk down to the bottom of Steep Ravine Canyon is inspiring, Lange noted, with "room for only those in need of sea and sky and infinity." One cabin (there are only 10) is wheelchair accessible; none have electricity, but they do have outside running water. Bring your own provisions. To reserve (up to eight weeks in advance), contact ReserveAmerica, toll-free tel. (800) 444-7275, and request an application form. You can also make reservations online; point your browser to www.cal-parks.ca.gov.

Inns in Western Marin
Even those without wheels can explore the seaward coast of Marin County in comfort and fine style—by hiking or walking the whole way from the Golden Gate Bridge with little more than a day pack and staying along the bay at a combination of hostels, campgrounds, hotels and motels, and the area's very nice bed-and-breakfast inns. (How far to go each day and where to stay depends upon time and money available.)

For area lodging referrals and information, also contact **Point Reyes Lodging,** tel. (415) 663-1872 or toll-free (800) 539-1872; or **Inns of Point Reyes,** tel. (415) 663-1420.

Classic **Ten Inverness Way,** 10 Inverness Way (on the town's block-long main street), tel. (415) 669-1648, is comfortable and cozy. Rooms feature excellent beds, handmade quilts, and private baths; there's a stone fireplace in the living room, wonderful full breakfast, private hot tub. Premium-Luxury.

In a woodsy canyon just outside town, **Blackthorne Inn,** 266 Vallejo Ave. in Inverness Park, tel. (415) 663-8621, www.blackthorneinn.com, offers simple Japanese-style furnishings in four-level "treehouse" accommodations with decks, all splitting off the vertically spiraling staircase. Good buffet breakfast, hot tub available. The peak experience here is a stay in the Eagle's Nest, the aptly named octagonal, glass-walled room at the top of the stairs. Luxury.

Also in Inverness Park, consider **Holly Tree Inn & Cottages,** 3 Silverhills Rd., tel. (415) 663-1554 or toll-free (800) 663-1554, which offers four rooms in the inn, plus a cottage on the premises (all Premium-Luxury), as well as the off-site **Sea Star Cottage** and **Vision Cottage** (both Luxury).

Up on Inverness Ridge is **The Ark,** tel. (415) 663-9338 or toll-free (800) 808-9338, a rustic cabin with bedroom, sleeping loft, woodstove, and kitchen. Luxury. Other cottages available through the Ark's same telephone numbers include woodsy **Rosemary Cottage,** which has a woodstove and hot tub (Premium-Luxury); and **Fir Tree Cottage,** a spacious two-bedroom house perfect for families or two couples (Luxury).

Fairwinds Farm, 82 Drakes Summit, tel. (415) 663-9454, is a fairly modern Early American cottage on five acres with forest, garden, and pond, a good family setup with two beds in the bedroom, a double bed in the loft, and queen sofa bed in the living room. Full kitchen (breakfast fixings supplied, plus snacks, even a popcorn popper), fireplace, hot tub, deck. Playhouse for children, barnyard animals, too. Expensive-Premium. Near Tomales Bay, **Marsh Cottage,** 12642 Sir Francis Drake Blvd., tel. (415) 669-7168, features a fireplace and a fine view, plus kitchen with breakfast supplies. Premium.

Farther south, **Roundstone Farm,** 9940 Sir Francis Drake Blvd., Olema, tel. (415) 663-1020, is an American country-style cedar farmhouse on a 10-acre horse ranch, rooms with private baths, fireplaces, European armoires, down comforters. Premium. Also quite nice is **Bear Valley Inn,** 88 Bear Valley Rd., Olema, tel. (415) 663-1777, a restored two-story Victorian ranch house with three country-style guest rooms upstairs, woodstove and oak flooring in the parlor. Rates available with or without full breakfast. Expensive-Premium.

For nostalgia with all the modern amenities (try to get a room away from the highway), the 1988 **Point Reyes Seashore Lodge,** 10021 Hwy. 1 (in Olema), tel. (415) 663-9000, is an elegant re-creation of a turn-of-the-century country lodge, a three-story cedar building with three two-story suites and 18 rooms, all with down comforters, telephones, and private baths, many with whirlpool tubs and fireplaces, most with a private deck or patio. Continental breakfast. Premium-Luxury.

The place for a genuine West Marin-style stay is a very modern facsimile historic hotel, a superb 1989 replica of the original **U.S. Hotel,** 26985 Hwy. 1, Tomales, tel. (707) 878-2742, a bed and breakfast with a hands-off hotel style, just eight rooms with private baths, continental breakfast served in the second-floor lobby. Expensive-Premium. The top bed-and-breakfast choice in Bolinas is **White House Inn,** 118 Kale Rd., tel. (415) 868-0279, a New England-style inn with two guest rooms sharing two bathrooms in the hall, continental breakfast. Premium.

The original 1912 **Mountain Home Inn** restaurant, 810 Panoramic Hwy. (on Mount Tamalpais), Mill Valley, tel. (415) 381-9000, has been transformed into an elegant three-story woodsy hotel with upstairs restaurant and bar. Fabulous views. Some of the rooms have fireplaces or jacuzzis. Rates include breakfast in bed. Premium-Luxury.

When Sir Francis Drake steered the Pelican to shore near here in 1579, he claimed everything in sight on behalf of Elizabeth I, Queen of England. For a taste of more modern true Brit on your way down from Mount Tam, stop at the **Pelican Inn,** 10 Pacific Way (Hwy. 1 at Muir Beach Rd.), Muir Beach, tel. (415) 383-6000. This is a very British Tudor-style country inn, a replica of a 16th-century farmhouse, where guests sit out on the lawn with pint of bitter in hand on sunny days or, when the fog rolls in, warm up around the bar's fireplace with some afternoon tea or mulled cider or wine. Hearty pub fare includes meat pies, stews, burgers, homemade breads, various dinner entrées. Restaurant and pub open 11 a.m.-11 p.m. daily except Monday. Not authentically old (built in 1979), the Pelican is still authentic: the leaded-glass windows and brass trinkets, even the oak bar and refectory tables come from England. There's usually a months-long waiting list for the seven rooms here. Luxury.

EATING WELL IN WESTERN MARIN

Inverness and Vicinity

After a relaxed afternoon spent reading in **Jack Mason Museum and Inverness Public Library** on Park Ave. (open limited hours, tel. 415-669-1288 or 415-669-1099), head out Sir Francis Drake Blvd. from Inverness to **Johnson's Oyster Company,** tel. (415) 669-1149, for a tour and some farm-fresh oysters. Open Tues.-Sun. 8 a.m.-4 p.m.; free admission. **Barnaby's by**

the Bay, 12938 Sir Francis Drake (at the Golden Hinde Inn just north of Inverness), tel. (415) 669-1114, open for lunch and dinner (closed Wednesday), has daily pasta and fresh fish specials, barbecued oysters, clam chowder, and crab cioppino.

Back in Inverness, **Gray Whale Pub & Pizzeria,** 12781 Sir Francis Drake, tel. (415) 669-1244, is the place for pizza, also salads, good desserts, and espresso in a pub atmosphere. Open 9 a.m.-9 p.m. daily. Or, try one of the town's two popular restaurants: **Manka's** at the Inverness Lodge (call for directions), tel. (415) 669-1034, which serves rustic American-style fare (marvelous rooms upstairs, two cabins also available), or **Vladimir's Czechoslovak Restaurant & Bar,** 12785 Sir Francis Drake, tel. (415) 669-1021, which serves good Eastern European food in an authentically boisterous atmosphere. (Yell across the room if you want dessert; that's what everyone else does.)

Marshall, Point Reyes Station, Olema

Popular in Marshall, along the east side of Tomales Bay north of Point Reyes Station via Hwy. 1, is **Tony's Seafood,** 18863 Hwy. 1, tel. (415) 663-1107. The food's quite fresh: they clean the crabs and oysters right out front.

Famous for its Pulitzer Prize-winning newspaper, the not-yet-too-yuppie cow town of Point Reyes Station is also noted for the mooing clock atop the sheriff's substation at Fourth and C. The bovine bellow, a technical creation of Lucasfilm staff, actually emanates—like clockwork, at noon and 6 p.m.—from loudspeakers atop the Old Western Saloon at Second and Main Streets. For "udderly divine" bakery items, from French pastries, bran muffins, and scones to cookies, stop by **Bovine Bakery,** 11315

Hwy. 1 (Main St.), tel. (415) 663-9420. The **Station House Cafe,** 11180 Main (at Third St.), tel. (415) 663-1515, is the local hotspot, a cheerful country café serving breakfast, lunch, and dinner daily but particularly wonderful for breakfast, especially on foggy or rainy days.

Both a good restaurant and lodging stop, the **Olema Inn,** at Hwy. 1 and Sir Francis Drake Blvd. in Olema, tel. (415) 663-9559, is a grandmotherly kind of place serving basic good food and soups as well as California-style cuisine. Open for dinner Fri.-Sat. at 6 p.m. and for lunch and dinner during the summer. For plain ol' American food, head for **Olema Farmhouse,** 10005 Hwy. 1 in Olema, tel. (415) 663-1264: good burgers and hefty sandwiches, daily fresh fish specials.

Bolinas

Bolinas is noted for the locals' Bolinas Border Patrol, an unofficial group dedicated to keeping outsiders out by taking down road signs. Once *in* Bolinas, however long that may take you, the gravel beach here is clean and usually uncrowded. The colorfully painted **Bolinas People's Store,** 14 Wharf Rd., tel. (415) 868-1433, is a good stop for snacks and picnic fixings. **Bolinas Bay Bakery & Cafe,** 20 Wharf Rd., tel. (415) 868-0211, is a popular breakfast and lunch stop famous for its cinnamon rolls, croissants, breads, and other fresh bakery items. **The Shop Cafe,** 46 Wharf Rd., tel. (415) 868-9984, is comfortable and cozy on a foggy or rainy day. (At lunch, try the black bean soup.) When you're ready for a casual pint of Anchor Steam, belly up to the bar at **Smiley's Schooner Saloon,** 41 Wharf Rd., tel. (415) 868-1311, a classic dive bar that's as local as it gets. Mind your manners and have some fun.

EASTERN MARIN AND VICINITY

Though the marshlands and open areas fringing the northern and eastern portions of San Pablo Bay could almost be included, the San Francisco Bay's northernmost boundary is actually Marin County. More than just the structural anchor for the other side of San Francisco's Golden Gate Bridge, eastern Marin has somehow become the psychological center for "the good life" Californians pursue with such trendsetting abandon. This pursuit costs money, of course, but there's plenty of that in Marin County, which boasts one of the highest per-capita income levels in the nation. Jaguars, Porsches, and more exotic automobiles are among Marin folks' favored means of transport, and BMWs are so common here that the late *San Francisco Chronicle* columnist Herb Caen long referred to them as Boring Marin Wagons.

Jokes about Marin County change, but other things stay the same. The weather here is unusually pleasant, mild in both summer and winter. Also, Marin au naturel is incredibly diverse. From Mill Valley west to the Bolinas Lagoon near Point Reyes, seven different ecological communities are typical: chaparral, grassland, coastal scrub, broadleaf forest, redwood and mixed evergreen forest, salt marsh, and beach strand. Almost one-third of the county is public parkland—national, state, and local.

CITIES AND SIGHTS

Sausalito

Sausalito is a community by land and by sea, a hillside hamlet far surpassed in eccentricity by the highly creative hodgepodge of houseboaters also anchored here. Though, for a time, mysterious midnight throbbings from the deep kept Sausalito's houseboat community awake night after summer night—with some locals even speculating that these nocturnal noises came from a top-secret CIA weapon being tested underwater in Richardson Bay—it eventually turned out that the racket was simply due to romance. Singing toadfish have become to Sausalito what swallows are to Capistrano, migrating into

Richardson Bay from the shallows each summer for their annual mating song—comparable, collectively, to the sound of a squadron of low-flying B-17 bombers. People here have adapted to this almost indescribable language of love, and now welcome these bulging-eyed, bubble-lipped lovers back to the bay every year with their Humming Toadfish Festival, a celebration conducted by residents dressed up as sea monsters and clowns, playing kazoos.

Aside from the pleasures of just being here, stop in Sausalito at the U.S. Army Corps of Engineers' **San Francisco Bay Model,** 2100 Bridgeway, tel. (415) 332-3870, a working 1.5-acre facsimile of the Bay and Delta built by the Corps to study currents, tides, salinity, and other natural features. We should all be grateful that the ever-industrious Corps realized it couldn't build a better bay even with access to all the bulldozers, landfill, and riprap in the world and settled, instead, for just making a toy version. Interpretive audio tours are available in English, Russian, German, Japanese, French, and Spanish. Guided group tours (10 or more people) can be arranged by calling (415) 332-3871 at least four weeks in advance. Open in summer Tues.-Fri. 9 a.m.-4 p.m., weekends and holidays 10 a.m.-5 p.m.; the rest of the year, Tues.-Sat. 9 a.m.-4 p.m. Free.

Also in Sausalito: the **Institute of Noetic Sciences,** 475 Gate 5 Rd., tel. (415) 331-5650, an organization of mostly mainstream scientists dedicated to exploring the more mysterious machinations of the human mind—that foggy frontier at the edge of the California cosmos concerned with biofeedback, mental telepathy, telekinesis, altered states of consciousness, and mental imagery in physical healing. Among Sausalito's armada of houseboat residents and bayside shops is **Heath Ceramics Outlet,** 400 Gate 5 Rd., tel. (415) 332-3732, open daily 10 a.m.-5 p.m., a wonderful array of seconds and overstocks for fine dishware fans.

Sausalito (or San Francisco, from Crissy Field via the Golden Gate Bridge) is a perfect place to start a serious Bay Area bike tour. For a 20-mile trip, head north along the paved bike path (Bay Trail), following the green "bike route" signs along the left arm of Richardson Bay to fairly new Bayfront Park in Mill Valley. Continue north to (busy and narrow) E. Blithedale Ave., and follow it east two miles or so to less-busy Tiburon Boulevard. From that thoroughfare, jog south along the bay on Greenwood Cove Rd., picking up the two-mile Tiburon Bike Path at its end. To make it a complete circle, take a ferry from Tiburon (see Bay Tours below) past Angel Island and Alcatraz to Fisherman's Wharf in San Francisco. From here, head back via the Bay Trail, up the grade (fairly steep) to the Golden Gate Bridge and over the bay, then back into Sausalito via the Bridgeway Bike Path.

Easier bike trips from Sausalito include the several-mile trip into Mill Valley, via the bike path past the houseboats and mudflats and marshes to Bayfront Park (picnic tables and benches available). Then backtrack to Miller Ave. and roll into town, right into the midst of a pleasant plaza-style shopping district. To get to Tiburon, from Bayfront Park follow the route described above.

For more information about Sausalito attractions and practicalities, contact: **Sausalito Chamber of Commerce,** 29 Caledonia St., Sausalito, CA 94965, tel. (415) 331-7262, open weekdays 9 a.m.-5 p.m.

Tiburon

Tiburon ("shark" in Spanish), once a ramshackle railroad town, is an affluent bayside community most noted for the Audubon Society's 900-acre **Richardson Bay Audubon Center and Sanctuary,** 376 Greenwood Beach Rd. (in the Belvedere Cove tidal baylands), tel. (415) 388-2524. Wonderful for birdwatching and nature walks, also picnicking (pack out your trash); day-use fee $2. Tiburon is also home to Dr. Gerald Jampolsky's **Center for Spiritual Healing,** tel. (415) 435-2281, a well-respected organization that emphasizes the emotional and spiritual aspects of healing in the face of catastrophic illness and events. The wooded 24-acre **Tiburon Uplands Nature Preserve,** south of Paradise Beach Park on Paradise Dr., tel. (415) 499-6387, includes a natural history loop trail and great bay views from higher ground. Absolutely spectacular for spring wildflowers, though, are the few acres surrounding the 19th-century gothic

church at **Old St. Hilary's Historic Preserve,** 201 Esperanza (at Mar West), tel. (415) 435-2567, open to the public Wednesday and Sunday 1-4 p.m. April-Oct., otherwise by appointment only. Nearby Belvedere is one of the nation's 10 most expensive outposts of suburbia.

For more information about Tiburon attractions and practicalities, contact: **Tiburon Chamber of Commerce,** 96 Main St. #B, Tiburon, CA 94920, tel. (415) 435-5633.

Mill Valley

Mill Valley is another affluent North Bay bedroom community, this one rooted on the eastern slope of Mount Tamalpais. The big event here every autumn is the **Mill Valley Film Festival,** the biggest little film festival outside Telluride, Colorado, with screenings of local, American independent, international, avante-garde, and various premiere films. For more information about the festival, contact the festival office at 38 Miller Ave., tel. (415) 383-5256. For information on other Marin art events, contact the **Marin Arts Council,** 251 N. San Pedro Rd., Building O, San Rafael, CA 94903, tel. (415) 499-8350, which publishes a free monthly *Marin Arts-Guide* and the quarterly *Marin Review* (available free to council members but also often available at local chambers of commerce).

Area Nature Preserves

Inland on the Tiburon Peninsula near Corte Madera is the **Ring Mountain Preserve,** another Nature Conservancy success story. A protected tract of native California grasslands around a 600-foot-tall hill known for its unusual serpentine soils and rare endemic plants, geological peculiarities, and Native American petroglyphs, Ring Mountain is known particularly for the rare Tiburon mariposa lilies—they grow nowhere else—that now thrive here, in a population estimated at 32,000 plants. To get to Ring Mountain, take the Paradise Dr. exit from Hwy. 101, then continue east to the preserve's entrance, 1.75 miles down the road. For more information, contact Marin County Open Space, 3501 Civic Center Dr., Room 415, San Rafael, CA 94903, tel. (415) 499-6387. Also in Marin is the **Spindrift Point Preserve** near Sausalito; for more information, call the Nature Conservancy at (415) 777-0487.

Once-bustling China Camp now survives as a state park.

San Rafael

San Rafael is Marin's biggest little city and the county seat, a Modesto-like community where scenes from George Lucas's *American Graffiti* were shot (on Fourth St., restaurant row). San Rafael is known for its downtown mansion district; for the 1947 replica of the **Mission San Rafael** (second to last in California's mission chain), 1104 Fifth Ave., open daily 11 a.m.-4 p.m.; and most of all for the **Marin Civic Center** just off Hwy. 101, Frank Lloyd Wright's last major architectural accomplishment. The center, home to the county's administrative complex and quite the tour de force, exemplifies Wright's obsession with the idea that all things are (or should become) circular. Surrounded by 140 acres of lovingly groomed grounds, the county fair is held here on the fourth weekend of every July.

The **Marin Civic Center/Marin County Certified Farmers' Market,** toll-free (800) 897-3276, takes place here Thursday and Sunday 8 a.m.-1 p.m., year-round, rain or shine; this is as good a place as any to sample public opinion on recent proposals to abandon the civic center. Docent-led civic center tours are available, but call (415) 499-6646 at least several days in advance. The center is wheelchair accessible, open weekdays 8 a.m.-5 p.m. (excepting legal holidays). To find out about major events and entertainment programs, request a current copy of the quarterly civic center arts magazine, *Marin Center.*

Another San Rafael attraction is the 11-acre **Guide Dogs for the Blind** campus, 350 Los Ranchitos Rd. (off N. San Pedro Rd.), tel. (415) 499-4000, where German shepherds, labradors, and golden retrievers are trained to "see" for their human companions. Monthly "graduations," which include tours and demonstrations of guide dog selective obedience work, are open to the public. Altogether it's a moving experience, especially when the 4-H children who raised these dogs to their pretraining age of 15 or 16 months show up to say goodbye, as the graduates depart with their new owners.

For more information about the area, contact the **San Rafael Chamber of Commerce,** 817 Mission Ave., San Rafael, CA 94901, tel. (415) 454-4163, open weekdays 9 a.m.-5 p.m.

Nearby Greenbrae is neighbor to **San Quentin State Prison,** home since the mid-1800s to sociopaths and other criminals, though more than 100 union members and organizers of the Industrial Workers of the World were also imprisoned here after World War I. San Quentin's disciplinary dungeons were closed in 1935. The new museum here and the Boot Hill prison cemetery—posthumous home now to a veritable Who's Who of Very Bad Guys—are open for (very popular) public visits.

Stop by the prison gift shop at San Quentin's entrance for inmate-made arts and crafts—from San Quentin T-shirts and hats to belt buckles, rings and other jewelry, artwork, and novelties. Head on through the entrance to visit the **California State Prison Museum,** housing artifacts, memorabilia, historical photographs, and records documenting the prison's history. For hours and information on both, call (415) 454-1460.

China Camp State Park
After the gold rush, many of California's Chinese turned to fishing as a way to make ends meet. Chinese fishing camps were common all along the northstate's coast, and 30 or more flourished on the more remote edges of San Francisco Bay. The Chinese were quite successful at plying their trade in the state's waters—so successful that by the 1900s enforcement of anti-Chinese, anti-bag netting fishing laws essentially killed these Asian communities. Partially restored China Camp, once the Bay Area's largest Chinese shrimp center, is the last of these old fishing villages. The community, where John Wayne's *Blood Alley* was filmed, survives now as a memory complete with history museum, renovated buildings, and rebuilt rickety piers. The only actual survivor is **Frank Quan's bait and sandwich shop,** which serves up fresh bay shrimp when available (put in your order early, especially on weekends). The park's 1,600 acres of oak forest, grasslands, and salt marshes also offer hiking, picnicking, and walk-in developed campsites, $12-16 per night. Reserve through ReserveAmerica, toll-free tel. (800) 444-7275.

Hiking trails at China Camp include the Shoreline Trail, which starts near the historic district and heads across Point San Pedro Rd., then forks—the left path leading to a view, the right path onward to the northwest, through the grasslands and chaparral. Good views all the way. Backtrack and you've walked an easy four miles. Or, from the entrance to Back Ranch Meadows Campground outside the park, take the Bayview Trail and climb up a ravine to an access road, returning by the Back Ranch Meadows Trail, more than three miles altogether.

China Camp State Park is open daily, sunrise to sunset; day-use fee is $3. The museum is open daily 10 a.m.-5 p.m. year-round. To get

here, take the San Pedro Rd. exit from Hwy. 101 and continue for several miles past the Marin Civic Center. For more information, contact: China Camp State Park, Rt. 1 Box 244, San Rafael, CA 94901, tel. (415) 456-0766.

Novato
Two museums in Novato are worth a stop: **Novato History Museum,** 815 De Long Ave., tel. (415) 897-4320, a monument to the town's pio-

---

HEAR YE, HEAR YE— WHERE'S THE FAIRE?

To experience the Middle Ages modern style, head for the long-running **Renaissance Pleasure Faire,** sponsored by the Bay Area's Living History Center, toll-free tel. (800) 523-2473 for current details and tickets. Held almost forever in Novato's Black Point Forest just off Hwy. 37, of late the Faire has been on the move—looking for a new permanent home. In 1999, the Faire's 33rd year, it settled into the old Nut Tree spread in Vacaville. Wherever it is these days, Northern California's own Renaissance Pleasure Faire is held on weekends from September through mid-October, 10 a.m.-6 p.m.

During the Faire, life in the local shire features an authentic return trip to 16th-century England, on the world's largest stage—a mile-long Elizabethan village with 16 separate neighborhood villages inhabited by thousands of corporate executives, computer programmers, housewives, and other amateur medievalists (including paying guests) dressed and acting in historical character and speaking only "Basic Faire Accent."

In keeping with Northern California history, Sir Francis Drake himself presides over each day's opening ceremonies; the queen leaves the shire by late afternoon. But in between, the activity never ends. There are madrigal groups and musical processions; games, juggling, singing, and dancing; full-contact fighting and jousting; feasts of broiled beef, beer, and fresh-baked bread, mixed inimitably with other aromas—incense and herbs and flower essence—in the air. At last report, admission was $17.50 adults, $15 seniors and students with current ID, and $7.50 children ages 5-11 (under 5 free). Call for current details and directions.

CALIFORNIA DEPARTMENT OF PARKS AND RECREATION

*Angel Island State Park,
once the Ellis Island of
the West*

neer past, open Wed.-Thurs. and Saturday noon-4 p.m. (free), and **Marin Museum of the American Indian** and park at 2200 Novato Blvd., tel. (415) 897-4064, a small but fascinating place with friendly staff and hands-on exhibits and other displays about Coast Miwok and Pomo culture. Open Tues.-Sat. 10 a.m.-3 p.m., Saturday noon-4p.m., closed Sunday. Free.

Just north of Novato is **Olompali State Historic Park,** P.O. Box 1016, Novato, CA 94948, tel. (415) 892-3383, a 700-acre ranch with broad historic significance. At one time it was a major Miwok trading village, a fact archaeological finds have verified. Sir Francis Drake and his men may have passed through, since a silver sixpence circa 1567 was discovered here. A Bear Flag Revolt skirmish occurred at the Olompali Adobe in the mid-1800s. Olompali's tenure as a ranch is obvious, given the weathered barns and the Victorian home of the one-time ranch manager. Restoration and park development are still under way, but the public is welcome to stop for a picnic and a hike to the top of Burdell Mountain, offering some good views of San Pablo Bay.

Olompali is open daily 10 a.m.-7 p.m. Day-use fee: $2. To learn more about Olompali's fantastic history, pick up a copy of ***Olompali in the Beginning*** by June Gardener. Getting here is easy from the north; from Hwy. 101, just take the marked exit (north of Novato proper). From the south via Hwy. 101, exit at San Antonio Rd. and head west, then backtrack to the park on Hwy. 101.

Angel Island State Park

Still sometimes called the "Ellis Island of the West," at the turn of the century Angel Island was the door through which Asian immigrants passed on their way to America. Japanese and other "enemy aliens" were imprisoned here during World War II, when the island's facilities served as a detention center. Explore the West Garrison Civil War barracks and buildings at the 1863 site of Camp Reynolds—built and occupied by Union troops determined to foil the Confederacy's plans to invade the bay and then the gold country. Among the buildings, the largest surviving collection of Civil War structures in the nation, note the cannons still aimed to sea (but never used in the war because Confederate troops never showed up). On weekends, volunteers in the park's living history program—with the help of apparently willing visitors—fire off the cannons, just in case the South rises again.

Though most visitors never get past the sun and sand at Ayala Cove (where the Cove Cafe offers lunch, coffee, and beer), also worth a stop are the 1899 Chinese Immigration Center, quarantine central for new Asian arrivals, and World War II-era Fort McDowell on the island's east side near the Civil War battlements. Often sunny in summer when the rest of the Bay Area is shivering in the fog, outdoorsy types consider Angel Island's hiking trails its chief attraction. (The eucalyptus trees being felled on Angel Island are nonnatives first planted in the 1860s and now being removed so natural vegetation can be reintroduced.) On a clear day, the view from the top of Angel Island's Mount Livermore is spectacular—with three bridges and almost the entire Bay Area seemingly within reach.

For unbeatable scenery (and sometimes brisk winds), picnic atop Mount Livermore. The intrepid can even camp on Angel Island, which features nine hike-in environmental campsites. Call park headquarters for information and reservations. (Campstove or charcoal cooking only—no fires.) If you're coming, come light, since you'll have to manage it on the ferry and pack it all into camp, at least a mile hike. The **Tiburon-Angel Island State Park Ferry,** berthed at the pier on Main St. in Tiburon, tel. (415) 435-2131, is available to island-bound hikers, bikers, and backpackers daily during summer (and often into autumn, weather permitting), but only on weekends during the rest of the year. The **Blue & Gold Fleet,** tel. (415) 773-1188, also offers Angel Island runs from San Francisco's Pier 41.

For more information about island hikes and docent-led tours of historic sites, also current ferry schedules, contact: **Angel Island State Park headquarters,** 1455 E. Francis Blvd., San Rafael, CA 94501, or P.O. Box 866, Tiburon, CA 94920, tel. (415) 435-1915. For information on tram tours of the island, as well as mountain-bike and kayak rentals there, call (415) 897-0715. For information about island tours for the disabled and about fundraising and other volunteer work to continue the island's restoration, contact: **Angel Island Association,** P.O. Box 866, Tiburon, CA 94920, tel. (415) 435-3522.

ASK MR. JELLY BELLY

A particularly sweet treat in Fairfield is the tour of the Herman Goelitz Candy Company and adjacent **Jelly Belly Visitors Center,** where the phrase "bean counter" takes on immense new meaning—especially just before Easter, when the factory here produces more than a million jelly beans every hour. These aren't just any jelly beans. Former President Ronald Reagan made them internationally famous, when he started to eat Jelly Belly beans to help kick his pipe-smoking habit. And a Jelly Belly was the first jelly bean in space. These are the original "gourmet jelly beans." The company boasts 40 flavors on its regular roster—buttered popcorn, root beer, pink bubble gum, jalapeño, and many fruit flavors among them—and produces many more for its seasonal lists. Jelly Belly is always experimenting with new possibilities, these known as "rookies," which each get a one-year tryout.

At the end of the factory tour, you'll probably meet up with a few rookies. But first you'll follow the **Jelly Belly Candy Trail,** looking down on the production floor to see how the beans are made. You'll also find out how the company comes up with all those flavors. You'll even get to sample the merchandise. There's a fully stocked Jelly Belly store and a Jelly Belly restaurant.

Free tours are offered several times daily (except major holidays, April 1, and two weeks in summer). For current information, call (707) 428-2838. To take a virtual Jelly Belly tour, the website is www.jellybelly.com. Mr. Jelly Belly will happily answer all your questions.

NORTH BAY DIVERSIONS

Bay Tours

In addition to the North Bay's astounding coastal access opportunities, particularly in western Marin County, there are also many ways to enjoy San Francisco Bay. In San Francisco, both **Blue & Gold Fleet,** tel. (415) 773-1188 or (415) 705-5555, and **Red & White Fleet,** tel. (415) 447-0597 or toll-free (800) 229-2784 (in California), offer bay ferry tours. Or design your own tours using the bay's ferry system. Blue & Gold's San Francisco-based ferries offer regular commuter service connecting Fisherman's Wharf to Sausalito, Tiburon, Vallejo, Angel Island, and Alcatraz. The Golden Gate Bridge District's fun triple-decker **Golden Gate Ferries,** tel. (415) 923-2000, come complete with indoor and outdoor seating and full bars, and connect the San Francisco's historic Ferry Building with both Larkspur and Sausalito, with departures about once each hour on weekdays (early morning through evening), less frequently on weekends. Golden Gate ferries feature special roundtrip "Lunch for the Office Bunch" midday runs from San Francisco to Sausalito and back with live lunchtime jazz or rhythm and blues, on

THE BAY BEYOND MARIN

San Pablo Bay National Wildlife Refuge

Also along the shores of San Pablo Bay—to the northeast, between the Petaluma and Napa rivers south of Hwy. 37—are the salt marshes, mudflats, and open waters of the San Pablo Bay National Wildlife Refuge, a winter refueling stop for migrating shorebirds and waterfowl, also permanent home to two endangered species: the California clapper rail and the salt marsh harvest mouse. Largely undeveloped but accessible—under certain strict conditions—for boaters and hunters, the only easy access for the general public is at **Tubbs Island,** originally acquired by The Nature Conservancy. To get here, park (well off the road) along Hwy. 37 just east of its intersection with Hwy. 121 (and just east of Tolay Creek) and walk. It's almost three miles (one-way) to these marsh ponds and nature trails on the northern edge of San Pablo Bay. Open during daylight hours only, no restrooms available, bring your own drinking water. For more information, contact: San Pablo Bay National Wildlife Refuge, P.O. Box 2012, Mare Island, CA 94592, tel. (707) 562-3000.

Six Flags Marine World and Vicinity

Vallejo sprawls across the point where the Napa River flows into San Pablo Bay, near the Mare Island Naval Shipyard. Vallejo is also home to Six Flags Marine World, a big-time theme park next to the Solano County Fairgrounds. A popular venue for family-style fun, Marine World features some 30 rides—including Boomerang, Hammerhead Shark, Kong, Roar, and Voodoo—and 35 marine and land animal exhibits. Among the most intriguing experiences are the tamest, including strolls through the fluttering **Lorikeet Aviary** and the glassed-in **Butterfly Habitat.** Trained-animal performances and other shows round out the action here. Marine World is open daily in summer, weekends only in fall and spring, and is closed entirely Nov.-Feb.; call or see the website for current days and hours. At last report, admission was $34 adults, $25 seniors, and $17 children (under 48 inches tall). There's a parking fee, too. For more information, contact: Six Flags Marine World, Marine World Parkway, Vallejo, CA 94589, tel. (707) 644-4000, www.sixflags.com/marineworld. For more information about Vallejo and vicinity, contact: **Vallejo Chamber of Commerce,** 2 Florida St., Vallejo, CA 94590, tel. (707) 644-5551, www.vallejochamber.com.

Northeast of Vallejo and north of Suisun Bay is Fairfield and adjacent Travis Air Force Base with its **Travis Air Force Base Heritage Center Museum,** tel. (707) 424-5605, www.travis.af.mil/, open 9 a.m.-5 p.m. weekends and 9 a.m.-4 p.m. weekdays, an impressive indoor-outdoor collection of old aircraft—including a handmade 1912 wooden biplane, cargo planes, jet fighters, and bombers.

---

selected Fridays from early June through early October. (For more information about ferry transportation, see Transportation: Getting Around Town in the San Francisco: An Introduction chapter.)

For very special sightseeing beyond San Francisco Bay, a responsible nonprofit organization offering guided whalewatching boat tours and other nautical expeditions is the **Oceanic Society** based at Fort Mason in San Francisco, tel. (415) 474-3385, with local whalewatching trips and Farallon Islands tours. Advance reservations required. The organization considers these tours part of their public education work on behalf of whales, and some trips support ongoing whale research. Whalewatching boats leave from either Half Moon Bay (three-hour trip) or San Francisco (six hours) and head out to the migration paths near the Farallon Islands.

Bay Recreation

Weather and wave conditions permitting, dedicated kayakers, rowers, sailors, whaleboaters, and windsurfers are as at home on the bay as the ferries and big ships. **Sea Trek** in Sausalito at Schoonmaker Point, tel. (415) 488-1000 or (415) 332-4465, is a big-league kayaking center offering something for everyone: classes for all skill levels (beginners' classes, two-hour classes to improve basic skills, day-long "Open Bay" classes and family instruction also available), kayak rentals, guided day trips, and overnight camping excursions. **Open Water Rowing Center,** 85 Liberty Ship Way in Sausalito near Sea Trek, tel. (415) 332-1091, requires equipment renters to have previous experience or certification, or to take their two-hour beginners' or intermediate class before setting out for serious adventures to Tiburon, Angel Island, Alcatraz, or out through the Golden Gate.

Quite special is **Environmental Traveling Companions** in San Francisco, tel. (415) 474-7662, with its kayaking program (and other outings) for the physically disabled, including overnight kayak-camping on Angel Island.

To rent sailboards for windsurfing, head for Sausalito. A variety of companies rent sailboards and offer lessons.

STAYING IN EASTERN MARIN

For a fairly complete listing of Marin County accommodations and other North Bay information, contact the **San Rafael Chamber of Commerce and Visitors Bureau,** 817 Mission Ave., San Rafael, CA 94903, tel. (415) 454-4163. Best bet for budget travelers in eastern Marin County is the **HI-AYH Marin Headlands Hostel,** in Building 941 at Fort Barry in Sausalito, tel. (415) 331-2777, urban enough—just five minutes from the Golden Gate Bridge—but also rural, 103 beds in a 1907 building in an otherwise abandoned fort in the midst of Golden Gate National Recreation Area. Basic dorm-style accommodations with hot showers (family room available by advance reservation), but facilities also include a great kitchen, dining room, common room with fireplace, even laundry facilities, game room, tennis court, and bike storage. Quite popular in summer and on good-weather weekends, so reservations advised. Budget (extra fee for linen rental, or bring a sleeping bag). To get here: if coming from San Francisco, take the Alexander Ave. exit just north of the Golden Gate Bridge (if southbound toward the bridge, take the second Sausalito exit), then follow the signs into GGNRA and on to the hostel.

To spend considerably more for a nice stay in the same general neighborhood, the recently refurbished Spanish-style **Hotel Sausalito,** 16 El Portal, tel. (415) 332-0700 or toll-free (888) 442-0700, offers 16 Victorian-style rooms and continental breakfast. Premium-Luxury. Practically next door and right on the water is the

Inn Above Tide, 30 El Portal, tel. (415) 332-9535 or toll-free (800) 893-8433, a luxurious boutique hotel with just 30 rooms. Great views of the city and bay. Luxury. Another possibility is Sausalito's most mythic hotel, **Casa Madrona,** 801 Bridgeway Blvd., tel. (415) 332-0502 or toll-free (800) 567-9524, both its historic (vintage 1885) and modern sections built into the hillside and connecting by quaint pathways. Newer rooms are plusher, generally speaking, but all are unique and inviting; some have spectacular views of the bay and some have fireplaces. The cottages are the epitome of privacy. Buffet breakfast. Luxury. Perched on the hillside above town, the **Alta Mira Hotel,** 125 Bulkley Ave., tel. (415) 332-1350, offers rooms with a view in a magnificent Spanish-Colonial inn; also separate cottages. Moderate-Luxury.

Other more urban North Bay accommodations include the eclectic 1910 Victorian **Panama Hotel,** 4 Bayview St. in San Rafael, tel. (415) 457-3993, with bed and breakfast-style rooms with or without private baths, continental breakfast. Moderate-Premium. Also in San Rafael: **San Rafael Inn** motel at 865 Francisco Blvd. E, tel. (415) 454-9470 (Moderate); **Wyndham Garden Hotel,** 1010 Northgate Dr., tel. (415) 479-8800 (Expensive); and **Embassy Suites,** 101 McInnis Pkwy. (near the Civic Center), tel. (415) 499-9222 or toll-free (800) 362-2779 (Premium-Luxury).

EATING WELL IN EASTERN MARIN

San Rafael is a good place to start your culinary explorations. At the Civic Center in San Rafael is the **Marin County Certified Farmers' Market** at the Civic Center, Hwy. 101 and San Pedro, tel. (415) 456-3276, held year-round on Thursday and Sunday 8 a.m.-1 p.m. There are other farmers' markets scheduled throughout the region; call for current details.

The **Rice Table,** 1617 Fourth St., tel. (415) 456-1808, serves a 14-dish traditional Indonesian *risttafel*—appetizers, main dishes, and *pisang goreng* (banana fritters) for dessert—for about $17 per person (two-person minimum); a smaller five-course feast, separate entrées, and vegetarian fare (call ahead for details) are also available. Open Wed.-Sun. for dinner. The long-time local standard for Thai food is **Anita's Kitchen,**

534 Fourth St., tel. (415) 454-2626, open Mon.-Sat. for lunch and dinner, though **Royal Thai,** 610 Third St., tel. (415) 485-1074, also gets raves. For Chinese, you can't go wrong at either **Chrysanthemum,** 2214 Fourth St. (almost in San Anselmo), tel. (415) 456-6926, or **China Dynasty,** 1335 Fourth St., tel. (415) 457-3288.

Still in San Rafael, for very good Afghani fare, try **Bamyan Afghan Cuisine,** 227 Third St., tel. (415) 453-8809, open for lunch weekdays, for dinner nightly. If a Moroccan menu appeals, **Kasbah,** 200 Merrydale Rd., tel. (415) 472-6666, offers lamb, chicken, and couscous in traditional recipes, served amid exotic decor. Belly dancing. Open Tues.-Sun. for dinner. For the real thing, Mexican-style, head to the superb **Las Camelias,** 912 Lincoln Ave. (between Third and Fourth Streets), tel. (415) 453-5850, or the taco café-style **Taqueria La Fiesta** nearby at 927 Lincoln, tel. (415) 456-9730. Also in San Rafael, locals swear by **Adriana's,** 999 Andersen Dr., tel. (415) 454-8000, which serves exceptional pasta and heart-healthy chicken, fish, and seafood at lunch and dinner. And some say **Il Davide,** 901 A St., tel. (415) 454-8080, has the best Italian food in the county. Don't miss the outrageous tiramisu.

In San Anselmo, Mediterranean cuisine extraordinaire is the specialty of **Insalata's,** 120 Sir Francis Drake, tel. (415) 457-7700. Look for such delectables as couscous, braised lamb shank, and an assortment of tapas. The restaurant also won top-decor honors in a *Pacific Sun* readers' poll. Open for lunch and dinner daily. For outstanding French cuisine in San Anselmo, try **Filou,** 198 Sir Francis Drake, tel. (415) 256-2436, an unpretentious place open for dinner Mon.-Saturday.

Popular in Corte Madera south of San Rafael is **Il Fornaio,** 222 Corte Madera Town Center, tel. (415) 927-4400, an elegant Italian-style restaurant and bakery with wonderful pastas, rabbit, chicken, and fish cooked in terra cotta, plus other specialties. Another upscale Corte Madera chain is **McCormick & Schmick's** seafood reastaurant, 55 Tamal Vista (off Hwy. 101 at the Market Place Shopping Center), tel. (415) 924-6774.

In a beautiful Victorian north of Corte Madera in Larkspur, the **Lark Creek Inn,** 234 Magnolia Ave., tel. (415) 924-7766, is considered one of the state's best restaurants, with hearty Americana like Yankee pot roast as well as California continental-style mixed grill, seafood, and other specialties. For more casual fare, consider the **Marin Brewing Company,** 1809 Larkspur Landing Circle, tel. (415) 461-4677, beloved for its microbrewery ales as well as its pizzas, calzones, and salads. Live music on weekends. Farther north, in Kentfield, the place for breakfast or lunch is the **Half Day Cafe,** 848 College Ave. (across from the college), tel. (415) 459-0291, serving omelettes, good sandwiches, and just about everything else. Open daily.

In Mill Valley, the **Cactus Cafe,** 393 Miller Ave., tel. (415) 388-8226, is a locally loved hole-in-the-wall serving inexpensive Mexican food—the real thing, quite good. **Jennie Low's Chinese Cuisine,** 38 Miller, tel. (415) 388-8868, serves a decent lunch beginning at 11:30 a.m., also open for dinner.

Still big news in Mill Valley these days is the refurbished and revitalized **Buckeye Roadhouse,** 15 Shoreline Hwy. (at the Stinson Beach-Mill Valley exit from Hwy. 101), tel. (415) 331-2600, brought to you by the folks behind the Fog City Diner and Mustard's. The roadhouse is part of a very hip social scene (especially in the bar), with contemporary and quite good American fare served up in the cavernous dining room of this hybrid diner/hunting lodge. Try Sunday brunch, lunch Mon.-Sat., or dinner any night.

Mill Valley's **Avenue Grill,** 44 E. Blithedale Ave., tel. (415) 388-6003, is also hip and happening, good for pastas and hearty American-style specialties. **Piazza D'Angelo Restaurant,** 22 Miller Ave., tel. (415) 388-2000, is up there among the Bay Area's best authentic Italian restaurants, serving excellent food—like linguine with fresh mussels in marinara sauce, homemade tortellini in chicken broth, and meat specialties including carpaccio—for reasonable prices.

Fred's Place, 1917 Bridgeway in Sausalito, tel. (415) 332-4575, is a surprising local institution, a no-frills coffee shop where 500 or more people compete all day for Fred's 30 seats. Serving unpretentious food à la American grill—with an excellent Monterey Jack omelette and other standards plus Polish sausage and bratwurst, fresh-squeezed orange juice—Fred's is the place, for millionaires and houseboaters alike. People even wait outside in the rain to get in. Open only for breakfast and lunch, weekdays 6:30 a.m.-2:30 p.m., weekends 7 a.m.-3 p.m., no checks or credit cards.

But the **Casa Madrona Hotel** restaurant, 801 Bridgeway in Sausalito, tel. (415) 331-5888, offers the best food around, at breakfast, lunch (weekdays only), and dinner, Marin-style California cuisine using only the freshest available ingredients. For fine fare away from the tourist throngs, try tiny **Sushi Ran,** 107 Caledonia St., Sausalito, tel. (415) 332-3620. For great views, alfresco dining, and a full menu of margaritas, consider popular **Margaritaville,** 1200 Bridgeway, tel. (415) 331-3226, offering casual atmosphere and great California-style Mexican food daily for lunch and dinner (if you like it hot,

try the exquisite Camarones à la Diabla). Other popular Sausalito restaurants include the **Spinnaker,** 100 Spinnaker, tel. (415) 332-1500, and **Horizons,** 558 Bridgeway, tel. (415) 331-3232— both upscale, on-the-water places specializing in great seafood.

Sam's Anchor Cafe, 27 Main St., tel. (415) 435-4527, is the traditional bayside eatery and bar scene for yachting types, open daily for breakfast, lunch, and dinner. Tiburon has an almost endless string of moderate to expensive bayside restaurants stretched out along Main. Nothing beats **Guaymas,** 5 Main St., tel. (415) 435-6300, with upscale and imaginative Mexican food, but you can try **Servino Ristorante Italiano,** 114 Main, tel. (415) 435-2676, serving decent pastas and fresh fish specials.

BOOKLIST

The virtual "publisher of record" for all things Californian is the **University of California Press,** 2120 Berkeley Way, Berkeley 94720, tel. (510) 642-4247 or toll-free (800) 777-4726 and fax (800) 999-1958 for orders, www.ucpress.edu, which publishes hundreds of titles on the subject—all excellent—and a number of titles about San Francisco and the Bay Area, some of which are included below.

Other publishers offering California titles, particularly general interest, history, hiking, and San Francisco Bay Area regional travel titles, include **Chronicle Books,** Division of Chronicle Publishing Co., 85 Second St., Sixth Floor, San Francisco 94105, tel. (415) 537-3730 or toll-free tel. (800) 722-6657, www.chroniclebooks.com, and **Heyday Books,** 2054 University Ave., Ste. 400, P.O. Box 9145, Berkeley 94709, tel. (510) 549-3564, fax 549-1889, www.heydaybooks.com. **Foghorn Outdoors,** Avalon Travel Publishing, 5855 Beaudry St., Emeryville 95608, tel. (510) 595-3664, fax 595-4228, www.foghorn.com, publishes a generous list of unusual, and unusually thorough, California outdoor guides, including Tom Stienstra's camping, fishing, and "getaways" guides.

Sierra Club Books, 85 Second St., Second Floor, San Francisco 94105, tel. (415) 977-5500 or toll-free tel. (888) 722-6657 for orders, www.sierraclub.org/books, and **Wilderness Press,** 1200 Fifth St., Berkeley 94704, tel. (510) 558-1666 or toll-free tel. (800) 443-7227 for orders, fax (510) 538-1696, www.wildernesspress.com, are the two top publishers of wilderness guides and maps for California. Among their titles are some particularly useful for exploration of the San Francisco Bay Area. Particularly useful from the Sierra Club, for example, is Peggy Wayburn's *Adventuring in the San Francisco Bay Area.* Wilderness Press publishes some good regional hiking guides, including *East Bay Trails* and *North Bay Trails.*

Contact these and other publishers, listed below, for a complete list of current titles relating to California.

The following book listings represent a good basic introduction to Northern California and San Francisco Bay Area history, natural history, literature, recreation, and travel. The interested reader can find many other titles by visiting good local bookstores and/or state and national park visitor centers. As always, the author would appreciate suggestions about other books that should be included. Send the names of new booklist candidates (or actual books, if you're either a publisher or an unusually generous person) for *San Francisco Handbook,* along with other possible text additions, corrections, and suggestions, to: Kim Weir, c/o Moon Travel Handbooks, Avalon Travel Publishing, 5855 Beaudry St., Emeryville CA 94608.

COMPANION READING, GENERAL TRAVEL

Ashley, Beth. *Marin.* San Francisco: Chronicle Books, 1999. An intimate tour of the territory just north of the Golden Gate Bridge, a story told with an assist from personal interviews with long-time residents and lavishly illustrated with 130 full-color photographs.

Bright, William O. *1500 California Place Names: Their Origin and Meaning.* A revised version of the classic *1000 California Place Names* by Erwin G. Gudde, first published in 1949. University of California Press, 1998. This convenient, alphabetically arranged pocketbook—now in an expanded and updated edition—is perfect for travelers, explaining the names of mountains, rivers, and towns throughout California.

Bronson, Po. *The Nudist on the Late Shift and Other True Tales of Silicon Valley.* New York: Random House, 1999. The extent that the technological innovations and inventions now streaming out of the San Francisco Bay Area's Silicon Valley are changing U.S.— and world—societies is all but impossible to chronicle. But Po Bronson gives it a go, bravely taking his readers on a personal non-fiction tour through the silicon heart of the beast. To sample Bronson's fiction, try *Bombardiers* and *The First $20 Million is Always the Hardest.*

Conrad, Barnaby. *The World of Herb Caen: San Francisco 1938-1997.* San Francisco: Chronicle Books, 1999. Pulitzer Prize-winning *San Francisco Chronicle* columnist Herb Caen, the city's most enduring cultural icon, knew—and revealed, via three-dot journalism—his Baghdad-by-the-Bay better than anyone. This book celebrates his singular life, and the singular impact that life had on his beloved San Francisco.

Flamm, Jerry. *Good Life in Hard Times: San Francisco in the '20s and '30s.* San Francisco: Chronicle Books, 1999. Life may have been hard, but in his personalized history Flamm says there was nonetheless a sense that anything was possible in San Francisco's good ol' days—that period of time bridging the gap between the two world wars.

Garchik, Leah. *San Francisco: The City's Sights and Secrets.* San Francisco: Chronicle Books, 1995. An impressive celebration of San Francisco's charms, by a *San Francisco Chronicle* writer and editor with some of the city's most respected photographers.

Gudde, Erwin G. Edited by William O. Bright. *California Place Names: The Origin and Etymology of Current Geographical Names.* Berkeley: University of California Press, 1998. Did you know that *Siskiyou* was the Chinook word for "bobtailed horse," as borrowed from the Cree language? More such truths await everytime you dip into this fascinating volume—the ultimate guide to California place names (and how to pronounce them). A revised and expanded fourth edition, building upon the masterwork of Gudde, who died in 1969.

Hammett, Dashiell. *The Maltese Falcon.* New York: Vintage Books, 1992. Reissue ed. More *noir* than even Humphrey Bogart, who starred in the Hollywood version of this classic mystery, Sam Spade is Dashiell Hammett's tough-as-nails San Francisco private dick. Also central to Hammett's *The Dain Curse* and *The Glass Key,* in this story Spade attempts to unravel the enigma of the Maltese Falcon, a solid-gold statuette originally crafted as a tribute to the Holy Roman Emperor Charles IV. While trying to find the falcon, Spade's partner is murdered, the coppers blame him for it, and the bad guys are determined to get him too. Then, of course, there's also the beautiful redhead, who appears and just as mysteriously disappears. Whodunnit? And why? Other classic Hammett reads include *The Continental Op* and *The Thin Man.*

Hansen, Gladys. *San Francisco Almanac.* Second revised ed. San Francisco: Chronicle Books, 1995. Finally back in print after a too-long hiatus, this easy-to-use source for San Francisco facts was written by the city archivist. Contains a detailed chronology, maps, and bibliography. Also fun: what some famous people have said about San Francisco. Fascinating, too, is the author's *Denial of Disaster: The Untold Story & Unpublished Photographs of the San Francisco Earthquake & Fire of 1906,* co-authored by Emmet Condon, 1989 (Cameron & Co.).

Hart, James D. *A Companion to California.* Berkeley: University of California Press. Revised and expanded, 1987 (OP). Another very worthy book for Californiacs to collect, with thousands of brief entries on all aspects of California and more in-depth pieces on subjects such as literature.

Harte, Bret. *The Writings of Bret Harte.* New York: AMS Press, 1903.

Helmreich, Stefan Gordon. *Silicon Second Nature: Culturing Artificial Life in a Digital World.* Berkeley: University of California Press, 1998.

Herron, Don. *The Literary World of San Francisco and its Environs.* San Francisco: City Lights Books, 1985 (OP). A well-mapped "pocket guide" for do-it-yourself walking and driving tours to sites where literary lights shine in and around San Francisco, their homes and haunts. This is the companion guide to the excellent *Literary San Francisco* by Lawrence Ferlinghetti and Nancy J. Peters. Also by Herron: *The Dashiell Hammet Tour: A Guidebook.*

Houston, James D. *Californians: Searching for the Golden State.* Santa Cruz, CA: Otter B Books 1992. Good prose, good points in this collection of personal essays about Californians in their endless search for the meaning of their own dream.

Kerouac, Jack. *Subterraneans.* New York: Grove Press, 1989. Considered by some to be Kerouac's masterpiece and first published in 1958, this is a Beat exploration of life on the fringes, a novel largely set in the San Francisco Bay Area. Others, however, prefer *The Dharma Bums* (1958) and *Big Sur* (1962).

Landauer, Susan. *The San Francisco School of Abstract Expressionism.* Berkeley: University of California Press, 1996. Landauer argues that the emergence of Abstract Expressionism was not a New York invention, but was rather a simultaneous—and bicoastal—post-World War II artisitic event.

Lee, Anthony W. *Painting on the Left: Diego Rivera, Radical Politics, and San Francisco's Public Murals.* Berkeley: University of California Press, 1999. An enlightening look at San Francisco's boldly political art and artists of the 1930s and 1940s.

Le Guin, Ursula K. *Always Coming Home.* Unbelievably, this book is now out of print. Ms. Le Guin gained fame as a science fiction writer, for novels including *The Left Hand of Darkness* and *The Dispossessed.* Her formal literary recognition includes the Hugo, Gandalf, Kafka, Nebula, and National Book awards. *Always Coming Home* is perhaps Le Guin's masterwork, and a special treat for those who love California—particularly Northern California (sometimes referred to, in a regionally chauvinistic sense, as "Superior California"). The geographical borders of the land she describes (and maps) in this imaginative explo-

ration of "futuristic anthropology" just happen to coincide with those in *Northern California Handbook.* Must reading for anyone helping to remake the California dream.

Le Guin, Ursula K. *Dancing at the Edge of the World: Thoughts on Words, Women, Places.* New York: Grove Press, 1989. This delightful collection of essays includes some rare side-long glances into the soul of the northstate—and why not? The daughter of UC Berkeley anthropologist Alfred L. Kroeber and Ishi's biographer Theodora Kroeber, Le Guin offers a unique perspective on California as a place, then, now, and in the times to come. Particularly enjoyable in this context: "A Non-Euclidian View of California as a Cold Place to Be"; "The Fisherwoman's Daughter" (about, among other things, her mother); and "Woman/Wilderness." In addition, the foreword to *Northern California Handbook,* "World-Making," appeared here first.

Loewenstein, Louis. *Streets of San Francisco.* Berkeley: Wilderness Press, 1996. The story of some 1,200 San Francisco street names, which reflect the city's diverse heritage and history.

Michaels, Leonard, David Reid, and Raquel Scherr, eds. *West of the West: Imagining California.* New York: HarperCollins Publishers, 1991. Though any anthology about California is destined to be incomplete, this one is exceptional—offering selections by Maya Angelou, Simone de Beauvoir, Joan Didion, Umberto Eco, Gretel Ehrlich, M.F.K. Fisher, Aldous Huxley, Jack Kerouac, Maxine Hong Kingston, Rudyard Kipling, Henry Miller, Ishmael Reed, Kenneth Rexroth, Richard Rodriguez, Randy Shilts, Gertrude Stein, John Steinbeck, Octavio Paz, Amy Tan, Gore Vidal, Walt Whitman, and Tom Wolfe.

Miller, John, ed. *San Francisco Stories: Tales of the City.* San Francisco: Chronicle Books, 1995. Everybody loves San Francisco. And some of the country's best writers have loved writing about San Francisco. This selection of stories collects some of the best short writing on San Francisco in the past 150 years or so, from Jack London to Jack Kerouac, Mark Twain to Hunter S. Thompson and Amy Tan.

Miller, John, and Tim Smith, eds., with an Introduction by Martin Cruz Smith. *San Francisco Thrillers: True Crimes and Dark Mysteries from the City by the Bay.* San Francsico: Chronicle Books, 1995. A darkly thrilling anthology of edgy stories, both fiction and nonfiction, that capture San Francisco's'dark side, including the classics *Vertigo* and *Ironside.* Illustrated with surrealistic period photographs by Francis Brugiere.

Rodriguez, Richard. *Hunger of Memory: The Education of Richard Rodriguez.* New York: Bantam Books, 1983. California-born Rodriguez got into all kinds of trouble by suggesting, in this book, that affirmative action and bilingual education do a disservice to children of immigrants to the U.S. He uses his own experience by way of illustration. As an intellectual biography of an immensely gifted writer, a long-time editor at San Francisco's Pacific News Service and frequent essayist on PBS's *The News Hour, Hunger of Memory* chronicles his education—when he starts school in Sacramento, knowing a sparse 50 words of English, and when he completes his formal studies in the elite reading room of the British Museum. He chronicles the high costs of social assimilation, including sadness at the increasing distance from his own family, but also exemplifies the freedoms that come with the mastery and love of language. Less controversial is Rodriguez's lyrical *Days of Obligation: An Argument with My Mexican Father,* a fascinating extended essay on contemporary California—and much of the U.S.—as caught between optimism and pessimism, Protestantism and Catolicism, youth and old age.

Selvin, Joel. *San Francisco: The Musical History Tour—A Guide to Over 200 of the Bay Area's Most Memorable Music Sites.* San Francisco: Chronicle Books, 1996. *San Francisco Chronicle* music critic Joel Selvin takes us on an entertaining up-close-and-personal tour of the clubs, homes, recording studios, and final digs of many of the city's music greats, from Jerry Garcia and Jimi Hendrix to Linda Rondstat.

Snyder, John. *San Francisco Secrets: Fascinating Facts About the City by the Bay.* San Francisco: Chronicle Books, 1999. A quirky collection of fascinating facts and both trivial and significant truths about San Francisco—another good book for natives to study, and for visitors to tote home as a memento.

Stryker, Susan. *Gay by the Bay: A History of Queer Culture in the San Francisco Bay Area.* San Francisco: Chronicle Books, 1996. Chronicling the origin and evolution of lesbian, gay, bisexual, and transgender culture in San Francisco and environs, this book was published to coincide with the opening of the Gay and Lesbian Center—the first of its kind in this country—in the new San Francisco Public Library.

WPA Guide to California: The Federal Writers Project Guide to 1930s California. (OP). The classic travel guide to California, first published during the Depression, is somewhat dated as far as contemporary sights but excellent as a companion volume and background information source.

HISTORY AND PEOPLE

Atherton, Gertrude. *My San Francisco, A Wayward Biography.* Indianapolis and New York: The Bobbs-Merrill Company, 1946. The 56th book—written at the age of 90—by the woman Kevin Starr has called "the daughter of the elite" whose career of historical fiction "document[ed] . . . itself . . . in a careless but vivid output. . . ." A delightfully chatty browse through the past, filled with dropped names and accounts of Atherton's own meetings with historic figures.

Bonadio, Felice. *A.P. Giannini: Banker of America.* Berkeley: University of California Press, 1994. Fascinating biography of Amadeo Peter Giannini, son of Italian immigrants, ruthless financial genius, friend of "the people," and founder of San Francisco's own Bank of America. This is the story of the man who was the first to extend credit to working stiffs, and who also shared the bank's wealth with bank employees.

Bronson, William. *Earth Shook, The Sky Burned.* San Francisco: Chronicle Books, 1997. Originally published by Doubleday, 1959. A San Francisco classic—just the book to tote home as a memento of your San Francisco vacation. This moving story of the city's devastating 1906 earthquake and the four-day fire that followed includes more than 400 on-the-scene photographs.

Cole, Tom. *A Short History of San Francisco.* Lagunitas, CA: Lexikos, 1986. Very accessible, thoroughly entertaining overview, with clean design and some great old photos and illustrations.

Ellison, William Henry. *A Self-Governing Dominion, California 1849-1860.* Berkeley: University of California Press, 1978.

Heizer, Robert F., and M.A. Whipple. *The California Indians.* Berkeley: University of California Press, 1971. A worthwhile collection of essays about California's native peoples, covering general, regional, and specific topics—a good supplement to the work of A.L. Kroeber (who also contributed to this volume).

Heizer, Robert F. *The Destruction of the California Indians.* Nebraska: University of Nebraska Press, 1993.

Holiday, James. *The World Rushed In: The California Gold Rush Experience: An Eyewitness Account of a Nation Heading West.* New York: Simon and Schuster, 1983. Reprint of a classic history, made while new Californians were busy making up the myth.

Horton, Tom. *Superspan: The Golden Gate Bridge.* San Francisco: Chronicle Books, 1988. How the Golden Gate Bridge came to be, illustrated with anecdotes and photographs—a very compelling history of an inanimate object.

Hutchinson, W.H. *California: The Golden Shore by the Sundown Sea.* Belmont, CA: Star Publishing Company, 1990. The late author, a professor emeritus of history at CSU Chico known as Old Hutch to former students, presents a dizzying amount of historical, economic, and political detail from his own unique perspective in this analysis of California's past and present. Hutchinson saw the state from many sides during a lifetime spent as "a horse wrangler, cowboy, miner, boiler fireman, merchant seaman, corporate bureaucrat, rodeo and horse show announcer, and freelance writer."

Jackson, Helen Hunt. *A Century of Dishonor: A Sketch of the US Government's Dealings (with some of the Indian tribes).* Oklahoma: University of Oklahoma Press (Trade), 1995. Originally published in Boston, 1881.

Kroeber, Alfred L. *Handbook of the Indians of California.* New York: Dover Publications, 1976 (unabridged facsimile version of the original work, *Bulletin 78* of the Bureau of American Ethnology of the Smithsonian Institution, published by the U.S. Government Printing Office). The classic compendium of observed facts about California's native peoples by the noted UC Berkeley anthropologist who befriended Ishi—but also betrayed him, posthumously, by allowing his body to be autopsied (in violation of Ishi's beliefs) then shipping his brain to the Smithsonian Institution.

Kroeber, Theodora. *Ishi in Two Worlds: A Biography of the Last Wild Indian in North America.* Berkeley: University of California Press, 1988. The classic biography of Ishi, an incredible 20th-century story well told by A.L. Kroeber's widow, also available in an illustrated edition. Also very worthwhile by Kroeber: *Inland Whale: California Indian Legends.*

Lennon, Nigey. *The Sagebrush Bohemian: Mark Twain in California.* Shooting Star Press, 1994. An entertaining, enlightened, easy-reading biography from a true lover of Samuel Clemens's writings as Mark Twain.

Lewis, Oscar. *The Big Four.* Sausalito, CA: Comstock Editions, 1982. Originally published in New York, 1938.

Margolin, Malcolm. *The Way We Lived.* Berkeley: Heyday Books, 1993. A wonderful collection of California native peoples' reminiscences, stories, and songs. Also by Margolin: *The Ohlone Way,* about the life of California's first residents of the San Francisco-Monterey Bay Area.

Milosz, Czeslaw. *Visions from San Francisco Bay.* New York: Farrar, Straus & Giroux, 1982. Essays on emigration from the Nobel Prize winner in literature. Originally published in Polish, 1969.

Perry, Charles. *The Haight-Ashbury: A History.* (OP). A detailed chronicle of events which began in 1965 and led up to the Summer of Love, with research, writing, and some pointed observations by the author, a *Rolling Stone* editor.

Royce, Josiah. *California from the Conquest in 1846 to the Second Vigilance Committee in San Francisco 1856.* Temecula, CA: Reprint Services Corporation. Originally published in Boston, 1886.

Sinclair, Upton. *American Outpost: A Book of Reminiscences.* New York: 1932.

Starr, Kevin. *Americans and the California Dream: 1850-1915.* New York: Oxford University Press, 1906. A cultural history, written by a native San Franciscan, former newspaper columnist, one-time head of the city's library system, professor, historian, and now state librarian. The focus on Northern California taps an impressively varied body of sources as it seeks to "suggest the poetry and the moral drama of social experience" from California's first days of statehood through the Panama-Pacific Exposition of 1915 when, in the author's opinion, "California came of age." Starr's 1985 *Inventing the Dream: California Through the Progressive Era,* second in his California history series, addresses Southern California. Annotations in both suggest rich possibilities for further reading.

Starr, Kevin. *Endangered Dreams: The Great Depression in California.* New York: Oxford University Press, 1996. "California," Wallace Stegner has noted, "is like the rest of the United States, only more so." And so begins the fourth volume of Starr's imaginative and immense California history, in which the author delves into the Golden State's dark past—a period in which strikes and unions were forcibly suppressed, soup kitchens became social institutions, and both socialism and fascism had their day. The "therapy" that finally cured California involved massive transfusions of public capital in the form of public works projects. Yet some things don't change: San Francisco is still a strong union town, and Los Angeles barely tolerates unionism.

Stevenson, Robert Louis. *From Scotland to Silverado.* (OP). An annotated collection of the sickly and lovelorn young Stevenson's travel essays, including his first impressions of Monterey and San Francisco, and the works that have come to be known as *The Silverado Squatters.* Contains considerable text—marked therein—that the author's family and friends had removed from previous editions. A useful introduction by James D. Hart details the journeys and relationships behind the essays.

Stone, Irving. *Jack London: Sailor on Horseback.* (OP). Originally published in Boston, 1938.

Stone, Irving. *Men to Match My Mountains.* New York: Berkeley Publishers, 1987. A classic California history, originally published in 1956.

van der Zee, John, and Boyd Jacobson. *The Imagined City: San Francisco in the Minds of its Writers.* San Francisco: California Living Books, 1980 (OP). Quotes about San Francisco pulled from the works—mostly fiction—of 37 writers, both widely known and locally celebrated. Accompanied by photos and a page-long biography of each author, as well as historical photographs.

NATURE AND
NATURAL HISTORY

Alt, David, and Donald Hyndman. *Roadside Geology of Northern California.* Missoula, MT: Mountain Press, 1999. Second Edition. The classic glovebox companion guide to the northstate landscape.

Bakker, Elna. *An Island Called California: An Ecological Introduction to its Natural Communities.* Berkeley: University of California Press, 1985. An excellent, time-honored introduction to the characteristics of, and relationships between, California's natural communities. New chapters on Southern California, added in this revised edition, make *An Island* more helpful statewide.

Barbour, Michael, Bruce Pavlik, Susan Lindstrom, and Frank Drysdale, with a foreword by Pulitzer Prize-winning California poet Gary Snyder. *California's Changing Landscapes: Diversity and Conservation of California Vegetation.* Sacramento: California Native Plant Society Press, 1993. Finalist for the Publishers Marketing Association's 1994 Benjamin Franklin Award in the Nature category, this well-illustrated, well-indexed lay guide to California's astonishing botanical variety is an excellent introduction. For more in-depth personal study, the society also publishes some excellent regional floras and plant keys.

Berry, William, and Elizabeth Berry. *Mammals of the San Francisco Bay Region.* Berkeley: University of California Press, 1959. Among other regional titles available from UC Press: *Evolution of the Landscapes of the San Francisco Bay Region,* by Arthur David Howard; *Introduction to the Natural History of the San Francisco Bay Region,* by Arthur Smith; *Native Shrubs of the San Francisco Bay Region,* by Roxana S. Ferris; *Native Trees of the San Francisco Bay Region,* by Woodbridge Metcalf; *Rocks and Minerals of the San Francisco Bay Region,* by Oliver E. Bowen, Jr.; *Spring Wildflowers of the San Francisco Bay Region,* by Helen Sharsmith; and *Weather of the San Francisco Bay Region,* by Harold Gilliam.

California Coastal Commission, State of California. *California Coastal Resource Guide.* Berkeley: University of California Press, 1997. This is the revised and expanded fifth edition of the California coast lover's bible, the indispensable guide to the Pacific coast and its wonders—the land, marine geology, biology—as well as parks, landmarks, and amusements.

California Coastal Conservancy, State of California. *San Francisco Bay Shoreline Guide.* Berkeley: University of California Press, 1995. This is it, the definitive guide to the entire 400-mile Bay Trail shoreline route, from its piers to its paths and parks. Comprehensive and user-friendly, with full-color maps and illustrations.

Clarke, Charlotte Bringle. *Edible and Useful Plants of California.* Berkeley: University of California Press, 1977. With this book in hand, almost anyone can manage to make a meal in the wilderness—or whip up a spring salad from the vacant lot next door.

Cogswell, Howard. *Water Birds of California.* Berkeley: University of California Press, 1977.

Collier, Michael. *A Land in Motion: California's San Andreas Fault.* Berkeley: University of California Press, 1999. An intriguing geologic tour of the world's most famous fault, which runs the entire length of western California—and right through the San Francisco Bay Area. Wonderful photographs.

Dawson, Vale, and Michael Foster. *Seashore Plants of California.* Berkeley: University of California Press, 1982.

Duremberger, Robert. *Elements of California Geography.* Out of print but worth searching for. This is the classic work on California geography.

Fitch, John. *Tidepool and Nearshore Fishes of California.* Berkeley: University of California Press, 1975.

Farrand, John Jr. *Western Birds.* New York: McGraw-Hill Book Co., 1988. This birding guide includes color photographs instead of art work for illustrations; conveniently included with descriptive listings. Though the book contains no range maps, the "Similar Species" listing helps eliminate birds with similar features.

Garth, John S., and J.W. Tilden. *California Butterflies.* Berkeley: University of California Press, 1986. At long last, the definitive field guide and key to California butterflies (in both the larval and adult stages) is available, and in paperback; compact and fairly convenient to tote around.

Grillos, Steve. *Fern and Fern Allies of California.* Berkeley: University of California Press, 1966.

Hedgpeth, Joel W. *Introduction to Seashore Life of the San Francisco Bay Region and the Coast of Northern California.* Berkeley: University of California Press, 1969.

Heizer, Robert F. *The Natural World of the California Indians.* Berkeley: University of California Press, 1983.

Hickman, Jim, ed. *The Jepson Manual: Higher Plants of California.* Berkeley: University of California Press (with cooperation and support from the California Native Plant Society and the Jepson Herbarium), 1993. Relatively hot off the presses but at least 10 years in the making, *The Jepson Manual* is already considered the bible of California botany. The brainchild of both Jim Hickman and Larry Heckard, curator of the Jepson Herbarium, this book is a cumulative picture of the extraordinary flora of California, and the first comprehensive attempt to fit it all into one volume since the Munz *A California Flora* was published in 1959. The best work of almost 200 botanist-authors has been collected here, along with exceptional line drawings and illustrations (absent from the Munz flora) that make it easier to identify and compare plant species. This book is the botanical reference book for a California lifetime—a hefty investment for a hefty tome, especially essential for serious ecologists and botanists, amateur and otherwise.

Hill, Mary. *California Landscape: Origin and Evolution.* Berkeley: University of California Press, 1984. An emphasis on the most recent history of California landforms.

Klauber, Laurence. *Rattlesnakes.* Berkeley: University of California Press, 1982.

Leatherwood, Stephen, and Randall Reeves. *The Sierra Club Handbook of Whales and Dolphins.* San Francisco: Sierra Club Books, 1983.

Lederer, Roger. *Pacific Coast Bird Finder.* Berkeley: Nature Study Guild, 1977. A handy, hip-pocket-sized guide to birding for beginners. Also available: *Pacific Coast Tree Finder* by Tom Watts, among similar titles. All titles now available through Wilderness Press.

McCauley, Jane, and the National Geographic Society staff. *National Geographic Society Field Guide to the Birds of North America.* Washington, D.C.: National Geographic Society, 1993. One of the best guides to bird identification available.

McGinnis, Samuel. *Freshwater Fishes of California.* Berkeley: University of California Press, 1985. Including a simple but effective method of identifying fish, this guide also offers fisherfolk help in developing better angling strategies, since it indicates when and where a species feeds and what its food preferences are.

McMinn, Howard. *An Illustrated Manual of California Shrubs.* Berkeley: University of California Press, 1939. Reprint ed. An aid in getting to know about 800 California shrubs, this classic manual includes keys, descriptions of flowering, elevations, and geographic distributions. For the serious amateur botanist, another title for the permanent library.

Miller, Crane S., and Richard S. Hyslop. *California: The Geography of Diversity.* Palo Alto, CA: Mayfield Publishing Company, 1999. Second Ed.

Munz, Phillip A., and David D. Keck. *A California Flora and Supplement.* Berkeley: University of

California Press, 1968. Until quite recently this was it, the California botanist's bible—a complete descriptive "key" to every plant known to grow in California—but quite hefty to tote around on pleasure trips. More useful for amateur botanists are Munz's *California Mountain Wildflowers, Shore Wildflowers,* and *California Desert Wildflowers,* as well as other illustrated plant guides published by UC Press. Serious amateur and professional botanists and ecologists are more than ecstatic these days about the recent publication of the *new* California plant bible: *The Jepson Manual,* edited by Jim Hickman. (For more information, see above.)

Ornduff, Robert. *Introduction to California Plant Life.* Berkeley: University of California Press, 1974. An essential for native plant libraries, this classic offers a marvelous introduction to California's botanical abundance.

Orr, Robert. *Marine Mammals of California.* Berkeley: University of California Press, 1989. Revised ed. A handy guide for identifying marine mammals along the California coast-with practical tips on the best places to observe them.

Orr, R.T., and D.B. Orr. *Mushrooms of Western North America.* Berkeley: University of California Press, 1979.

Pavlik, Bruce, Pamela Muick, Sharon Johnson, and Marjorie Popper. *Oaks of California.* Santa Barbara: Cachuma Press, 1991. In ancient European times oaks were considered spiritual beings, the sacred inspiration of artists, healers, and writers since these particular trees were thought to court the lightning flash. Time spent with this stunning book will soon convince anyone that this truth lives on. Packed with photos and lovely watercolor illustrations, maps, even an oak lover's travel guide, this book celebrates the many species of California oaks.

Peterson, Roger Tory. *A Field Guide to Western Birds.* Boston: Houghton Mifflin Co., 1990. The third edition of this birding classic has striking new features, including full-color illustrations (including juveniles, females, and in-flight birds) facing the written descriptions. The only thing you'll have to flip around for are the range maps, tucked away in the back. Among other intriguing titles in the Peterson Field Guide series: *A Field Guide to Western Birds' Nests* by Hal Harrison.

Powell, Jerry. *California Insects.* Berkeley: University of California Press, 1980.

Raven, Peter H. *Native Shrubs of California.* Berkeley: University of California Press, 1966.

Raven, Peter H., and Daniel Axelrod. *Origin and Relationships of the California Flora.* Sacramento: California Native Plant Society Press, 1995. Reprint of the 1978 original, another title most appropriate for serious students of botany.

Robbins, Chandler, Bertel Brown, Herbert Zim, and Arthur Singer. *Birds of North America.* New York: Western Publishing, 1983. A good field guide for California birdwatching.

Roos-Collins, Margit. *The Flavors of Home: A Guide to the Wild Edible Plants of the San Francisco Bay Area.* Berkeley: Heyday Books, 1990. Just the thing to help you whip up a fresh trailside salad, a botanical essay, field guide, and cookbook all in one.

Sale, Kirkpatrick. *Dwellers in the Land: The Bioregional Vision* Georgia: University of Georgia Press, 2000. New edition of one of the first books putting forth the bioregional philosophy, envisioning a world based not on political borders but on natural geographic regions.

Schoenherr, Allan A. *A Natural History of California.* Berkeley: University of California Press, 1992. With introductory chapters on ecology and geology, *A Natural History* covers California's climate, geology, soil, plant life, and animals based on distinct bioregions, with almost 300 photographs and numerous illustrations and tables. An exceptionally readable and well illustrated introduction to California's astounding natural diversity and drama written by an ecology professor from CSU Fullerton, this 700-some page reference belongs on any Californiac's library shelf.

Stebbins, Robert. *California Amphibians and Reptiles.* Berkeley: University of California Press, 1972.

Wiltens, James. *Thistle Greens and Mistletoe: Edible and Poisonous Plants of Northern California.* Berkeley: Wilderness Press, 1988 (OP). How to eat cactus and pine cones and make gourmet weed salads are just a few of the fascinating and practical facts shared here about common northstate plants.

ENJOYING THE OUTDOORS, RECREATION, TRAVEL

Bakalinsky, Adah. *Stairway Walks in San Francisco* Berkeley: Lexikos, 1998 (distributed by Wilderness Press). This updated San Frabcisco classic offers 27 neighborhood walks connecting San Francisco's 200-plus stairways, choreographed by a veteran city walker and walking tour guide.

Blue, Anthony Dias, ed. *Zagat San Francisco Bay Area Restaurant Survey.* New York: Zagat Survey. This annually updated collection, a compilation of "people's reviews" of regional restaurants, is a fairly reliable guide to what's hot and what's not in San Francisco and surrounding Bay Area destinations.

Brant, Michelle. *Timeless Walks in San Francisco: A Historical Walking Guide.* Berkeley: Brant, 1996.

Clark, Jeanne L. *California Wildlife Viewing Guide.* Helena, MT: Falcon Press, 1996. Second ed. This revised and expanded guide tells you where to go for a good look at native wildlife, and what to do once you're there. Color photos, overview maps.

Delehanty, Randolph. *San Francisco: The Ultimate Guide.* San Francisco: Chronicle Books, 1995. Second ed. Explore San Francisco on one of 16 self-guided walking tours, from the exclusive enclave of Russian Hill to the hustle-bustle heart of Union Square on foot and by cable car.

Doss, Margot Patterson. *New San Francisco at Your Feet.* New York: Grove Press, 1990. One of a series of popular Bay Area walking guides by the same author, including: *The Bay Area at Your Feet,* 1987 (Lexicos); *There, There: East San Francisco Bay at Your Feet* (OP); and *A Walker's Yearbook: 52 Seasonal Walks in the San Francisco Bay Area,* 1989 (Lexicos).

Fong-Torres, Shirley. *San Francisco Chinatown: A Walking Tour.* San Francisco: China Books, 1991. Definitely an insider's guide to Chinatown, escorting visitors through the neighborhood almost step by step while filling in fascinating details about the history and culture of the Chinese in California. Fong-Torres also includes a culinary education, even abundant recipes for simple and authentic Chinese cuisine. (For information on "Wok Wiz" culinary tours led by the author and her staff, see this book's Walking Tours section in the Delights and Diversions chapter.)

Forée, Rebecca Poole, et al., eds. *Northern California Best Places.* Seattle: Sasquatch Books, 1998. Third ed. Though this reviewer also contributed to the first edition of *Best Places* and therefore isn't entirely objective, this massive compilation of detailed restaurant and accommodation reviews offers some entertaining insights as well as great local guidance in all price categories—always a plus.

Gordon, Lynn. *52 Adventures in San Francisco.* San Francisco: Chronicle Books, 1994. Fifty-two playing cards offer fun ideas for a day out in San Francisco.

Hosler, Ray. *Bay Area Bike Rides.* San Francisco: Chronicle Books, 1994. More than 50 bike rides throughout the greater Bay Area— all the way to Napa and Sonoma Counties— useful for both mountain bikers and touring cyclists.

Jeneid, Michael. *Adventure Kayaking: Trips from the Russian River to Monterey.* Berkeley: Wilderness Press, 1998. Tired of fighting that freeway traffic around the Bay Area? Try a kayak. Under decent weather conditions—and with an experienced kayaker to clue you in—you can get just about everywhere.

Kirkendall, Tom, and Vicky Springs. *Bicycling the Pacific Coast.* Seattle: The Mountaineers, 1998. A very good, very practical mile-by-mile guide to the tricky business of cycling along the California coast (and north).

Levine, Dan. *Avant Guide San Francisco: Insider's Guide for Cosmopolitan Travelers.* New York: Empire Press, 1999. Get the inside scoop on San Francisco: from nightspots in the Mission to the best place to catch breakfast in the Haight. A great guide in a series that includes guides to London, New York and Prague.

Margolin, Malcolm. *East Bay Out.* Second ed., Berkeley: Heyday Books, 1988. Published with the cooperation and sponsorship of the East Bay Regional Parks District, this excellent guide focuses as much on the *feeling* as the facts of the East Bay's remaining wildlands, also urban parks and diversions. Highly recommended.

Martin, Bobi. *Kidding Around San Francisco: A Fun-Filled, Fact-Packed Travel and Activity Book.* John Muir Publications, 1996. This guide covers fun stops for kids and includes puzzles and other activities to keep children entertained on the plane or in the car.

McConnaughey, Bayard H., and Evelyn McConnaughey. *Pacific Coast.* New York: Alfred A. Knopf, 1986. One of the Audubon Society Nature Guides. More than 600 color plates, keyed to region and habitat type, make it easy to identify marine mammals, shorebirds, seashells, and other inhabitants and features of the West Coast, from Alaska to California.

McConnell, Doug, with Jerry Emory and Stacy Gelken. *Bay Area Backroads.* San Francisco:

Chronicle Books, 1993. Day trips and more throughout the greater Bay Area—and beyond—brought to you by the host of the San Francisco Bay Area's most popular local television show.

McKinney, John. *Coast Walks: 150 Adventures Along the California Coast.* Santa Barbara: Olympus Press, 1998. The new edition of McKinney's coast hiking classic contains plenty of new adventures, from Border Field State Park at the Mexican Border north to Damnation Creek and Pelican Bay. Along the way you'll also learn about local lore, history, and natural history—a bargain no matter how you hike it. Maps and illustrations.

McMillon, Bill, and Kevin McMillon. *Best Hikes With Children: San Francisco's North Bay.* Seattle: The Mountaineers, 1992.

Ostertag, Rhonda, and George Ostertag. *California State Parks: A Complete Recreation Guide.* Seattle: The Mountaineers, 1995. Moving from north to south, this readable companion serves as a good general introduction to the state parks—and guide to what to do while you're there, with an emphasis on hikes. Here California is divided into six regions. Helpful maps, some entertaining photos.

Parr, Barry. *San Francisco and the Bay Area.* Oakland: Compass American Guides, 1996. With its dazzling prose and impressive intellectual intimacy, Parr's general guide to The City and vicinity is one of the best available and enjoyable, even for California natives, as companion reading.

Perry, John, and Jane Greverus Perry. *The Sierra Club Guide to the Natural Areas of California.* San Francisco: Sierra Club Books, 1997. Second ed. A just-the-facts yet very useful guide to California's public lands and parks—though, without an update, less useful with the passage of time, given numerous changes at all levels of public lands management in California. Organized by regions, also indexed for easy access.

Pitcher, Don. *Berkeley Inside/Out.* Berkeley: Heyday Books, 1989 (OP). The definitive general guide to Berkeley, featuring an abundance of practical facts and insider insights as well as Malcolm Margolin's Historical Introduction.

Pomada, Elizabeth. *Fun Places to Go with Children in Northern California.* San Francisco: Chronicle Books, 1997. This long-running guide, now in its eighth edition, is based on the premise that as important as it is to find a comfortable place to eat with kids, equally important is finding appropriate places to take them before and after meals. For aficionados of California's Victorian homes and buildings, the author's *Painted Ladies* series, co-authored with Michael Larsen, is quite charming too.

Rusmore, Jean. *The Bay Area Ridge Trail: Ridgetop Adventures Above San Francisco Bay.* San Francisco: Wilderness Press, 1998. This update of the original edition offers abundant adventures for hikers, bikers, and horseback riders, along 38 completed segments of this in-progress trail. Includes area maps, trailhead directions, and complete trail descriptions.

Rusmore, Jean, et al. *Peninsula Trails: Outdoor Adventures on the San Francisco Peninsula.* Berkeley: Wilderness Press, 1999. This updated third edition covers all parks and open-space preserves from Fort Funston south to Saratoga Gap. Also by Rusmore and Francis Spangle: *South Bay Trails: Outdoor Adventures Around the Santa Clara Valley.*

Socolich, Sally. *Bargain Hunting in the Bay Area.* San Francisco: Chronicle Books, 2000. The ultimate shop-til-you-drop guide, now in its 13th edition, including discount stores, outlets, flea markets, and the year's best sales.

Stevens, Barbara, and Nancy Conner. *Where on Earth: A Guide to Specialty Nurseries and Other Resources for California Gardeners.* Berkeley: Heyday Books, 1997. Ever wondered where to get that unusual color of iris or that exotic azalea, or where to find the state's best native plant nurseries? Wonder no more. California gardeners won't be able to live for long without *this* essential resource.

Stienstra, Tom. *California Camping: The Complete Guide.* San Francisco: Foghorn Outdoors, 1999. Eleventh ed. This is undoubtedly the ultimate reference to California camping and campgrounds, federal, state, and local. Included here are Stienstra's "Secret Campgrounds," an invaluable list when the aim is to truly get away from it all. In addition to a thorough practical introduction to the basics of California camping, this guidebook is meticulously organized by area, starting with the general subdivisions of Northern, Central, and Southern California. Even accidental outdoorspeople should carry this one along at all times.

Stienstra, Tom. *California Fishing: The Complete Guide.* San Francisco: Foghorn Outdoors, 1995. This is it, *the* guide for people who think finding God has something to do with strapping on rubber waders or climbing into a tiny boat, making educated fish-eyed guesses about lures, ripples, or lake depths, and generally observing a strict code of silence in the outdoors. As besieged as California's fisheries have been by the state's 30 million-plus population and the attendant devastations and distractions of modern times, fisherfolk can still enjoy some world-class sport in California. This tome contains just about everything novices and masters need to know to figure out what to do as well as where and when to do it.

Stienstra, Tom. *Great Outdoor Getaways to the Bay Area and Beyond.* Emeryville: Foghorn Outdoors, 1995. A gem for anyone who needs to get outdoors and who prefers areas not already tramped by everyone else in California. The book's organization is unique, too, allowing readers to locate that great escape by map, activity, and specific destination (particular forest, mountain, or park). Usually updated annually.

Unterman, Patricia, *Patricia Unterman's Food Lover's Guide to San Francisco.* San Francisco: Chronicle Books, 1997. Now out in an updated second edition, this is a marvelous guide to gustatory bliss by the Bay—written by the *San Francisco Examiner* food critic, also owner of the Hayes Street Grill—includes cheese shops, coffee emporiums, and favorites cafes and restaurants,

Wach, Bonnie. *San Francisco As You Like It: 20 Tailor-Made Tours for Culture Vultures, Shopaholics, Neo-Bohemian, Fitness Freaks, Savvy Natives, and Everyone Else.* San Francisco: Chronicle Books, 1998. A hefty helping of more than the usual tourist fare, from The Politically Correct and Avant-Garde Aunts tours to Current and Former Hippies and Queer and Curious. And a good time will be had by all.

Wayburn, Peggy. *Adventuring in the San Francisco Bay Area.* San Francisco: Sierra Club Books, 1995. Revised ed. A fine guide to outdoor activities in the nine Bay Area counties, as well as the islands of San Francisco Bay. Appendixes list frequent and occasional bird visitors, as well as California state parks, environmental organizations, and nature classes, all with addresses and phones.

Weintraub, David, with a foreword by Galen Rowell. *East Bay Trails: Outdoor Adventures in Alameda and Contra Costa Counties.* Berkeley: Wilderness Press, 1998. This complete and up-to-date guide to Alameda and Contra Costa Counties is particularly useful for hikers, but also offers out-there guidance for mountain bikers and equestrians.

Weintraub, David. *North Bay Trails: Outdoor Adventures in Marin, Napa, and Sonoma Counties.* Berkeley: Wilderness Press, 1999. Once you get there, this substantial guide to North Bay trails will help you get around.

Whitnah, Dorothy L. *An Outdoor Guide to the San Francisco Bay Area.* Berkeley: Wilderness Press, 1997. Third revised ed. A well-worth-it, nuts-and-bolts guide to Bay Area open space. Includes distances and grades for trail hikes as well as directions for getting there. Especially handy for those without a car, because it discusses public transit options for each destination. Another useful book by Whitnah: *Point Reyes,* a very good and comprehensive guide (with an introducton by John Carroll) including trails, campgrounds, and picnic areas.

ACCOMMODATIONS INDEX

RESTAURANT INDEX

INDEX

ENTERTAINMENT

EVENTS

MUSEUMS

MUSIC

TOURS

A Day in Nature: 60
Alcatraz Cellhouse Tour: 62-63
Alcatraz Tour: 61
All About Chinatown Tours: 60
Barbary Coast Trail: 58
Blue and Gold Fleet: 61-63
Chinese Cultural Center: 59
City Guides walking tours: 58-59
Cruisin' the Castro: 59-60
Dashiel Hammett Literary Tours: 59
Filoli Mansion: 121-122
Footnote's Literary Walks: 59
49 Mile Scenic Drive: 63
Foundation for San Francisco's Architectural Heritage: 59
Friends of Recreation and Parks: 59, 72
Golden Gate Bay Cruise: 61
Gray Line: 60
Great Pacific Tour Company: 61
Helen's Walk Tours: 59
Hornblower Cruises and Events: 62
Javawalk: 60
Jelly Belly Factory: 185
Johnson's Oyster Company: 178
Levi Strauss & Co.: 50
Mangia North Beach!: 60

Most Twisted Streets Tour: 64
Natural History of the Presidio: 67
Oakland Heritage Alliance: 144-145
Oceanic Society: 62, 186
Pacific Heights Walks: 59
Palo Alto-Stanford Heritage: 125
Precita Eyes Mural Art Center: 59
Presidio Main Post Historical Walks: 67
Quality Tours: 61
Red & White Fleet: 61-62
Roger's Custom Tours: 59
Ruby Tom's Glorious Food Culinary Walk Tours: 60
San Francisco Bay Model: 180
San Francisco Performing Arts Center: 59
Sea Trek: 186
self-guided tours: 63
Steepest Streets Tour: 63-64
Three Babes and a Bus Nightclub Tours: 61
Tower Tours: 61
Victorian Home Walk Tour: 59
walking tours: 33, 58-60
Wok Wiz Chinatown Walking Tours: 60

139
Stevenson, Robert Louis: 30, 34
Stockton Street 33
Stonestown Galleria: 80
Strauss, Joseph B.: 8, 67
Strybing Arboretum and Botanical Gardens: 70
Summer Festival of Performing Arts: 78
Sunol Regional Wilderness: 165
Sunset: 126
Sunset District: 44-45
Sutro Baths: 65
Sutro Library: 45
Sweeney Ridge: 121

T
taxi travel: 17
Tech Museum of Innovation: 131-132
tectonic plates: 2
Telegraph Hill: 37-38
Telephone Pioneers Museum: 54
telescopes: 138-139, 149
Temple Emanu-El: 43
Tenderloin District: 6, 23-25
Tet Festival: 24
Theater Artaud: 25, 74
theater district: 24-25, 74
Theatre on the Square: 25, 74
Theatre Rhinoceros: 25, 74
TheatreWorks: 128

Thornton Beach: 116
Three Babes and a Bus Nightclub Tours: 61
Tiburon: 61, 181
Tiburon Uplands Nature Preserve: 181
Tien Hau Temple: 33
Tiffany: 22
Tilden Regional Park: 157-158
TIX Bay Area: 24, 73
Tomales Bay State Park: 174-175
tours: 58-64, 185-186
Tower Outlet: 56
Tower Tours: 61
Transamerica Pyramid: 27
Transmission Theatre: 56
transportation: 15-21, 140, 154-155
Travis Air Force Base Heritage Center Museum: 186
Treasure Island: 7
trolley (San Jose): 139
Tubbs Island: 186
TulipMania: 76
Turbo Ride Simulation Theatre: 39-40
Twain, Mark: 38
Twin Peaks: 52
Twinkie defense: 51

U
U.S. Courthouse: 28-29
Underground Railroad: 43-44
UnderWater World: 40
Union Square: 22, 98-99
Union Street Spring Festival Arts and Crafts Fair: 77
United Nation Plaza: 28
University Art Museum: 156, 161
UC Berkeley: 156-157
University of California at San Francisco Medical Center: 43
University of San Francisco: 43
USS *San Francisco* Memorial: 65

V
Vaillancourt Fountain: 26

ABOUT THE AUTHOR

Kim Weir is a California native. She is also a journalist and writer. A curious generalist by nature, Weir is most happy when turning over rocks—literally and figuratively—or poking into this and that to discover what usually goes unnoticed. She lives in Northern California.

Weir's formal study of environmental issues began at the University of California at Santa Barbara and continued at California State University, Chico, where she studied biology and obtained a bachelor's degree in environmental studies and analysis. Since all things are interconnected, as a journalist Weir covered the political environment and the natural and unnatural antics of politicians. Before signing on with Moon Publications, she also held an editorial post with a scholarly publishing company.

Weir is a member of the Society of American Travel Writers (SATW). Her award-winning essay on ecotourism was published in the 1993 international *American Express Annual Review of Travel*. She is also a graduate student, a member of the initial class of the new California State University consortium MFA in Creative Writing program.

CONTRIBUTOR PAT REILLY

Pat Reilly is a business manager for *Wired* magazine and has written for several local and national publications. After falling in love with San Francisco on sight, she moved to the city after spending half her life in the north of England. She lives with her husband and his collection of obscure turntables, '80s CDs, and an overwhelming dependence on BBC radio.

AVALON
TRAVEL
publishing

BECAUSE TRAVEL MATTERS.

AVALON TRAVEL PUBLISHING knows that travel is more than coming and going—travel is taking part in new experiences, new ideas, and a new outlook. Our goal is to bring you complete and up-to-date information to help you make informed travel decisions.

AVALON TRAVEL GUIDES feature a combination of practicality and spirit, offering a unique traveler-to-traveler perspective perfect for an afternoon hike, around-the-world journey, or anything in between.

WWW.TRAVELMATTERS.COM

valon Travel Publishing guides are available at your favorite book or travel store.

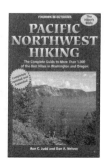

MOON HANDBOOKS

provide comprehensive coverage of a region's arts, history, land, people, and social issues in addition to detailed practical listings for accommodations, food, outdoor recreation, and entertainment. Moon Handbooks allow complete immersion in a region's culture—ideal for travelers who want to combine sightseeing with insight for an extraordinary travel experience in destinations throughout North America, Hawaii, Latin America, the Caribbean, Asia, and the Pacific.

WWW.MOON.COM

Rick Steves

shows you where to travel and how to travel—all while getting the most value for your dollar. His Back Door travel philosophy is about making friends, having fun, and avoiding tourist rip-offs.

Rick's been traveling to Europe for more than 25 years and is the author of 22 guidebooks, which have sold more than a million copies. He also hosts the award-winning public television series Travels in Europe with Rick Steves.

WWW.RICKSTEVES.COM

ROAD TRIP USA

Getting there is half the fun, and Road Trip USA guides are your ticket to driving adventure. Taking you off the interstates and onto less-traveled, two-lane highways, each guide is filled with fascinating trivia, historical information, photographs, facts about regional writers, and details on where to sleep and eat—all contributing to your exploration of the American road.

"Books so full of the pleasures of the American road, you can smell the upholstery."
~ BBC radio

WWW.ROADTRIPUSA.COM

TRAVEL ✦ SMART® guidebooks are accessible, route-based driving guides focusing on regions throughout the United States and Canada. Special interest tours provide the most practical routes for family fun, outdoor activities, or regional history for a trip of anywhere from two to 22 days. Travel Smarts take the guesswork out of planning a trip by recommending only the most interesting places to eat, stay, and visit.

One of the few travel series that rates sightseeing attractions. That's a handy feature. It helps to have some guidance so that every minute counts."

~San Diego Union-Tribune

Foghorn Outdoors

guides are for campers, hikers, boaters, anglers, bikers, and golfers of all levels of daring and skill. Each guide focuses on a specific U.S. region and contains site descriptions and ratings, driving directions, facilities and fees information, and easy-to-read maps that leave only the task of deciding where to go.

Foghorn Outdoors has established an ecological conservation standard unmatched by any other publisher."
Sierra Club

WWW.FOGHORN.COM

CITY·SMART™

guides are written by local authors with hometown perspectives who have personally selected the best places to eat, shop, sightsee, and simply hang out. The honest, lively, and opinionated advice is perfect for business travelers looking to relax with the locals or for longtime residents looking for something new to do Saturday night.

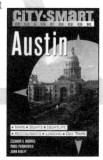

There are City Smart guides for cities across the United States and Canada, and a portion of sales from each title benefits a non-profit literacy organization in its featured city.

www.travelmatters.com

User-friendly, informative, and fun:
Because travel *matters*.

Visit our newly launched web site and explore the variety of titles and travel information available online, featuring an interactive *Road Trip USA* exhibit.

U.S.~METRIC CONVERSION

1 inch = 2.54 centimeters (cm)
1 foot = .3048 meters (m)
1 yard = 0.914 meters
1 mile = 1.6093 kilometers (km)
1 km = .6214 miles
1 fathom = 1.8288 m
1 chain = 20.1168 m
1 furlong = 201.168 m
1 acre = .4047 hectares
1 sq km = 100 hectares
1 sq mile = 2.59 square km
1 ounce = 28.35 grams
1 pound = .4536 kilograms
1 short ton = .90718 metric ton
1 short ton = 2000 pounds
1 long ton = 1.016 metric tons
1 long ton = 2240 pounds
1 metric ton = 1000 kilograms
1 quart = .94635 liters
1 US gallon = 3.7854 liters
1 Imperial gallon = 4.5459 liters
1 nautical mile = 1.852 km

To compute celsius temperatures, subtract 32 from Fahrenheit and divide by 1.8. To go the other way, multiply celsius by 1.8 and add 32.

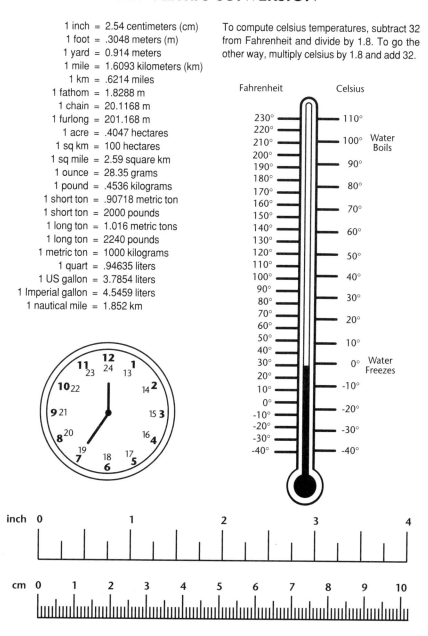

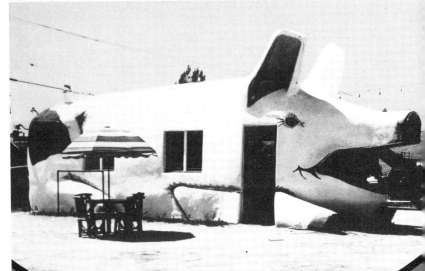

Next time, make your *own* hotel arrangements.

Yahoo! Travel

Do You
YAHOO!
?